GU00991987

Making Volunteers

Princeton Studies in Cultural Sociology

SERIES EDITORS:

Paul J. DiMaggio, Michèle Lamont, Robert J. Wuthnow,
Viviana A. Zelizer

A list of titles in this series appears at the back of the book

Making Volunteers

CIVIC LIFE AFTER WELFARE'S END

Nina Eliasoph

PRINCETON UNIVERSITY PRESS · PRINCETON AND OXFORD

Copyright © 2011 by Princeton University Press

Requests for permission to reproduce material from this work
should be sent to Permissions, Princeton University Press

Published by Princeton University Press,
41 William Street, Princeton, New Jersey 08540

In the United Kingdom: Princeton University Press,
6 Oxford Street, Woodstock, Oxfordshire OX20 1TW

All Rights Reserved

British Library Cataloging-in-Publication Data is available

Library of Congress Cataloging-in-Publication Data

Eliasoph, Nina.
Making volunteers : civic life after welfare's end / Nina Eliasoph.
    p.   cm. — (Princeton studies in cultural sociology)
Includes bibliographical references and index.
ISBN 978-0-691-14709-3 (hbk. : alk. paper)   1. Voluntarism—United States—Case
studies.   2. Young volunteers in community development—United States—Case studies.
3. Volunteer workers in community development—United States—Case studies.
4. Community development—United States—Case studies.   I. Title.
  HN90.V64E425   2011
  361.0068'3—dc22   2010048925

Printed on acid-free paper. ∞

press.princeton.edu

Printed in the United States of America

10 9 8 7 6 5 4 3 2 1

Contents

Acknowledgments

LIKE ANY SCHOLARLY BOOK, this one is the fruit of many minds. Ilana Gershon, Jack Katz, and Laurent Thévenot each combed through many chapters, line-by-line; I am grateful to each of them for convincing me to make big changes, however ornery I may have been at the time. Many generous and thoughtful people read and gave helpful comments and critiques on field notes, multiple drafts, or papers that I wrote while puzzling my way through the book, including Daniel Cefaï, Paul Dekker, Mike Edwards, Andreas Glaeser, Lynne Haney, Ron Jacobs, Michèle Lamont, Caroline Lee, Patricia Paperman, Isaac Reed, Michael Schudson, Tommaso Vitale, Ed Walker, and Robert Wuthnow.

Faculty and staff at the University of Wisconsin and the University of Southern California have provided friendly and intellectually stimulating homes. A year at Princeton shifted my agenda when I discovered the literature on the nonprofit sector, thanks in part to Stanley Katz. The University of Wisconsin conducted a brave experiment in adjusting the "work-family balance," by giving me a half-time, tenure-track position. To my mind, the experiment was a great success, and a blessing that I hope other academic parents get a chance to taste.

I have been lucky to have so many smart undergraduate and graduate students who make sure that my mind stays on its toes. One of the wonderful things about students is that they can become colleagues. I hope that Julian Charles, Jade Lo, Eeva Luhtakallio, and I continue to walk (or bike) the same path together for a long time.

Speaking of walking, I have traded stories about nonprofits, volunteering, and Empowerment Projects, while strolling at night to listen to crickets, sipping tea, savoring long meals, or exploring strange neighborhoods, with many beloved friends and colleagues: Hanan Afi, Jeffrey Alexander, Gianpaolo Baiocchi, Bob Bellah, Marc Breviglieri, Marion Carrel, Ann Crigler, Marcy Darnovsky, Sophie Duchesne, Mitch Duneier, Merija Eisen, Myra Marx Ferree, Shelly Freiberger, Lew Friedland, Tom Goodnight, Neil Gross, Camille Hamidi, Arlie Hochschild, Leslie Hustinx, Dway May Ju, Ann Mische, Mary Nicholas, Jane Pilivian, Marion Smiley, Ann Swidler, Iddo Tavory, Carole Viaud-Gayet, Erik Wright, and Philip Ziegler.

While doing the research and writing, I gave several talks, many based on my raw fieldnotes before I had discovered what they meant. At Northwestern, UC Berkeley, UC San Diego, Yale, Radcliffe, the University of

Chicago, Vanderbilt, the École des hautes études en sciences sociales, the Institut d'études politiques, the Royal Dutch Academy of Sciences, the Université de Lyon, the Université de Lille, and Helsinki University, fellow scholars helped me figure out what all my funny and sad stories meant.

Eric Schwartz, at Princeton University Press, has been a wonderful editor of the sort that is reputed no longer to exist: wise, subtle, kind, and often able to discern and organize my thoughts more clearly than I have—a true master of his craft.

My children Olivia and Leo have provided endless entertainment, and have nobly argued with me in my most cynical moments, to show me, based on their own experience, how volunteers can change people's lives. Nobody slept a lot, which is as it should be, because Nobody is our cat. My loyal husband, colleague, and lifetime collaborator, Paul Lichterman, and I have been together for twenty-five years now. Together, we have created articles, courses, reading groups, gardens, children, and a cozy home for enjoying each other's love, insight, and care. I am more thankful for him than words can express here.

I greatly appreciate the many people who allowed me to observe, and participate in, their gatherings. This book is dedicated to the "Emily's" of the world—the sensitive and energetic youth workers portrayed in this book who work so valiantly in such difficult circumstances to make people's lives better, and often succeed. I hope this book helps make it easier for them to fulfill their missions.

Introduction: Empower Yourself!

CLARION CALLS TO "serve your community" come at us from every direction lately. From the heights of national government to the lowly offices of nonprofits,[1] from universities to elementary schools, from breakfast cereal companies to toilet paper companies,[2] we hear summons to volunteer, to participate, to build grassroots, multicultural community, and to become empowered. In everyday practice, these alluring ideas materialize in surprising ways, sometimes with consequences that are nearly the opposite of anyone's intentions.

Youth programs are ideal places to witness those transformations. A program like Community House,[3] for example, is a free after-school and summer program for low-income, mostly minority youth in Snowy Prairie, a mid-sized city in the American Midwest. One day, Community House won an award from the local Rotary Club—money to help buy a minivan. The group was *told* that it won the award for having done "service to the community," and this made sense, since members had helped organize litter cleanups, food drives, and other events. Everyone was delighted with how well the award fit with the mission of empowering underprivileged youth. But when they got to the awards luncheon, the proud Community House youth volunteers read, on the list of award recipients: "Community House: Van to transport needy youth." Emily, Community House's adult organizer, told me, "If I'd have known [the list was gonna say that], I wouldn't have brought my kids at all. I wish they had not seen that. I don't pity them! If I did, I'd spit on them. You can't pity people." Organizers and youth would often grow furious when such messages about statistics and crime were said within earshot of youth volunteers. Nonetheless, this kind of mistake was frequent and predictable in these organizations.

It made sense that these mistakes were common. Calling the youth "volunteers" made sense because it was a way of highlighting their civic spirit and independence. Calling the youth "needy" made sense too, even though it seemed insulting to point out their dependence at the luncheon.[4] It made sense because Community House's funding came from government, nonprofits, and private donors, who needed evidence that the funds were being spent wisely. After all, Community House could not use charitable contributions, or taxpayers' money, to buy "a van to transport really rich youth," or "youth who are perfectly fine." To deserve the van, these youth had to be needy. Crisscrossed moral inspirations—these and others as well—collided at the awards luncheon. When the organizations' missions tangled up like this, it was not just a random quirk. Crisscrossed promises justified these programs' very existence.

Programs like Community House have a veritable mantra, calling for engagement that is:

- Civic, participatory, open and inclusive, egalitarian, voluntary
- Innovative, multicultural, diverse, aimed at getting you to "break out of your box" and "stretch your comfort zone," and at promoting leadership, choices, and options
- Inspiring, in the here-and-now, not dwelling on the past
- Community-based, local, grassroots, comfortable, personalized, natural
- Transparent, unbureaucratic, not reliant on distant experts, not abstract, not hierarchical, not managed or controlled from the top down

Preface each of these words with the word "potential": potentially civic, potentially innovative, potentially comfortable, and so on. As we will see, "potential" is the most important "keyword"[5] that makes it all run.

This refrain is what I will call *Empowerment Talk*. It is a theme, and variations on it are heard around the world, wherever officials try to cultivate grassroots community empowerment, from the top down. Any American who has volunteered lately has heard it.

With its blend of government, business, volunteer, and nonprofit support, and its mantra of empowerment, Community House is typical of a newly prevalent type of organization that we can call the *Empowerment Project*. An Empowerment Project is an organization that has short-term, flexible funding from a "hybrid"[6] of private, public, and/or nonprofit sources, and that uses Empowerment Talk. Not all organizations that use Empowerment *Talk* are Empowerment *Projects*—many businesses and schools use it, too.[7] Conversely, not all organizations that have hybrid sponsorships use Empowerment Talk.

Empowerment Projects have many morally magnetic missions. By "morally magnetic," I mean that most Americans, myself included, find them to be simply and almost irresistibly good, for reasons that we assume don't need much further explanation. One set of puzzles, however, is that these morally magnetic missions sometimes undermine each other. Many projects' short-term funding adds to the difficulties of blending the hopeful missions. But since Empowerment Projects have to be innovative and flexible, their funding is very often short-term. Since time is short, fundraising is almost constant, success has to come fast, and documenting and publicizing every success has to be nearly constant.

When we say "voluntary association" or "social service agency," what we often have in mind is this kind of semi-voluntary, semi-government, semi-nonprofit, flexible, transparent, short-term organization whose refrain is Empowerment Talk. More and more common since the 1970s, both in the United States and around the world,[8] organizations like these are transforming volunteer work and government, simultaneously. Though they are not entirely new in the United States, they are newly prevalent here. Compared to Europe, Canada, and other wealthy nations, however, the U.S. government provides only the most minimal services, if any at all, for the elderly, children, college students, the poor, the mentally ill, the physically ill, and the disabled. The United States has never had "big government," and still does not. Part of the American government has always included a thin, decentralized web of nonprofit and for-profit organizations, not just one big central state. Now, however, this hybrid form of government has seized policy makers' imaginations both within the United States and around the world, fueling a dramatic, exponential, global rise of Empowerment Projects.[9] Projects like Snowy Prairie's youth programs are typical embodiments of "neo-liberal" governance.[10]

What can we expect from this increasingly prevalent kind of semi-civic life? Missteps like those in the story about the van for needy youth, for example, were not mistakes, as I had thought the first ten times I heard them. Rather, they reveal one of the typical "patterns in the rug" that I recognized only after hearing them over and over again. By getting inside the programs and patiently waiting for definite patterns like these to appear, we will see how this newly prevalent kind of civic life is being born.

Predictable Methods of Putting the Puzzle Together: Organizational Style

Participants kept going without becoming impossibly tangled up in the crisscrossed missions. How? The "van for needy youth" scenario shows tensions and, by default, shows typical ways of easing them: Emily's teens got the van because they were independent civic volunteers. They got it also because they were needy, *not* yet independent. For Emily, who adored these teens, they were also neither independent nor dependent, but attached, almost part of her. In the youth programs, the most polite method of unknotting these tensions, between treating the young people as "active volunteers," as "needy wards," and as "intimate family members," would have been to avoid mentioning the volunteers' neediness at the awards luncheon. This was a very firm bit of etiquette, but the mistake was hard to avoid, since it was hard to keep all the missions spatially separate from one another.

Notice: the teens *already knew* they were poor. Everyone knew it; the teens themselves said so in other situations. So did Emily. The problem was not that they had just learned something new and sad about themselves. The offense was in the *saying it*, aloud, here in front of the youth volunteers and adults, here at this luncheon.[11]

Having multiple, often contradictory missions is not at all unique to Empowerment Projects—most organizations do. In organizations that make their missions explicit (as opposed to friendships or families, for example, that do not have by-laws and missions statements), competent actors have to know how and when to invoke which mission, how to keep them separate, or blend them, or ignore them—when and how to do *something* about the missions—at least enough to keep the organization going, with members and onlookers sharing general ideas about how to act appropriately and what to expect next.

To become competent participants, people got a feel for their organizations' unspoken etiquette: to learn not to call the young people needy *here*, in this place, but to call them needy *there*, in that *other* place; to call them needy on this grant application, but not in this thank-you speech; to this person, not that person. They had to learn how to feel and express bonds between one another, and how to talk about these bonds differently in different places within the organization. They had to learn how to imagine their organization on a wider social map, and how to talk about this map differently in different places within the organization. When people got a feel for all of these "how's," they mastered what I call an *organizational style*, learning:

> *who* could say or do *what, how, to which audience,* and with what kinds of props or *equipment*.[12]

Participants in any ongoing organization need an intuitive feel for the ground on which they are walking together, implicitly answering, "What are we doing here together here, now? Who, if anyone, is watching this activity?" and "What is appropriate to say here versus there?" What do we intuitively feel this relationship to be a 'case of' at this moment?[13]

All of this is the "organizational style." People learn patterned ways of harmonizing predictable discords between an organization's varied missions, just as a listener can recognize, within the first few notes, that John Coltrane's harsh, squeaky rendition of "My Favorite Things" is not the same as Julie Andrews' honey-smooth version in *The Sound of Music*. The listener cannot guess every single move in advance, but can hear *continuity in style*—in the different musicians' typical *methods* of connecting the notes. Snowy Programs had one typical style of connecting the notes; the concluding chapter will show that while Snowy Prairie organizers' method of connecting the notes was probably common, other styles are possible, too. However, people's methods of connecting the notes are not infinite, not simply random improvisations; if they were, each participant would have to relearn how to participate afresh, from scratch, upon entry into each new program. Finding the pattern in the rug means finding participants' typical methods of varying the themes.

FINDING YOUTH PROGRAMS: WHERE I WENT AND WHAT I DID

I spent almost five years in Snowy Prairie's youth programs, beginning with the first event of a city-sponsored youth volunteer program. I was excited. The event was a somber ceremony, beneath an American flag on a windy, freezing hillside, to commemorate a terrible, nationally televised school shooting.

Connie, the adult who organized this event, invited the ceremony's participants to a meeting to plan the city's annual Martin Luther King Day celebration, and I volunteered to help her. Her teen volunteers had come from after-school programs, including Community House. Having met Community House's leader, Emily, in those meetings, I started volunteering there, as well. Connie introduced me to the meetings of the Network of Youth Organizations, and I started volunteering in its member organizations, and attending the NOYO's meetings.

My initial question was that since the world seems to be in such a hopeless condition, how does anyone imagine raising hopeful youth? I wanted to see what moral, cultural resources American adults could muster or create for the purpose. I spent many hours at the tiger cage at the local zoo, listening in on adults and children talking about the posters that explained extinction and habitat destruction. I also went to schools' Current Events classes, and a nature education program for elementary school kids. I soon realized that I wanted more than abstract discussion, however; I wanted to see how adults tried to put their hopeful ideas in practice, where the adults could, I thought, neither melt into hopelessness nor issue vague pep talks about "making a difference," but had to think of something to *do*, *today*, with young people. So I looked for some volunteer or activist groups. But could hardly find any. Instead, I found myself in a galaxy of Empowerment Projects. This form of organization was initially unfamiliar to me. Participants called them "volunteer groups," but they were not.

Thus, my question soon changed. I realized that getting a feel for the *form* of these organizations was, itself, the main lesson that participants—youth and adults alike—were learning. Watching them learn it captivated me, and I dropped the other research sites so I could see how these strange hybrids worked. After having been surprised by the ubiquity of this strange hybrid form, I discovered that policy scholars had already started documenting their spectacular growth over the past fifteen years. I realized that I was witnessing these organizations' infancy, during which routine patterns were developing and solidifying.

After casting my net very widely, I settled into a few Empowerment Projects. Like me, organizers often started with volunteer work, then moved from one hybrid organization to another. My path followed a typical path through a constellation of Empowerment Projects.

My home base was a set of free after-school homework clubs,[14] and summer day camps for disadvantaged youth. They promoted civic engagement in two ways: *adults* volunteered in them, and some of their *youth participants* conducted community service projects.

- Community House had about sixty members. It met in a tiny, one story building. Its narrow entry hall had tables to collect food for the hungry—usually day-old bread and scabby potatoes. Down a half a flight of stairs were a high-ceilinged basketball gym, some brightly lit vending machines, and a tiny kitchenette. Down another half flight were three dim basement rooms: one for participants to do their homework, another for doing art projects, and a third for playing games. I attended Community House's afterschool and summer programs, events and meetings, at least one day a week for four and half years.

- Two Casa Latina programs: One, run by Nan, met in a big school cafeteria. It had sixty members. The other, run by Laura, met in a small classroom, with about twenty-five members. Both were for Spanish-speaking youth; Casa Latina was the umbrella organization that sponsored the two. I attended each for one afternoon a week, for at least a half a year.

- Chippewa Middle School after-school program, run by Kristin and Karen, had about sixty members. It also met in a big cafeteria. I went one afternoon a week for two years.

Through the after-school programs, I also became involved in a set of civic engagement projects for socially diverse youth. Among these, I especially focused on the Regional Youth Empowerment Project (Regional YEP) and the Martin Luther King Day Planning Committee. Both had about twenty members. I attended all of their monthly meetings, and most of the community service activities that they conducted between meetings.

This web of organizations might seem confusing, and it was. Participants were often members of two projects that met one right after the other, in the same room, and this sometimes made it hard for members themselves to distinguish between one organization and another.

I also attended adult planners' meeting, including:

- The Network of Youth Organizers (NOYO): About forty-five program leaders, city and nonprofit officials came to any given monthly lunchtime meeting, each representing one of about a hundred organizations. I attended almost all of their monthly meetings for four years and several subcommittee meetings, workshops, and classes per month.
- The Certificate Course for youth workers was the most intensive NOYO course I attended. It was a twelve-week, four-hour-per-week course for about forty organizers who worked in a very diverse set of youth programs, from the Girl Scouts to a program for teens who were in trouble with the law. Earning the certificate could qualify the youth worker for a higher-paying job.

In the after-school programs, I helped with homework, played capture the flag, checkers, ping-pong, and "ice-breakers," went to dances and movies; baked banana bread with participants; and generally did whatever other adult volunteers did. In the youth civic engagement projects like the Regional YEP, I helped plan events such as food drives, and public events like Martin Luther King Day, awards ceremonies, and litter clean-ups in parks; painted posters, and gathered food for the needy. I attended big, public events—Juneteenth, Cinco de Mayo, Martin Luther King Day and others—that the youth groups helped to plan. I also helped with Community House's fundraisers, such as dinners and rummage sales.

Many of Snowy Prairie's youth programs were exceptionally good by U.S. standards. They won grants partly because some local officials kept up to date on research on youth and on civic engagement. Snowy Prairie had a low crime rate, good public schools, and a large middle class. Programs there were probably easier to run than they would be in a city with less money, fewer educated officials, a smaller middle class, more linguistic diversity, a bigger gang problem, worse public schools, or worse poverty. Snowy Prairie was one of the best places in the country for youth programs, and Community House was one of the best in Snowy Prairie.

Diversity

The after-school and summer programs involved disadvantaged, mostly minority youth. The evening civic engagement projects also included college-bound, mostly white, mostly relatively affluent youth. In those civic engagement projects, the two sets of youth were supposed to conduct volunteer work as equals, side-by-side. While it was taboo even to acknowledge noticing the distinctions at all, they silently motivated many interactions, so I have to name them here, however rude that may have been to do on site: The one set was mostly poor, and mostly but not all non-white.[15] The other set was even harder to classify: while most were not poor, some were very poor, rural whites. While almost all in this second set were white, a few were Asian, and one was Latino; none were black.

Organizers did not like to make distinctions like these, but when forced to, on a grant, for example, they named the first set "disadvantaged youth." Organizers never *had* to name the second set in order to justify funding, so this set was just called "youth." Following organizers and participants themselves, I will, throughout the book, name members of this second category only by what they were *not*—by an absence, a lack of a marker: the "non-disadvantaged youth."

And finally, I should introduce myself, because I was at all of these meetings. Rather than telling you about my whole self and my personal history, I can just say how I appeared in these meetings: as a mom with two young children (and some kind of professor or teacher, though I think the professor part seemed implausible, considering how excessively self-effacing I am), always introduced as "someone who really likes kids," or "cares about youth," who likes to play, always ready to laugh at a bad joke (these last three are, in fact, deeply "me"), probably white, "casual" in dress, and present mainly in the capacity of adult volunteer, though with a better attendance record than most.

How Empowerment Projects Amplify Participants' Feelings of Doubt

Initially feeling inspired by Empowerment Talk's promises, I became more and more equivocal. Organizers did not want to stifle volunteers' creativity, so they repeated, in words that varied slightly from one meeting to the next, that their organizations were "open and undefined, up to you to decide 'whatever'." I admired their motive, but finally had to recognize that the seeming openness posed a problem: finally had to recognize that the seeming openness posed a problem: in organizations that claim to be "open and undefined, up to you to decide 'whatever'," everything you do tends to look like a direct expression of your deepest self, your inspirations, your "gut feelings," your traditional culture, and your very unique form of diversity. You must be able to express complicated and possibly ambivalent feelings about it all, quickly and unequivocally. With all their seemingly limitless blending and exposure, Empowerment Project participants cannot easily hide behind any prescribed roles. It might feel like being naked in public. Empowerment Talk turned nearly inside out when used in Snowy Prairie's Empowerment Projects.

Publicly and explicitly justifying one's volunteer efforts so frequently makes it hard not to doubt one's own motives. As we will see, being thrown together with people from diverse backgrounds makes it hard to avoid noticing how emotionally powerful class and race differences can be. Since participants are supposed to be learning about and celebrating "cultural diversity," they constantly have to explain and display their cultures; needing to explain and display one's culture under so many criss-crossed spotlights encourages participants to question their cultures. All the public, speedy presentations aimed at multiple, hurried, distant audiences makes it easy for participants to see themselves through the wrong end of the telescope—the wrong ends of many telescopes. In Snowy Prairie's hurried performances aimed at distant audiences, there is no time to express or explore the doubts, puzzles, or ambivalence that this participation itself generates. In this way, as we will see, Empowerment Projects increase people's chances for people to feel doubt,[16] vertigo, and possibly fruitful perplexity, but diminish their chances to explore them together in comfortably long-lived relationships.

So, participants rarely taste the delights that Empowerment Talk promises, but they do learn other lessons and skills. While not the programs' intended lessons, some may be useful nonetheless. Participants learn how to produce and value pleasant small talk with people whose lives are vastly different from their own, how hard it is to ignore these differences, and how deep the currents of class and race inequality run. They learn how to listen politely to, politely doubt, and promptly ignore, the adult volunteers who come to help their afterschool program, promising to become like "beloved aunties" to them, but with only two hours a week for four months to spare for the purpose. They learn to doubt organizations' grandiose claims more generally. They surreptitiously learn how their programs got funding and they learn how to stage public events that make their programs appear worthy in those funders' eyes. They learn how to display enthusiasm for each new short-term project, and how to juggle multiple organizations' discordant timelines. They learn how to document and publicize diversity quickly, for multiple, distant, hurried audiences. They learn very specific skills for civic engagement, such as how to take notes and chair a meeting, but not how to develop passionate opinions or to refine political ideas. They learn to maintain a tentative, doubting, distant relation to their own culture, enough to be able to display it to hurried spectators. Above all, they learned to treat the past as irrelevant and keep their hopes relentlessly focused on limitless, hopeful future potentials that they doubt will ever materialize. This, then, is how we arrive at our puzzling inversion of Empowerment Talk's hopes.

Learning to make conversation with strangers is an important skill for anyone; not all relationships ought to be deep and heavy. Some of the lessons, however, seem to be useful mainly for creating citizens who will placidly accept contemporary governments' increasingly short-term projects; who will not panic about short-term employment in an unsteady job market; who will feel calm about short-term marriage; not become too passionately attached to any people or ideas: citizens who will change their souls rather than their conditions. These lessons are also unintended consequences of participation, not the lessons that Empowerment Projects aim to teach.

Some of the programs' lessons come from mixing many missions at once. Though possibly perplexing, those lessons are not harmful. The harmful consequences came from these projects' short time horizons. Policy makers take note: temporary funding meant constant fundraising, documentation and constant publicity. This made volunteering seem, too often, like a loud public ad for the youth programs, rather than an intrinsic good. Speed-up undermined these programs' potential benefits.

To see what should or could change, we need slow, patient observation. Our first step, then, is simply to observe how people experience these projects in everyday life. Only after taking this first step can we know where to anticipate useful lessons and moments of predictable failure in them. Viewing these programs from the inside, over the long haul, we can see what they can and cannot realistically do. Through patient observation, we can see how they could fulfill more of their hopeful missions, making volunteering truly soul-changing and world-changing.

CHAPTER 1

How to Learn Something in an Empowerment Project

COMMUNITY HOUSE BEAUTIFULLY ILLUSTRATES Empowerment Projects' complex tangle of crisscrossed sponsorships and crisscrossed missions. It is a very successful Empowerment Project, coming close to fulfilling all the missions at once. Most of its funds come from the government, from nonprofit organizations, and from private donations. A small amount of money comes from its many fundraisers, which involve selling burrito or lasagna dinners, used clothes, old stuffed animals with dirty fur, and rumpled, second-hand books. So, to survive, the program has to act a bit like a state agency, a bit like a nonprofit, a bit like a charity, and a bit like a business. Such programs have to act like state agencies, expertly documenting their successes at preventing disadvantaged, minority youth from entering the futures which social scientists predict for their ranks, of drug abuse, poverty, teen pregnancy, and crime. Programs like these also have to act like civic associations, both by inviting adult volunteers to come help young people do homework in the after-school programs, and by encouraging youth members to conduct volunteer work themselves, on weekends, evenings, and holidays. In addition to acting like state agencies, businesses, charities, and civic associations, the programs are supposed to be "family-like," as organizers put it, thus further blending the kinds of obligations that participants might expect from one another.

The projects also have to "promote our diverse, multicultural community," as flyers and other publicity often advertise. To promote "bonding among diverse youth," organizers like Emily encourage disadvantaged youth from her after-school program to attend evening meetings of county-wide youth civic engagement projects like the Regional Youth Empowerment Project—planning and conducting litter cleanups or gathering food for the hungry—side-by-side with non-disadvantaged youth.

When the disadvantaged youth joined their non-disadvantaged peers in these volunteer projects, the blending grows yet more complex. The two sets of youth volunteers enter the programs on different trajectories, heading toward different projected futures. Most of the poor and minority volunteers like those from Community House come to the evening civic engagement projects in a group, with fellow members of their afternoon "prevention programs" for "at-risk youth." An important implicit goal of these prevention programs is, as the "van for needy youth" story illustrates, to prevent *them* from becoming future problems themselves. The relatively affluent, mostly white youth volunteers, in contrast, come partly for the purpose of plumping up their CV's for their future college applications, since they know that college admissions committees will want evidence of an applicant's good citizenship. Volunteers in this category usually come to meetings alone, driving their own cars, rather than as part of a larger group. *Their* volunteer work has different sponsors— including their families, who do not need to be publicly convinced to spend money (on transportation, food, adult planners' help, for example) to make these young people into good volunteers and good citizens. No one could avoid noticing these inequalities, but talking about them was taboo, resulting in another typical, everyday tension in Empowerment Projects.

Empowerment Projects are supposed to blend different kinds of people and different kinds of organizations—civic association, state agency, non-profit organization, family, and cultural tradition. Since funding is usually short-term, all of this blending has to happen flexibly, rapidly, and transparently, with documentation for multiple sources, each with a separate form. Organizers celebrate all this melting of stiff boundaries, finding it exciting and empowering. But the blending also produces tensions, as it is often hard to juggle this many different types of relationships all in one place, all at once—as the anger in the awards luncheon shows.

MORALLY MAGNETIC MISSIONS, PREDICTABLE PUZZLES

A tangle of hopes gives Empowerment Projects their "family resemblance."[1]

Like any kind of organization, an Empowerment Project has to make big, beautiful, public promises, both to participants and to outside onlookers. Organizations often do not fulfill their lofty promises, and, as this book will show, when one promise is met, it often conflicts with another of the many promises, yielding unintended consequences.

While these morally magnetic stories do not guide action in any straightforward way, they are not irrelevant, either. They nourish organizers' powerful passions, without which Empowerment Projects would be dry and empty—and much more expensive, since paid organizers often lovingly work for free on weekends and evenings.[2] And even when people do not feel inspired, they still have to do *something* to appear to carry out an Empowerment Project's missions.[3]

When focusing on promoting *civic engagement*, people are supposed to associate as independent equals, in an organization whose door should always be open to any newcomers. When hoping for *safe, comfortable intimacy*, people are supposed to be like family, *not* with an always-open door, not so flexible that their relationships should easily end when the grant ends. Emily, for example, knows how fast the hair on her kids' arms grows. When aiming for *flexibility, innovation, inspiration,* and *multiculturalism*, people are supposed to connect as respectful, curious strangers, open to new adventures, not necessarily comfortably, but "stretching their comfort zones" and "getting out of their boxes"—the farther out, the better.

In principle, organizers approve of all of the many missions, but in everyday practice, fulfilling them sometimes feels wrong—to organizers, youth participants, or both.[4] Despite their feelings and their moral judgments, organizers still have to keep trying. *All* of the morally magnetic missions become harmful or beneficial, depending on how people manage to blend them with the other missions.

In principle, for example, flexible innovation means "breaking out of boxes" and "promoting diversity," which Snowy Prairie organizers relish. But in the conditions of an Empowerment Program, it also means constant fundraising for short-term funding, which organizers do *not* relish. Fresh projects get seed money, and old, stale projects are continually trimmed away; everyone has to be eager to start a new project all the time, even when their previous project is just getting off the ground. Youth volunteers have to want to combat homelessness for six months; next, they have to feel inspired to combat racism or promote literacy, depending on the next funder's agenda. Intimacy has to materialize fast, too, because programs can end when temporary funding ends.

In principle, Snowy Prairie organizers hope to *help the needy*, but saying it directly makes them uncomfortable. They do not want to speak of their work in those terms in front of the youth; to organizers' ears, "help" and "needy" sound disrespectful. They have to speak in those terms, however; as partly government-funded agencies, they have to demonstrate transparency, clearly documenting that they help the needy.

In principle, organizers also consider *transparency* and *innovation* to be fine ideals, but as we will see, these hopes often materialize as a nagging pile of forms on organizers' desks, for new grants every six months, each demanding slightly different data. Organizers dutifully supply the data and then, with an ironic lilt to their voices, mock their own comical precision: numbers of youth volunteers, numbers of minority youth volunteers (which means categorizing and labeling them, which organizers loathe to do), number of adult volunteers, tons of food delivered to the needy, numbers of recipients served, hours and minutes of service rendered to the community by the programs' volunteers, number of pregnancies and crimes and addictions successfully prevented.

In principle, organizers hope to promote *civic engagement*, but sometimes, as we will soon see, even this magnetic mission can be destructive, in practice, when temporary volunteers try to forge instant intimacy with disadvantaged youth. And when it is destructive, organizers still have to try to fulfill this mission, because funders want quality assurance,[5] which means, in *these* types of organizations, systematic accounting, to demonstrate that these are *not* stiff, top-down bureaucracies. Empowerment Projects' twisted task, then, is to demonstrate to distant bureaucrats that they are grassroots, intimate, and non-bureaucratic.[6]

This book tells how these morally magnetic missions transfigure when they materialize in the everyday lives of Empowerment Projects.

What Organizations Fit the Category "Empowerment Project"?

Different Empowerment Projects develop different organizational styles, but the family resemblance is clear: An Empowerment Project is an organization that blends most or all of these missions, using a complex mix of government, nonprofit, and private funds to transform whole groups of people's personal feelings and sense of self, to cure them of their social ills by "empowering" them. These projects' goal is to bring people closer to government, to bring people closer to each other, so that the participants can make decisions in a democratic way. The projects aim to make people take responsibility for—or unfairly make them feel responsible for—their own fates.[7]

Included in this newly recognizable, newly prevalent constellation of organizations are "participatory democracy" projects that invite local citizens not just to contribute to local decision-making, but to transform their attachments, their feelings of belonging, responsibility, community, and self.

Included also are many current economic development schemes. In the past ten years, governments, intergovernmental organizations like the World Bank, and non-governmental organizations have been aiming to build democracy and better economies, simultaneously, by bringing citizens closer to each other, and bringing citizens closer to government.[8] The idea is that changing "the culture" and "empowering" poor people to run small businesses or cooperatives—in Cairo, or Santiago, or rural Malawi, for some examples[9]—will promote economic development. This approach took off when development experts began noticing that an active economy develops in informal places: the people who gather in the local chorus, or the café, also network with one another—the shoemaker finds himself across the table from the shoelace maker and they make a deal, based on feelings of trust.[10] Empowerment Projects draw upon these informal ties as resources for creating a better economy. These projects' common phrases include: "If you give a man a fish, you feed him for a day. If you teach a man to fish, you feed him for a lifetime,"[11] "asset-based community development," "capacity-building," "participation," and "community."

Without emphasizing the "civic" side as much, some projects bear a family resemblance to Empowerment Projects that is a bit less immediate, but clear, nonetheless. For example, alternative women's prisons with mixed government-nonprofit funding sources encourage prisoners to transform their desires and become "empowered" to eat healthful food, avoid drugs, and get a good education. While the prison project does not aim to cultivate grassroots political participation, it aims to transform intimate feelings of a whole group, and to teach the women to "take responsibility" for social conditions, even those that are beyond their control.[12]

Not included in the galaxy of Empowerment Projects would be social service organizations that receive mixed funding but do not aim to promote personal transformation and empowerment. For example, a preschool that takes care of clients, but in which "fostering community ties within the organization is not part of [the] focus,"[13] or a health clinic whose employees harbor no dreams of transforming clients and their communities, would *not* be in this strangely intimate, civic territory that I am calling the Empowerment Project.[14] A purely corporate-sponsored volunteer project, such as Disney's Showyourcharacter.com, or Georgia-Pacific's "Angels in Action" award—of a year's supply of toilet paper for exceptional youth volunteers—would not be an Empowerment Project; funding comes only from one private source, and is mainly a clever form of public relations. Many American school districts require community service as a condition of high school graduation. While they use Empowerment Talk, student participation in them is not optional, and they usually do not have multiple funding sources, so they are not Empowerment Projects.

Organizers often expect Empowerment Projects to work the same way everywhere, regardless of conditions, as if "where there is a will, there is a way," as if keeping your eyes on the prize will get you there. This book shows how keeping your eyes on the prize can work, in certain conditions, but not just *regardless* of conditions. To make it work more often, participants would have to ask themselves why they had not gotten to the elusive prize yet. They would have to comb through their past and present conditions, to locate obstacles to the prize. This rarely happens; participants have usually run off to join another project before any serious questioning has begun. This disregard for past and present conditions is a central theme of this book—a predominant color braided through our rug.

Through reading studies of similar projects around the world, I saw that Empowerment Projects routinely face similar crisscrossed requirements, but have different routine, everyday, patterns for meeting them. In most, the hope of being able to start with a blank slate is a recurrent theme. When organizers try to empower people, they often assume that if a program worked well in affluent, egalitarian Denmark, for example, they can export it and make it work in Albania. They do not carefully consider how it matters that the two places have very different degrees of class inequality, different degrees of ethnic diversity, different charitable practices based in religion, family, civic association, and/or government, different etiquette, different levels of literacy, different degrees of access to running water, electricity and the Internet.[15] So, our second step is to notice participants' everyday, routine ways of keeping their organizations going, as if no past or current conditions might get in their way.

AN ARCHEOLOGY OF AMERICAN EMPOWERMENT PROJECTS

Empowerment Projects missions have strong, long-lived roots in American history.[16] Americans have long treasured "local, close-to-home civic engagement," "soul-changing inspiration," and "innovation and multiculturalism" as sources of good citizenship and good personhood.

Organizers' eagerness to link civic engagement with comfortable, intimate domestic life has a long history. When French observer Alexis de Tocqueville visited the youthful America in the 1830s, he was amazed and amused at peppy, optimistic Americans' eagerness to fix local problems without any help from a centralized government. His example is a man who has to decide, with his neighbors, whether a road should be built in front of his own home. While it would be "hard to pull a man out of his own self, to interest him in the fate of the whole state," it is much easier for him to get involved in a local, close-to-home issue, in which, "he discovers, without even knowing it . . . a tight link between his private interest and the common interest."[17] In this long-standing American tale, the man's efforts to protect his domestic comfort imperceptibly slide into a broader concern for the whole society. The man's circle of concern expands. It may never have been as effortless as Tocqueville makes it seem, to move from private to public, but the parable is a powerful inspiration for American ideas about volunteering, nonetheless. If we were archeologists, this would be one layer in Empowerment Talk's sedimented riverbed of morally alluring stories.

Snowy Prairie organizers' eagerness to honor deep, spiritual inspiration also has long roots in American culture. In a canonical essay, "Self-Reliance," Ralph Waldo Emerson[18] says that it is a moral duty to "Insist on yourself; never imitate . . . (for) God is here within."[19] Organizers wanted youth to "get in communication with the internal ocean," as

Emerson put the idea. This internal ocean stretches, infinitely blue, past the limiting, constricting horizons of social institutions, to a place where each individual stands whole, free of social conditions, independent. In this image, moral vision cannot come from waiting for some bureaucrat or pious church official[20] to tell you about goodness; the only reliable source of morality is the sacred ocean within, the place where rivers of deep personal feelings, intuitions, and passions merge in a communion where "the most personal is the most universal." In Emerson's extreme, mystical, solitary, cosmic vision, all ideas and all people are one vast unity. Empowerment Projects somehow have to tame inspiration, to make it useful for mundane, day-to-day organization-building.

Snowy Prairie organizers' faith in innovation and multicultural experimentation has deep American roots, too. Social reformer Jane Addams reflected on her hands-on volunteer work with immigrants in early twentieth-century Chicago, saying that in a diverse society, it is citizens' "moral duty" to explore, to throw themselves into close contact with people who are very different from themselves, to seek out situations that she says should, if experienced slowly, delicately, with sensitivity, leave them feeling "perplexed." Addams' thinly veiled self-portrait painfully describes how the "daintily clad charity visitor" starts off wanting to help poor immigrants without questioning her own morals, but soon discovers that if she wants to help the poor, she has to challenge her own moral assumptions. If, for example, a poor family has to choose between forcing their children to drop out of school to take paid jobs, versus becoming homeless as a family, Addams realizes that her initial indignation about child labor, based on her own elite upbringing, rings false, because she has misunderstood how their moral decisions make sense in their real-life conditions of poverty. To help them, she realizes that she has to change her own life, by changing the society that they all share. In this example, she has to make child labor unnecessary by becoming a political activist, advocating for minimum-wage laws, so the parents can make enough money without relying on their children's wages.[21] What initially seemed like harmless, apolitical volunteer work undermines the charity visitor's taken-for-granted sense of reality. Addams says it is her moral duty to question the ground while walking on it, and not just to question it, but to *change* the ground—to change laws regulating the economy, in the minimum wages example.

Addams' life illustrates Snowy Prairie organizers' ideal model for soul-changing, world-changing volunteerism. Such slow, delicate, tentative groping is indeed possible for a very long-term, paid organizer like Emily, but not for adult volunteers or youth volunteers. And as we will see, fighting to change laws like Addams' minimum-wage battle is not possible in these organizations, since organizers assume that they have to avoid political conflict. Addams' vision shines through Empowerment Projects, but like Emerson's stringent vision, hers is tamed: Empowerment Projects speed it up, vacuum any political conflict out of it, and make it accessible to people who may not be ready to change their souls.

It may seem as if Empowerment Projects' treatment of the young is not new, either. Following a strong current in American child-rearing patterns,[22] Snowy Prairie organizers do not want to pass down any oppressive, pre-set rules or rituals to youth, refusing, for example, to give curious teens in the Martin Luther King Day planning committee any hints about how the holiday has been celebrated in the past. Organizers want youth participants to take the future into their own hands—"never imitate," as Emerson said, to "make the road by walking it," as activists since the civil rights movement have said,[23] to "learn by doing," as American schoolteachers say. If, they think, young people just started doing things together, working together, they will learn to get along, and will make discoveries that no adult could ever have imagined. Organizers consider this process to be better than imposing any dusty, confining old rules and limits on the young.

Another aspect of Empowerment Projects echoes common, long-standing patterns of child rearing: If the caregiver makes the young person feel more independent than he or she actually is *so far*, the young person may feel strong and proud, and may grow into the feeling, growing to fit the projected image. Making her feel competent and confident by attributing more capability to her than she actually has may be a normal part of good, respectful nurturance. This feeling of "prospectancy" may be the necessary leavening in a hopeful, buoyant personality.[24]

These fears and hopes are new neither for American social policy, nor for American civic life, nor for American childhood. They are built into the very structure of our government. In other wealthy nations, policy makers and voters assume that the face-to-face process is not enough; that citizens cannot *become* equals in the civic realm if they enter it as extreme unequals in the first place—if some are too poor, too sick, too uneducated, homeless, or disabled to enter on equal footing. Rather than waiting for private charities or nonprofits or volunteers to take up the slack, those other nations developed sturdy—or "expensive and inflexibly centralized and disrespectful," depending on your point of view—social safety nets. Voters in those countries have considered equality worth the price if it means that no one has to enter civic life through the servants' door, as a second-class citizen. Most Snowy Prairie organizers favor welfare, but they *also* hope to lessen inequality directly, themselves, right now, before government policies might change. They hope that people can *become* equals by working together, step by step, regardless of their divergent starting points. They hope that respectfully treating people "prospectantly," as if they are independent equals will begin to make them so, and might even set them on the path of upward mobility.

Snowy Prairie's organizers echo Emerson's, Tocqueville's, and Addams' and others' long-lived, potent tales of good citizenship,[25] along with our deepest intuitions of how to raise creative and competent children. Empowerment Projects' many missions might then seem like timeless manifestations of American culture: Tocquevillean civic engagement + Emersonian inspiration + Addams' experimentation and multicultural curiosity + common child raising patterns. But the result is not a simple addition problem.

These old, nearly sacred ideals transform when they materialize in Empowerment Projects. In them, volunteers' "internal ocean" is explicitly put to use as, for example, a form of pregnancy and drug abuse prevention. Emerson's vast ultramarine ocean has a rapidly approaching deadline on the rushed Empowerment Project's short time horizon. Addams' slow cultivation of moral perplexity transforms, as well: civic participation, inspiration, and appreciation of diverse cultures all have to be rendered transparently visible, for quick and easy assessment by multiple, distant, hurried audiences. The tradition of honoring youthful freshness also transforms, in these short-term projects: it has high financial stakes and has to be constantly publicized.

THE FLIGHT FROM THE BUREAUCRAT'S GHOST

Our local organizers often tell a tale that derides distant experts—specifically, the government planners of the 1950s and '60 s who bulldozed the charming, mixed-use, slightly ramshackle ethnic neighborhood of three-story wooden houses near Community House to build efficient, impersonal high-rise housing projects. Organizers say that those tidy modern projects destroyed local, grassroots, informal comfort, where the friendly old neighbor could sit on a stoop keeping an eye on the kids as they freely roamed, where the corner grocery store, the school, and home blended together, in the exuberant, creative life of the street.[26] Distant experts knocked down the homey neighborhoods without noticing what was good about them.

The old twentieth-century bureaucrat's ghost haunt organizers, motivating them to try to bring government close to the people and bring the people close to each other. With visceral disgust, organizers and funders alike revile anything that smells of inflexible experts, inflexible government, rigid rules, and rigid roles, people who are trapped in the past. Instead, they want open-ended, spontaneous voluntary participation; appreciation of diverse cultures; a bridging of differences between rich and poor, white and non-white, expert and average non-expert citizens; they want intimacy and exploration. They want organizations that can break down borders and hierarchies, not be trapped by past expectations but be open to limitless, seemingly impossible dreams. They want youth volunteers to open up their imaginations, in organizations that they say are *open and undefined and up to you to decide 'whatever.'*

Organizers' desperate flight from the bureaucrat's ghost does not necessarily yield the rosy outcomes for which they hoped. Making rigid distinctions and relying on experts had predictable opportunities and dangers in the "modern" organizations of the mid-1900s. Trying to do the opposite, and imagining that everything and everyone can effortlessly blend, brings predictable opportunities and dangers to Empowerment Projects.

Now, volunteering has become flexible, temporary, "loose connections."[27] Volunteers are supposed to be capable of helping the needy quickly, and without any need for expertise. Diverse participants are supposed to be able to bond quickly and easily, and separate just as easily. The past is no longer supposed to be a rigid model. On the contrary, it is supposed to be completely irrelevant. Instead of making stiff judgments based on narrow rules, organizers have difficulty pronouncing any judgments at all. In this, Empowerment Projects echo trends that resonate throughout society, with its temporary jobs, temporary marriages, temporary government programs. They embody a future-oriented, doubt-filled spirit that filters through many aspects of contemporary life—a point to which we will return in the conclusion.

Empowerment Projects promote ideals that once were uncommon, fresh, radical, and "anti-establishment." Now, these ideals are common, established principles in all sorts of organizations.[28] And so, in the course of volunteering, I was struck with the possibility that I was witnessing how big processes were materializing, step by step, in little organizations like Snowy Prairie's youth programs, in themes and variations all over the country and perhaps around the world.

Typical Puzzles in Empowerment Projects

Part One portrays puzzles of *cultivating civic, open equality.* Part Two portrays the puzzles of *cultivating intimate comfort and safety.* Section 3 describes the twists and turns in *promoting multicultural experimentation.* Since organizers were supposed to be fulfilling these missions at once, while also helping the needy and being both transparent and flexible, starting at any of these three points ends up looped together with the others, where they all meet. So, my three categories follow organizers' attention, my gaze following the aspect of the Empowerment Project that they themselves lit up most brightly at the moment.

Within part one, chapter 2, "Participating under Unequal Auspices," shows what happened when the two different sets of youth volunteers were supposed to meet as equals in the civic engagement projects. Disadvantaged youth often overheard the public speeches about them, documenting their programs' effectiveness in preventing crime, drug abuse, and pregnancy. So it made sense that they spoke of themselves as outcomes and variables; they understood that they themselves were considered the main problem to solve. Non-disadvantaged youth assumed, in contrast, that they were supposed to solve the problems of distant others. The two sets of volunteers could not talk about this inequality together, but they had to know about it, just in order to make sense of action in the programs.

In chapter 3, "'The Spirit that Moves Inside You': Puzzles of Using Volunteering to Cure the Volunteer's Problems," we see that when the soul-changing spirit flickers inside you, it can be exciting. It can also be frightening. Since organizers also had to help needy or troubled youth volunteers, volunteering usually had to be easy, not frighteningly soul-changing.

Chapter 4, "Temporal Leapfrog: Puzzles of Timing," portrays the programs' possibly mismatched time lines, and shows how participants aligned them by focusing on future potential. Sometimes this temporal leapfrog worked, for example, when organizers patiently kept treating needy, troubled youth participants as if they were self-propelled leaders, even before they really were self-propelled leaders. After a year or so, some of them grew into the "prospective" hope. But sometimes this focus on future potential came at the expense of any focus on the past or present. For example, hungry, homeless recipients of youth volunteers' aid might not be able to wait until volunteers become inspired and competent enough to find them food and shelter. There were other temporal disconnections as well: organizers needed to apply for grants over the summer—often on specific topics such as tobacco prevention, promotion of the arts, or literacy—before new youth volunteers arrived each September. Another temporal disjuncture was that organizers tried to "build community" by "drawing on community," "build leadership by drawing on leadership," treating "the community," "leadership," "good choices," and other potentials "simultaneously as diagnosis and cure."[29] This chapter shows how even with these mismatched time frames, people still managed to coordination everyday action.

Chapter 5, "Democracy Minus Disagreement, Civic Skills Minus Politics, Blank 'Reflections,'" opens with some organizers' passionate dream: to encourage youth volunteers to care about politics and "the big picture."

Doing so would have required discussion and possibly led to conflict, which most organizers considered depressing and difficult, not inspiring and easy. There was not enough time for reflective discussions, anyway. So, the youth programs all just conducted projects with which no humane person could disagree—gathering mittens and cans of tuna for the poor, but not asking why there is hunger, for example—thus severing any connection between civic volunteering and political engagement, and tending to breed, paradoxically, hopelessness about finding any solutions beyond one mitten at a time.

Part Two follows organizers' activities that aimed to cultivate intimacy, comfort, and safety. Chapter 6, "Harmless and Destructive Volunteers," portrays adult volunteers who came to help in the summer and after-school homework programs. Adult volunteers' presence symbolized, in funders' eyes, that a program enjoyed local grassroots support, so paid organizers could not shut out these volunteers. However, when they came to the after-school programs for one or two hours a week for a few months or a year at most, their short-term, optional, sporadic efforts at creating intimate bonds with youth participants undermined the intimate atmosphere that a devoted paid organizer like Emily managed to create.

Chapter 7, "Paid Organizers Creating Temporally Finite, Intimate, Family-like Attachment," shows how some of the paid organizers became intimate with some of their program's members. Organizers wanted to become family-like with all of their program participants. But they were not expecting to share a lifetime with them, and their intimacy was on display for public judgment. Nevertheless, some full-time, long-term paid organizers managed to become "like family" to their youth program participants. Puzzles of loyalty—another set of temporal puzzles—ensued.

Chapter 8, "Publicly Questioning Need: Food, Safety, and Comfort," focuses on desires that organizers were not supposed to call "needs," but I do: for food, safety and comfort. Part of an organizer's job was to make participants question their feelings, and to treat all desires as "choices." Empowerment Projects invited participants to draw on deep, intimately comfortable feelings, but also to challenge these feelings, never taking anything for granted. The projects put participants' feelings on display, lit up and explicit, in the glare of multiple, crisscrossed lights. In this shadowless light, organizers could, without offending any of the program's multiple audiences, say neither that their participants had any unmet "needs," nor any bad habits and desires, nor could they explain why participants had ever any unmet needs or bad habits or desires in the first place. The programs were supposed to do more than fulfill basic needs, but were supposed to retrain participants' habits, to learn to satisfy their need for food in healthful ways, for example. Organizers found that funders would not pay for food unless the request for funding cast "food" as something more important than a mere "need," saying that good nutrition enhanced brain development, prevented obesity, or established a homey feeling in a program. Programs still hardly ever got any food, but did offer many theoretical lessons about food.

Chapter 9, "Drawing on Shared Experience in a Divided Society: Getting People Out of their 'Clumps,'" shows organizers' heroic efforts to get the socially diverse youth volunteers to bond quickly, easily, and comfortably. Organizers hoped that sharing their tastes, habits, and desires would help, but the only desires that these diverse and unequal youth ever said they shared were for pizza and blue jeans. Paradoxically, these exercises showed participants just how uncomfortable diverse, unequal people felt when they were thrown together: an important sociological lesson in just how deep social divisions go. It was an important lesson, but not what the programs aimed to teach.

Part Three examines the promotion of *multicultural experimentation and diversity*. Chapter 10, "'Getting Out of Your Box' versus 'Preserving a Culture': Two Opposed Ways of 'Appreciating Cultural Diversity,'" shows that, for people who considered themselves minorities, multiculturalism meant safety and protection—protecting a tradition by staying apart from the mainstream. For people who felt "mainstream"—usually white, middle-class—it meant exploring and mixing, not staying apart.

Chapter 11, "Tell Us about Your Culture: What Participants Count as 'Culture,'" shows how participants used the terms "culture" and "diversity." People used these terms so constantly, they seemed to mean everything and nothing. While Empowerment Talk summons us to draw on our unique cultures, no cultures fit the bill. All were too hard to understand quickly, or were considered too sexist, racist, hierarchical, inaccessible, constraining, frozen, or ossified. Participants had to cleanse their cultures before allowing them to enter the open, flexible, optional, transparent, egalitarian civic arena. While the term "cultural diversity" never led to exploration of anyone's religion, history, or language, this chapter shows that this cleansing still had an effect. It made the differences feel transparent, weightless, and easy to doubt.

Chapter 12, "Celebrating . . . Empowerment Projects!" describes the bewildering, over-stimulating form of Empowerment Projects' public events. In roughly similar words, all flyers for these events invited people to "celebrate our diverse, multicultural community." The events had no center stage, but loud music from multiple stages, each playing its own music. Organizers would not specify what the celebrations were about, intentionally leaving it "open and undefined." Nonetheless, anyone who attended a few of them knew exactly what to expect: a jumble of nonprofit, activist, and government programs—drug abuse programs, high blood pressure prevention programs, prison rights projects, home heating projects—making the celebration of "our multicultural community" seem like a public service announcement offering instruction in how to avoid the heartbreaks that disproportionately touch the poor and the ill. "Our diverse, multicultural community" became, in everyday usage, a way of avoiding a conversation about poverty, and simultaneously, of celebrating Empowerment Projects.

Having quietly, patiently, watched and waited for patterns in the rug to appear, throughout these chapters, we can now piece together practical proposals. Based on this now-solid ground that helps us see what we can reasonably hope for or expect from them, the conclusion offers some urgent proposals for Empowerment Projects.

PART ONE

Cultivating Open Civic Equality

The groups that Alexis de Tocqueville described were "classic volunteer groups": unpaid local folks who banded together in an open-ended group, to fix or accomplish something for their local community. Classic American voluntary associations usually brought together people who were already homogeneous in terms of race and class.[1] They aimed to fix something in the community, not to cure the volunteers of their psychological problems by empowering them. Classic volunteer groups did not have to justify themselves to any external funders. Classic volunteers could start with something small, local, and uncontroversial, and expand to something big, political, and controversial. As the next four chapters will show, Empowerment Projects are very different on all these scores.

Some writers wax nostalgic for those old-fashioned, unfunded, local volunteer groups, and see these newly prevalent Empowerment Projects, with their dependence on money and external authorities' approval, as a downfall. At the moment, about forty years ago, that government funding for voluntary associations began to increase, a nonprofit executive worried:

> [T]ruly voluntary associations are desperately needed for the revitalization of the democratic process, but they cannot be supported by government funds since government funding immediately contaminates their nature and is self defeating.[2]

For the executive, grassroots voluntarism is the soul of America; the word "contaminates" is no accident.[3] The interesting and useful question, however, is not an up or down, a yes or a no, but a "how." Empowerment Projects do not necessarily kill the civic spirit—or bring it to life, either. When they blend their many missions, civic life does not simply lose or gain ground: rather, the ground changes.

CHAPTER 2

Participating under Unequal Auspices

INTERVIEWING SOME YOUTH VOLUNTEERS who were helping out at a local event, a reporter asks a question that was intended to give a boy a chance to display his generous volunteer spirit:

Reporter: Why are you here today?

Wispy black boy, maybe fourteen years old: I'm involved instead of being out on the streets or instead of taking drugs or doing something illegal.

The wispy boy's response was not a mistake. For poor and minority youth, finding an implicit answer to the question, "Why am I in this group?" was easy: I am slated to do poorly in school and in life, and my after-school group exists for the purpose of helping me defy my conditions. I am a problem. For non-disadvantaged youth, there were other unspoken answers: I am here to help others (and perhaps boost my chances of getting into the college of my choice).[1]

Volunteer work was supposed to bring the different types of youth together: even though participants were not equals in the rest of their lives, just getting their hands dirty, doing the work, walking the walk, was supposed to set them on equal footing right now, in the moment. In practice, creating this haven meant learning how to ignore the differences, joining together as equals by leaving the past behind.

This practical solution created its own puzzles and its own form of inequality. It was hard for underprivileged youth to appear entirely civic, self-propelled, and independent, since their programs had to document exactly how much money had been spent on helping them. Disadvantaged youth overheard organizers' constant fundraising efforts, which often included expertly documenting their neediness. Their dependence was publicly visible. It came with a dollar amount. For them, the missions of promoting civic engagement, helping the needy, and transparently documenting their projects' effects blended, often uncomfortably, but sometimes offering surprising insights, almost surreptitiously acquired. If underprivileged youth heard data about poverty and racism, they might see the big picture and feel pride at having beaten the stiff odds, surmounting the obstacles that they faced as members of an unjustly deprived racial or class category.

The non-disadvantaged youth volunteers, in contrast, never heard any-one publicizing the importance of spending money on preventing them from becoming criminals and drug addicts. Their dependence and need for protection was invisible, not subject to public questioning, though one could glimpse, in small, hidden interactions, the dedicated parents on whom they privately, almost secretly depended. According to this second category of youth volunteers, it was urgent that the Empowerment Proj-ects' money be spent in a "civic" way, on helping someone else, not on the volunteers themselves. Many came to the projects hoping to find inspira-tion, to be touched to the core, deeply transformed. So, initially at least, they might appear to fit the mold of classic volunteers better.

Yet, the non-disadvantaged volunteers, too, had an agenda beyond helping others and seeking inspiration. Admission to a good university is not automatic in the United States, as it is in some other nations; these non-disadvantaged youth had to market themselves to future college ad-missions offices, using volunteer work to "signal"[2] that they were good, active, caring, and knowledgeable people. Knowing that they were sup-posed to feel motivated by pure inspiration and altruism, they nervously questioned themselves and each other about whether they were really involved just to puff up their resumes, to market themselves.

The two sets of youth had different hidden reasons for being there, dif-ferent sources of pride and shame, different ways of relating to broader political issues, and even different ideas for what community service proj-ects to conduct. The chapter portrays these knots of tensions, showing how social inequality materialized here in a way that may be typical in Empowerment Projects, wherever the implicit rules of engagement for the two distinct sets of volunteers are so very different.

What Brings You Here? Implicit Answers

Poor and Minority Youth: I Am Preventing Myself from Becoming a Problem

I kept hearing minority youth making what I thought was a mistake when they described their volunteer work. At first, I though they misun-derstood the question. "Safe Night" was a prophylactically named eve-ning event to provide teens with a safe place to go at night instead of drinking, taking drugs, or having sex. Participants ranged from about eight to fifteen years old.

A middle-aged white volunteer got up in front of the racially mixed group of about 100 youth, passing around construction paper cut-outs in the shape of hands. She asked them to write five things—one on each finger—that they could do to serve their community.

Most gave the standard, expected answers: "Shovel snow for old people, baby-sit, help at a nursing home, go grocery shopping for someone who can't, help clean up a park." But many black kids said things like "get a job," and "do my homework."

After hearing these apparent misunderstandings numerous times, I saw a striking "pattern in the rug." These disadvantaged volunteers accurately perceived that they themselves were considered the community problem. Occasionally, impoverished white youth from rural or suburban areas said the same thing. I never heard young people who were neither poor nor minority say it.

Similar prevention programs exist nationwide, in which organizers and youth explain volunteer work in similar terms.

The Dream Shop, an afterschool program for girls age ten to 15 from an impoverished neighborhood in East Dayton [Ohio], is making a dramatic difference in the lives of the participants, reports Cox News Service. The majority of the families living in the census tract where the Dream Shop is based are poor and Appalachian, with grim prospects for the future and a high teen pregnancy rate. Approximately 180 girls have joined the Dream Shop since it started. . . . Many work on *community service projects* [my italics—notice the very next sentence). "We haven't had a single pregnancy yet, and all the girls are still in school," said [an organizer]. The girls in Dream Shop are educated about a range of health issues, including smoking, dental hygiene and sexuality. "That's the thing I like about the Dream Shop. It's like kept me off the street. It's easy to say 'no' whenever I need to," said Samantha Brower, 15.[3]

A similar inspiration fuels prevention programs around the country. Here is one from Nevada, where a school district had started a mariachi band, so students could learn to play this kind of Mexican folk music. Critics said the program was too expensive:

Supporters dismiss the critics. They say the program has the power to keep at-risk students—many of whom are Latino—engaged in school . . .

Javier Trujillo, project coordinator for mariachi instruction in the Clark County School District, said $25,000 was "the average price to keep a juvenile in the prison system per year. Now you apply that same amount of money to education[4]—you're impacting thousands of student lives.". . .

"I'm not on the streets trying to do bad things," said [a student, Edsel] Lemus, who plays the vihuela, a guitar-shaped lute . . . several students boosted their grades . . .

"There are not that many opportunities for at-risk Hispanic kids to be successful," [the band's leader said].[5]

Many schools no longer automatically receive funds for music classes, so they have to compete for grants.[6] Of course, the young musicians, like the young volunteers, may, as a by-product, learn to take pleasure in the music, or the volunteering. Sensual pleasure in the present—in the music itself—may very well overtake the music's future-oriented utility.[7] However, as these multiple excerpts from field work show, the public message was very hard to ignore since it was reaffirmed so frequently, by many voices. The sensual feel in the present and the public justifications about the distant future, both felt real.

Seeing the pattern in the rug is easiest when the pattern is interrupted: At Casa Latina, an after-school program for Spanish-speaking 11–14-year-olds, the adult leader Laura sometimes invited youth to help solve the *world's* problems, rather than only treating the young people as the problem themselves. One day, Laura asked her teens to write messages on a banner that she was going to bring to a pro-bicycle, anti-car rally. When she, and I, and the other volunteers heard this interaction, the jolt of recognition of the absent common pattern made us all laugh aloud:

Laura had written on the banner "La Tierra = La Vida" ["The Earth = Life"] and she also handed out a list of ten incriminating "Facts about the Car"—like pollution, depletion of natural resources, poor working conditions for auto workers, and sprawl.

Most of the kids misunderstood her point. They wrote and drew statements [in Spanish] like "don't drive drunk," "don't ride a bike drunk," "don't smoke while riding a bike," or even, "ride a bike to lost weight!"

Laura's teens expected to be asked to prevent themselves from becoming problems—not to get drunk, fat, or high. They did not expect an invitation to act as independent civic equals who would protest the world's problems, and not just fix their own personal problems. They were so unprepared for Laura's invitation, they misinterpreted it. Everyone knew, but could not say that, whether skating, singing, or fishing (as in other programs nationwide), the funding came with the purpose of preventing them from becoming problems. Without knowing this prediction of future disaster, one could not participate competently in the programs. It was what brought them together—with each other, and with their beloved organizer, Emily—in the first place.

This message delivered a possible moral insult to disadvantaged youth. The puzzle was to act as if disadvantaged participants were in the civic engagement project for the same reasons that other participants were, even when it was not quite true yet. This was puzzling when, for example, youth from Community House's free after-school program attended evening meetings of the Regional YEP just to have somewhere to go at night. To NOYO's adult organizers, but never to youth participants, Emily sometimes said that some of those quiet participants just wanted to stay away from abusive or unpleasant relatives. Empowerment Talk extends the hope that becoming volunteers will strengthen these youth, protecting the helper from misery, as it did in the case of Daisy, the girl who become an extremely active volunteer after having been close to suicide at age thirteen.

Organizers hoped that the story about civic empowerment would eventually fit youth like twelve-year-old Raul, even if it did not do so just yet. Raul came to meeting after meeting, doing nothing but twiddling his mini-sized Nacho Doritos™ bags, trying to balance one full Nacho Doritos bag upside down on top of an empty one. He never looked up and never said a word except at one meeting, when he mentioned that he was going to Mexico soon, to visit his father and other relatives. Since he did not do any volunteer work, either, it may have been unclear why he attended these meetings. Once in a while, his half-sister Bonita complained about their mother's drug-dealing and mean boyfriends, so organizers guessed that his civic participation was helping him, as a form of therapy, but no one could be sure of Raul's reason for coming, and asking him would be hurtful and extremely tactless.

Focusing on potential, by attributing more capabilities to them than he or she currently has, is, as noted in the introduction, a normal part of any good nurturance. In Empowerment Projects, however, this normal nurturance took a peculiar form. Caregivers' normal, gracious, gentle, barely perceptible tact transformed an organizational mandate, with high financial stakes and many spectators watching as organizers doled out all the not-yet-quite-well-deserved praise. Here, the stakes were not just about the individual's feelings of self-respect, but the program's survival. Programs publicly had to demonstrate that they had made the volunteers more independent, within a short time frame. Others were watching as well; there were youth volunteers who were there not for the purpose of preventing themselves from becoming problems, but to solve problems outside of themselves. Those volunteers, who were usually in the "non-disadvantaged" category, were supposed to be equals to the disadvantaged youth. The non-disadvantaged youth were not supposed to be using civic participation as a form of therapy, and had to learn that different rules applied to the disadvantaged youth. They had to learn to hear lavish praise of the quiet, inactive volunteers like Raul and filter it through this unspoken knowledge, in order to understand the organizers' habit of attributing independence to disadvantaged youth when it was not true— at least not yet.

Tactful, wise organizers were skilled at marching through youth volunteers' resolute silence; such organizers patiently waited for months and even years till the curative effects of civic engagement caught hold, if ever. In the meantime, these skillful organizers let meetings keep going *as if* youth participants were *already* active civic volunteers. For example, after one year's annual Martin Luther King Day celebration in January, several disadvantaged youth still wanted to keep meeting through the winter. This puzzled but pleased adults, so they complied with the request, even though the youth volunteers who had begged to hold the meetings then proceeded to sit in stone silence at the meetings that they themselves had requested:

Sheila [adult leader of Martin Luther King Day planning committee this year]: Do you want to do a community service project? (No one answers.)

Emily [the much-beloved Community House leader]: What's the weather gonna be like? Does anyone know? (No one answers.)

Emily: What do you think about doing a community service day? (No one answers.)

Sheila: Should we do something on April 8, like last year? What day is that? Is it a Saturday? (No one answers.)

Emily: Do you want to do a project?

Kid: Like a walk-a-thon, bowl-a-thon, slide-a-thon?

Another kid: Or a bike-a-thon, or that kind of thing? Like we did last time?

Emily: Yeah, or a run—we'd just have to figure out which and reserve a space and get sponsors. So what do you think, guys, should we do something like that? (Kids say yes, whispering.)

After another meeting like the one with the Doritos tower, Emily told me:

A lot of my kids couldn't follow the Regional YEP meeting at all. In the car on the way back [she drives kids in her own car], they were asking, "Huh, what happened? What did we decide?"

NE: I've heard the same thing after other meetings. But it's hard to make those meetings do all things for all kids, because some kids just whizz so quickly, I can't even follow.

Emily: Exactly! And most of my kids aren't going because they're really into it—a lot of them are going because they just don't want to go home. It doesn't hurt to go, and I figure maybe something will rub off on them.

Most organizers braved magnificent silences like Raul's and the post–Martin Luther King Day volunteers'—carefully not pressuring youth participants into exhibiting any discernable reasons for attending meetings, not prying into their mysterious reasons for participating. Some day in the future, it may or may not become clear, but in the meantime, showing respect required assuming that no one can fully know why anyone else volunteers, and no one should ask. *Not* asking was the usual, acceptable organizational style. To me, this seemed like a respectful way of harmonizing the Empowerment Projects' crisscrossed missions of promoting civic engagement and helping the needy.

Some organizers, however, made volunteers' active, verbal, articulate participation mandatory—a disrespectful violation of the graceful organizational style. For example, Miracle, an African American girl, had never spoken in a meeting. At a Regional YEP meeting one day, she said something!

Cindi, another teen volunteer: Erin, that should go in the minutes that Miracle said more than five words!

Davey: Hey, are you making fun of her??

Tandy: She never *talks* and she's so *nice*.

Erin [this year's paid adult organizer]: She *is* sweet.

(Miracle burrows deep into her hooded sweatshirt and looks down, as if she is about to cry.[8])

At another Regional YEP meeting, Erin asked for volunteers to head a committee. When no one stepped forward, Erin clumsily "volunteered" Miracle, saying, "You'll have to do it some day. You'll have to say something in a meeting some day. What do you think, kids, doesn't she?" Once again, Miracle scrunched up her long neck and burrowed her head into the oversized hooded sweatshirt that she always wore. Erin's goal was to make Miracle into a "leader," but Erin got the organizational style wrong. She was being too direct. Rob Strauss, Erin's boss who often attended meetings, scowled, as did several youth participants.

Non-disadvantaged Youth: We Are Here to Help Other People, Not Ourselves

At every meeting of the socially diverse Regional YEP, organizers told participants that they were doing community service *just by coming to meetings*. This message did not make sense to the non-disadvantaged youth. In one meeting, the group was planning a fundraiser, and the question was what to do with the funds they hoped to raise. A county agency had also already given the group some money. Erin said, "You could either give it to yourselves, to raise money to put on a party for yourself—that's a kind of service, you deserve it. Or you could donate the money to a charity that you would pick."

At another meeting, Erin said: You're *doing a huge community service just by being here.* You guys are a bargain. Paragon County gets a lot of wonderful things out of what you're doing here. [This was right after only two kids had shown up for a major volunteering event that the group had planned and promised to host. What are the wonderful things that Paragon County gets from the group?" I wondered: Benefits to those present? free food for the needy once a year? raised consciousness? good role models for other youth?]

At another meeting, describing a project that another youth group was doing, Erin says to her kids, "It's making kids [she meant the teen volunteers in the room] feel good about what they're doing, which is the purpose."

For non-disadvantaged youth, the idea of just turning the government money straight over to a charity, as Erin suggested, did not make sense, because they wanted to add something. They did not assume that their alternative to "just being here" would be taking drugs and committing crimes, so they did not imagine needing to be "impacted," as prevention programs put it, but to *have* an impact. For example, the usually calm VJ got angry when many members of the Regional YEP volunteered to go the Pediatric Hospital, claiming to be excited by the project, and then only four showed up. The hospital visit took place on a raw, cloudy day.

In most rooms, pale, still, young children lay propped up in beds, watching frenetic daytime TV. Faint winter sunlight slanted across the bare walls of their rooms, while parents sat in chairs lined up on the walls. "Could anything in the world cheer them up?" I wondered, gloomily, wondering which children were terminally ill, and feeling chilled and randomly lucky that I am not in those parents' position at this very moment.

In one bustling room, about twenty busy volunteers were coloring posters from the current Disney blockbuster *How the Grinch Stole Christmas,* and cutting out paper and plastic decorations to hang on the bare walls and ceilings. Most volunteers were from the University and had not met before this one-day event that they had found listed in a "volunteer opportunities calendar." All volunteers were warmly greeted by an extremely cheery hospital employee who said her job was to "coordinate the social and psychological aspects—like coordinate volunteers and do activities."

I was sitting at the big table near VJ and Teeyen, who was not a member of the group yet. We joked about how much easier it would have been to buy decorations, how making them "really sloppy" would make them look more "handmade," so that it would really look like "someone cared," as VJ put it, half ironically.

After our afternoon's labor, shiny Mylar candy canes and stars dangled from the fireproof ceiling, lights and tinsel hung next to the intake forms on the reception desk; our posters lined the walls, between the fire alarms, safety warnings, biohazard boxes, and medical instruments. I wondered if it was cheery, and wondered how a sociologist could measure that. Afterward, I sat with VJ and Teeyen in the bright hospital basement cafeteria, eating frozen yogurt. Teeyen was a new volunteer in the "disadvantaged" category, since she lived in a housing project, was not white, and was very poor. From her adoring gaze at VJ, it was obvious that one of her motives for volunteering that day was that she had a crush on her tall, handsome Pre-Calculus tutor. After this day, though, she began attending meetings, thus illustrating an entry route that I never heard discussed, and would have been hard to promote, though it is probably one of the most common routes.

VJ fumed that other members of the Regional YEP were coming just to pad their resumes, or meet people, or feel important, not to do the work.

VJ: Only four people showed up! Jenny and Joey came for about a half an hour yesterday. They said they were gonna come from 11 to 3 but they left at about 11:30! Then today we were the only ones. People say they're interested but then they don't sign up to come.

Teeyen: It's like the community service project at school. People come to meetings but no one signs up to do any of the projects.

VJ: It should be like Honors Society—You have to do three community service projects a semester and if you're absent three times, you're out. People want to just be able to say they were on the Regional YEP for their vita. We got all this money—$2,000. How are we gonna spend it? What about buying books and toys for kids in the hospital, and distributing them? Would that be a way to spend it?

NE: I don't think that's what people had in mind—more like, putting up posters to get other people to donate something, or use the money to make something else happen, not just to buy stuff for people.

VJ: Yeah, but how many posters? $2,000 is a lot of posters.

Teeyen: T-shirts? Some of it *is* going for t-shirts. But that's a lot of t-shirts. I thought the money was for giving ourselves parties and doing things for ourselves, to reward ourselves for doing things in the community.

VJ: Yeah, but that's still a lot of money and besides, we haven't done anything in the community yet.

NE: I have a friend who teaches at Washington Middle School who said a lot of kids want to go but don't have transportation.

Teeyen: There's a van for that.

VJ: But I don't know if we'd have to pay the driver for miles. Is it worth it? I mean, if someone's way out there, is it worth it to send a van all the way there to pick them up?

NE: Well, I guess if you're the person all the way in Rutherford or something, you might feel kind of isolated.

VJ: I mean, would it be cost-effective to fly someone in from Los Angeles, California to come to the Regional YEP meeting? I mean, people come to meetings but they don't do anything else. What's the point? [a few more backs-and-forths] . . . we haven't *done* anything yet. People just come to meetings, and don't do anything, or they sign up and don't come—like for the Sun Corp fair, people signed up but only two people came.

Backstage, youth volunteers had conversations like this, puzzling over the meaning of the public monies and the value of volunteering, but when adult organizers were present, the discussion ended quickly with exclamations like Erin's: "Of *course* you're worth it!"

To VJ's mind, spending the money on his own mental health was not "worth it," since VJ did not consider himself to be "a potential problem," but rather, as a "potential solution to someone else's problem." The fact that public money was spent on volunteering gave non-disadvantaged teens like VJ a sense of urgency to make sure the money was well spent. In this way, they were learning to make civic decisions, to ask, "Is this a good way for our society as a whole to be spending its money?"

Hidden Damage: Helping Non-disadvantaged Volunteers

Since non-disadvantaged teens like VJ wanted to give help, not receive it—to help sick children, old people, poor children, animals, or plants—they reserved their wrath for participants whom they perceived as being like them socially—white and/or not poor—who did not help others, and worse, who might be trying to pad their resumes. VJ never expressed anger about volunteers like Raul, with the Doritos bag. VJ assumed that Raul was in another category.

Non-disadvantaged but troubled volunteers could easily fall through the cracks, then, since they neither visibly deserved help nor gave help. Two active, non-disadvantaged volunteers, VJ and Jenny, invited everyone to eat at Hardcore Pizza to discuss this problem: the Regional YEP had begun in September, and by December, the group still had not done any service projects. Only five members came, all in the "non-disadvantaged" category. The pizza dinner became a venting session, with teens complaining bitterly about some other (non-poor, white) members who disrupted planning meetings, or signed up to do projects and then did not show up. As Jenny put it, the group should "have some standards, some requirements, not just be open to anyone":

> Jenny [describing two white, middle-class kids in the group]: "They only count for half a person each! Just half, not a whole person! . . . There could be a rule that you have to do two service projects a year or something." This idea was repeated three times that evening; another time, Jenny said the group should have "higher standards for enrollment." VJ and Jenny had discussed it many times before.
>
> "The meetings are already too big—the bigger they are, the more out of control they'll get" [Jenny said this several times, too]. Getting more people isn't the problem, but getting them to do something other than go to meetings is.

They said that if volunteers like Davey were not *performing*—a word usually reserved for a salesperson or worker who is not meeting a quota— he should be kicked out. From VJ's and Jenny's perspective, therapy for non-disadvantaged, disruptive participants like Davey was not worth funders' money: Davey did not have an "excuse," as they put it.

It would have been hard to turn Davey's neediness into a public issue. Since he was not, on the face of it, a member of any disadvantaged category, publicizing his neediness would inevitably have to be personal, about his family, about his psychology, maybe about his body (and there was, indeed, some discussion about how skinny he was). Nothing could be said to clarify the mystery. At a mid-day gathering of youth workers, Erin and Ju, an Urban League employee, discussed Davey:

> Erin: It's hard, because you don't want to tell people to leave, but that's what we'll have to do.
>
> Rob Strauss (just entering): What happened? Someone was disrupting the meeting last night?
>
> Erin: Let's keep it positive.

Emily said that she has that problem with her kids too. She said, "It's hard to get them to focus. That's part of why I want them to participate: to learn to concentrate."

Organizers knew, theoretically, that misery, suicide, violence, and drug addiction are not limited to the poor or the non-white; that people with hidden problems need protection, too. They sometime reminded each other that nearly all of the perpetrators of big school shootings have been white, middle-class boys. A speaker at one event told a long story describing a neglected, alcoholic teen whose uncaring parents drove an expensive new Volvo, contrasting him with a teen whose parents were desperately poor but loving. His point was that the first teen had a worse problem than the second. He insisted on it, as if it were a surprise, a *counterintuitive* revelation that certainly did not go without saying. Similarly, when organizers were talking about white volunteers from a village outside of Snowy Prairie, who had disrupted some meetings, one said:

> A lot of little towns have a big drug problem—it's not just all cute and storybook there. Who are *we* to tell these kids what to get out of the program? What would they be doing instead? (puzzling aloud) It's gotta be doing *something* for them, or they wouldn't keep coming back.

However much the organizers cared about non-impoverished kids, preventing their misery was not the main public justification of most programs' funding. There was a bit of funding for programs in impoverished villages, but programs' survival did not depend on funding for helping youth whose parents drove Volvos, no matter how neglectful their parents were.[9] There was no form to fill out about it.

Still, organizers had to allow everyone to come, even youth like Davey, even if for unfathomable reasons. There was a practical reason, which was that programs had to be open to all possible volunteers, and the larger the numbers of youth, the better, so even if organizers had wanted to throw Davey out, it would have been hard. But beyond that, kicking him out would have violated one of organizers' most emotionally compelling dreams, of protecting even those youth whose injuries are mysterious and hidden.

For Non-disadvantaged Youth: Nervousness about Self-marketing

The non-disadvantaged youth volunteers worried that they, or their peers, were using volunteering instrumentally, to beef up a resume for future college admissions; they scrutinized themselves and each other for signs of this motive, teased each other about it, and sometimes grew angry with each other because of it. While they could not discuss this motive overtly, they indirectly made its importance obvious when, for example, they made very sure that their volunteer hours were always accurately recorded. At the pizza dinner just described, a new member, Andrew, asked VJ if the group kept "records" of what it did. VJ just naturally assumed that Andrew was asking about getting credit, but Andrew had actually been asking about how to learn from the past:

> VJ, the experienced youth volunteer: No one is keeping a record for the group, but individually, you send in your hours, on those sheets. If you need them signed, you can go to Mary, if you're working in the hospital.

> Andrew: No, I meant is there a record for the future, so you can go back next year and look at what you did and how it went and how you got there and who to contact.

Though it offended teens like VJ, adult organizers had to emphasize this motive, because one of their missions was to level the playing field, by giving disadvantaged youth access to information about how to get into a good college, by telling them directly what teens like VJ had already absorbed in more indirect ways.[10] Erin, as organizer of the Regional YEP one year, was an especially enthusiastic proponent of the plump resume. She repeated messages like this at every meeting:

> Being on the Regional YEP is important for when you're putting together a resume for colleges. They really look at that kind of thing. The President's Award is really huge. It tells them you not only work when you have to; you work when you want to. Coming to these meetings counts—when you're sending in your sheets with your hours [spent volunteering] on them, count these meetings. It's so much fun you forget that you're doing a good deed.

DIFFERENT OPPORTUNITIES FOR PRIDE AND RISKS OF SHAME: VISIBLE PUBLIC SUPPORT VERSUS BEHIND-THE-SCENES SUPPORT

Independently Helping Others

Non-disadvantaged youth could feel proudly independent when they volunteered, knowing that they had freely chosen to help others. The Regional YEP held a food drive one Martin Luther King Day. Standing in an upscale grocery store next to the fresh flower display one frigid winter day, behind a shopping cart semi-full of donated Cheerios, canned minestrone soup, and toilet paper for the food pantry, Siobhan, who was not disadvantaged, smiled at the food that she had bravely coaxed out of busy shoppers. "I feel really great! I feel like I really did a lot of good work today."

Non-disadvantaged youth volunteers could also feel more independent than disadvantaged volunteers; their support was less publicly visible. Caroline, for example, beamed with pride at an awards ceremony for teen volunteers; her mother had driven her to all the Regional YEP meetings; made sure that Caroline had sent in documentation of each hour she worked; driven her to each volunteer engagement, made sure she had made "good choices"; and made sure that Caroline had felt free in making all of her choices. The fact that her mother was doing all of this work, funded by her own family income, was not up for public scrutiny; her mother's expenditure of time, fossil fuel, and effort was not a public, political issue on which anyone would need to vote or justify in public. In fact, part of what made her mother's care so good was that it seemed so freely and happily given; she made it seem not to be "work" at all. She hid in the crowd so that Caroline could shine for having helped other people, in her own spare time, fueled by her own inspiration. Such pride could blossom when a caregiver provided quiet, invisible support, subtly clearing the way for the youth volunteer to feel autonomous and thus, eventually, to take responsibility.[11]

Outstripping the Odds, and Being a Good Representative of One's Category

While they rarely spoke of taking pride in helping distant others, disadvantaged youth volunteers had other sources of pride. First, if they were "minorities," they could feel like proud representatives of their racial or ethnic category. As Marisol put it in another of the many publicity-oriented questionnaires that Community House youth filled out about their civic involvement, she worked as a volunteer in order "to show that our community is not as bad as its reputation." In contrast, in various questionnaires, non-disadvantaged white teens wrote that they hoped that their volunteering would show that *teenagers* were not as bad as the reputation of *teenagers*.

Second, disadvantaged volunteers could feel proud for having beaten the odds. Knowing the grim statistical predictions for people in their social category, disadvantaged youth assumed that using civic engagement to give themselves a boost made perfect sense. Samia, for example, frankly stated in meetings that she was using her volunteer work to get what she knew she deserved: a scholarship to college. When the local newspaper gave them yet another questionnaire, the teens at Community House crafted their responses together:

Samia (laughing): Would it be arrogant if I said, "I volunteer to get money to go to college?"

Emily: Maybe you could put it differently, like "I volunteer to work toward future possibilities for myself?"

Nancy [employee of United Way]: Say, "I volunteer to secure a place for myself in the future." Or no: "to secure a scholarship." Or no: "I volunteer to secure a place in college."

Samia sets to writing: "Secure a scholarship?" What did you say I'm saying? What were your words again?

[Nancy repeats what she had told Samia to write]

The resulting newspaper article mentioned the volunteers' ethnic and racial backgrounds, and said where they lived, thus making it clear that they were poor. These youths' motive—using volunteering to get money for college—was worth cheering, when coming from someone who was as smart, motivated, and in need of money as Samia was. Samia was *supposed* to use volunteering to earn the money, through her own hard work. Volunteering could lessen her feeling of, and appearance of, dependence. The result was another harmonious, possibly respectful reconciliation of the Empowerment Project's missions of promoting civic engagement and helping the needy.

Three years later, Samia did indeed receive a small scholarship. Another news article reported on this triumph, thus boosting Community House's already good public image even more, demonstrating to potential funders that their money would be well spent.

Pride in Independence for Disadvantaged Youth: Incessant Bake Sales, Car Washes, and Lemonade Stands

Another common solution to the problem of disadvantaged youths' conspicuous, publicly displayed dependence was to make the youth participants raise the funds for their programs themselves. Earning the money was supposed to make them look and feel more independent. This resolution of Empowerment Projects' tensions was much less harmonious than the one just described, however, because the fundraising never raised any significant amount of money, and what money it did raise was unreliable. As moral and economic education, Community House's constant spaghetti dinners, burrito dinners, car washes, rummage sales, and other fundraisers gave members potentially good lessons in self-sufficiency, creativity, counting change, and tallying profits against expenses. They were like the American family tradition of the Sunday lemonade stand in the front yard—the lemons, sugar, cups, and ice cost more than the earnings, but if the parents can afford it, it can be worth the sociable entertainment and the lessons in economics and arithmetic. It was the same in the youth programs—projects like those were sometimes great fun, but, as an organizer joked at one meeting, "the forty-seven dollars our bake sale raised paid for the ingredients. But the cookies sure were good!"

If the children do not raise enough money, nobody says that a family should collapse, but in a program like Community House, the urgency and relentlessness of the fundraising made collapse look like a very real possibility. This made it hard to avoid thinking of the goal as being *money*, rather than a lesson and a fun afternoon activity. Instead of feeling like a solution to inequality, a route to empowered self-sufficiency, the endless fundraising became yet another kind of deprivation. Disadvantaged young people had to raise funds for their own upkeep; their wealthier counterparts did not.

At one meeting among adults, Emily suddenly grew angry when she thought that the young people's fundraising strayed from the lemonade stand motif:

> Emily proudly told the Board of Directors [a group of volunteers, mostly older women, that meets monthly, in the evening] that a local pizza joint, Hardcore Pizza, offered to donate a dollar for every whole pizza customers bought, if they mentioned Community House's name. Triumphantly, she added, "It was the KIDS who went and asked Clementina (that's the owner's name) themselves! They really took initiative!"
>
> We all exclaimed about how great that was, that the kids were so self-reliant.
>
> Emily added, "That's what I keep teaching them—to be self-reliant, take initiative."
>
> We all agreed enthusiastically that that was important, just what kids need, etc.
>
> Emily abruptly changed key, to a distinctly minor one, saying, "*All* the kids *ever do* is fundraising—all our workshops are on fundraising, how to write grants how to get money. There's like no cultural enrichment or music or arts programming or anything."

She continued, in the resentful tone of a mother who cannot provide the best for her children, to describe the stimulating, expensive art, music, and theater school that wealthier children attended. Another time, she said it was "unfair" to make her kids raise funds for their own care, while non-disadvantaged youth automatically have more "options," more room for personal "inspiration," as Empowerment Projects promise, to choose chemistry or ceramics, cooking or bassoon. Emily's complaint was not a sign that she favored "hand-outs" to the poor, as some might imagine.

On the contrary, she very strictly and frequently told participants that they should "*not expect something for nothing*," neither from adult volunteers nor from anyone else. When, for example, adult volunteers cooked with participants, Emily made sure that the young people cleaned the kitchen themselves.

Then, on top of it, after participants had succeeded in making this clever fundraising deal with Hardcore Pizza, the pizza place went bankrupt! The lessons about self-sufficiency had to have very low stakes; the program's fate could not depend on funds raised in lemonade stand–like lessons. Most funding agencies recognized this and did not actually expect youth volunteers' fundraising to make the programs entirely self-sustaining, but the nonstop fundraising sent youth participants a different message.

In a twisted way, the unspoken message that they perceived was very correct: the programs' existence *did*, in fact, depend on kids' nonstop fundraising, because the fundraising worked as a symbol for funders who thought that becoming self-propelled volunteers who plan fundraisers would help prevent disadvantaged teens from becoming social problems. Here again, while volunteering was supposed to equalize the two sets of youth, the incessant fundraising amplified a certain, specific kind of inequality between them.

DIFFERENT USES OF ABSTRACT KNOWLEDGE

Learning about Experts' Statistics as a Form of Direct Experience for At-Risk Youth

To feel proud about having beaten the odds, disadvantaged youth had to know what the odds were. For that, broader sociological knowledge was necessary. When, for example, African Americans were asked to speak "from their own personal experience," they often presented *statistics*. At one Juneteenth celebration (Juneteenth celebrates the freeing of African American slaves in Texas; the news of freedom did not arrive in Texas until two years after the Emancipation Proclamation), for example, a thirteen-year-old black school boy stood on the podium and said:

> Most blacks can't control themselves because they have such low expectations on them. There is a 50 percent dropout rate, so the community makes it tough for black males like me. It's very tough to get off that thing they set up for us.

Learning about dropout rates can help someone like this boy see how he fit into the world. Even though he spoke of himself as a "black male," with the clinical scent that the phrase bears, at least the statistics gave him a sense that he was not alone.

Messages about statistics and inequality were emphatically not the messages that most white organizers hoped to teach. They hoped instead for youth to leave the past behind, and for all races to treat one another as already equal. When speaking out publicly, youths' words were supposed to be "from the mouths of babes." But participants in the Empowerment Projects eagerly read the unspoken signs, so they could know where they stood.

African American adults who addressed youth Empowerment Projects also often started their speeches with heartfelt lists of grim statistics: dropout rates, incarceration rates, poverty rates, unemployment rates, illiteracy rates, single parenthood rates, teen pregnancy rates. They ended the speeches with rousing calls to boost graduation rates and voting rates among "*our* youth"—implicitly meaning blacks, though they could not say it directly—no matter who the audience was. At one annual Martin Luther King Day event, for example, an African American speaker devoted half of his blazing, furious speech to statistics. "There are exactly 201 black males in ninth grade in the Snowy Prairie public schools. Based on these statistics, only ten will graduate with college degrees." At the end, he ominously declared that if you wanted to learn more about racial inequality, you could read a book, and he held one up. This speech made it clear that when he discovered statistics documenting the depth of these racial inequalities, it was, itself, a shocking, direct, *personal* experience, an external verification of his personal intuitions, and a trumpet call to civic participation. In contrast, whites could not give such speeches without risking sounding like they were condemning blacks; and when whites heard such speeches, they considered them to be abstract descriptions of blacks, as we will see more directly in a few pages. Learning about oneself through statistics, and as a member of a category, can certainly be a route to empowerment, though it is definitely not the kind of empowerment that Empowerment Talk promises.

At the same time, disadvantaged youth tended to minimize the problems that poor people face; they needed to prove to themselves that deprivation is surmountable and does not inevitably lead to needy dependence, because they, themselves, were often the unspoken referent. They did not necessarily feel damaged, did not want to feel damaged, and certainly did not want to publicize any damage, if there was any. For example, Dominic's mother dealt drugs and sometimes took drugs all night long. Landlords evicted his family from one apartment after another. They moved in with relatives, sleeping on their sofas, but finally, the relatives also threw them out. Dominic was flunking school, for reasons that Emily said were "obvious," enumerating the list I just gave. But her youth group judged Dominic culpable anyway, still holding him responsible for his choices, since his home life was not much different from many of their home lives.

Community House participants rarely talked about politics in the sense of "public policy" or elections, but when they did, their conversations were like their discussions of statistics: rather than imagining "politics" as a far-away thing that affects someone else, politics seemed close and personal. One was about the election of President Bush; one boy exclaimed, "He'll take away our rights!" Emily, once again, had to take the other position, reassuring them by saying that there were many checks and balances to prevent him from taking away all their rights. In their very personal, passionate treatment of statistics and politics, it was important for *someone* to take the position that the danger was somehow not insurmountable. It was a game that had to reach an equilibrium: when Emily did not take the opposing viewpoint, the young people did; when the young people did not, Emily did.

Since disadvantaged youth were often physically lumped together, it was easier for them than for non-disadvantaged youth to see themselves as members of categories. At the Prairie Restoration Project for elementary-age children, for example:

> The kids from Echo Park [a program like Community House for disadvantaged kids] don't have their names on the attendance roster. They all come in a pack in a school bus, and they all got free yellow t-shirts with the name of their program on it, so they're all wearing the same outfit.

In contrast, non-disadvantaged children's individual names appeared on an attendance roster, they wore varied clothing, and they trickled into the room individually, after having been dropped off by their parents. Each morning, one parent or another described to me the long, fascinating, funny, or poignant conversation they had had on the way to camp, with the detail and wonderment that comes with love—intimacy that Empowerment Project organizers hoped to democratize, even to youth whose parents were not so loving, or were in another country, or dead. Through hundreds of little, tiny reminders like these, the participants in the unique shirts appeared as individuals, while participants in the uniform shirts appeared as members of categories and representatives of "their community," as Marisol had put it.

Apolitical Structure Talk: Non-disadvantaged Youth's Relation to Politics

The non-disadvantaged youth had a very different relationship to politics and political problems. They used what we can call "Apolitical structure talk" to speak abstractly about distant others' problems, often exaggerating them with a dramatic flourish. Apolitical structure talk demonstrates that the speaker understands politics rationally, coolly, dispassionately, without taking any of it personally or applying it to anyone he or she personally knows. People who use it can sound sophisticated, piling on evidence to depict a hopeless political world, making it easy to feel as if there is absolutely nothing they can do until structural conditions change, and that the hopeless conditions have nothing to do with their lives. By "exempting"[12] themselves from the hopeless world, the speakers come out clean and blameless.

While making posters for the Regional YEP's food drive, wielding a paintbrush loaded with gloppy yellow tempera paint, sixteen-year-old VJ masterfully performed an arms-length analysis, as if he was already imagining himself as a potentially powerful policy maker. He was chatting with the other teens at his table, casually describing an essay he wrote for his Advanced Placement English class. He had argued that the murder in *Native Son*, in which the poor black servant possibly accidentally kills the white mistress girl, was *absolutely inevitable* given the servant's social conditions. From his panoramic perch, showing that he understood the effects of social conditions was a way of saying, "I am compassionate, broad-minded, and smart. I can paint a completely coherent picture of society."

Many university students who came to volunteer in the after-school programs also sounded like this. Keith, a white volunteer homework helper, was a Political Science major who came to Community House for a few months. He eagerly told the elementary school children that their textbooks were full of absolutely nothing but lies, and that the whole society is racist from top to bottom. It was clear that he was proud of his new knowledge, but had not quite gotten far enough to ask himself how his proud display of solidarity might undermine the third graders' faith in their homework or in their teachers—or in him.

DIFFERENT IDEAS FOR VOLUNTEER PROJECTS: DRAWING ON SEPARATE EXPERIENCES

Organizers continually asked youth volunteers to identify problems that affect *all* youth, not just *some* youth. Despite organizers' best intentions, the non-disadvantaged volunteers' ideas sounded more universal to organizers. These youth often felt more comfortable speaking in front of a group. It was as if their ideas were pre-formatted for easy insertion into the public arena. As a result, their suggestions more often became the kernels of the groups' projects. This created another kind of hidden inequality.

For example, the purpose of one Regional YEP project was to make sure that teenagers who drove from town to town at night were subject to the same laws in each town. As it stood, in some towns, it was illegal for sixteen-year-olds to be outside after 10 o'clock; in others, the age or hour was different; in others, night driving was illegal for teens, but walking was not. The Regional YEP wanted uniform rules throughout the county. It took me *months* to notice that the most active Community House participants were surprisingly uninvolved in this project. In field notes, I chastised myself for being so oblivious:

> It was only when I heard Marisol [from Community House] rolling her eyes and muttering to Samia about how she "didn't care, didn't know, had never been to New Stockholm [one of those towns with the early curfew rules]," that I, terrific sociologist that I am, noticed that the *whole issue was for kids who drive!* It was for kids who drive from one suburb to another at night; kids who have cars and live in suburbs, not in Snowy Prairie's dense public housing projects where most of the Community House kids lived.
>
> After Marisol said that, I realized that I had never heard of some of these hamlets, either. There would be no more reason for Marisol or Raul to go to one of those snowy all-white villages at night than for I, and no way for them to get there, even if they wanted to. How could I have not put this together before hearing Marisol grumble, six months into the project?

Community House members did not have drivers' licenses. Why had they not objected sooner? It would have sounded too much like a personal complaint and would have rudely dampened enthusiasm. I never heard any organizers noticing that the project made sense only for teens who drove. Erin had told me earlier that year that many participants did not have cars, but in this situation, she forgot, probably having been carried away with enthusiasm for the youth leadership that she hoped to build.

The point is *not* that the adults did not *care* about inequality; it was just hard for them to notice it in this case, as it was for me. When they did notice that a proposed project benefited only non-disadvantaged youth, they slammed the brakes on it. One Regional YEP meeting opened with the question of what project to do next. VJ and Jenny suggested telling the high schools to put AP[13] grades on a 5.0 scale.

VJ: UCLA demands a 4.3 average!

Jenny: By putting it at 4.0, students don't challenge themselves enough. Putting it at 5.0 gives incentives to take harder classes.

Erin agrees: Someone who is taking auto shop might get A's. Some student senate/congresses are already doing that [putting grades on a 5.0 scale].

Rob Strauss, the head of county youth programs, was usually extremely enthusiastic when teens made any suggestions at all, or took any initiative at all. He strongly believed in the principle of participation, as a good in itself. This evening, he just sat silently, with a slight grimace. After the meeting, indirect criticizing the project, he told me that he wanted projects to include *all* youth, not just a few, not just those who were already leaders and at the top of their classes. Probably, he was imagining a certain race and class of youth in those AP classes, but he could not say that, even behind-the-scenes to me.

Usually, the fact that youth had gotten together to do *something* was all that mattered to adults, regardless of a project's substance, but in this case, Rob Strauss's conspicuous silence made his disapproval clear, though he never gave the youth volunteers any hints to explain it. After VJ and Jenny suggested the project a few more times, the Regional YEP still did not take it on. Eventually, lacking any enthusiasm from these usually enthusiastic adults, VJ and Jenny dropped the proposal.

Different Maps of the City

Even deciding on a meeting place indirectly revealed inequality between youth volunteers. There was no socially neutral space to meet. For a while, the Regional YEP met at Community House, but some organizers, and most non-disadvantaged, suburban youth, said it was dirty and inconvenient, since it was not near their neighborhoods or any highway exits that would make access by car easy from the city's green-lawned periphery.

> By day, Community House basement rooms house a program for sixteen- to eighteen-year-olds who had been kicked out of high school. The dirty walls are covered with their infantile projects—crayoned leaf prints, lumpy collages about pop music stars of the past, "reports" on other countries like, "Life in Britten" with a picture cut out of a magazine of a queen and a castle (one of the suburban YEP kids joked, "Britten: rhymes with 'kitten!'")—projects like those a seven-year-old might bring home.
>
> So we moved the meetings, to the bleak gym of the Prevention Center, way out in the outskirts of town. This was more convenient for the suburban youth because it was right off the six-lane highway they took to drive their cars into downtown Snowy Prairie from the various suburban neighborhoods and towns. Glaring ceiling lights, which one youth member described as "interrogation lamps, like in a torture scene," made us all look as if we had blank eye sockets. Some older men, all black, had a GED class ["General Equivalency Degree," that helps

people who have not finished high school to graduate, sometimes 20 or 30 years after they dropped out] in the next room down the grim hall.

The scene alone, and the difficulties in choosing a place to meet, says something: The PC Building made volunteering seem somehow clinical, a prescription, a vaccination.

So, the group voted to move the meeting place a third time, a couple of months later, this time about twenty minutes away, to a posh office building with cushioned swiveling armchairs, plush carpeting, framed prints and original art on the walls. But *that* was too far from Community House; the Community House kids—who had all voted against the move—would always be late, since they would have to wait until Emily closed up Homework Club at 6, to drive them to the meetings that *started* at 6 across town. So, the meetings moved a fourth time. There is simply no neutral common ground in segregated cities like this!

The two sets of volunteers even seemed to hold different maps of Snowy Prairie, literally making it hard for them to give each other directions to local addresses—especially when disadvantaged youth tried to describe where they lived. If, for example, a disadvantaged member usually took the bus and a non-disadvantaged member drove, they had different ideas of time and distances. They had different landmarks: the library, university, or upscale mall for non-disadvantaged youth versus the disadvantaged youths' internal maps that focused on the bus transfer center, free health clinic, and the Burger King in front of the hidden Buckingham Estates housing project. Buckingham Estates could be found only if one knew that the sole entrance was through one particular Burger King parking lot. The housing project was hidden *behind* it, with no city street connecting it to another city street. Everyone could locate the first list— the library and the mall—even if it was a little hard for the disadvantaged youth. Non-disadvantaged youths' maps simply did not include places like Buckingham Estates, and more generally, the lives of the disadvantaged members were opaque to their more affluent counterparts.

Sometimes, the baffled non-disadvantaged teens puzzled amongst each other over interactions that they did not understand. But if they intuited that the mystery was somehow related to other youth volunteers' poverty or ethnicity, no one gave them the tools to finish making the connection. For example, VJ told Jenny and some others, in a small meeting of some YEP members, that Bonita and Marisol sometimes gave the same phone number on contact sheets, and sometimes gave different ones. He said that when he tried to call Bonita's house (or apartment—he was not sure which, he said) (which was apparently only sometimes also Marisol's, he said) to remind her of a meeting, some guy answered who asked, "Bonita who?" and practically would not let him talk. VJ speculated that the guy was not her dad, because the next time he called, some other guy answered. He could not figure out why there were so many phone numbers and so many guys and why they were so worried about his talking to her, but he could not ask these questions—especially not to Bonita herself—without being impossibly rude. I silently wondered to myself if the number of guys and the quickly changing addresses had something to do with her parents' and uncles' stream of migration in and out of Mexico. If you want to make sense of families that are different from your own, one way is to ask questions, but since adult organizers had not designed a way to make the questions seem less rude, posing them was awkward (and possibly could reveal legal problems, in this case, if the relatives did not have green cards, though the non-disadvantaged youth may not have known what a green card was).

Organizers and disadvantaged youth could each talk about inequality to their own groups in a concrete, local way. It was only the non-disadvantaged youth who could not decipher it. Bringing people together as equals was hard in these baffling conditions, but organizers assumed that talking about the differences might have taken too much time, or be uninspiring.

TRYING TO IGNORE INEQUALITY

These Empowerment Projects existed partly because of social inequality, but did not have enough time for a complex, potentially explosive discussion of it. They could not scare away any needy, fragile youth who might be healed if they became volunteers, and organizers assumed that discussion would scare them away. So, developing an organizational style that could smooth over inequality without having to discuss it was urgent.

One approach was simply to minimize the inequality, or change the subject. After one Martin Luther King Day event, Liz and I were with some middle-schoolers who had to conduct a "service" project because they had broken a school rule. Liz, their music teacher, had gotten roped into leading the group.

> We were walking through the icy parking lot to Liz's new, sparkling teal-blue minivan. Liz was going to drive us to Community House, to sort books for a charity drive. Liz is white and the kids are all non-white. They are relentlessly quizzing her about how she can afford such a large vehicle, teasing her, asking her where she lives, how big her house is, comparing her neighborhood to theirs.

She kept answering that it was not so big, not so expensive, not so fancy, not very different from their car, home, neighborhood. Rather than acknowledging the differences, she was trying to be egalitarian by minimizing them, but it was obvious to all that she is in a different class (partly because they know that her husband is a lawyer).

Evading the question made sense, however. The difficulty of explaining inequality in Empowerment Projects was driven home to me when the Urban League, an organization for the promotion of African Americans' rights, held its annual Martin Luther King Day Pancake Breakfast in a high school cafeteria. Most of the two hundred or so people who came were non-white, but a few white social workers, teachers, politicians, program leaders like Emily, and government officials like Rob Strauss always attended, probably making it Snowy Prairie's most racially diverse public gathering. Most of the event was a ceremony for minority youth who received awards from various NGOs for having outstripped all odds. The premise of the event was impossible to explain to non-disadvantaged, white audience members:

> A few of the middle-class whites [the politicians, teachers, social workers, many of whom I recognized] attended with their own children. One white kid—maybe seven years old—ruminated to his politician father: "Why do they get awards for playing flute and getting B's? What's so great about that?" The father whispered a response; it was very short and I couldn't hear it.

How could the father realistically explain this event to his son, who did not consider playing flute and getting B's to be very amazing? It would be impossible without offering a whole sociology class and lots of statistics, directly addressing poverty and racism's grave effects, if there are any, on the everyday lives of children. Discussing it would have required a whole semester's worth of sociology classes!

The programs' usual solution was absolutely no discussion of inequality, so knowledge about it came oozing out of the seams where the "civic" and "protection of the needy" sides of the programs were loosely stitched together. For example, the youth-led celebration of Martin Luther King Day became an inspiring symbol of interracial unity in Snowy Prairie. The local community television station played the event over and over again for weeks, displaying the diverse youth audience as a symbol of hope for racial harmony and the spirit of volunteerism. But up close, the symbol wobbled under the weight of big social divisions between the two sets of youth.

While waiting for the morning speeches to start, the non-disadvantaged teens sat at their tables talking about their cars, talking about where they parked their cars, about what kind of repairs their cars needed, about where they were driving after the event, talking on their cell phones (this was several years ago, when few people in Snowy Prairie had them), buying the conference center's overpriced coffee, bagels, fruit, and jam. Meanwhile, the disadvantaged kids arrived in big clusters, in community center vans or city buses. They could not afford the food, so they had to wait to eat for four more hours, when free pizza and soda was distributed. Age differences overlay race and class differences: the event was designed for kids ages twelve and up, and indeed, all the non-disadvantaged youth were in their mid-teens. In contrast, the disadvantaged youth were of all ages, down to age four, because, as organizers sometimes remarked, their working parents needed a free, safe place to send them, on this day off for schools that was not a day off for most workplaces. The non-disadvantaged youth had only themselves to take care of; the disadvantaged youth had to worry about their younger brothers and sisters. Physically and socially, the two sets of young people came on different routes, and rarely mingled.

The event's theme of universal, unconditional love, equality, and unity took on a strange flavor in this setting. Every year, all participants were given folders with this quote from Martin Luther King, Jr. inscribed on them:

> Everybody can be great. Because anybody can serve. You don't have to have a college degree to serve. You don't have to make your subject and your verb agree to serve. You don't have to know about Plato and Aristotle to serve. . . . You only need a heart full of grace. A soul generated by love.

Speakers echoed the theme of grace and service, of moral wholeness regardless of your station in life. One said, for example, that "if you serve, you are blessed, regardless of your I.Q. or socioeconomic status" (leaving me to wonder if some kids thought, "Oh, good, so even though I'm dumb, I can serve!?"). Inspiration and civic engagement could, according to this message, cure you; you are helped when the spirit moves you to help others. The spoken message, however, was nearly the opposite, aimed at the importance of doing well in school, going to college, being sure that your subject and your verb agree.

Implicitly, speakers imagined the African Americans as the audience for this spoken message, and this message, aimed at one set of youth, transformed as it entered another set of youths' ears. One speaker, the black president of the local Urban League, pitched a message aimed straight at the African American youth:

> Achievement matters. One out of two African Americans will drop out of high school in Snowy Prairie. . . . [He gives more statistics about the awful dropout rates among blacks, and then adds some about Latinos.]

And at another Martin Luther King Day event, the same speaker said, after offering similar statistics:

> If we don't start taking achievement seriously, we'll continue to get what we've got [here is that implicit "we" again], and that's unaccept-able. They're the next group of people that's gonna take care of us in the twilight of our years. I'll want someone who got B's, not D's, taking care of me, who was there when the lesson was taught about how to take care of people, not out on the street or having a party. I'd want someone who ACHIEVED!

So, you might not need to know about Plato and Aristotle to serve, but at least you need pretty good grades! Participants overheard stories that were intended for others. In order to make sense of these interactions, the non-disadvantaged youth had to know that getting B's was a good goal for *someone else*, but not for them; as we heard earlier, their aim was a higher-than-A average achieved through AP credits.

These messages, aimed at one set of youth but overheard by another, further divided the already racially segregated audience in this segregated city. In the first speech, the speaker went from citing statistics to scolding a knot of black boys who were fidgeting and laughing in the back, point-ing to them and saying to them—and to everyone else, of course— *"There's the problem right there."*

When one audience was not separate from another, one story split in two. They heard the same message, but got very different things from it. Both sets of youth knew what social categories were relevant, and who was the intended audience, or the speeches would have been gibberish. They could not mention knowledge of their differences, but they had to use that knowledge, anyway, just to decipher speech and action in Em-powerment Projects. Empowerment Projects' diversity and blending made accidental crisscrossings of messages frequent. Youth volunteers came to recognize this strange new form of inequality, when they kept interacting on predictably unequal footing.

Jokes about Inequality: The Baby-Blue Cardigan with Pearlized Buttons

However taboo it was to mention inequality, it was impossible to hide, and so, an element of organizational style developed: the disadvantaged youth volunteers produced a constant undertow of jokes about their non-disadvantaged counterparts. At one Regional YEP meeting, Marisol, from Community House, got up and announced, loudly and proudly:

> *All* members of the Regional YEP will get a shirt to wear at events: A light-weight, baby blue cardigan with pearlized buttons!

She triumphantly held up the model sweater and grinned. Before the meeting, the Community House girls giggled among each other before any of the white kids had arrived, saying that it was "the ugliest sweater you've ever seen." The whole thing was a joke.

But at Marisol's announcement, the meeting room filled with alarm.

Jenny, baby blue eyes blazing with fury, demanded, "What will the boys wear?"

Siobhan [the studious white girl with whom I gathered groceries, who was bound for an excellent private college in the fall]: *I* would wear that kind of thing!

Lisa (another white kid from a suburb): I would, too!

Another white girl, sounding really worried: But what would the *guys* wear?

A fourth white girl: They're not *pink*, they're *blue*. That's why they're blue!

The Community House girls did not let on that it was a joke, and kept it afloat over months of meetings. Finally, they had to apologize, clarifying that it was just a joke, based on a dirty sweater they had found at Community House.

The sweater in question was just the kind of thing Jenny wore. Whenever she spoke in meetings, usually about her full schedule of tennis, field hockey, and other sports, or about her car, her thin face glowing white and pink above her baby-blue clothes, the big, dark Community House girls sat (somehow, always behind her) like the Greek chorus, clad in black and red, slick or sexy but never pastel-colored or femme, making silly faces. At one Regional YEP meeting,

Jenny bounced in, looking nervous and tennis-y, blond hair and braces gleaming. You had to laugh at the contrast, and Marisol and Samia did [though I didn't!]. They mumbled to each other, "Oooh, they have *tennis* at Sandstrom High. Ooooh, *tennis* at Sandstrom High. Well, gotta go get into my game of *tennis*." Jenny didn't hear, but I was sitting right next to Marisol, so I did.

At another meeting:

Marisol, Bonita, and Marie were arranged in a semicircle behind Jenny, and when she announced that everyone should come to Sandstrom High's tennis game, the Greek chorus behind her started giggling, seemingly out of control. Marisol hid her mouth in her hand and looked down after a while, but her eyes were crinkled up into a big giggle.

Covertly, they had made the baby-blue cardigan with pearlized buttons into a symbol, significant only to them, flagging the differences between the two teams.

What I had not put together, until scrutinizing my field notes a year later, was that a very similar baby-blue cardigan had appeared at a meeting once before. A charity used part of this Regional YEP meeting as a focus group, to get ideas for its upcoming Holiday Gift drive (nonprofits and charities often used the Regional YEP as a focus group). Erin suggested

> a V-neck like yours (looking at VJ). VJ, always the fashion model, gets all his clothes from Abercrombie and Fitch.

> Someone else added: Baby-blue cardigans like the one Jenny's wearing [from the Gap, which was relatively expensive at the time, compared to other local clothing stores].

Of course, the Community House girls snickered, and it may have been here that their joke about the baby-blue cardigan with pearlized buttons began (though the one that the girls found at Community House looked very much like Jenny's, it must not have been, or she would have been happy that they had found her long-lost sweater).

Samia, Bonita, and Marie often joked about racism when they were hidden from their non-disadvantaged, white counterparts. The three girls were in one of the basement rooms at Community House, doing their homework, with the door closed. A meeting was about to begin in the room, and I entered early, inadvertently bursting in on their privacy. There was a parody list: "Marie's Favorite Things to Say," on the blackboard:

> "I'm not a racist—I don't care what color you are!" (mocking teachers' standard line at Snowy Prairie High School. Marie, venting to me a year later, repeated that pious line, saying it was part of her reason for hating school, almost dropping out, and doing poorly her last year—which was a shame considering how smart she was).
> "I (heart) Jesus and you should too." (mocking Christians)
> "Snowy Prairie is the best place on earth." (mocking everyone)

Also backstage (when Emily and I were the only adults there) were the standard American jokes about different kinds of race traitors and conformists: caramel apples (brown on the outside, white on the inside), bananas (yellow outside, but white inside), etc., that most Americans know.

Very young or inexperienced African American volunteers sometimes spoke directly about wealth and poverty in front of non-disadvantaged youth and organizers, but quickly learned to stop, to put their comments backstage, or to transform them into low snickers. The Martin Luther King Day planning committee decided to send participants to work in soup kitchens, but then discovered that soup kitchens would be closed on the holiday:

> A black volunteer: We could do it in someone's house, if it's reeeeally big. (Turning straight to the two white sisters in the meeting) You'all have a big *house*?

> One of the white sisters: No, but there's a mansion nearby.

I saw the repressed knowledge of differences between the two sets of youth burst into outright conflict once, in an evening meeting to plan the year's Martin Luther King Day. As in other meetings of the civic engagement projects, disadvantaged volunteers introduced themselves by naming the programs (like Community House, Urban League, or the Boys and Girls Club) through which they had come. Non-disadvantaged youth introduced themselves by saying more varied things about themselves, as individuals: what schools they attended, or that they liked to volunteer, or what issue concerned them. As usual, the non-disadvantaged youth had come alone, in their own cars, not in groups, in community center vans. As usual, the non-disadvantaged volunteers were all teenagers, while the disadvantaged youth ranged in age, from age seventeen down to six. All together, about thirty youths and five adults sat at folding tables in the Teen Community Center, a storefront drop-in center with windowless walls decorated with murals portraying faces of racially diverse teens interacting joyously.

I was at a table with a group of black elementary school students who were in an after-school group organized by the Urban League. By about 9 o'clock, they were getting overtired and fidgety—most had not been home since 7 a.m. Their organizer, an affectionate, petite white Americorps volunteer, kept gently saying, "Are you listening?" and "I don't want you hurting the table" to a tired-looking eight-year-old who kept writhing in his seat and hammering on the table.

Finally, Denali, the daughter of two lawyers, exploded in frustration, chastising the writhing, hammering, fidgeting, inattentive crowd. She said that if kids were really going to organize the event and not leave it to adults, then they had to take it seriously and pay attention. Usually, the organizational style deflected such outbursts.

CONCLUSION: BEING A PROBLEM, OR SOLVING OTHER PEOPLE'S PROBLEMS?

Empowerment Projects prescribe civic volunteering as a method of gradually overcoming inequality, step-by-step, by working together, shoulder-to-shoulder. The process helped youth like Samia, the Community House participant. She beat the odds, became a proud, effective, and dedicated volunteer, and eventually won a university scholarship. Focusing on hopeful potential, they acted as if Raul might very well become a dedicated volunteer some day, though he was not one yet. In the meantime, it kept him safe for the evenings at least, and possibly coaxed him into becoming an active volunteer some day. At its best, this process not only helped someone like Samia win the university scholarship; it also sometimes helped disadvantaged youth learn how they fit into the bigger picture and to see that their outstripping the odds was itself an achievement about which they could be proud.

While some volunteers like Raul might grow into the high expectations that organizers had for them, the process did not make social inequality vanish. Bringing diverse youth together also created a kind of inequality. "Being" a problem is nothing new for African Americans: "How does it feel to be a problem?" W. E. B. DuBois famously asked at the turn of the twentieth century (1998 [1910]). It is not new, but was playing out here, in organizations in which participants had to speak *as if* they were equals when everyone knew they were not, and when they knew that they were together because of programs that existed for the purpose of preventing some but not all of them from becoming problems.

To understand how racial or class inequalities come to feel real in Empowerment Programs, we have to examine how participants enter the scene, for different purposes, with different invitations in hand. The two different sets of youth enter the civic engagement projects on different routes, riding in on different trajectories from different pasts and toward different predicted futures.[14] In Empowerment Projects, their trajectories momentarily crossed, and they were supposed to leave those pasts and futures behind, to bond as equals, new and fresh and untainted by past or current conditions. Their unspoken differences—differences that everyone recognized anyway—drove a wedge between them. However organizers tried to resolve the perplexities of "showing respect" in such socially diverse groups, their answers did not obliterate inequality, but incarnated it in new ways. Participants ferreted out the reasons for their own participation, and for their organization's existence, no matter what organizers said explicitly to the contrary. Learning to do this was, in itself, a valuable lesson, though not the intended one.

CHAPTER 3

"The Spirit that Moves Inside You": Puzzles of Using Volunteering to Cure the Volunteer's Problems

"BEING WILLING TO FAIL EVERY DAY": PUBLIC SPEECH ABOUT THE SPIRIT THAT MOVES INSIDE YOU

A favorite speaker at Snowy Prairie's volunteer events was a Jamaican musician, a born-again Christian, Ezeky'el. At one event, his assignment was to describe the inspiration for volunteering and tie it to the day's theme of "leadership." Pacing across the school auditorium's stage, building up a sweat, tossing his clean dreadlocks, he said:

> Leadership. That's what they want me to talk about. It means taking risks, joy *and* pain, risking getting lost. You have to know what it is to be lost. How many of you have been lost?
>
> (enthusiastic shouting from the audience, as if at a prayer revival meeting)
>
> So you know how it is to be lost. Leadership: It's failing. Failing every day ... Leadership: It's sharing—some days it feels like give, give give ... it's a spirit that moves inside you. *Nobody can see it, but you know it's there.*

"What a moving message," I thought to myself. "This is why volunteering is so important! You recognize the unfathomable mystery of each other; 'nobody can see it, but you know it's there.' What is respect, if not awe before this human mystery?"

Empowerment Talk suggests that volunteering is good because it is soul-changing, and organizers embraced this mission. To fulfill this mission of deeply inspiring and transforming the volunteers, volunteering would be *hard*. To fulfill the mission of helping needy volunteers themselves—youth who were "not the usual leader type," who lacked confidence—however, organizers had to make sure volunteering was *easy*.

These two missions came into possible tension with each other, and with a third: helping others, which usually requires knowledge, or even expertise, not just inspiration. There was a possible three-way dissonance between inspiring all of the volunteers, helping the needy volunteers, and having the expertise or know-how to help other people. These possible discords, and their various resolutions, harmonious and otherwise, are the topic of this chapter.

Soul-Searching and Inspiration versus Easy and Accessible Help for the Needy Volunteer

Youth Empowerment Projects in Snowy Prairie never *did* those kinds of soul-changing projects that Ezeky'el proposed. It would be too hard and would scare off potential volunteers. The contrast became clear when youth participants divided up into smaller groups right after his speech, when Samia, Bonita, Marie, and Marisol, Emily's four most active volunteers, led a workshop that they had designed on "How to Start a Group."

Marisol stood at the head of the classroom, in front of a group of about thirty teenagers, many resting their heads on their desks, looking pale, tired, and grumpy—grumpy because it was early morning on a school holiday, and many were there because their parents had made them go, so that they would not be home having sex and taking drugs. The day's slogan, written on folders and posters, was: "It's a Day On, Not a Day Off," but many participants would have preferred a day off.

Marisol: How many of you have ever volunteered? (Lots raise hands.)

Marisol: What did you do?

Voices from audience pitch in:
Concessions stand at a soccer game.
Cleaned litter on a highway.
Volunteered at Snowy Prairie Festival.
Blood drive.
Volunteered in my church.

Organizer of a rural Youth Center, turning to the kid who said he cleaned a highway: *Is* it a lot of work, or not too bad?"

Youth participant: It's a mile stretch, you go 3–4 times a year; it's not too bad.

Next, there was a long discussion about how easy it was to pick up highway litter, about dates, and about how you did not have to do it in the winter.

These easy, half-day activities did not easily mesh with the unfathomable, mysterious good that was supposed to come from selflessly serving, buoyed on the vast internal ocean where Emerson said that the most personal meets the most universal. Programs needed to attract as many youth as possible, by making it sound easy, comfortable, and fun, not risky, terrifying, or "failing every day," as Ezeky'el put it. The needy young people whom organizers most wanted to reach were those who were already failing, and organizers guessed that they would not want to set themselves up intentionally to risk even more failure. And so, all youth participants knew that their volunteering was almost never full of "risks and pain." You could not get "lost."

Of course, having the litter picked up is better than not, but that was not the groups' main point. Their hope was that just having a taste of volunteering might whet a few participants' appetites for more serious, soul-changing work. Organizers spoke about the projects such as litter cleanups as if they were *just like* the kind of self-directed, soul-changing, soul-threatening work that Ezeky'el described.

The Regional YEP's visit to the Pediatric Hospital was typical of the tension between doing something soul-changing and difficult, doing something easy that could help them overcome their own problems, and helping others. At the group's meeting, VJ, a non-disadvantaged volunteer, described in a proud but humble voice:

> I went to Disneyland over spring break and there was this family that had taken their child there. She was terminally ill, and going there was her one big wish. She was so skinny and pale, but she was so happy to be there! They let me go around with her one day—I'll never forget it—I was just so—I mean, I couldn't go to work for four days after that. I couldn't leave the house without thinking of this little girl and everything she was going through. I wrote about it for my college entrance essay and gave it to my English teacher. He really liked it—he said it was so touching, it actually made him shed a tear.

His story evoked the heartbreaking, spiritual ideal that Ezeky'el's speech had evoked—something life-changing, frightening, touching one's soul, coming straight from a common humanity, personal, fervent, direct. Such experience was rare, and to be treasured (in VJ's case, it also turned out to be good for the college application, as the English teacher's tear attests).

The youth group was excited by the idea, and thought of throwing a party for the sick children, but it turned out the hospital had rules about visitors. A party would be too much work for the hospital: it would expose both volunteers and patients to unpredictable germs, and each ingredient of each brownie and cupcake would need approval, for patients who were on special diets. So the volunteers decided that reading to the sick children would be good. But then, they learned that volunteers younger than eighteen years old required intense supervision, and that would have demanded a large investment of the hospital staff's time—too large, unless the youth group could pledge to volunteer weekly for a year or more, which was a promise that the volunteers could not make since turnover in the group was too high for that. Something more than inspiration was needed; expertise that might develop in the course of a long time commitment was also needed. Without that, there was almost no possibility of direct contact with the patients.

VJ reported to the group, "This policy might change soon, especially if the Regional YEP shows itself to be responsible. So, in the meantime, the hospital suggested helping decorate the walls for Christmas." Fellow volunteers eagerly approved the new plan.

When the time came, only four of the twenty or so Regional YEP teens participated, along with about fifteen local university students, who had also come for a one-day, plug-in volunteering opportunity through their own service-learning program. Still, the original inspiration was so perfectly in harmony with Empowerment Talk, Regional YEP members and organizers often retold the tale of the hospital visit for at least three years (minus the part about only four Regional YEP members coming).

Some easy, non–soul-changing projects were so appealing, they attracted too many volunteers who gathered too much stuff. In a meeting of the Community House Board of Directors, we talked about the annual rummage sale, which always included hundreds of pounds of books. The director said, "The guy who donates used books runs a used book store, and can give as many books as we can take in our cars, as many trips as we want to make." Similarly, sorting and storing many tons of food takes space and time, so the food bank coordinator did not even want youth volunteers just to gather as much food in one day as they possibly could.

Helping the Volunteers Help Themselves versus Helping the Volunteers Help the Recipients of Their Aid

Since volunteers' inspiration was itself so highly prized, volunteers were showered with gratitude, no matter how unhelpful they were. This made it hard for them to learn from experience.

Trudy, the paid staff person at the Community House, at the program's annual rummage sale: We used to have these people who would send beads—big, hand-made beads. They would send a whole big bag full of them. But the kids just didn't like them. We would tell them that the kids just loved the beads. And every year, they'd send more beads, and we'd bag 'em up at the end of the day and send them on to St. Vinnie's [a second-hand store]. You know, they felt so good about what they were doing, contributing the beads to us, and we didn't want to make them feel bad, so we'd just say, "Oh, yes, the kids just loved them!"

Nina: What happened—do they still send them?

Trudy: No, they were very elderly, and just got too old to make the beads.

Community House members had to be grateful for each ugly bead . . . even if they ended up throwing them in a bin to give to a second-hand store. "Do Something!" was the name of one local Empowerment Program. This way, whether or not they were helpful, volunteers could symbolize the idea that "someone out there cares," as organizers put it.

Deluged with praise, youth and adult volunteers alike could not easily learn from their mistakes, because no one could point them out. An Americorps volunteer[1]—a music major, fresh out of college—helped arrange a Christmas toy give-away, in which poor, minority children would receive wrapped gifts. The event went on and on, starting in late afternoon and continuing till long past children's bedtimes on a school night, without any food except cookies and chips.

> The multipurpose room of a mega-church was divided into different "stations"—you could make glittery cards here, do face-painting there, sit on Santa's lap and have a photo taken in another location, and so on. Carrying their huge winter parkas and boots and mittens and scarves and hats and snow pants through the hot din, about 400 people waited patiently on line at each "station," and waited again for each kids' toy. So if they had three kids, they had to wait three separate times. But the young Americorps volunteer did not want it to feel bureaucratic, and did not know how to arrange such a big event. Families had arrived before 6, so they could be sure to enter their kids' names on the toy give-away list. An experienced planner might have calculated in advance that it would have taken thirty-three hours for each child to sit on Santa's lap and have a photo taken!

I had come with my own kids, and was carrying my one-year-old. Sweat was cascading down his back and over my forearm.

> By the time we left, it was 9 p.m., past most kids' bedtimes, and these are the same parents who teachers so often accused of not making sure their kids get enough sleep—how unfair! When we made our exit, no one had eaten dinner yet. There was no food except for some chips and cookies, and the toys had still not been given out. Luckily, my kids had not expected to get toys, so there was no promise for me to undo. It was a school night, and many kids still had to take two buses to get home.
>
> The amazing thing was that people hardly complained. One grandma very gently complained by mentioning that she would have to take two buses home, and by pointing to her overexcited granddaughter who had eaten too many cookies, but she was quick to say that it wasn't too bad.

Whether she did not complain because she was accustomed to such treatment, or because she figured that I was white and therefore had helped organize the event (since no white people were there as recipients, but only as volunteers, social workers, and police), or because it seemed unfair to complain about receiving a gift, I cannot say for sure. Whatever the reason, it was clear that the parents and grandparents who stayed with the increasingly wild children had to shower gratitude on the young, sweet Americorps volunteer.

An experienced organizer would have made sure that the families got home earlier, and would have given them dinner if they had stayed past dinnertime. Details about food, heat, noise, time, sleep, numbers of buses, and bedtimes had not occurred to the young Americorps volunteer (though someone had made sure that there were two police cars parked in front). Perhaps this volunteer had never taken a city bus in Snowy Prairie or he would have known that the wait for the bus was long, and frostbite on a December night was a definite risk. The next day, the children's teachers would probably blame the parents when the children were sleepy and crabby, after staying up three hours past the bedtime that schools recommended.

Right before I left the sweaty Holiday Toy Give-Away, I asked the Americorps volunteer how he thought the evening was going. He sounded unequivocally proud. I quickly realized that he assumed that the question itself was a form of congratulations for his voluntary efforts, so an expression of pride was his appropriate response. The event was good for inspiring a spirit of voluntarism *in him*, and possibly making him into the kind of person who would continue, throughout his life, to do good civic work. The volunteer spirit was there, even if the details were wrong. If the Christmas toy give-away had been held by a government agency, recipients could have criticized it for its inefficiency, or might have said the state should have used its funds differently; this situation short-circuited any such complaint.

Volunteers who paid to be in volunteering programs—helping poor people in faraway places, for example—were even less likely to have an opportunity to learn from their mistakes. At a regional environmental educators' conference, held in Snowy Prairie, a speaker described his eco-tourism outfit's project of getting teen volunteers to help save Costa Rican sea turtles. The obvious comparison was with a normal vacation to a tropical beach hotel. When someone in the audience asked if knowledge of Spanish was required, the leader said no, though he added that sometimes, local residents did not understand what the volunteers were doing, and told a story about locals getting in a fistfight with a participant from his program. Nobody questioned whether flying volunteers to Costa Rica was worth the pollution and the offense to the natives.

The volunteers' parents would be paying, so no elaborate public justification was necessary.

One way to smooth over the tension between helping needy volunteers and helping needy others was to let the volunteers make decisions without worrying about the decisions' effects on the needy recipients of aid. Planning a trip to a sister city in Nicaragua, for example, organizers invited Snowy Prairie youth to plan projects before they knew anything about the village—whether the village had running water or a health clinic, for example. When they got there, they were, according to Emily who went with them, surprised and chagrined to learn that the Nicaraguans had their own ideas of how the Snowy Prairie volunteers might help. Much like when the youth volunteers fed the homeless, the symbol—of eager, hopeful youth taking initiative—was more important than the concrete action. Once again, inspiring the youth volunteers and helping the faraway recipients of their aid were two missions that did not quite match.

These examples have all shown how challenging it was to balance needy volunteers' evanescent inspirations with the needs of recipients. Valuing inspiration's effect on the volunteers worked well for picking up litter. Litter has no feelings and never disagrees with the volunteer who cleans it up. Valuing inspiration's effect on the volunteers worked for decorating the hospital, but less well for making direct contact with the patients. It worked still less well for people who have sensitive, strong feelings, such as the Costa Ricans did about wealthy volunteers invading their beach. It works even less well when the recipients of aid need something at regular intervals—food, for example—or might die if their urgent needs are not met immediately, regardless of the volunteer's inspired feelings, as the next chapter will show.

CHAPTER 4

Temporal Leapfrog: Puzzles of Timing

RATHER THAN DRAWING ON any experts' distant, abstract knowledge from the outside, organizers hoped that volunteers themselves would find wisdom by drawing on the "inner ocean," the deep, still place within, their hidden source of insight. Organizers called it "drawing on strengths." They hoped that anyone who glimpsed this now-hidden place would easily and quickly recognize it as desirable and good, and would be able to use the inspiration to make change in their communities and in themselves.

This posed puzzles for timing activities in Empowerment Projects. First, the organizations needed money, and grant applications often had to be completed months in advance, usually in the summer, before most of the youth leaders arrived in the fall, to start leading. Organizers could not get money until they had a project in mind, and they could not have a project in mind until they knew whether the potential funding was for drug prevention, promoting the arts, literacy, good nutrition, or for something else. Funding was usually temporary seed money, to encourage innovation, on constantly changing themes. To smooth out this temporal dilemma, adult organizers and youth volunteers alike often pretended that youth volunteers had invented projects that the adult organizers had invented; organizers, in turn, were following funders' lead. Slowing down our camera, we will see how youth volunteers learned this complex dance into future "youth leadership."

Empowerment Projects aim to build leadership by drawing on leadership, build community by drawing on community, build good desires by drawing on desires that the person already feels. A second set of temporal puzzles arose when participants treated the lack of leadership, community, wholesome pleasures, and good choices as problems, and also as solutions to those same problems. To align these possibly discordant time lines, organizers riveted their attention onto a potential future, in which people already had a better community, already had made better choices, already were in touch with that inspirational inner ocean. In a game of temporal leapfrog, organizers asserted that participants were already doing good things, that community already existed, that youth volunteers were already having fun creating community. Leadership, community, fun, volunteering: the uses of the words became obvious in practice. Organizers hoped that telling a youth volunteer "you *are* a leader" would create a happily "self-fulfilling prophecy."[1] It was a way of making tiny adjustments to the discordant time lines, as if, implicitly, most of life took place in *"the future perfect"*: The future perfect is a verb tense: will + have + past participle, indicating an action that already will have been completed at some point in the future: "this *will have happened*." This implicit tense was a very predictable element of the organizational style— a clear pattern in the rug.

Third, volunteers, funders, and organizers often treated volunteer work as a symbol of volunteers' good will; some recipients, however, urgently needed something more than a symbol. Focusing on the future might help someone like Raul, the Nacho Cheese Doritos tower builder in the first chapter; he might become a leader in the future, if organizers continued to be tactful and not force him to "participate" too actively, too soon. Often, though, organizers' hopeful prophecies had dimmer prospects for success: their focus was on future potential even when needy recipients of aid needed something right away, before the potential volunteer became inspired and developed the know-how to be an effective helper. Empowerment Projects focused on future potential even when a group had almost no potential of becoming self-sustaining, active volunteers—disabled old people, for example. Money was scarce for people who could not display any potential, like the disabled seniors.

The programs' usual solution to all of these temporal disconnections was a relentless, unreflective focus on future hopeful potential. Empowerment Projects' steady gaze at hopeful potential included a taboo against looking backwards, to unearth the sources of unhealthy feelings. When people lacked community, or made bad choices, or had unwholesome desires, organizers could not say why participants did not have the right kinds of community, preferences, and desires already. The *past* was cut off. It was taboo to say that focusing on long-term future potential might not be the best solution if people are hungry today and cannot wait till the hopeful prophesy comes true; conditions in the *present* often had to be treated as irrelevant. In the short-lived Empowerment Projects with their evanescent memberships, participants could not project much of a *future* together, so those happy potentials had very little time to materialize.

In these timeless conditions, feelings began to seem like symbols, launching pads for something else, means to other ends, valuable for what they boded for an abstract future, more than for how they felt in the present. In Empowerment Projects, volunteering becomes a symbol of this future potential, with no hints about why we are not yet living in that brighter future, and thus, only a few, dim hints about how to get there.

Yet, the Empowerment Projects managed to keep going. This chapter shows how.

PLANNING IN THE "OPEN AND UNDEFINED, UP TO YOU TO DECIDE 'WHATEVER' ORGANIZATION"

Crisscrossed Calendars

Our first set of timing puzzles arose when youth volunteers' calendars and funders' calendars did not easily match. Inspiration had to happen quickly, and on schedule, and a program's very survival depended on it. Since funding was usually temporary, and fundraising constant, if a program lost its grant to combat tobacco, racism, homelessness, or gangs, organizers quickly had to retool and apply for another grant on another theme—promoting music, good nutrition, or literacy. In this quest for elusive funds, adults had to plan projects *before* the youth leaders joined the groups. Youth leaders followed the adult organizers, who followed the money. The youth leaders were not forced to follow, but if they did not, as they pointed out, their events would be held in grimy school cafeterias rather than pleasant places like the city's spacious, grand, but expensive conference center.

A lunchtime meeting of program organizers and local officials illustrates these temporal disjunctions. The early August meeting was held to plan a week of youth service projects that would "showcase youth leadership," adults said. The point, as one organizer put it, was to get more money for youth programs by showing county officials that "kids appreciate the money, and that they want them to 'up' it next year." In planning meetings, away from youth volunteers, adults often drew elaborate flow charts and time lines, so they could time events like this Community Service Week for exactly the right moments to influence legislators, nonprofits, and voters. Over the course of several meetings, Bing, an old 1960s community activist who now worked in city government, had drawn several complicated, overlapping time lines on the whiteboard or newsprint, showing which legislators, nonprofits, and other funders make decisions about which funding, with which deadlines. His maps also showed that each organization's lead time was different, saying that even after your organization won funding, you might not actually get your hands on it for a long time. Also, some funding was only "seed money" for getting a project off the ground and going for a short time only, after which it would have to find funding elsewhere; government funding was harder to get but usually more enduring, though he said that that was changing, too. Many of these decisions were made in autumn.

At this August meeting, we adults suggested to one another that youth leaders conduct a food drive, mitten drive, toy drive, a visit to a nursing home, and a visit to a homeless shelter. After more discussion of possible activities, an organizer suggested changing the date, so that youth leaders could have more of a say in the planning. That was impossible. A city official said;

> The original idea was to affect the city and county budgets that are drawn up in the fall, to shine a light on all the good things we *could be doing if we had money*.

> Jerrard (a minister of an African American church youth program that received government money): This week is to show that we're doing these things, that kids are not out on the street, or causing trouble, that we need more money. That's what we're ultimately doing this for. (With a grin) Maybe we could get police records on lower youth crime that week, because youth are busy doing community service.

> A little later, Georgia, a magenta-haired youth worker, dressed in shredded black clothes and big hiking boots: I'm wary of planning everything for people who are not at the table [teens who would not start coming to meetings till September] because it's not realistic.

> Miriam, a very long-term, dedicated youth worker, agreeing: When you plan like that and they weren't there, and then you say, "Oh, but it was such a good idea!" but it wasn't *their* idea.

Since different youth participants came to the programs each school year, organizers had to guess, based on *this* year's group, what *next* year's group might want. In April of another year, a group of organizers met over lunch, to begin planning autumn activities.

> Dubiously, an organizer said, "I could *try* to have youth lead these projects, but 80 percent of my kids are graduating in May." She said she could not predict what the new kids would want. "And if they didn't plan it, they won't want it anyway," she added, now quite certain.

At another meeting, she observed that her group's membership changed weekly. Such a group could not plan ahead, but still had to make it seem as if all its youth members were taking leadership.

Adult organizers diligently tried to encourage each youth group to think for itself, to start fresh, "never imitate," as Emerson put it. Hoping not to confine volunteers' imaginations, organizers carefully avoided telling them what had been done in the past.

> Bing: There is this President's Award challenging kids to do one hundred hours of community service.

> Teen volunteer: What is that? Do you just do it by yourself?

Bing: It's doing service to people, whether with a church group or baby-sitting for a family that can't afford it or volunteering at St. Matthew House—We're leaving it pretty *open and undefined*.

Teen: Got it.

Some may have "gotten it," but most still wanted to know what was usual and expected. In meetings of the Martin Luther King Day Planning Committee, for example, youth volunteers kept asking about the history of the holiday and how it had been celebrated in the past. Adult organizers, in turn, kept trying to divert the question, *not* telling volunteers what had been done in the past, insisting that *whatever* had been done about the holiday in the past, the past was now irrelevant and the holiday was free of the weight of history. This excerpt from my field notes is very repetitive, and that is the point (and I deleted several more repetitions).

A newcomer youth: Who thought up last year's Martin Luther King Day? When did it start?

Rob Strauss finally answers: Oh, do you know the story? It started in 1986, celebrated by participating in your community, free community suppers. But there was not as much emphasis on service; it was more about recognition and celebration. The "youth service" focus is a new thing.

Olympia, a fairly new youth participant: Is the "service event" on Martin Luther King Day because it's an opportunity, because it's a day off from school anyway? Or are those things happening on that day because it's a day that's about Martin Luther King?

Roberta, the Recreation District coordinator: That is a good question— whether it's a day for doing things we're doing anyway, or if it's about Martin Luther King, and all these things are happening because of him and his teachings [notice: she affirms Olympia by saying that it's a good question, but does not answer it, on purpose, because of what Rob says next]:

Rob: "Ownership," "control," "initiative." You *could* make his life more central. *It's up to you.*

Roberta: It's up to you to decide which and plan accordingly. But there's no money yet, so you have to keep that in mind. [What follows is another volley of questions from volunteers about what had been done in the past, and more putting the ball back in the volunteers' court. After that, someone asks how it was funded last year.]

Roberta: Local funders and a big grant—Snowy Prairie was one of the few cities to get all it asked for. But it depends on what we plan. Those of you who want to be actively involved in planning [looking seriously at the young people]: What do you need to get done by August?

[Youth volunteers don't answer, so adults fill in, bandying around ideas about who would be available, and not too expensive, to invite to speak at the event.]

Roberta (back to the agenda): What I'm saying is, you guys have a lot of control."

[. . .]

One youth volunteer, asking adult organizers: Will the theme be "hunger" again?

Another youth volunteer: Will it be at the Snowy Prairie Convention Center again?

Another: Will there be speakers and service (like the year before)?

After this questioning continues for a while, an adult organizer responds to all the questions: You can do what you want with it. Or not do anything with it.

One teen suggested inviting Coretta Scott King and another suggested a local high school principal; no one mentioned the different likely costs involved.

Inexperienced youth volunteers assumed that adult organizers knew the right answers and were just withholding them, the way teachers might withhold the answers to a quiz. Quickly, however, they learned that the organizers' refusal to tell them what had been done before was intentional; it *was* the lesson. Organizers hoped that if youth volunteers started from scratch, in complete control, their creativity and inspiration would grow.

Teenagers generally like innovation, and some portion of the programs' insistence on innovation was perhaps due to volunteers' age, rather than the fact that Empowerment Projects required it. This year's stationery has to be different from last year's, so that this year's group could exercise its own creativity, and the youth artist could get a chance to express herself. In meetings held to plan the third youth-led Martin Luther King Day, Emily, the leader of Community House, emphatically told us *not* to have the same topics or leaders for workshops as last year. She warned us that if we did, Martin Luther King Day would get "stale real quick." The old mural at Community House had to be painted over, rather than repaired, since *this* year's group did not paint it, and they considered the '70 s clothes, hair-do's, and TV images in the painting to be out of style. Teens' zeal for innovation and the programs' zeal for innovation seemed, at first, to mesh perfectly: someone got a grant to repaint the old mural at Community House, and teens seemed relieved.

In an Empowerment Project, however, teens' desire for innovation twists: here, since the funding for an adult artist capable of eliciting and controlling youth participation kept disappearing, and/or artist/organizers kept disappearing, the fifteen-year-olds who attended the series of "brainstorming sessions" to imagine the new mural were twenty years old by the time the mural was done. The temporal disjunction between the initial inspiration and the stop-and-start budget made it both almost impossible and yet mandatory to keep galloping ahead toward the "fresh and new."

One novice adult organizer kept eagerly making a mistake by not emphasizing innovation. At a few planning meetings, she kept repeating that Nickelodeon, the TV network, had a "whole package for promoting youth volunteering, that included a van that they send from one town to another." Experienced organizers kept ignoring her. Getting a prepackaged program missed their point entirely. Similarly, when an organizer was composing a letter about an upcoming event, the first draft said, "Youth groups have been invited to send youth to participate in the event." The second-to-last draft said, "Youth have been actively involved in planning, so it has been a very youth-initiated process." Adult organizers learned to appear to take the back seat to those youth leaders, no matter how late the leaders arrived.

In another meeting, organizers tried hard to get youth volunteers to take control, but the youth volunteers did not know what kind of money was available, and they wanted to know. Adults could not make the money question disappear. Roberta was late, and the youth leaders were waiting for her to lead.

Connie [adult organizer]: What should we do till Roberta gets here?

Jim [employed by Urban League]: The goal is to get *youth* to organize, so let's just get *them* to talk! [but they don't; finally, Roberta arrives and apologizes for "interrupting," as if the meeting could have started without her, which, of course, it could not]

Destiny [adult organizer]: How much money do we have?

Jim and Roberta both say, at once: About $10,000.

Jim: Do you have an agenda?

Roberta: First: if there's no funding, do we still want to do it?

Destiny: I think so.

When an adult organizer said, "You can't get it [the grant] till you know what you want it for," Roberta looked straight at the youth volunteers, steering the discussion back to the essential topic: "I know you can't commit individually, but *ideally*, how would youth be involved in the planning process? If you could plan the ideal youth involvement, what would it look like?" Finally, after Roberta's insistent prodding, a middle-school age volunteer very tentatively suggested basing it in schools, as if she were timidly guessing an answer on an oral test. In meeting after meeting, Roberta insistently, subtly, repeatedly tried to steer the conversation back to the question of "what youth want, ideally, regardless of funding and sources," as she explained it to youth volunteers in another meeting.

The programs' unceasing focus on funding was a condition for their survival, and no matter how hard they tried to ignore it, organizers' awareness of these conditions slipped out, almost unconsciously. At a lunchtime meeting, they did not even notice that their inspirations corresponded with the funding cycle:

> Bill, the leader of the 4H Club (a national youth organization with several local chapters): We met last night. It was a very interesting discussion that lasted almost till midnight, about youth leadership and about what *adults* need to do to be more inclusionary of diverse youth. I was so wound up from this discussion, I couldn't get to sleep till almost two!
>
> He reviews, from the amazing notes he took the last time, the premises of the philosophy of "youth leadership" that constituted our guiding set of principles, saying: Visualize this coalition in four years.
>
> Someone asks, "Why 'four years' in particular?" [His answer was that it corresponds to the cycle of funding and evaluation in 4H.]
>
> [After this detour (or *is* it a detour?) into the funding schedule, we are back to the more philosophical discussion.]
>
> Bill: What would tell you that this coalition (convening on the topic of youth leadership) has been successful? What outcomes?

Experienced youth volunteers knew they should act as if their personal inspiration was the sole motor of the Empowerment Projects, they knew they should not ask about history, or demand practical information about future plans and future finances. Volunteers had to learn to make it look as if the organization was "open and undefined," and that the service projects were propelled solely by their personal, heartfelt inspiration, while also carefully second-guessing what would appeal to funders, on the funders' calendars, and matching their inspirations to their careful assessments.

*A How-To: Spotlighting Inspiration while Second-guessing
Funders' Expectations*

This process usually began with adults securing money, first, by reading a grant application—for drug abuse prevention or literacy promotion, for example. Then, they would imperceptibly hand it over to the youth volunteers, who would take it up as if they themselves had planned it. In an August meeting of adult organizers, for example, Rob Strauss asked whether to include a food pantry as one of the organizations involved in the proposal he was writing. Erin said that working on hunger would fit the bill, since it would fulfill a real, measurable need:

> Reading aloud from a federal grant's guidelines (the Corporation for National and Community Service): "We expect well-designed activities that meet compelling community needs and lead to measurable outcomes and impact."
>
> Sheila: We need to beef this part up.
>
> Rob Strauss adds: To say what service projects people actually did.
>
> Sheila: Do we need to get feedback from recipients? And from students: "Did this actually change you in any way?"
>
> Emily: Yeah, like impacts based on spirit? Like *"Did it affect your spirit?"*
>
> Sheila: Yeah, like "Did it change anything for you?"

Sheila then told the story of Daisy, the youth volunteer who had been nearly suicidal till she was initiated into volunteering at a Martin Luther King Day event when she was thirteen years old. That day, Daisy found meaning in life, Sheila said.

Organizers and officials recognized that measuring the "impacts based on spirit" of any single project, in a short time span presented a big problem. At another meeting, a city official ironically fabricated an imaginary post-test question: "Because you ate pizza and got to socialize on Friday night, do you feel better about ... yourself?" She added, "The effect is more intangible." Though they questioned the plausibility of measuring effects on the spirit, they also had to do it in pre- and post-tests, because those were the quick, transparent messages that funders needed.

Back to the August meeting's discussion of the grant application: Rob said that he did not think that that is what the grant application meant, adding, "They want something measurable."

> Roberta: We could say, "We delivered a ton of food for 70 families, painted the YMCA Annex."

Rob: I think that's what they mean: *real changes* [this was a reference to Emily's question about "impacts based on spirit," which were, he unintentionally implied, not as real].

Erin [paid adult organizer of the Regional YEP]: But what could we say: "We read to seniors at senior centers?" That sounds kind of vague.

Rob: I don't know what kids think, but I think that the association of food with service makes sense. Do you think kids would want to keep the focus on hunger?

Sheila: I'm guessing that hunger comes up every year.

Erin: Definitely!

By the end of the meeting, Rob read a draft of that section of the application:

"Youth will read to 1,000 people. Collect two thousand pounds of food." These are real— *graspable*—by participants, and by media.

A month later, the Martin Luther King Planning Committee started up for the school year, and Rob subtly introduced the volunteers to the idea of collecting food. When no one took up his suggestion to form this committee to collect food, he had to suggest that *he* join the committee, which the youth leaders had not (yet) formed!

I'd like to join a volunteer committee, specifically, to try a food drive, to get a ton of food to food pantries and homeless shelters, Sundale kids could go to the Walmart there, Snowy Prairie kids could go to Food-a-rama, I'd like to work on that. If any of you wanna work with—

(he paused, and I actually held my breath, because I had been consciously asking myself if he would say "with *me*," because that was *exactly* what he could *not* say—it would make him seem to be leading—so he left out the word "me" and rearranged the sentence)

—want to work on that, I'd like to join.

None of the youth leaders in the room joined this committee. Just two adults joined Rob.

In the next meeting, as if by magic, youth volunteers took on the project as if they themselves had planned it: Samia, an active participant from Community House, reported to the Regional YEP:

They [she was referring to the youth-led Martin Luther King committee, of which she was a part, yet she called it "they"] are going to organize volunteer projects such as food drives at grocery stores.

Jenny (a new volunteer that year): Is Martin Luther King Day focusing on hunger and literacy or just hunger?

Emily: Both. And there's a third thing, but I can't remember what it is.

How had Samia known to focus on hunger? It had happened behind the scenes, between meetings, with Emily in her tiny, private office, where Samia and the most active Community House volunteers met to plan the meeting's agenda. Emily had simply told them that the plan was to gather food, and Samia was satisfied to know the plan. As we will see in the following chapter, Samia was learning many important civic skills in this hidden little room, so her contentment was well-founded, but it was not based on the personal inspiration Empowerment Projects hope to elicit.

Through this organizational style, the clashing time lines seemed to merge, as Samia simply did not say that the decision was made by Rob Strauss, the city official! Samia had mastered the style: learning to display a self that looked self-directed. Our question is when and how the face might grow to fit the mask, as it did for Samia over the next few years.

"Leaving it pretty open and undefined" was a phrase that organizers used, not as an abdication of authority, but as a way of exercising the specific kind of authority that Empowerment Programs exercise. In these projects, which were not very "open and undefined" at all-youth volunteers like Samia learned to play along with the official, nearly mandatory, not at all "open and undefined" story that attributed volunteering to their personal inspiration, while second-guessing what authorities like Rob Strauss wanted her to plan. To make this feel real, organizers gently, almost imperceptibly, reminded participants to pretend to invent projects from scratch, making the time frames merge.

What If the Needy Need Something before Any Inspired Volunteers Learn How to Help?

Organizers hope was that eventually, the needy people of today would become the eager volunteers of tomorrow; when needy people help needy others, the helpers become empowered, in an endless chain of empowerment, moving constantly into a hopeful future. In the meantime, however, the needy volunteers might not *yet* be very helpful to the needy recipients of their aid *today*, or tomorrow, or the next day, before the volunteers both felt inspired and learned how to be helpful. Here was another possible temporal dissonance.

Organizers dreaded having to work with the head of the local food bank, Ann Barth. In frustration, they would say that she never "got it" that the goal was "democracy" and "letting youth lead." Ann thought the point

was to get food to the hungry and homeless, and had stringent requirements that put the needs of the hungry first, so every time she came to a
meeting, she annoyingly asked when they would get the food, and how
much food would get to whom, and whether it was nutritious; and since
storage space was not infinite, and even packaged foods are perishable,
she often complained about getting too much at once and then not getting any for a long time. After one such meeting, Rob Strauss complained:
"She's missing the point: it's all about leadership, and democracy." Service
projects served two sets of clients: one hungry today, the other happy to
demonstrate that they care, on their own schedule. For the volunteers, the
donations were symbols, showing that they cared and could take initiative; for the hungry recipients, the donations were immediate necessities.

Once in a while, teen volunteers gently made fun of the process of
scheduling volunteer work regardless of recipients' needs. This problem
of timing became most visible when volunteers wanted to help on days
that the social services agencies were closed altogether. The Regional YEP
wanted to feed the homeless on a school holiday, but many soup kitchens
were closed on holidays. A new volunteer wryly muttered, "People aren't
hungry that day."

Since these Empowerment Projects had to show funders that they were
helping to develop good character in large numbers of volunteers, organizers had to make sure that all potential volunteers could find a problem
to solve, on the day and hour that they were available to solve it. When
an exciting, easy volunteer opportunity arose, too many youth volunteers
often signed up, requiring organizers to adjust the flow of volunteer
work. VJ's idea of playing with or reading to sick children at the hospital
was *too* popular, as Erin announced:

> The only problem is that too many people in our group want to go—
> we can only have ten or twelve [the problem became moot when hardly
> anyone showed up . . .]. We could contact other hospitals so everyone
> gets a chance to go.

At another meeting, Emily asked if anyone knew of a project going on in
Snowy Prairie that could use one hundred people right away; she had
some eager youth volunteers. Nancy, from a large nonprofit, said, with a
little laugh, "Drat! I just gave one away. Shoveling snow, for the Mercer
Senior Center." Similarly, too many volunteers offered to clean up the
riversides on Clean Ducks Day. Organizers in the noontime meeting discussed whether the day's coordinator would be overwhelmed if too many
youth volunteers came:

> Erin: How many does she want?

> Rob Strauss: Could we rachet it up to 400?

Roberta: She said, "Not 1,200."

Magenta (a youth worker at Mercer Community Center, joking, pretending to beg for more slots): "Hey, we need more litter!"

Another adult: She has a network of environmental groups, so we supply the team and—

Erin: But seriously, we should not over-recruit for her and cause her problems. Now wouldn't *that* be a nice problem to have!

So organizers had to find something else for volunteers to do that would be just like cleaning litter from riverbanks.

No Help for People Who Have No Prospects of Becoming Civic

Funding agencies were inspired by programs that taught the needy recipients of aid to help themselves. They were not inspired by people who would never become empowered, never become volunteers, never become self-sufficient. A severe timing clash arose between Empowerment Projects and people who had no prospects of helping themselves: the need was immediate and had no potential of transforming in the potential future.

At one meeting of local social service agencies directors, including the heads of several youth programs, the city's biggest nonprofit funding agency announced its new policy: from now on, United Way would empower people rather than providing direct, immediate aid for needs like food or nursing care. Several heads of programs grew furious. One became so angry, she started to cry, saying that her clients—mentally and physically disabled old people—would never become self-sustaining, that this nonprofit had been funding her organization for years, and that her people had nowhere else to turn since the government had also cut funding.

The United Way head insisted that everyone can become empowered, if even in a small way. With a reassuring smile, she gave the example of disabilities rights activists, who she said had empowered themselves, even though they were in wheelchairs. The sobbing head of the program for disabled seniors protested that her situation was not the same! And then the meeting swiftly got back on track, to a discussion of how to apply for seed money for the nonprofit's sustainability projects.

Empowerment Projects' promise is that treating people as if they are independent, capable, responsible civic actors will help make them so. When funders tried to be encouraging by attributing happy potential pep to people like the disabled seniors, the missions of civic engagement and helping the needy clashed. It was hard to imagine a nearby "future perfect," in which the old people "would already have been cured" enough to help themselves.

TELLING SELF-FULFILLING PROPHECIES: DRAWING ON COMMUNITY, YOUTH LEADERSHIP, FUN, AND GOOD CHOICES IN ORDER TO CREATE COMMUNITY, YOUTH LEADERSHIP, FUN, AND GOOD CHOICES

Issuing hopeful self-fulfilling prophecies is certainly not unique to Empowerment Projects. This has been noted already and is worth repeating: trying to make a child feel as if she has liked an activity or a new food, after the parent has subtly fed her the idea or the food, is something that parents and teachers do all the time—yum-yum, strained yams! The assumption is that if you treat a person as if he or she can make good choices, the person might grow into the expectation, the face will eventually grow to fit the mask. In Empowerment Projects, however, these happy prophecies have to work on a larger scale, with higher financial and organizational stakes, with multiple spectators observing their expression, with objects that, unlike yams, do not quite yet exist: "community," "nurturance," "youth leadership," "fun," and "good choices." Let's see how these attributions of potential work in the cases of these five key aspirations.

Potential Community, Community Meals, and the Problem of Take-out Containers, Drawing on Community to Create Community

The idea of using "the community" to solve the problem of "lack of community" sometimes puzzled youth volunteers. In the Martin Luther King Day planning committee, Roberta invited youth participants to draw pictures to symbolize the holiday's message. Roberta said that it should be about "building community":

> Olympia, a teen, asks quizzically, "With building community, it's not like food—it's not something you can really touch."
>
> Roberta: That's a good question; that's something to think about and talk about with your friends. What about ice-breakers, like in those books? Actually, that makes community, brings people together who wouldn't normally come together.
>
> Rob Strauss, her boss, the head of the County Youth Programs: Oh, yeah, I like ice-breakers. They're fun.
>
> Roberta [later that meeting] explaining to kids what "leadership" is: "The City Youth Commission feels there's a need to teach students to be leaders so maybe they'll go back to their communities and start

projects that they've always wanted to do but didn't know how to do or didn't have the leadership skills to start."

The "leaders" could "*go back to their communities*" even though the organizers had just said, in this meeting as well as in many others, that a lack of community was the cause of the problems. Could the potential future leaders go back to potential future communities when neither existed yet?

Sometimes, it worked in small ways, when done quietly and unobtrusively. After a series of school shootings across the nation, five members of the NOYO spent many meetings drafting a Letter to the Editor of the local paper. These discussions were "very philosophical . . . enough for a thesis," exclaimed one, with infectious delight. We all agreed, but we got stuck when we tried to imagine a solution that did not blame anyone, and arrived at "the community" as the answer:

> Jerrard, a black minister who runs a church-based youth program that is partly funded by the government, has been talking about the importance of neighborhood adults, who can be the "whole village" that it takes "to raise a child": It just takes someone who cares to turn a kid around. Literally. I see the school over here [nods in one direction], and the kids walking this way (nods in opposite direction) and all he has to do is honk and say "Go back to school" and they turn around.

> The question being discussed is how to cultivate this sort of local circle of adults for kids when it is not already there.

> Jeanne, the coordinator of a relatively expensive, nonprofit after-school and summer program: [saying that they can't single out one group, parents, teachers, or anyone else for blame . . .] We all need to be involved in raising our children. We need to create more opportunities for parents to be more actively involved in our programs and as a result to be more actively involved in their children's lives.

> A white suburban organizer: Parents don't know each other. Something as little as carpools could help.

> Jerrard: Block parties.

> Jeanne, reading a sentence she has composed to express this sentiment: "To accomplish these goals we need the involvement of all parents, schools, community citizens, elected and appointed officials."

> Roberta, of the Snowy Prairie Recreation District, says that it doesn't say concretely what they should do. "I don't know if we have anything concrete to do."

Jeanne: That was one of my many pages [chuckling].

Kelly, a young white youth worker: "We want to engage you," or something—not sure what the English would be.

By the end of three thought-provoking, open-ended discussions spread over a few weeks, we arrived at a solution: We agreed that we should not say anything about the already-existing community, but just focus on potential. One draft said that we should create community by beginning dialogues in our communities:

> We challenge all of the communities within Paragon County to do one of these—we challenge/encourage you to begin dialogues in your own communities, to do town suppers. For further info, contact the University Extension town suppers.

> NE: What does "communities" mean here? . . . [what if] people who don't already feel like they have it would read this and go, "I don't have community already"?

I said that for me, personally, hearing "school district" might be more welcoming, since I knew my kids were in one, and I was not sure what else to think of as my community.

> Kelly: It's true, if you're having a time in a lower socioeconomic bracket and don't feel part of a community. Or (as if surprisingly) if you're in a higher socioeconomic place and feeling that alienation!! [earlier that afternoon, Jeanne had reminded us of non-disadvantaged kids' alienation, and potential to become criminals—like the kids in a school shooting that was in national headlines that year]

The hope was that respecting the community that people already had would encourage them to bring more of it into existence. The problem was that this same community had also created, or at least not cured, school shooters. Organizers did not want to act like distant experts, and could not offend any of their audiences. They were determined not to pass judgments or even to use the words good and bad, except in "scare" quotes: "good" and "bad." So they had to leave the meaning of the word—"community"—empty and open, waiting to be filled by potentially comfortable interactions that would build upon one another in ways that no one could predict or spell out.

A couple of years after the discussions about school shootings, Community House did indeed hold three community dinners, and miraculously, that is just what happened, in a very small, nearly invisible way. About twenty people came to each dinner, ate with whomever they came with, and left with the same. Employees from youth centers came and sat together, exchanging stories about their work. Teens came with their friends and sat together. Each family that came sat at its own table. At one dinner, a really outgoing mom of an after-school program participant traveled from table to table, making short conversations at each one, but that high level of sociability was otherwise unknown.

These dinners provided a cheap, cozy place to go on a snowy night: a humble and simple good in itself. If they built community, it was the way a local café, post office, or public library might: by increasing the chances that neighbors will run into each other and maybe recognize each other on the street some day.[2] If they built community, it was by giving program organizers a place to exchange tales of their work. This community-building would have been hard to measure quickly.

To work this way, these dinners had to have low costs and low stakes: If hosting them had cost more than the price of the noodles and tomato sauce, more documentation would have been required, but documenting their impact quickly and transparently would have been impossible. They had to be small: If more people had come, it would have been better for publicity, for showing potential, but then it would have been even harder to meet anyone. In a way, an event like this might succeed best by failing on conventional terms: if only four people had come, they may very well have gotten to know each other, thus "building community," but then the event would have been considered a failure.

If the stakes and costs are very low, and conditions favorable, community dinners like these might create companionship without blaming anyone, without dwelling on the troubling past, without mapping out a constraining, overly certain path forward, thus embodying Empowerment Projects' ideal of a prospective, open-ended focus on potential.

Under the wrong circumstances, however, community dinners can cause problems. In a free, once-a-week, late afternoon program at a community center, there were different youth every week; different ages, different genders, different mixes. Participation was fleeting, making it hard to create that "community" feeling. Sheila reported, in one meeting, that she had gotten the idea of community dinners from the Search Institute, a national nonprofit whose website suggested that community dinners would, she said, "rebuild social bonds" in order to "develop community assets." Usually a serene person, she sounded frustrated:

Kids come just because there's food, that's free—sometimes their parents send them to get the food to bring back to their house. They come running at around 5:00 when the food comes out, and then it takes a while to get organized . . . They come and they don't really care what it's about—they're like "Oh, yeah, great, what's for snack?" Sometimes, they bring take-out containers!

Organizers cleverly parried the kids' clever move by making a new rule that the food had to be eaten at the Community Center, so that participants would not continue to shovel it into family-size take-out containers. Sheila left her voluntary position, though, before she could see whether the solution was working.[3]

Clearly, this was not the right kind of community in which to hold community-building dinners. Maybe a better one with better people in it would be a better place for building community! When people could not reflect together on what caused the community's current problems, and to make judgments about what to preserve and what to change, "community" started to sound like a slippery word, a theoretical ideal, a perky abstraction. Lumping together all the habits and conditions and future potentials and naming it all "community" made it hard to see any path forward, from the neighborhood's current conditions to the projected abstraction.

Potential Nurturance

Organizers had to publicize the good work that their programs potentially could do—"to shine a light on all the good things we *could be doing* if we had money," before they actually did the good things. This meant hosting big, fun, highly televisual public events. For example, one meeting of a NOYO subcommittee included a typical list of annual events to show that youth programs were doing good work and needed funding to do more of the same:

> Roberta: Martin Luther King Day, youth services—there were over 400 students.
>
> Jerrard [listing more big public events]: Third Annual Youth Empowerment Week—that had thousands of participants.
>
> Kelly: Juneteenth.
>
> Roberta: Clean Ducks Day.

One purpose of these events was to raise funds so that programs could eventually afford good but invisible things like the "impacts based on spirit" that Emily had mentioned in the August meeting described earlier; or dreary, non-innovative things like upgrades to Community House's roof, or repairs for basement leaks. Emily never managed to find funds to replace the center's moldy, ancient wall-to-wall carpeting or the dangerous climbing structure on the small playground. Even after a child fell through the rickety structure and broke an ankle, the center still could not gather the funds to replace it. Only an innovative extreme makeover would have sufficed; simple replacement was much harder to fund.

Was the shiny publicity *itself* the good work, or was the purpose of the publicity to raise funds that would pay for more important but less visible ongoing caregiving? In some ways, doing the publicity could be both: involving youth volunteers in the planning was, indeed, a way to take care of them: they could not get pregnant or take drugs while they were in meetings planning events, and they could very well learn management, note-taking, and other organizational skills, as well as a sense of personal efficacy.[4] On the other hand, as we saw earlier, the ceaseless fundraising did not give participants a chance to cultivate any other talents. Organizers often treated the publicity as the good work, itself, and this posed a timing puzzle. Here again, their method of keeping their eyes on future potential often included ignoring the particulars of the present and of the unique individuals therein—while some young people's inner light might shine when they publicize big events and plan all the logistics, others' might shine when they do chemistry or play the flute. The splashy events advertised potential good work, as if to imply that they represented something larger and more ongoing, but sometimes, planning the event was the only thing that participants did together, at the expense of other possible activities. For those youth whose potential talents and passions lay elsewhere, the splashy events symbolized something for which there was no original.

Potential Leaders

Organizers proudly refused to accept the normal equation in which "leader" = "popular, college-bound, athletic, tall, non-disadvantaged, and already anointed by peers or teachers as leader." Whatever the words may mean in a dictionary, however, they absorb meaning in everyday patterns of use. Youth volunteers discovered that someone who was called a "youth leader" was not tall, handsome, athletic, and popular. Instead of projecting a happy future (a hope that you become a "leader"), the word began to project a miserable predicted future of crime, early pregnancy, and poverty.

The new definition yielded predictable misunderstandings, though, such as when Roberta asked the Regional YEP volunteers to discuss, "When did you first realize that you were a leader?" and "What are a leader's qualities?"

Kids were supposed to break into groups to discuss the question, but many did not grasp it, drawing a blank about the question, or arguing against the question's whole premise. Only the kids who really were "leaders" in the normal use of the word answered the questions. Some groups answered the second question as if "leader" meant "person who gets called a leader," and said things like "bossy, popular, good-looking," and even "tall"!

After the groups of four reconvened, Roberta, who had sensitively discerned some kids' blank puzzlement over the question, asked, "Maybe you don't even think of yourself as a leader."

Many of the kids said that they didn't!

Meanwhile, the NOYO started a subcommittee for discussing youth leadership. Eight organizers met monthly, holding stimulating discussions about how to unearth potential leaders, as opposed to "stereotypical leader-types," as they put it:

> The manager of a high-end nonprofit art and music school (she clearly missed the other organizers' point): A lot is written on what makes a good business leader in management.

> Erin snaps back: This is somewhat different, because some kids don't seem like leaders but then become leaders, so you can't identify them beforehand. You want to provide opportunities for *all* kids.

Calling everyone a potential leader is supposed to harmonize the missions of using volunteer work to help the volunteers versus using volunteer work to help others. This temporal adjustment works simply by changing the definitions of the words "leader" and "volunteer." Leaders used to need followers. No longer. Now, everyone can be a leader. But instead of harmonizing the missions, the word "leader" just changed meaning, to fit into its rigorous new conditions. Organizers often said that their programs were not "prevention programs" but were "leadership programs." At the monthly lunchtime meeting of the NOYO, about twenty-five youth workers were listening to a nervously enthusiastic woman introduce a summer program that she said is "like a summer camp." Strenuously, she asserted, "This is *not* a 'prevention program'!"

> People *used* to call it a prevention program but I don't want you to limit your ideas to thinking of it as drug and alcohol prevention. It's a "*Leadership Development Program*," encouraging youth to think about problem-solving, and health and wellness . . . it's not a prevention program at all! We teach them "youth development" and "developing assets in their community [phrases from Asset-Based Community Development].

> They learn that there's many different conditions in the community that help them make decisions—healthy *or* unhealthy. At the summer program, they pick a condition that they want to work on. Then, they make a plan of action, saying how they'll work on the condition they've

identified. When they leave, they feel, "This is a safe community. I can blossom, I can grow, I can say what I want to to say."

One of the programs this summer will be about . . . underage drinking because it's funded by DOT (the Department of Transportation), but don't think the action plans are usually like that. Action plans are usually very broad, not "prevention." [She says that whether it continues will depend on funding.]

It's an exciting program that shows results, and it's working!! We did a pre- and post-test: students who aren't drinking or involved with drugs when they come in aren't involved six months later. That might not seem so special, but if you took another group that was drug-free, and retested them six months later, drug use would have gone up. So, we have some of those "statistical data" that I know some of you need (with a little ironic grin).

First she said it was not a prevention program, and then she described its activity aimed at preventing alcohol abuse, and then gave data on how well it worked as a prevention program. She was trying hard to smooth away the tension between treating participants as independent civic actors and treating them as needy dependents who need protection. It was hard, however, to make a prevention program into something else when one of the program's audiences demanded evidence that the program prevented drug abuse.

Organizers' effort to rename their programs "leadership programs" was, ironically, too successful!

In a small meeting about promoting "youth leadership," Roberta, the thoughtful city official, explained: "We need to appeal to a broader range, more 'middle' group, more diverse, ethnically, culturally, and socioeconomically. Up till now, our effort has been to bring in low-income, disenfranchised kids. So now we don't have any middle-income, middle-potential kids. A lot of kids see a stigma attached to our programs [which were called 'youth leadership programs'], like 'that's where all the bad kids go.' So now we need to pull back and appeal to the middle, too."

To know where they stood, youth volunteers scanned the organizations for landmarks. Volunteers did this no matter what organizers called the programs. As we saw in the first chapter, "leadership" was a hopeful prediction for the future for one set of youth volunteers; for the other, "leadership" was a statement about the present. Posing this hopefully self-fulfilling prophesy about the relationship between a "leadership program" and "a prevention program" often had a paradoxical effect; instead of making everyone a leader, it made "leadership program" sound like another word for "prevention program," making civic involvement sound like a kind of therapy for deprived or maladjusted people. This became predictable, redefining all of Empowerment Talk's keywords: civic, volunteer, leader, need, fun.

Potential Fun

Calling wholesome activities "fun" was another hopeful prophecy, foretelling a feeling that did not quite exist yet. Sometimes it worked and sometimes it did not.

Erin, an adult organizer, used fun-talk compulsively, in spurts, calling all sorts of activities "fun." Here are one meeting's first eight examples (not counting "awesome," "cool," "happy," "excited," or "blast" and other synonyms for "fun"). Yes, I counted once, after noticing how often she said "fun"! After counting twenty, I stopped, though the meeting was not even half over.

> Erin: *All* these jobs are fun. My goal in life is to have fun, to do work and have fun.

> [Later] Erin: "I'm so happy to be here. I'm so excited. This group is so cool. We're gonna have a lot of fun. The elections [for officers for the group] last time were a little grueling but we got a lot done and we have a lot of great projects planned. It's gonna be an awesome year!"

> [Later in the meeting, someone asks what Martin Luther King Day was about last year. A kid says it had workshops and speakers at the Snowy Conference Center and after lunch kids went to do community service.]

> Another kid says, "It was really fun."

> Erin seconds him: It was really, really fun. It was really a blast, a fun day.

> Later, Erin finished off another set of remarks with: "I have a fun little thing we're gonna do for fun later."

I saw no evidence that this nonstop fun-talk worked. Rather, I witnessed a great deal of mocking of it. One evening, I was late for a meeting that was in a locked building.

Dan and Aaron, two boys in the Regional YEP, are opening the downstairs doors for late-comers.

> I say to them, "Ooh, but you're missing the meeting!"

> "Naaah," says Dan, voice dripping with irony, "we're not missing a meeting, we're just missing Erin telling people how much fun the party will be." They laugh.

At another meeting, the discussion was about what kind of music would be at an event:

A girl: Ska, sort of.

Erin: Fun stuff .

Dan: "Funk stuff?" (Joking, knowing full well that she had said "fun.")

Erin says, "No, *fun*, kids'll love 'em."

As a summary statement, she often said, "If it isn't fun, it isn't good; we only do projects that are *fun*!" An exception was a blood drive, which Erin justified by saying that it would save lives. But then she quickly added that it would be "fun," too, partly because it would be in a mega-mall, and she named several chain stores where they could shop after helping nurses extract the blood.

It makes sense that young people would volunteer only if it was "fun." The hope was to make desire and duty coincide. It sounds harmless and even beneficial, until one hears youth volunteers' jeering discussion about old people's diapers.

Erin: There's gonna be a party on Youth Service Day—do you guys want to do some kind of service project?

Paul [an active youth member]: We could change diapers at a senior center (joking).

Dan [another active youth member]: YEWHF!

Erin [the adult] (Laughs): But we could play bingo with senior citizens.

Dan: Last time I played bingo with a senior citizen, he ate one of the chips.

Youth volunteers made mean jokes about old people at another meeting, too, and both times, Erin laughed along. She did not reprimand them because she was trying to make participants feel comfortable, to keep enthusiasm up, not judge or criticize. She was making it clear that nobody needed any special skills, or had to make any commitment, or do any soul-searching or risk-taking.

Unlike Erin's sudden flash floods of "fun-talk," Emily's efforts at changing desires were a persistent drip, accreting over the course of years, not minutes. The effects would have been hard to measure in time for the next grant. For example, whenever she heard someone using the words "gay," or "weird," or "dorky" as insults, she would repeat, "So? So *what* if he's gay?" or "So, what's wrong with 'weird?' Weird is good (or ". . . dorky")." Smiling, she would mock the speaker: "'My pencil broke.

This pencil is *so gay*!' 'My paper ripped. This paper is *so gay*!' 'My dog peed on the rug. My dog is *so gay*!'" A quick survey of these youth would have revealed that they had already heard this lesson many times, at school at least once a year. The proof of the pudding is in the eating, however: they had heard the lesson at school, but had they learned it, or did they still use the word "gay" to mean "creepy and bad"? Remarkably, while the school messages did not sink in, Emily's messages about gay and weird and dorky, repeated hundreds of times over several years, did: I heard some participants giving Emily's lesson to their peers, using Emily's words, even when they were out of Emily's earshot.

In long-term relationships, organizers argued with youth about what they *should* call "fun" or "weird." Erin, in a short-term relationship, could just repeat the word "fun" twenty times in thirty minutes and be satisfied that she had done her job; there, abstract ideas about how easy it is to change desires could reign, because there was not enough time to see the abstractions contradicted. Only in the hidden safety of a program like Emily's, after hundreds of rehearsals, could participants' feelings slowly transform.

Such a program work by constant repetition, over years, *not* by innovation. And so, by *some* of Empowerment Projects' measures, Emily's would not be considered a good program, because in it, repetition, not innovation, was key.

Just to give a feel for this drum's steady, repetitive beat: One midsummer day at Community House, Emily began the campers' lunchtime with a toast to "Things We Enjoy!" Like other organizers, Emily avoided using the words "good" and "bad," but she nonetheless made it clear that she really meant a toast to "things we *should* enjoy." So, when some participants offered unsavory ideas, just to tease her, she vetoed their suggestions!

> This week is "Holiday Week," so today's pretend holiday was New Year's (it's July—Emily is just trying to have some fun—last week, kids dressed up in funny outfits and put on pretend fashion shows—how does she think up all these things?). Emily poured us all cranberry juice for making a toast and lit candles that she stuck into a halved banana. She said everyone should hold up their cup (paper cups donated by Beanie and Cecil, a regional café chain) and give toasts.
>
> Holding up her paper cup, she went first: Here's to Community House and all the people in it!
>
> She called on someone else, who said: Here's to all the people who are nice and treat people with respect and listen.
>
> Next kid: Here's to video games.

Emily: Oh (looking disappointed), I'm sorry. I can't toast to that. Let's have another serious toast.

She calls on Chemise, who says: To all the people who don't listen.

Emily says: No, can't toast to that one—how about a serious one?

Next she calls on Dorene, who mumbles: To all the people who are sitting down. Emily didn't hear, so I repeat (I'm standing a couple of inches behind Dorene, who is sitting), and Emily (giving up, a bit, on the hope of non-sarcastic toasts) says, "All the people who are sitting down!" (and raises her cup).

Since Emily was with her group all the time, she had the freedom to disagree with them:

> Emily had the kids make a list of "forty rap songs with 'positive' lyrics." The kids knew what 'positive' meant, so they didn't have to ask. She didn't say, but we all knew. It meant, roughly: no drugs, crime, bragging about money, or violent sex (like, no "Must Be the Money" songs—it's the hit song of the summer, whose words are hard to understand but include the "n" word and the refrain, that *is* understandable, is about getting high in a fancy car). Kids who did not make a list could not come along on the next field trip, which was going to be really fun—to a big city.

Emily could give them a homework assignment like this; she could risk contradicting and even offending them, because she expected to keep seeing them for months and maybe even years. They were attached to one another, *dependent* even, and could make up later.[5] Without that attachment, short-term organizers like Erin laughed along with the cruel jokes about old people, as a way of simulating camaraderie.

Potential Good Choices

"You will make good choices" was another common self-fulfilling prophecy in these Empowerment Projects. It seems respectfully to attribute immense power to the young people: you have the power within yourself to change. At one Martin Luther King Day celebration, all seven adult speakers repeated the theme of "choice," hoping to impress the disadvantaged youth in the audience that no matter how deprived they were, they could transcend their social conditions. The word "choice" was supposed to invite youth to take responsibility for their action and to see they could have done otherwise. Sometimes this seemed harmless, and possibly respectful, but sometimes, it was a way of blaming the victim.

A respectful speaker like Emily gently made the "how" of her predictions obvious. Our hero Emily stood in front of the microphone and said, "You guys have made a very good choice by being here today." Emily's telling participants that they had made a choice seemed more respectful than treating them as captives. It was an encouragement to do something that they had, in fact, already done and knew how to do—a pat on the back. However, everyone knew that most of the four hundred participants were not there voluntarily. As Roberta had pointed out in a meeting of adult organizers, Martin Luther King Day is a school holiday but not a holiday for most parents. She had said, "Face it, that's why a lot of kids are there: because it's someplace parents can send their kids for a day."

Another speaker at this Martin Luther King Day, a black police chief, emphasized "choice" in a more chastising way than Emily did. He did not offer a "how." The first part of his canned, well-rehearsed keynote speech made good choices sound both very easy and utterly unfathomable:

> Let me tell you a story about a kid who was the fourteenth of sixteen kids, with a single parent. He was bullied around in second grade and could have chosen to fight back. He made a choice not to fight back, but to befriend the people who bullied him. And a volunteer stepped into his life, a teacher, who saw that he wanted to learn . . . stayed after school with him. Then in fifth grade he made another choice. This time, the gangs in his neighborhood told him he had to join. But instead, he made another choice. He joined his church, this fourteenth of sixteen kids . . . then his mother made a *choice* to send him to a school that was 90 percent white . . .
>
> This kid grew up on the Southside of Chicago, had no father around, grew up on welfare, could've made all the excuses in the world not to do anything. I am here because I made the right choices.

Next was a question and answer period.

> Question from a teen volunteer: How hard was it for you to make those choices, not to do all those things and just say no?

> Answer: It was *very* hard. See, I didn't tell you about the *bad* choices I made (everyone laughs), I didn't want you to hear about this. I knew that the choices I made wouldn't affect just me; they'd affect my friends and family. When I made choices, I didn't want to look bad in front of everyone else, have people telling my mother that I'd made the wrong choice, and be a burden on my friends and family.

Miriam, an Emily-like organizer who had been working in her youth program for over a decade, challenged him:

> Q: Why do we give advice but don't give youth the tools to do it? We tell them what to do but don't tell them how—we tell them what they

should do but don't give them the resources to do it. I'm in a bind here, because I can't always be around to tell them how.

A: I'm a community policing specialist, I teach the community how to self-sustain itself so they don't need police to come around and say, "you do this and you do that," so they can do it themselves.

He then went on to the next question.

In the rehearsed part of speech, the chief spoke in a sing-song voice, as if he were telling a fairy tale, but during the Q and A, his voice grew sharper and sharper, stabbing each word. The anger overtook him, so that when asked, "Where is your vision from?" he answered, "Other volunteers. There weren't enough *volunteers*. I felt like I was *cheated* because not enough *volunteers* stepped in, and that's why I volunteer now." Fielding another question about his brothers and sisters, whose lives did not turn out well, his voice grew furious.

As his anger billowed, his choices started to sound more and more like miracles that befell him from on high. The police chief never said *how* he made all those good choices, or what any of his bad choices had been. Instead, he quickly switched the topic to answering *why* he made good choices. Giving a "why" answer instead of a "how" probably did not help any audience members who needed to know a "how": *how* to deflect bullies in second grade, *how* to resist gangs in high school, and most mysteriously, *how* to be chosen by a dedicated volunteer in fifth grade. He could not mention why so many more bad choices were available—and were made—in the Southside, a famously impoverished part of Chicago, than they were elsewhere, though the audience had to know that in order to decipher his tale.

Future Potential with No Means of Reaching It

At first, what bothered me about this emphasis on "choice" was that it seemed to ignore the effects of poverty and racism—to blame the victims. But then I realized that the problem was not the emphasis on participants' potential to make good choices itself; rather, it was the emphasis on "choice" in a vacuum, emphasizing "choice" without suggesting that some living conditions might make it easier for people to make good choices, emphasizing "choice" without hinting at any patient, slow, possibly painful methods of reflecting on internal desires, making "choices" for sex and drugs sound like quick shopping decisions. It was the assertion of "choice" without any reflection on why anyone had ever made, and sometimes even taken great delight in, bad choices. While ultimately no one can change unless they change themselves, just exhorting people to change ignores all the reasons that they have not yet changed. He dematerialized "choice."

This became viscerally clear to me when I caught myself giving my own children the same message that I had initially felt uneasy hearing at Martin Luther King Day the year that all the speeches had focused on "achievement" and getting B's, not D's. Later that day, I grumbled to Emily that that was *not* King's main message!

Emily readily agreed, but said that, for these kids, it was an important message. I still said I was not so sure it was the right message for *this day*, as she and I started walking toward the evening portion of the day's events. At the entrance, I stopped.

"Aren't you coming?" Emily asked.

I said no, I had to get home to make sure that my eight-year-old did her math homework. I then chastised myself as a hypocrite: here I am, rushing home on Martin Luther King Day, of all days, to nag my own child to do her math homework for tomorrow, but I seem not to care if Community House children "achieve." The event ended past schoolchildren's bedtimes, but I had forgotten to care about these other children's bedtimes. From this, I realized that, like the organizers, I could not imagine raising decent children, or being a decent person, without the idea that "personal responsibility" is possible. No matter how poor I might become, or how deprived or even *disabled* my child was, I could not imagine giving up on that idea, even if it is partly fiction.

Catching my own hypocrisy made me realize that the message about responsibility and achievement was not the problem. Rather, the problem was that organizers were sending this message in conditions that made it almost impossible to fulfill. In fact, since they were keeping children up so late on a school night, the conditions for delivering the message undermined the very message they hoped to convey. Organizers were so busy keeping their eyes on the prize, in the glowing future, that they were ignoring tomorrow's day at school, when heads would droop onto desks.

Naming actions "choices" is certainly not unique to Empowerment Projects. Teachers and parents over-used the term, too, also probably redefining it in practice. The difference was that outside of an Empowerment Project, it was usually a simple command, and came with very obvious means of implementing it. For example, one afternoon at Laura's Casa Latina's programs, a curvaceous thirteen-year-old, Mauricia, was very busily flirting with a boy. This group met in the room that was Mauricia's English teacher's classroom during the regular school day. Mauricia and the boy were sitting on top of each other on a futon that probably was supposed to suggest comfort and intimacy, and the two horny teenagers were taking the suggestion too seriously.

Her teacher happened to run in, after hours, to pick up something she must have forgotten. Upon seeing Mauricia and the boy giggling on the futon, the teacher barked, "Mauricia, are you making good *choices*? You have homework to do. I don't want to see your name on the board for back work. I see your name is not on for this week's work. Good. You turned yours in this week. Now you just have to catch up on the two weeks before this one."

The teacher glared at Mauricia from under her frizzy gray page-boy hair-do, looking like a caricature of a crabby schoolmarm. The fact that she had to use the language of "choice" shows just how ubiquitous it was for professionals in Snowy Prairie at this moment. But in this case, the language of "choice" was irrelevant; it was simply a more professional way of saying, "Do what I say!"

The teacher exited, and then, needless to say, Mauricia continued to choose to flirt with the boy on the futon, rather than choosing to complete her homework.[6]

When the crabby schoolteacher barked it at them, teens heard the bark and saw their names on the blackboard under the "in trouble" heading. In those conditions, the word "choice" clearly meant "Do as I say!" Similarly, while I stood listening near the tiger cage at the zoo in early spring, I heard many parents saying, "I'm going to give you a choice: you can put your coat on right now or we can leave. Ok? If you don't have your coat on by the count of three, we'll leave: One. Two. Two and a half. Two and three quarters. Two and five-eighths. Ok, I'm just gonna put your coat on for you!" Outside of an Empowerment Project, Mauricia's teacher and the moms in front of the tiger cage gave their children the means of making the good choice, and forced it upon them if necessary.

Too Much Volunteering Disqualified the Volunteer, Who Was No Longer a Potential Volunteer

When asked to speak from their own personal experience and to exercise their unlimited imaginations, to "imagine you have a magic wand," youth volunteers drew on their experiences of working in Empowerment Projects: working on a time line, doing publicity, figuring out budgets, and applying for short-term grants. In our odd game of temporal leapfrog, when active volunteers learned these important lessons, they were no longer considered "at-risk" and were no longer considered representatives of what organizers called "the Youth Experience." They had become too unusual, and not as needy as other potential volunteers. The experienced and effective volunteers had to step aside. The missions of helping the needy volunteers and effectively helping others clashed.

Experienced volunteers' sense of time changed. Just before Martin Luther King Day, Samia said, "The words "Martinlutherking" are getting to be just like one word, like it doesn't mean anything, all we're doing is planning it." Planning a Martin Luther King Day activity at another meeting, Miracle suggested an activity. Wanda answered:

> But we're doing that at the Youth Leadership workshop. Martin Luther King Day is so soon after.
>
> Miracle: Not really.
>
> Wanda: It's October 26 for the one, and January 15 for the second. Oh, I guess it's not that close. I'm doing so much, I'm doing one thing right after another, it seems like it's just the day after to me!

I heard adult organizers say similar things—time and space became dematerialized and abstract:

> Bing: It's easy to get money from nonprofits that don't have to go through budgets and prioritizing committees and the County Executive.
>
> Jonathan, the NOYO member who ran the youth section of the city website: What kind of entity is the Youth Commission?
>
> Bing: It's not an entity—it's a committee (he draws a flow chart for money and time). So the Youth Commission is nothing.
>
> Another organizer: It's not a place, there's nowhere to go.
>
> Jonathan: To accept one hundred thousand dollars, you have to ask. It takes a number of months to work it through.
>
> Connie [adult organizer of this year's Martin Luther King Day celebration]: Thus, your suggestion to work through a nonprofit is more streamlined.
>
> Bing: The disadvantage is that if you get it built into the county government, it's more long term.
>
> Jeanne [head of public relations for a nonprofit afterschool program]: You have to plan so far into the future and have such a long time horizon, when the time actually comes it feels like: it's already past, it's not really happening, and you're on to planning the next six months!

Participants transformed; their sense of time collapsed. They felt dizzy at first, but eventually learned how to work on a complex, long-term schedule. This was an excellent lesson on how governments and nonprofits work, and it provided good training for work in a global economy. It is hard to imagine a person becoming powerful without this lesson, but it did not match Empowerment Talk's emphasis on local, personal, and unique. It also did not fit very well with the project of helping the needy; letting these no-longer-needy volunteers direct the work did not help a potential volunteer who was still needy, like Raul, the builder of the Doritos tower and the Skittles racetrack.

Samia and Wanda could no longer answer: "What would you do if money and time were not an issue?" Thus, to sign up the same four or five youth volunteers over and over again missed the point, according to officials like Rob Strauss. In a meeting between organizers, Emily offered up her four most active youth volunteers to help plan another event that showcased "positive youth engagement." Looking straight at Emily, Rob said, a bit sternly, *"And maybe we can get some people beyond 'the usual suspects'."* He meant Marisol, Bonita, Samia, and Marie. I heard him repeat this message in various other ways in other meetings. Emily glared and said nothing. Later, we will discuss Rob's frequent critiques of her apparent favoritism, but for now, the point to notice is that she offered those four eager volunteers because she wanted them to develop the talents that they had heroically dedicated themselves to learning. She knew that they loved this work, had a talent, and that they would still be in her program, and she knew that other participants' loves, talents, and schedules did not match as well.

Dedicated teen volunteers were supposed to get dumped out of the waterwheel while the new volunteers poured into the top. This echoed a familiar pattern; just as funding for programs goes for "seed money," not established programs, so did the programs have to focus on beginners, not advanced students. Youth who *actually* became leaders in the old definition of the term (someone who leads something) no longer seemed like "Representatives of Youth." And so, the more a teen volunteered, the less his or her experience counted as real. Some long-term dedicated organizers, however, sometimes smoothed out this temporal tension in another way: Emily, for example, continuously overrode Rob's suggestions and let Samia lead.

CONCLUSION: A HIGH-STAKES FOCUS ON POTENTIAL

Cultivating volunteers' inspiration and their skills takes time. It can take months before the inspiration seizes the potential volunteer, and many more months till the volunteer develops the skills to be effective. Volunteering can often be curative for some volunteers in the long run, and for them, it is clearly worth the wait. But the wait poses timing problems.

Participants tried to avert the potential temporal conflicts by trying to maintain an even flow of inspiration, by rarely becoming attached to any one particular project—the food for the homeless, the books for the preschool, the litter removal—and sometimes even forgetting what the goal was—is it hunger this year, or is it literacy? They adjusted the time lines by focusing on helping the needy volunteer. This could mean ignoring the needs of the recipient of the volunteer's aid, such as the hungry homeless people who needed food today, not next month.

Above all, they adjusted the temporal disjunctions by keeping their eyes fixed on limitless future potential, and by ignoring the past. When participants spoke as if all potential leaders had already become leaders, and all neighborhoods already were good communities, and young people consistently made good choices, it was as if the past did not weigh upon the present, and the present had already dissolved into the hoped-for future. The police chief's exhortations illustrate this firm organizational style of congratulating young people for having made a good choice before they had made it, when they had no intention of making it, or when they had had only one option from which to choose, when the speaker did not necessarily have the power or time to enforce it, and without giving youth the means to implement it.

Charging ahead into a hopeful future, these organizations did not encourage reflection on the conditions that made bad choices so tempting, that made inadequate community ties so common, or that turned some kids into non-leaders or school shooters. When participants are supposed to transform so quickly and unreflectively, the self-fulfilling prophecy can rarely self-fulfill. Emptied of history, lacking reflection on the past or the present, often lacking material to make the changes, armed only with hopeful gazes set forward on the soon-to-be-changed attitudes, the responsibility for fulfilling the happy prophecies could easily be flung back into the young person's interior and his or her weightlessly changeable "mind-sets" that were supposed to change in a flicker of insight.

CHAPTER 5

Democracy Minus Disagreement, Civic Skills Minus Politics, Blank "Reflections"

IN SNOWY PRAIRIE, a handful of organizers drew their boundless energy from the hope of connecting volunteering and politics, of encouraging youth volunteers to care about "the big picture," as these organizers often put it. However, many missions converged to prevent them from building this bridge between civic engagement and the bigger political picture. The result was that Empowerment Projects conducted projects about which any humane person would agree: pick up litter, gather food for the hungry, mittens for the cold—projects that were so indisputably good, organizers called them "no-brainers."

Paradoxically, this quest for easy, hands-on inspiration could easily lead to despair. Shining the spotlight only on indisputably good projects and on hands-on experience, organizers did not offer any practical solutions that youth volunteers—or organizers themselves—found plausible. We can define politics as the realm of "organized discord" in which people disagree about problems that they treat as not simply eternal and inevitable, but that they assume humans can solve—perhaps to stop global climate change and poverty-related disease, but not to eliminate all sadness, illness, and death, for example.[1] Without reflecting on politics, organizers could encourage volunteers to bring a can of tuna to feed the hungry, but they could not encourage them to ponder the problems' sources. The problems could easily seem overwhelming, when volunteers see that for every mitten they gathered for the homeless, another cold hand appeared. The absence of reflection and disagreement erased "the bigger picture," and made problems seem eternal.

It might seem obvious that organizers intentionally had to avoid conflict in order to avoid violating the U.S. tax code's regulation that requires nonprofits to be nonpartisan, but surprisingly, the groups never got close enough to a political conflict to worry about that.[2] Other barriers blocked the route before that risk even appeared. First, though a handful of organizers loved political dialogue, most found politics depressing, boring, and overwhelming, not at all inspiring, and they guessed that youth volunteers would feel the same way. They assumed that youth volunteers would consider hands-on, concrete projects to be more fun. Second, youth volunteers spent so much time publicizing and documenting their volunteerism, to prove their programs' worthiness to potential funders, little time was left for reflection or discussion. In fact, discussing how to publicize and measure their work took up more time in meetings than discussion of the work itself. Youth volunteers had to work on local, hands-on, easy projects that could be wrapped up quickly, in time for the next budget cycle, and that could accommodate high member turnover. The process left no time for slow, leisurely reflection, and it made disagreement too risky.

After describing organizers' hope of connecting volunteering and politics, and the frequently paradoxical results, this chapter ends with a surprise: to protect their programs, organizers brought youth participants to county budget hearings every year in the fall, to demand increased funding. This might look like direct political activism, but in a sleight of hand, organizers gave no hint that any decent person could be against increased funding of these youth programs, any more than someone could favor homelessness or the plague. The problem seemed natural and eternal. They gave no hint that the decision against increased funding had already, de facto, been made on the nonlocal level, when *national*-level policy makers decided how to spend most of our tax dollars—on wars, environmental protection, highways, parks, and the rest. Finances are not infinite; the youth programs existed because politicians and nonprofit offices funded them, instead of funding something else. Avoiding political controversy in Empowerment Projects required ignoring this ground on which the projects stood, ignoring these conditions of the programs' very survival.

Youth volunteers sometimes surreptitiously glimpsed important lessons about avoiding conflict, creating an image of transparency and flexibility, planning and managing—useful lessons, but not the lessons about linking personal inspiration to social change that fed some organizers' dreams.

Researchers have shown that volunteering early in life leads to a somewhat greater likelihood of voting in later years.[3] This may be so, but the passageway to politics that these Empowerment Projects opened up was narrow. It did not open out onto a broad political vista. Participation did not challenge participants' imaginations or opinions.

Some Organizers' Hope: Smoothly Connecting Civic and Political Engagement

An instructor of a workshop for organizers said, "If you work at a food pantry for your service project, the key to it all is to ask, 'why there is hunger and what can our society do about it?'" He said we *should ask the question*, but he did not *keep going*, to ask for possible answers. If he had, he might have discovered that, if they had any opinions at all, they may have disagreed, about the cures and the causes: Establish a minimum wage—if the cause is low wages? Make the government or corporations create jobs, or job-training programs, for the poor—if the cause is out-of-date or poor education? Build more mental hospitals—if the cause is mental illness? Make government or corporations provide food pantries and homeless shelters—if the cause is temporary lack of food? Combine all of these solutions, if the causes are mixed? Wait until a free-market entrepreneur finds ways to make a profit providing food and shelter? The discussion never got that far, because it would have required looking backwards, at past causes, in order to arrive at future solutions.

Waiting for volunteers to come to the rescue was always the programs' implicit answer, even though most organizers did not consider that to be a very good solution. In practice, however, the only problem that volunteers were asked to fix was the lack of community spirit. In one of the NOYO's first, most exciting meetings, Connie, the adult leader of the Martin Luther King planning group that year, advocated giving volunteers a less vague picture:

> Connie: It's a struggle to do what service learning really is about. It should be a process—but what we end up with is a series of "random acts of service"—from the individual youth's perspective, they don't get behind the planning of things. Except for a few leaders in the County Youth Committee, who do. So they go pick up trash, and that's nice and all, but it doesn't get at the *learning component*. And part of the problem is that it is tremendously labor intensive for leaders to get involved [. . .] SO, there's a lot of learning on behalf of the leaders and staff to get students to put in time to develop a sense of what "caring for your community" really *means*. And that's my sermon for the morning.

> Rob Strauss (tongue-in-cheek): Praise the lord!

> Jonathan [information technology guy for regional programs]: Right on! There's two sides to the concept of service learning: one is tied to the curriculum. Like a literature course, reading *The Grapes of Wrath* and then doing a project with migrant labor. It has to tie in, in a meaningful way. The more you split it off from the curriculum, the less good it is. "Ok, teacher, you're interested in labor history, here's some history happening right here, here's a strike right here." They probably don't teach labor history, but you get the idea. This is their place, where they're learning what *is* civic life. It's preparation for their role for society, by doing these kinds of projects. We should get kids thinking about civic responsibility and their role in society, by picking up the trash, sure, but go on from there, to *tie it to something broader*.

As introspective and imaginative as Connie and Jonathan were, even they could not make their dreams come true.

Blank Reflections

Youth volunteers filled out forms about their volunteer work: the forms asked where, when, and with whom, and then had a space for "reflection." I entered data from about four hundred such sheets, for two years' worth of Snowy Prairie youth volunteering—some of the sheets came from individuals, with only one name, some came from groups and had a dozen names, and some had just a group's name with no individuals listed. As the person who entered all this data, I saw that in all but a few cases, the reflection sections were *blank*.

The blank reflections made sense since there was no audience for them: Only one other adult ever read them; Sheila dipped into the pile to find some pull quotes, for publicity. As the data entry person, I was told that typing the reflections into the database was unnecessary. If youth volunteers reflected, it was on their own time, with no organizers acting as guides to help them sort through any troubling insights.

Three volunteers wrote more than a word or two in the "reflections" sections, and those three had some really touching thoughts. One had more or less the same touching thought from one week to the next, saying in each entry that it looked hard to be old and that the senior citizen whom she visited enjoyed being visited. Another, Daisy, was the remarkably thoughtful girl who had been suicidal before discovering her passion for volunteering. Her long reflections transformed over time. They were the painfully precise reflections at which some thirteen-year-olds can excel—about hypocrisy, narrow-mindedness, poor leadership. Slowly, she became a political activist, engaged in controversial issues. The third volunteer who actually reflected in the "reflections" section dug up invasive, non-native plants in a big park, every week for months. All the other volunteers went to a site once or twice—to be in a Holiday Show at the Senior Center, for example, or to pick up litter. When any volunteers other than the three girls just mentioned wrote anything, it was only a word or two: usually "fun," or "a blast." Otherwise, volunteers just left the space blank.

Learning How the Other Half Lives?

Organizers like Jonathan hoped that volunteers would grope, step-by-step, across an uncertain terrain, eventually grasping the conditions of other people's lives. This would fulfill Empowerment Projects' morally magnetic mission of promoting risky exploration, stretching one's comfort zone. However, getting inside of another person's life can be upsetting at first, as well as difficult and time-consuming. It would not appeal to everyone. In any event, it was not on the agenda as a concrete activity, but only as a distant hazy dream.

Aside from the girl who wrote in her "reflections" section about her six months of weekly contact with a senior citizen, volunteers here did not come into any sustained contact with recipients. While gathering food for the hungry, I asked Siobhan and Wanda if we should avoid food that required preparation, asking, "Do the people have some place to cook it, or are they homeless, or are they staying in a shelter with a place to cook? Could they use something like flour or baking soda?" I honestly did not know. Wanda and Siobhan didn't know, either. I wondered what town the food would go to. We did not know that, either. We decided that encouraging shoppers to donate expensive things like tampons and shampoo would be best. By the end, our shopping cart was almost full of donations.

When Erin, the adult organizer, came to pick us up at the end of the afternoon, Siobhan asked her, "*Do the people take the food to their homes to cook it, or does a food pantry cook it?*"

Erin said that she thought they could take the food home, but was not sure. She said no one knew yet which food pantry would get the food; it went all over Paragon County.

"*What I do know is that it will get measured by weight*," Erin added. The question of how to measure the volunteer work was at the top; it was the only thing that Erin knew about the food or its recipients. In retrospect, trying to put ourselves in the shoes of the hungry was a mistake. Pound per pound, canned peas would have been much better than tampons. Bottled water would have been best.

Similarly, Rob Strauss many times suggested that youth volunteers bring food for a food pantry to the Regional YEP's Halloween Party.

Rob: It's called Trick or Treat so Others Can Eat. You gather food to give to a food pantry or homeless shelter.

Erin [the adult organizer that year]: Like a can of tuna. Let's do that!

Erin chimed in so quickly and with such enthusiasm, no youth leaders could object. At the next meeting, when Rob made the same suggestion, the youth leaders again asked what it was.

VJ answered: It's like UNICEF.

Erin said, again: Yeah, like you bring a can o' tuna.

Youth volunteers asked if they would collect the can of tuna instead of UNICEF money[4] when they went trick-or-treating, pointing out that they could not collect both. Yes, it would be instead of UNICEF.

To empower youth, organizers assumed that something innovative, local, and hands-on would be better than something old, global, professional, and big like UNICEF. Organizers said that gathering food for local people would feel more close and real than sending money through UNICEF. However, gathering food did not bring volunteers into contact with local needy people, and the groups did not discuss local poverty. The can of tuna did not help volunteers learn about local lives. Collecting the can of tuna put youth volunteers closer to the can of tuna.

Should the answer be more face-to-face contact with poor and homeless people? No, not on these projects' short timelines, when it would just mean gawking at homeless people across a steam table, and then congratulating themselves on their selflessness and on their better fortune.[5] Face-to-face charity risks embarrassing or degrading the recipients, even over a long-term relationship; that is why some religious traditions say that anonymous donations are more respectful to the recipients.

As a means of helping the volunteers learn about poverty and homelessness, an alternative might be to embrace, and tame, the ensuing controversies, and some youth civic engagement projects[6] do that, showing that reconciling this dissonance requires letting youth volunteers learn about and reflect on impersonal causes—piecing together the bigger picture's patterns of "organized discord."

Participants Learn How to Avoid or Ignore Controversy and Sound Upbeat

Most youth volunteers considered avoiding political controversy easy. Jenny told me how the Regional YEP decided on which projects to do.

> We just do what we're interested in. *We do what there is to do.* Like nursing homes—like there's always gonna be a need for people to go to nursing homes.

> VJ: Like there are always ways to help at the hospital—you just have to contact this lady named Jan Hausenblock, or Shannon, and she'll have something for you to do.

Youth volunteers found a problem—illness, in this case—and they tried to alleviate suffering. The hospital visit was a good project because no decent person could object. In another project, youth volunteers went door-to-door giving out ribbons for people to wear and signs to put up, to show that they objected to sexual violence.

> One organizer in a NOYO subcommittee: It was nice to see there were so many young people out doing things on Positive Youth Day.

> Jonathan: Did it have an impact on enthusiasm?

"Did have an impact on enthusiasm?" was, along with questions about how to document the volunteer work, always one of the first questions, even for Jonathan, who had earlier mentioned reading *The Grapes of Wrath*.

Even in a story that included hatred and murder, controversy cleanly vaporized. In the yearly speeches at Martin Luther King Day, a typical presentation went something like this typical one:

> Martin Luther King fought against hunger and illiteracy, poverty and homelessness; he organized thousands for community service. Our democracy, our system, needs an army of volunteers, of do-gooders, and you are part of that army ... You've already shown, by being here today, that you're the kind of person who rises to a challenge.

Calling King a "do-gooder" was an odd choice of words. The phrase is usually used contemptuously to describe sweet but clueless old ladies who do not understand the people they serve.[7] Over and over, King was portrayed as a volunteer who offered simple solutions and with whom no one could disagree.

When teen volunteers were making up a trivia quiz about King for a contest during the annual celebration, they came up with facts such as: where he went to college, where he founded the SCLC, when he won the Nobel Prize, which president made Martin Luther King Day a national holiday—nothing that gave any hint about his broader ideas. I was helping the group by typing, and I asked if they knew about his positions on the Vietnam War or his support of labor unions. They did not, but, having had to memorize the entire "I Have a Dream" speech at school, they competed here to see who could recite it faster, and then, higher, and then both higher and faster, and then all did it together till they sounded like records played at the wrong speed, and then they broke down in giggles. Organizers may have considered King's political positions—about unions, foreign wars, and class inequality—irrelevant, and they may have thought that we all agree about racism (though millions of King's former enemies are still alive, aren't they?), and that all that we need to glean from his lessons is their general, vague spirit. But King's steady focus was on implementing dreams, not just having them.

All this is not to say that volunteering crushed the volunteer's political imagination; just that it did not cultivate it. In their food drive, Wanda and Siobhan politely greeted each customer saying, "Would you like some information about how to donate food to a food pantry for MLK Service Day?" People mostly said, "No, thanks," or "I already did," or "I don't have any money," or stared at the ceiling, or gave us a "Don't talk to me" face.

When one customer said, "I already did," Siobhan exclaimed, "I just can't understand how someone could not give food to a food pantry, when we're standing right here asking!"

Knowing that Siobhan was a top student, and wanted to be an international human rights lawyer when she grew up, I thought she might relish a small debate. I said, in various ways, that maybe people wanted to give money to politicians who would eliminate the need for food pantries by eliminating poverty. Siobhan's indignant reply: "Some people are just bad. They're just wrong. I mean, I just don't understand some people." She was learning how to plug into events like this one, but the Regional YEP had not once asked volunteers to ponder those big "why" questions that some organizers passionately hoped to teach.

MANY ADULT ORGANIZERS FOUND POLITICS DEPRESSING, NOT INSPIRING

I was standing with Sheila in an icy parking lot after a meeting. She said, "There was this peace event this Saturday, and I met a principal of New Stockholm School, who's a major peace activist. I'm big into 'peace.' But I'm not into the *politics*." This was one of the rare times I heard anyone use the word "politics," so my ears perked up.

Nina: Hunh? How you can separate them?

Sheila: She's like me. I find the politics depressing and discouraging, and a real downer. Like there's this Paragon County Peace and Justice Coalition, and they do things like "US OUT [notice that she does not even say what they are urging the US to get out of!]." And it's important to do that stuff. Someone's got to do it, but I'm just more into getting into peace through art and music—I'm glad they're doing that stuff. But I'm more the other way—so we made Valentines to send to kids.

She was a serene, back-to-nature kind of person, with a toddler and a farm in a semi-rural area. She said that she rarely watched TV, but happened to turn on *Oprah* one day.

These two little kids, a brother and sister, six and eight years old, started something they called Turkeys R Us. They heard that a lot of people couldn't afford a real Thanksgiving dinner and they said, "Hey, Mom, we're gonna raise 10,000 turkeys for poor people and we're gonna call what we're doing 'Turkeys R Us!'" [a take-off on the mega-chain Toys 'R' Us]. And they did it! You know, you get a six- and an eight-year-old asking for a donation for turkeys and you don't say no.

She said that Oprah had another kid on who was ten years old and already a sophomore in college, who said, "I want world peace, and I have a four-point program for making it happen."

She did not remember what the four points were, but loved his *attitude*. She was "deeply disappointed by last year's Kids for Peace Day because we didn't *do* anything." I looked quizzical.

We didn't do anything to help any kids! Like the year before there was the Candies for Kosovo, we made these packages and sent them. But this year there wasn't anything! And there are all these kids all over the world now who don't have *anything*.

She wanted to link up with a local refugee aid society, somehow, to get children what they really needed. We started naming places from which local refugees had come, taking turns: "Laos," "Vietnam," "Albania," "El Salvador," "Russia."

Now there's the earthquake in India, too. I feel a real deep, personal tie to that. Elsa's husband is from India—they've been there since December. I don't know if they were in the part of India that had the earthquake. But there are so many places that need things.

Like Sheila, most organizers loved youth work because it is hands-on, immediately useful, regardless of distant political conditions, and they did not want to wait for legislators: they wanted to make things better now, themselves.

This is the paradox: this hands-on response to urgency could lead to despair. For example, a speaker at a conference of regional environmental educators, held in Snowy Prairie, gave a presentation on how to encourage activism:

We generate 4 pounds of trash a day per person curbside, that's what we *see*, but there's 120 pounds per day that we *don't* see . . . 27 pounds of stone and cement a day, 19 pounds of coal, 11 pounds of wood . . . We in the First World consume 80 percent of the world's resources, but only 20 percent of the world's population is in the First World. In the United States, we consume 30 percent of the world resources, but only 4.7 percent of the world's population is in the United States.

Then she sang a song imagining the person in Central America who may have made her shirt—imagining the person's wretched conditions and asserting her intimate connection with that maquiladora worker. Her voice shook.

To illustrate her point about how we can make a difference, by taking *personal action*, she turned off the lights, saying that we could save fossil fuels that way. This was a windowless conference center room. So, her alternative required sitting in pitch darkness. She turned the light back on after a few seconds, of course.

I had heard these statistics several times, and wondered how I personally used 27 pounds of cement a day when I did not remember ever having used any. I finally found the source of the numbers: they came from dividing the number of pounds the whole nation uses by the number of citizens. That means "you" used "your" 27 pounds of cement to build airports, highways, parking lots, aircraft carrier landing strips, and military bases. Without engaging in public debate about issues like military and transportation policies, you will not be able to shrink your 27 pounds. The environmental educator's job was to inspire us to learn about the environment, to touch us emotionally, even to upset us, but she could not say how to fix it, except by personally using less cement today.

Further, when she suggested that we each *individually* save energy, and switched off the light in the windowless conference room, it only made things worse, since we all could see with our own eyes that sitting in a pitch dark room was no answer. Once again, an Empowerment Project organizer denied the conditions—electrical and architectural, in this case—that made the meeting possible. By ignoring the conditions that allowed us to gather together in the windowless room, she hoped to convey a message of hope, but sitting in the dark also conveyed the opposite feeling: a crushing sense of helplessness and hopelessness.

The Importance of the "No-brainer"

"Look at the positive and you'll see positive," was an idea I heard often, in various words. The day after the hospital trip, after he had complained so much about the volunteers' low attendance, VJ sent out an announcement on e-mail saying, "Thanks for everyone who visited the Pediatric Hospital. It was really fun and we got to meet a lot of new people."

The next day, Erin wrote, "The trip to the Pediatric Hospital was truly rewarding. Just seeing the smile on the little girl's face in the ICU made it worthwhile."

At the next Regional YEP meeting, VJ reported:

VJ: The hospital trip was overall a success. It went for two days—Saturday and Sunday—and there were a lot of people from the community, groups from the University, church groups, different high schools. We could go again next year.

Erin: We could start a tradition of going to the Pediatric Hospital. It was really cool.

VJ: Yeah, we could start a "tradition."

Erin: We really should do it again. It was really cool. It was awesome. It was so beautiful when we left—you should have seen the hospital, there were decorations on the ceilings and Andrea did this really huge painting on the wall. It really felt good, just to see those, there were all these sick little kids . . . "

Since no project was ever called a failure, or even critiqued in the presence of youth volunteers, enthusiasm was nearly guaranteed.[8] Mastering the organizations' style required learning this method of staying inspired.

The phrase "no-brainer" was one that Erin used often, emphasizing the obvious goodness of some projects. But finding a good no-brainer took a lot of brains. The Regional YEP launched a campaign to forbid local radio DJs from talking about how much fun it was to get drunk.

Erin, to the group: They get on the air saying, "Huh-huh, what's so bad about underage drinking? We did that when we were young." [. . .] when they're telling kids to do illegal stuff, it's a *no-brainer*. This is a good project . . . It's a good project, and I believe in it strongly.

Rob Strauss, the supervisor of regional youth programs, had been, behind-the-scenes, trying to steer her away from this project, sternly reminding her that it was very much not the "no-brainer" she had imagined, since the DJs could simply invoke freedom of speech, or that they could say that minors also overhear beer ads before they can legally drink, and car ads before they can legally drive. That was what the DJs soon did. Not knowing how to respond, to engage in a conflict, the youth group gave up.

Further blurring the connection between non-conflictive volunteering and politics, youth volunteers were often told that they "represented" the larger "youth community," even though no one had elected them. A city official came to a meeting of the Regional YEP to encourage us to attend a County Board Hearing, and starting by saying that she would tell us how the YEP fit into local political policy making. The city official introduced her lesson about representative democracy like this:

"I thought it would be neat if you could see what you do and how it fits with the various members of the Youth Commission. I see you as *representing high schools—AND middle schools!*"

She continued, saying that the group "represented all the youth of Paragon County."

How could this be? Could Marisol's brother, the only middle schooler in the group of about twenty that day, really be treated as the sole representative of all middle schoolers? No, of course not, but did he know that? And in what way *was* it legitimate, at least enough for the official to say it?

Youth volunteers probably assumed, if they were listening at all, that the legislator was just waxing enthusiastic—just one of those bubbly babbling adults who did not know how to talk to teens. If they were listening, however, they might have assumed that this un-elected boy could represent all middle schoolers, as long as he only worked on projects with which *everyone* would agree, like feeding the poor or caring for the sick. As a lesson in political representation, given by a political representative from the County Board about how legislators should make decisions, it was wrong.

Two Perilous Alternatives to Empowerment Talk and Political Avoidance

Laura, the organizer of one of the Casa Latina programs, sometimes talked to her middle schoolers about political controversies. While we have just seen that avoiding politics posed dilemmas in Empowerment Projects, discussing politics in them did, too. One afternoon, she told her group about a protest at an upcoming School Board meeting, whose topic would be whether Spanish-speaking students should be taught subjects like math and science in Spanish, or immersed in English till they learned it. She wanted her program participants to come testify.

> She introduces the idea by asking the kids whether it was better to be taught subjects like science and math in English versus in Spanish.
>
> Kids answer, "English!" which is not the answer Laura wants to hear.
>
> Then Laura asks: "Which way helps you learn English more quickly?" Some said they didn't know; some said again that being taught in English helped them learn English more quickly.
>
> She said: "But studies show that you Latinos learn better when you're taught in your own language!"

At first, her violation seemed to me to be a welcome relief from the stringent demands of Empowerment Talk. By bringing in statistical studies that contradicted members' direct personal experience, Laura violated the principles of Empowerment Talk, which invites participants to speak "from direct, personal experience" that no one can question. Laura was asking teens to take themselves as the objects of knowledge, not the inspired sources of it; to treat themselves as members of a social category, not just to draw on their own unique personal experience; to value knowledge, not just inspiration. Could it work here, in a program like this? It is hard to imagine how, without making a big change in the program's design.

Her approach had problems. When Laura asked about their direct experience, they responded that they learned better in English. She did not like that answer and ignored them, giving them impersonal, large-scale data, instead—a fine, deft move if she were in a debate club or social studies class, in which participants should presume that no single individual's impressions give the whole picture. In a program like this, there was no time or will to investigate both sides, thought both sides had good research to support them.[9] Since Laura's lesson was only one-sided, it was just another lesson in ignoring disagreement.

An even more perilous alternative to political avoidance appeared in some meetings of the Regional YEP. I was craving the gritty texture of youthful rebelliousness, and feeling forlorn that these fifteen-, sixteen-, and seventeen-year-olds seemed so tame, decent, docile, methodical, and practical, with all their attention directed to planning and budgets. One evening, a rebellious-seeming teen came to the Regional YEP, bristling with impossible, passionate, almost erotic urgency. I watched her squirm, giggle, and whisper in her molded plastic chair and her ripped black tights. Secretly, I felt relieved.

Then, noticing that the other, more dedicated youth volunteers were glaring at her, I silently chastised myself for feeling charmed. Trying to emulate the serious teens' responsible, adult-like internal demeanor, I sternly reprimanded myself, writing in my field notes later, "I really need to grow up! . . . The other kids (the non-utopian ones) are so wholesome, so sensible, they really *will* do good realistic things. Who needs the other kind—the dreamy rebellious ones? They're just 'impossible.' *Forget* about poetic, esthetic, impossible ideals."

When I chatted with the rebellious girl, Meghan, during the meeting's break, my initial delight and subsequent chagrin now turned into confusion. It turned out that she was very passionate regarding three issues: she was a born-again Christian, against legal abortion, and very much in favor of the death penalty. I personally disagreed with her positions, and yet was *still* a bit relieved to see a teenager acting as passionately as I imagined a teenager should act. Though I was still charmed that at least she *had* strong opinions, I could see that dealing with Meghan's vehemence made other youth volunteers uneasy. VJ, Bonita, and I had been talking, when Meghan and her friend Traci ran up, obviously trying to flirt with VJ by talking about a topic they knew he enjoyed: the recent election (a topic he never got to bring up during meetings, near adult organizers, of course). Explaining why they favored a recent political candidate, Traci said, "Well, I'm really in favor of capital punishment, for one."

Meghan looked VJ straight in the eye and said: "You run for president [of the Regional YEP]. Are you pro-choice?"

VJ started to answer: "moderately so, depending—" (but she kept going, saying), "Say no. Say no and I'll vote for you. Right, and I'm not pro-choice." (She continued, getting a little too close to VJ), "How could *anyone* kill a little *babeeee*? Babies are so cute, how could anyone kill one?" (She mock fluttered her eyelashes, giving a pretend "damsel in distress" look to VJ).

(VJ was kind of taken up short, as much by her strange demeanor as by her words, I think.)

Meghan changed the subject: Well anyway, that's not what I came over to talk about. For the hospital project, I was thinking that for Thanksgiving, we could . . ."

Empowerment Talk might welcome inspired, out-of-the-box, fiery, possibly painful passion. But harnessing its energy would be too dangerous unless organizers could figure out a way to build conflict into the project's design rather than trying to repress it. As we will see in the conclusion, such projects do exist, and scholars say they can change participants' lives. But they demand more intense commitments of time and emotion than Snowy Prairie's projects. There, volunteers' day-to-day participation in Empowerment Projects neatly tamed potentially offensive passion, and the "can of tuna" came to the rescue.

POLITICAL ACTIVISM WITHOUT REFLECTION

County Youth Committee officials attended a meeting about twice a year, to give short speeches urging youth to come to budget hearings. One gentleman started by saying, "You are the future of Paragon County," and went on to make a request:

There is going to be a budget cut this year, in the county budget. There are going to be a series of public hearings, and I hope you can come and advocate for youth.

Do you know what "advocate" means? It means say why you think youth is important. It's important that you come and say why youth programs are really great, so we can keep this position on the budget (gestures to Erin) and keep the Youth Community Centers open. Do you all know what the Youth Community Centers are? (A lot of kids say no.)

So you've got to stand up and say why these programs and that budget position is important—you've got to be advocates for youth services, because there's gonna be handicapped people and wheelchair people and people advocating for the mentally ill and a lot of people all asking for a lot of money. *But that's the ball game* [my italics].

I appreciate your coming out tonight, and I'd appreciate it if you could come to that meeting, some time at the beginning of October. You don't even have to speak. Just coming would say something.

So, every autumn, a big group of youth volunteers went to the County Budget hearing. I came home from one thinking that such political activism was a mixed blessing:

The kids were great—really articulate, persuasive, and attractive. Everyone congratulated them; they came with a big entourage of supportive adults. They got all dressed up and looked very put together, especially compared to all the disabled adults who could barely speak, or who went on long tangents about their Halloween costumes and their tastes in clothing and pets. The youth were more poised than the crying parents of disabled babies, who lost track of what they were saying in their testimonies [. . .]

One bright thought teens had: if you counted up the hours they put into community service, and thought of the minimum wage, they do a lot.

I hailed VJ on the sidewalk outside[10] [. . .] I said I went a couple of years ago and it was like this one—all these heartbreaking stories, really hard to listen to, really sad and upsetting. I asked him if he knew whether the groups were competing with each other for the budget or whether the whole budget could be expanded. Honestly, I didn't know, and nobody has *ever* explained it to the kids, and it wasn't explained at the beginning of the hearing!

Isn't that a remarkable non-lesson in civics? Rob [county official] said, a couple of months ago, "that's the way it is," about the budget, when he first invited the kids to go to the hearing. The county board member who came to the meeting at the beginning of the school year said the same thing [that the budget can't expand, that the youth are competing with the disabled babies and old people, that that's the ball game]. But I'm not sure either of them is right, and neither of them explained it.

VJ said, "It's a budget," and shrugged. "That's all there is. If someone gets more, someone else gets less."

I said, "I wonder if maybe all the groups were there to say that the whole budget for human services should go up—everyone there seemed to cheer for everyone else, and everyone was thanking other people for coming, as if we were in it together."

He said, "The only way to do that is to raise taxes," and he shrugged away that remote possibility. (Hesitatingly) "This isn't 'good' or 'bad,' but: I'm glad we weren't right after a real emotional one. This way we didn't have to worry about looking like we didn't really need it."

. . . The conversation ended by his saying, "There's no right or wrong answer to who should get it."

At the next meeting, I asked Wanda and Siobhan what they thought of the hearing.

"Long." "Too long." "Board members were asleep." And they imitated one hefty Board member, who snored while slumped over the table.

I said it wasn't clear to me whether we were competing over the same pie or not.

Wanda seconded my confusion, saying: "They *all* deserved more. Healthy Infants and Toddlers didn't want more, they just wanted to stay the same. I wouldn't want to be on the County Board and have to make that decision!"

Erin, the adult organizer, told me later that she thought *all* the programs could grow. But the teens had not heard her or anyone else giving that message, and neither had I. There was no discussion of the obstacles against this increased funding: who should do it? At what cost? Should the county pay and manage it, or someone else? Why haven't taxpayers voted for higher taxes if the need is as obvious as we think it is? The problem was that the issue could not be resolved without conflict, and without recognizing that it was not just local; unless the federal budget grew or got rearranged, some local programs would suffer. Every year for three years, there was the same miscommunication.

The County Board hearing provided a potentially powerful opportunity for a hands-on, local lesson in how and why governments make decisions. When organizers missed this golden opportunity, the teens were inexorably forced to conclude that they had to compete for funds—against disabled babies, mentally ill adults, and sick old people.

Empowerment Talk promises that hands-on, local, individual civic inspiration can sidestep political conflict. The result, in this case, was the inverse: a message that politics is a battle with no room for dialogue, a game with the rules already fixed, with no possibility of changing bigger policies so we could use less cement, or pay for both infant *and* elder care *and* teen programs. "That's the ball game." Like the environmental educator's pitch-black room, here was another recipe for despair.

In this and other chapters, I have reported all the conversations that could be called "political"—the realm of organized discord—that I heard during my four and a half years of volunteering in Snowy Prairie, except one, which was related to Emily's constant objections to calling pencils and dogs "gay" as an insult. Thirteen-year-old Bonita defended a lesbian politician to a fellow Regional YEP member, saying, "So what's wrong with being a lesbian?" She got embarrassed murmurs in response.

Organizers did not encourage such conversations. They quite often blurted out frustrations and worries about funding, but treated these worries as if they were just digressions. These seemingly tangential expressions of worry did not lead to discussion of the arguments surrounding funding: the obstacles against funding, or ways of convincing opponents, or reasons behind opponents' opposition, or broader questions—all the lessons missed in the trips to the county board.

Nonetheless, while participants learned to disconnect volunteering from politics, some learned very specific civic skills, in two specific conditions.

The Highly Circumscribed Task: Harmonizing Civic Equality and Protection of the Needy

In a perfect illustration of citizen education, young people learned how to interpret rules and apply them with moderation. This was not the radical, ambitious, utopian "youth leadership" that most organizers sought. Volunteers were *not* being asked to sip from that deep reservoir of universal knowledge and intense feelings that led to VJ's Disneyland-inspired Pediatric Hospital trip. It was not "open and undefined," not "up to you to decide 'whatever."

Instead, youth volunteers in these highly circumscribed situations were asked to do something humble and plain: to interpret rules within an existing organization. Instead of treating this as a self-fulfilling prophecy in the future perfect, they were given the tools to do the humble task. For example, a committee at Chippewa Middle School, composed of about five pre-pubescent teens who were either in foster care, in troubled families, or in serious trouble at school, had been given the power to make some small decisions for the school. This afternoon, the question was what to do about some kids in the after-school program who had gotten into a fight on a field trip to a miniature golf course. Rulebook in hand, Roberta, the subtle, unpretentious county official, led the meeting.

Roberta: These are the rules we've been using, but we don't have to stick to them.

The rulebook outlined four types of violations, ranging from "indecent language" to "harmful language" to "harming" to "life-threatening or illegal harming" ("Hammering on someone's arm is harming but not illegal or life-threatening, for example," Roberta explained).

Roberta called the field trip's problems "minor," not even the "second degree of unacceptable behavior."

Roberta or Kristin, one of the adult leaders of the after-school program, asked the students, "So what do you think should happen with the students who got in the fight on the field trip?"

Thirteen-year-old Carmen, who herself had recently returned from being suspended, surely and articulately answered in slightly accented English, "They should have to write a letter saying they're sorry and promising not to do it again."

Kristin, the adult leader of the after-school program in which the trouble had occurred, added, "And also one to the establishment, Noah's Park, or whatever?"

Carmen approved the amendment. Virgil also spoke up confidently (impressively so for an eleven-year-old, and especially an eleven-year-old who was in foster care) about what should happen after the first time and the second time a student "screws up."

Carmen, a regal girl with perfect posture and a pink and magenta feather dangling from her long hair, looked proud of her authority. In small, do-able lessons like these, youth volunteers could learn to imagine themselves as the kinds of people who could make rules for and be self-governing—a very bounded, limited, kind of self-government. Learning how to interpret laws and rules is crucial for citizenship. It could, theoretically, help youth understand conflict, especially conflict about how to interpret laws, though I never saw that result. In any case, the process of invoking this participation was very different from Empowerment Talk's invocation of vast, boundless inspiration.

Harmonizing Civic Openness and Family-like Comfort: The Intimate Context for Learning Civic Skills

Another kind of situation in which youth learned how to make decisions on behalf of others arose through a close, enduring, intimate attachment with a paid organizer. Community House participants learned to be effective volunteers through heavily directed, step-by-step cultivation and guidance with Emily. Like Carmen's decision-making, this was not the "open and undefined, for you to decide" empowerment that the projects usually encouraged. Also like Carmen's, this did not help participants learn to understand conflict. However, it taught them other skills that might eventually help them be effective if they were, someday, to become politically engaged. This was as close a connection between "civic" and "political engagement" as I found in the Empowerment Projects— an attenuated connection, but one that was at least not antagonistic to politics.

Participants learned "civic skills"[11] when Emily chaired meetings in her tiny office with her four most active volunteers. Samia typed the agenda, which Emily dictated.

> But Emily did not really dictate: she kept saying, "Is that all?" and, "Think: was there something else?" And "Did we decide that we don't have time for outreach?" and "Whose job was it to contact newspapers? Was it Bonita's?" These were questions for which Marie and Samia had definite answers.
>
> When writing up the minutes, Marie said, in a light parody of supplication, "Oh, Emily, tell us what to write. We need *you* to tell us what we did."

Civic skills that Emily's girls learned included: spelling, typing, computer proficiency, writing an agenda, and delegating work in complex organizations.

They also learned to value speaking in public, and to imagine themselves as the sorts of people who could do it. Asked by a local reporter to fill out a questionnaire about their volunteer work, they were not sure what to write. To help the others who could not think of what to write, Emily told Marisol to read what she had written: "When I talked in front of people, I didn't like all the little eyes looking at me, and if I messed up, I'd feel salty." Now, she said, she had learned to speak in public. These meetings taught civic skills, but not in Empowerment Talk's "open and undefined" kind of way.

These meeting defied the Empowerment Project's exigencies in another way: they were not open to everyone. Meetings amongst Community House members alone—not with the bigger, more diverse Regional YEP—felt like family gatherings. Moments before one typical meeting, seven members had been playing loudly on the computer, doing homework, gossiping, and jumping around. Emily called the meeting to order, which meant simply moving from the computer to the art table. It felt like a family moving from the living room to the kitchen table for dinner, but instead of eating, they were planning a five-day field trip to a big city.

They needed to raise funds, and to do that they had to establish themselves as an "organization." Emily told them to elect a president, vice president, secretary, and treasurer, but it still felt like dinner.[12] The group then made some plans for their trip, and went back to telling funny, fond stories about one younger girl in the after-school program who screamed too much—most recently, the cause was a worm on a field trip. In other words, there was no temporal or spatial separation between the "civic" mission and the mission of creating warm, intimate attachments.

Empowerment Projects value such intimacy, but here, there was a problem: it was not open to *all.* For example, when the Regional YEP was holding its evening meetings at Community House, the non-disadvantaged members seemed like intruders, through no fault of their own. As soon as they drove off, after one awkward and inefficient evening meeting, we six put our feet up on the table, tried on each other's glasses, joked about putting lice and rice in our hair, and launched a steady stream of jokes that would have been incomprehensible to a person who had not spent a long time at Community House. Relaxing, we also got down to business, making the detailed plans that the stiffer, larger group had neglected. The Community House girls had clammed up when non-disadvantaged participants had appeared, and that might appear on the face of it like class or race resentment. Those feelings certainly were in play at other moments. But the problem at this moment was that the non–Community House teens had barged in on these teens' private space.

From this comfortable nest, these youth volunteers could plan and manage civic projects. By one measure of an Empowerment Project's success, then, Emily's program was doing very well: she was teaching civic skills. By another measure, she was also doing well: the atmosphere was comfortable and intimate. It was hard, though possible, to mesh these two missions. And by yet another measure, Emily was not doing very well: secretly, Emily adored these girls more than she adored some other youth volunteers—another indication that the group was not perfectly open to all. This intangible feeling—let's call it love—ran against the principle of including all youth equally. "Don't just bring 'the usual suspects,'" as Rob Strauss had put it earlier.

The hitch was that heavily guided and highly personal attachments were these programs' *only* routes to learning civic skills. Non-disadvantaged youth often came to meetings already knowing these skills, and some already knew how to develop political opinions, perhaps having absorbed these skills in their own comfortable, intimate safe place—home. But if disadvantaged youth were not learning such skills at home, the learning had to happen in the Empowerment Projects, if it was going to happen at all. Here, intimacy fed civic engagement; civic engagement fed intimacy: a cycle. Thus, over the course of three years of attachment to a paid, more-than-full-time employee, four highly motivated girls learned "civic skills." This was not the story that these groups told themselves about how civic engagement develops, but it worked very well this way—though it still did not teach anyone to make the connection that Jonathan and Connie cherished in their dreams, between civic and political engagement.

Another Non-Action-Oriented Place for Talking Politics

Another place where it was possible to hold a political conversation was at school, in conditions that were very different from Empowerment Projects': classroom discussions did not have to lead to immediate action, there was time for disagreement, students were attached to the teachers, and no one could just leave if the going got rough. I attended current events classes for three years, in the three schools that most Community House, Regional YEP, and Casa Latina participants attended.

At school, they nimbly discussed the pros and cons of different policy solutions to problems including the death penalty, starvation, global warming, the protection of wetlands, the national debt, unemployment, illiteracy, child abuse, incarceration rates, serial killers, immigration, and "the worldwide disappearance of the frog." Over the course of just one semester, one teacher, Mr. Mueller, got up in front of his class of nine- and ten-year-olds, always in his plaid cotton/poly blend shirt, explaining those problems and then conducting a debate, aided by a remarkably thorough, engaging current events curriculum, Newscurrents. Mr. Mueller's nine- and ten-year-olds' capacities to reflect were impressive.

The situation made the difference. First, teachers' mission is to make students think and to assume that all students can learn to enjoy thinking, while Empowerment Projects have to attract all youth, even if they do not think of themselves as people who like to think. Second, teachers do not have to lure pupils in with attractive fun programs; they do not have to worry about terrifying or boring the students—though, while in these classrooms, the students genuinely appeared to love arguing about dramatic, horrifying, emotionally wrenching political issues. Third, while Empowerment Projects had to ignore conflict so that they could easily and quickly stage publicity events, the social studies classes did not have to arrive quickly at any concrete plan of action. Mr. Mueller did not have to arrive at a plan of action at all. So students could debate a single issue, such as nuclear war, or the preservation of wetlands in Florida, for a whole half hour and still not solve it. Engaging conflict this way might risk indoctrination, but these teachers brought out opposing sides very well. When they made their students vote on capital punishment, for example, or immigration, the students voted against what I knew was the teacher's position.

Surprisingly, then, for someone like me, who initially had been convinced by Empowerment Talk's ideals, the seemingly drab, routine, bureaucratic, expert-led, relatively coercive, enduring school setting fueled young people's political imaginations much more easily than the busy, active, hands-on Empowerment Projects did.

PARTICIPANTS' INSTITUTIONAL INTUITION IN AN "OPEN AND UNDEFINED, UP TO YOU TO DECIDE" ORGANIZATION

In the open meetings of the Regional YEP and the other civic engagement projects, youth volunteers quickly mastered the art of accepting organizers' statements about everything being "up to you to do 'whatever'" and being "open and undefined," while also calmly, coolly ferreting out the information they needed in order to make realistic plans. *That* was the knowledge that gave them power—knowledge of how to navigate the complex landscape of Empowerment Projects' intertwined missions.

Organizers often invited youth to "think of a social problem in your community" and *then* to imagine ways of solving it: two steps. But *before* thinking of social problems to solve, volunteers usually imagined the Empowerment Projects that were already in place. At one Martin Luther King Day meeting, for example, we broke up into small groups, to discuss what we could do that day that would be "on the themes of peace and nonviolence and the other themes that Dr. King promoted." I was sitting on a folding chair knee-to-knee with Wanda and Miracle, in a cavernous, dark gym at the Community Prevention Building on the far edge of town in a bleak building that also housed a program for grizzly old men who had been in jail. Lights glared down at us from the ceiling.

Our little group's assignment was to dream up ideas for one-hour workshops, about six of which would take place at once, in different rooms, on the day of the event. My subgroup thought by naming organizations. Emily introduced the assignment by handing us a sheet with examples:

"Health topics":
Healthy Self, Healthy Family [health promotion team, sponsored by: Paragon Tech University Health Services, and Paragon Tech University nutrition department]

"Community organizations":
Mercer Community Center, Franklin Community House [other community center programs]

Boys and Girls Club
West Snowy Prairie Positive Option Program [keeping kids off drugs]
Rainbow Family Resources Care Center
Paragon County Regional YEP

Wanda and Miracle said they were still not sure what the question was. Emily told us to think of topics first, and then think of people who could address them. But the girls could not think of the two separately, or in the proposed order. This was our list:

The 'No More Tobacco' Team of Paragon County. Miracle suggested it but Wanda kept saying it was boring. Miracle insisted that No More Tobacco was at another event she went to, implying that it must be a good idea to invite them.

Teen Peer Educators [another semi-government, semi-NGO, social work-oriented program, sponsored by schools and a grant].

Games for the World [an NGO that teaches "ice breakers"]
("But that was there last year, Wanda worried.)

Miracle barely audibly offered the only suggestion that did not have a ready-made organization to represent it: "How to Get a Club Started."

I asked: Are there any *issues* you want to talk about? Like stuff that's happening in the world? (Wanda looked puzzled.)

I stumble: Like, I don't know—war? Or whatever the opposite of that is—peace, I guess? Or the environment? Stuff like that.

In response, Wanda contributed: Drugs: Like the High on Life Team at The Truth Summit [two other Empowerment Projects].

Wanda was thinking *by naming organizations*. Instead of thinking of a problem first and then dreaming up a solution, youth volunteers would think of an organization that offered a solution first. When asked to "draw on your experience," they did exactly that, realistically drawing on their experience in Empowerment Projects, and matching their inspirations to the possibilities they saw on the horizon, learning to desire what they considered possible.

Adults unsuccessfully tried to downplay this institutional intuition, but it kept percolating to the surface, because without knowledge of politics and bureaucracies, getting the organizations to function at all would have been impossible. For example, in a youth program aimed at getting teens to educate their peers about the dangers of smoking, the organizer, Brian, said, over and over, "I might not be around." Brian wanted to start this program at other schools. "If I'm around," he kept saying. "There's this question of funding." He kept returning to this. He might not get funding for next year. He said it five times. First, he explained the finances in detail:

> If not me, then some other people might be laid off. There are four of us, two might get cut, some overlap—two people are basically doing the same job. There's someone from Paragon County and someone from Public Health basically doing the same job. So I might not have my job next year.
>
> [Later in the meeting]: Usually, the state gets $15 million for tobacco research and programs, but it'll be down this year, to $10 million, and half goes to the university. But I'm making this manual so you guys know what to do when I'm gone.

Since, for teens' purposes, people like Brian could vanish from their lives forever, for lack of funds—as Brian's funereal language about "when I'm gone" inadvertently declared—experienced youth volunteers diligently kept track of organizers' sources of income. Discussing an organizer who had left his job at Community House to work at an organization that Emily said was "privately funded," Marisol asked, "Is he making more money?"

"Yes, grrr," snarled Bonita, glancing supportively to Emily. Emily laughed.

Probably, most organizers would have considered Brian's speech to be a mistake, but interactions like these were surprisingly common and surprisingly educational mistakes. In them, organizers often unintentionally gave a lesson about how Empowerment Projects work. Overhearing so many discussions about planning, logistics, and documentation, youth volunteers could sneak a glimpse of a wider social landscape, and, in that way, learn something about the conditions for their programs' survival.

Figuring out how to document their work itself took so much time, almost none was left for reflection, either on the groups or on the broader society. For example, here, in the Regional YEP, is a discussion of the "President's Hundred-Hour Challenge"—a national award for youth who complete one hundred hours of community service in a year. This award loomed large in Snowy Prairie, partly because programs received funding based on how much volunteering they inspired. So, measuring those one hundred hours loomed large, as well.

In fact, in many meetings, youth volunteers devoted more time to the question of how to measure their volunteer hours than they spent on any other question. Dulce, an adult volunteer with the Urban League, opens one discussion of the President's award:

> A question we've been racking our brains about is how to keep track of the one hundred hours . . . so that at the end of the year we can have a record.

Polly, an employee of a health-promotion program, asked: Would you remember to send it in?

Kids: No.

An adult: What if you got a reminder?

Another adult: Or gave it to your group leader and they could send them all at once?

Another adult: Or if you forgot to get it signed, you could get a parent to sign.

The first adult: The problem is, who'll take the time for copying and pay for postage.

Diane [teen volunteer]: Is everyone gonna be affiliated with a group [in other words, part of a community center, not supervised by a parent]?

Connie [adult organizer of MLK Day]: So far, everyone is.

Dulce: Then, what are your thoughts—would you fill it out? Our idea was to get you to reflect on your service. Would that just be an added burden?

Liz [adult, Americorps volunteer]: After doing service, kids have this extra burden of "Oh, I have to fill this out, get a stamp from my mom." I know it sounds little but—or get group leaders to really keep on track, to avoid some negativity to putting in hours and getting disappointed when they don't all get recorded.

Olympia [13-year-old volunteer]: You could drop off huge piles in grocery stores, post offices—people could just pick them up.

Nadine [Olympia's twin sister]: Is this a nonprofit?

[A short discussion followed, detailing the laws that qualify a group as "a nonprofit."]

Polly: If I were a young person, I'd get a pile of sheets to mail in, because everyone was doing it, but then the next week I'd forget about it.

Diane [teen]: If you cared about community service, you'd do it.

Polly: There could be a "recognition" event in the group.

Dulce: And there'll be a midyear Recognition Event at the next Martin Luther King Day. But it has to be a personal commitment.

Polly: Will there be a "recognition" for, say, this person did 80, this did 20, isn't there a recognition after 20 hours, 40 hours, 60 hours?

It's like "here's the starting point and we're not gonna give you water at the five-mile point."

Dulce: We're volunteers, three people with full-time jobs—if you could volunteer (looking around the table) to enter this into the computer, make copies, typing, that would really help.

[Discussion of the funding for Martin Luther King Day's adult coordinator follows, after she offers to help until her job ends at the end of the fiscal cycle.]

Two points can be drawn from this long example. One is to notice how much time and surgical precision went into measuring the volunteer work. This precision even accounted for emotions: if, that is, the work was unpleasant, adults let the teens count the hours double. Youth volunteers got credit for eight hours of volunteering to clean up after a street fair even though they had only worked four, "because," said their adult organizer, "it was crappy, to put it politely." Similarly, at Community House one afternoon, Samia told me about the National Honor Society, which awards money for university scholarships:

Nina: You mean, if you volunteer a certain number of hours, you really will get money for college?

Samia: It's possible.

Nina: Is that part of a program?

Emily: It's the National Honor Society. But I wonder what counts. You've already done fifty hours that count for the "President's Hundred-Hour Challenge"; can they count for both?

In this way, youth could conceivably volunteer eight days a week, if they were recording volunteer hours for more than one program. And teens got "volunteer hours" for attending meetings in which they decided how to count volunteer hours, when, for example, Erin announced, "You're sitting right here, and that counts for one and a half hours. I have it written down, who was here, so you'll get credit for that."

The second point to draw for this example is that all this time and effort spent documenting the hours unintentionally but clearly showed youth volunteers what mattered in Empowerment Projects, in practice: measuring and publicizing. From these frequent discussions, participants developed an institutional intuition about how their organizations survived. Adults never guided them through any intentional reflection on it, however. Though they spent no time intentionally reflecting, discussions like these gave youth volunteers a chance to overhear brief tangents that helped form their institutional intuitions: tangents explaining what a nonprofit is, and reminding them that "the fiscal cycle" matters for their leaders, for example. Participants' intuition developed despite organizers' intentions.

Participants' unintended but incessant focus on funding sometimes surprised me so much, I sometimes thought that I had not heard correctly. At a meeting planning a mural at Community House, an adult introduced herself to me. She said her first name and then immediately said, "I'm the coordinator of volunteers at Fox School, and I'm also running an art program for disabled people. We got a grant for it." Financing was at the very top of her head, right up there with her name. This *was* the experience of working in these organizations; organizational affiliation and funding were as important for adults as their names.

Some youth volunteers learned about these sponsorships and were proud of how many acronyms they knew and how much they knew about which organization was connected to which; proud teens bandied the acronyms about in rapid fire in some meetings, while everyone else gazed in awe.

Part of their awe came from the extreme difficulty of orienting oneself on this horizon. Paid workers were sometimes called "volunteers." Someone like Wild River Running Dear, for example, made a living by writing grants to fund her work, so she was actually paid, but people called her a volunteer, the same way that Americorps volunteers are called volunteers. It was confusing. In cases like these, "volunteer" was an honorific title, which signified that she had the skills and credentials to make more money, but was making a financial sacrifice to help us. Calling her a volunteer signaled that she was freelancing, operating not as part of an agency, but by taking initiative to dig up sources of funding that other youth workers could not or did not.

To operate in Empowerment Projects, participants had to know where they stood , but gleaning this information was hard, and once they learned it, they could discuss the details only indirectly, only in tangents, or as part of a discussion of logistics, speeding along en route to getting something done visibly and quickly. They did not reflect on these conditions. Even though adults try so hard to encourage the youth to ignore the money, discord, and power, youth volunteers covertly got an inside glimpse into the seemingly boring institutions that shape the world—minus, however, any discussion of political conflict or any vision of political change.

CONCLUSION: DISCONNECTING VOLUNTEERING AND POLITICS

Surveys in many nations show that over the past twenty years, young people say they care less and less about "politics," while saying they care more about people and the planet.[13] This attitude resonates perfectly with Snowy Prairie's civic programs, which encouraged youth volunteers to care about people and not to care about politics.

Empowerment Projects draw on individual inspiration as the basis for civic engagement, suggesting that if it is genuine and deep enough, everyone will agree. Some organizers also wanted to make youth care about politics, but without acknowledging discord or seeing solutions beyond "one mitten at a time." Youth volunteers were so busy with the logistics of planning "no-brainers" and measuring volunteer hours, there was no time for reflection, anyway. In this way, Empowerment Projects made problems like poverty seem natural, not matters of dispute, not human creations that humans could fix. Civic and political engagement disconnected.

Without being guided through any conscious reflection, youth volunteers nonetheless often overheard organizers making plans for their organization's survival, and glimpsed a connection between their programs and broader political decision-making that way. Some Community House participants also learned skills that they could possibly use some day in the future, if they became politically engaged, but they learned them only in the context of long-term, exclusive relationships with organizers like Emily. In other words, the civic engagement projects opened up participants' wider political imaginations only when participants surreptitiously snuck below the radar of Empowerment Talk.

PART TWO

Cultivating Intimate Comfort and Safety

Organizers hoped to create havens of safety, intimacy, and comfort in their after-school programs. The comfortable, long-term attachment between Emily and some of her participants shows that a dedicated organizer in a stable, long-lived program could go very far in fulfilling this mission. At the same time, organizers had to invite a steady stream of short-term adult volunteers into their comfortable nests. Hoping to become intimate with participants, plug-in volunteers tended to undermine the intimate atmosphere in programs like Emily's.

Another challenge was to make participants feel comfortable and at home while trying to transform their feelings—to make sure, for example, that they did not feel comfortable with the junk food that their own parents and grandmothers lovingly fed them.

Harmonizing comfort with "out-of-the-box" experimentation was also a challenge, when people from vastly different social backgrounds were supposed to become intimate on the Empowerment Project's fast-paced schedule. What made one set of participants comfortable sometimes infuriated or disgusted the other; very diverse people probably will not feel very comfortable with each other right away, but in Empowerment Projects, "right away" was often all there was.

The next four chapters portray these discords and harmonies between cultivating intimate comfort, changing bad habits, encouraging experimentation with diverse others, and doing it all transparently and at a high speed. Learning how to make light, friendly small talk with people who are vastly different from themselves, how to discredit the volunteers' lavish promises and more generally, how to discredit an organization's lavish promises may all be useful lessons, especially in a flexible, speedy, unreliable work world. None, however, harmonize easily with the intimate comfort and safety that Empowerment Projects promise to provide.

CHAPTER 6

Harmless and Destructive Plug-in Volunteers

ADULT VOLUNTEERS JOINED Empowerment Projects hoping to have an inspiring, emotionally and morally transformative and fulfilling experience. Organizers and adult volunteers alike said that the volunteers should try to become "like beloved aunties" to the young people. The volunteers came to the after-school programs earnestly hoping to help, but they had only one or two hours per week to spare, usually only for a few months at a stretch.[1] Drawing inspiration from the idea that people are all the same underneath it all, adult volunteers had faith that they could become intimate quickly. In practice, everyone could not be so quickly and interchangeably available to everyone else. I call them *plug-in volunteers* because they hoped to be able to plug in and out as quickly and universally as plugs into sockets. After examining the ways that those volunteers' quests became harmful, this chapter points to some ways that other, non–plug-in styles of volunteering can, indeed, be helpful.

Adult volunteers' quest for a rewarding experience meant that they had to find youth participants who would be rewarding to help. If volunteering stopped feeling rewarding, the volunteer had no obligation to stay. So, in the first few minutes of one after-school homework program, adult volunteers would literally run to get seats next to participants who were easy to help, who actually had their textbooks and who were eager to do their homework. Volunteers would avoid participants who were hard to help or bond with. They ignored, for example, the miserable, greasy-haired, hard-to-talk-to white boy who sat alone at a big cafeteria table with seven empty seats, hunched in a dirty windbreaker, every afternoon, all winter. They ignored the abrasive black teenage girl who threw mud at a boy one day and threw paint at someone else another day. It was really hard for a volunteer to know what to do with these troubled youth. Helping them with their homework or their emotions would not be rewarding, or even possible, on the plug-in volunteers' tight schedules.

Some volunteers tried just having fun, joking, playing, and teasing, in hopes that just *making contact* would lead to an emotionally rewarding depth of intimacy at some future date. On the plug-in volunteers' schedule, this was even worse for a homework club member than being ignored, because it meant abandoning homework that afternoon, to chat, have a snowball fight, or play on the computer.

Plug-in volunteers, who were almost all white in Snowy Prairie, found contact to be especially inspiring if it crossed racial lines. They were most eager to help, and most curious about, the disadvantaged youth, but with so little time for them to learn about their big differences, the volunteers sometimes actually added to the young person's difficulties, as we will see.

For all these reasons, the four most studious, hard-working Community House participants routinely hid in a dark, somewhat moldy basement room to do their homework, and closed the door. There, the chatty adult volunteers could not find them and could not try to help them or bond with them. I was frankly shocked to find that the adult volunteers' efforts were so often harmful. To have a less disastrous effect, volunteers would either have to work more hours per week for a longer time span, or would have to trim their ambitions to tasks that did not promise to be intimate or soul-changing.

The Paid Organizers' Cultivation of Intimacy

Empowerment Talk promises that volunteers will be more effective than paid employees at creating warm, cherished, unique relationships. However, a paid employee like Community House's Emily was always with her program participants, not just one or two hours per week, but sixty or eighty. She knew the intricacies of her program members' latest crushes, knew all about their school, their specific teachers, their siblings, their parents' and their parents' and live-in relatives' comings-and-goings from other countries or regions. Emily knew how fast her kids' hair grew.

Though plug-in volunteers undermined her program's feeling of family-like, safe, comfortable intimacy, she had to keep inviting these volunteers, since they so potently symbolized grassroots, civic empowerment in the eyes of funding agencies that wanted evidence of programs' grassroots support. Opening up their programs' inner chambers to any adult who wanted to help for however long she or he wanted to help, organizers had to protect their programs' homey intimacy from the breezy civic volunteers, with their infinitely flexible schedules.

Before assessing the plug-in volunteers' efforts, we have to see the homey, intimate atmosphere that a really dedicated paid organizer managed to cultivate. Every day after school, Emily's kids came blasting into the Community House building, smelling of cold fresh air, reporting, one by one, on their school day. To their stories, Emily dispensed offhand advice and humor: "That guy is just trying to rip you off," about someone in one kid's daily tale. Later that day, when Bonita said she won $10 for doing well in math, Emily advised, "Why don't you save it all up, every time you get money, and buy something really good?' When Bonita said she wants to spend it on food at the nearby McDonalds, Emily said, "Well, at least don't get something really gross."

Unlike "really communicating" in a late-night, risky, exciting, inspiring tête-à-tête, Community House's kind of intimacy went with security, physical stability, and predictability. Community House's kitchenette, slightly hidden rooms, places on the basketball court that everyone knew belonged to one group or another—all this contributed to the familiar atmosphere. In contrast, organizers of programs that had no stable meeting place complained bitterly, saying that setting up afresh each day in an echoing cafeteria made it hard to do art projects and play board games, and made loyalty hard to cultivate. With stable staff and a stable place, a feeling of quiet comfort and long-term familiarity could arise.

In Community House's dingy rooms, one could easily observe the signs: when teens were sharing jokes and words that no one else could understand, finishing each other's sentences, and correctly guessing Emily's mood from the sound of her footfall even before she entered the room. Emily, in turn, knew her kids well enough to detect problems before anyone told her about them, or even before they happened: When there was a fight at a dance in the Community House parking lot one summer night, Emily and Miriam, her colleague from another community center, sniffed out trouble about two hours before anything happened.

If this portrait is starting to sound like an ad for a mood-enhancing pharmaceutical product, keep reading. Emily and her participants argued ferociously and made up soon after—or two months after. As in the minutiae of arguments between siblings, each argument was inconsequential in its details. One blow-up, for example, was about a boy who might have been two-timing on Marie and Marisol—Marie thought that Emily was on Marisol's side. Marie stormed out in the icy December evening alone, which was followed by a three-way, week-long silent treatment. Emily also nagged them about homework. She got frustrated. She turned red. Emily and her participants treated each other like family.

One could call their togetherness "intimacy," but not the kind that the word usually implies for Americans; not extraordinarily intense verbosity and heart-to-heart midnight whispers, not the special activity that Americans tend to call "really communicating."[2] Rather, it was the kind of intimacy that means familiarity and comfort with a unique person, place, or activity, which slowly accretes over time[3]—very different from the quick intensity that plug-in volunteers sought.

"MAYBE HE SHOULD FIND A DIFFERENT MENTOR"

My first hints that plug-in volunteers might be ineffective or even destructive came from the young people themselves. At an all-day workshop on how to be an effective volunteer, six high school students had been summoned to address about thirty adult volunteers, to tell them how to be helpful. These six students had all received the Ranscombe Scholarship, a local award for youth of color who had shown potential. The six teenage recipients were describing their former friends who had become trouble-makers or dropped out of school.

Question from adult mentor [a "mentor" was supposed to be an espe-cially dedicated volunteer who worked one-on-one with the same young person each week]: As Ranscombe Scholars, someone's been tracking you, making sure you stay on track. Do you feel it's helped you resist peer pressure and stay on track? *Do mentors make a difference?*

Blonde girl: [Clearly accustomed to this spiel after her years as a Rans-combe Scholar, she had begun the session by clarifying her ethnicity, by telling us that, even though she is blond and does not look stereotypi-cally "Hispanic," she says, her mother is from Mexico]: *Not really,* because people make their own choices. We [she and the wholesome friends she had just been describing] call the other [not wholesome] girls and invite them to do things and they always just blow us off.

Next, an adult mentor details her problems with the kid she is mentor-ing—he doesn't do his homework. She asks for advice.

A black teenage boy [This generic, possibly racist way of describing him represents the adult volunteers' perceptions in this situation, I think. Like the other adults, I didn't know these teenagers' names. Like the other adults, all I knew about this boy was what I saw and what I knew: that he had received a scholarship for youth-of-color. Should I describe him by something that he chose to represent himself—the baggy pants or the big shirt? No, in this situation, he was being treated as a "repre-sentative" of a category, and I do likewise here]: Maybe school is bor-ing. Maybe his class is so boring, he can't think of it. I know there are some classes. . . . .

Another black boy: People don't try. I think if someone—it has to be something—he don't believe in—it has to be him on his self.

Question from another adult: *How does a mentor make a difference?* How does a mentor make a personal connection? I meet with my mid-dle school kid once a week. What can I do with my kid to make the homework meaningful when I meet with him next Wednesday?

A black girl [echoing the statement I so often heard]: I know, just meeting once a week in the middle of the week is *not gonna be helpful.* I mean, I know if I have homework on Monday and Thursday, I'm gonna need help on it on Monday or Thursday. *Just once a week, that won't help.*

Another adult: It's about self-discipline. You can't always be there. He's gotta learn to organize himself so even when you're not there, he does what he needs to do.

The black girl: So maybe you could meet with him on Monday and Thursday—because if he has homework on those days, that's when he's gonna need help.

The blonde girl: That's where motivation comes in. He needs to motivate himself.

Female mentor: My schedule doesn't allow me to come in more than once a week.

The black girl: Maybe he should find a different tutor! (everyone laughs nervously, a little shocked) No, not like that! Like a (people chime in with her, saying "in addition," "not instead of") an *additional* tutor!

Adult moderator: He needs to learn time management. We all do—need to plan, know what needs to be done when.

That ended it for a while; their conclusion was that the boy's problems were ones that *we all share*—they were, according to the adults in this discussion, neither serious psychological problems that the mentor should help the mentee reflect upon, nor social problems that the mentee's living conditions created, that the mentor could help change. The mentors implied that this boy's problems were universal: We're all the same underneath. Their discussion affirmed the value of the volunteer's one hour per week, by saying that the boy could and should learn to help himself on the other days of the week.

A while later, they returned to the topic:

The blonde girl: It's really the parents, it all depends on the parents—the parents need to take responsibility.

Question from adult: *Is there anything volunteers can do?*

The blonde girl: *No*, it's mostly parents.

Adult sitting in front: When you're with a kid, you can let them know that they have "assets" [alluding to asset-based community development], and they can "build on them." Even if they're having a hard time with their math homework, or reading, everyone has something they can do well, whether it's something little, just point out to them, "Look at what you just did!! *You* can do *this*!!"

The blonde girl: *But that doesn't help either*. If they're already on the wrong side of the track, you can't get them back.

Later, the teens complained a little more directly about unhelpful mentors, and then, finally, an adult asked if there was some way for them to lodge a complaint about the unhelpful mentors, maybe with the school principal. The mentees said that it "doesn't feel right" to complain about someone who was there simply out of the goodness of their heart and was not getting paid. Needy recipients of aid could not complain about something that seemed costless—even if it did not feel costless.

Why did these teens keep denying that volunteers made a difference in their lives, no matter how many times the adults re-asked the question? There are two possibilities:

One is that teenagers want to feel independent, and recoil from acknowledging dependence on anyone, especially in front of a crowd of strangers—even if they really have benefited from someone's help. If this was the case here, then making the teens get up in public and acknowledge their dependence was a degrading ritual that could only produce shame and snip their budding independence.

Another possibility is that what the teens were saying was true: that time and repetition are irreplaceable, and those volunteers were ineffective. If that was the case, then providing real help for the needy teens clashed with the programs' mission of promoting plug-in volunteers' civic engagement.

I could not peer directly into teens' psyches to see if the first was true, but I observed, time and time again, that the second was.

Volunteers came and went rapidly, like guests who may or may not make a mess, and who will try to be nice to the children, but will not be much help in tasks that require familiarity with the children's lives. As a typical volunteer homework helper, I was often unhelpful, too. I often found myself having to *undo* advice that the Tuesday's volunteer had given, who had, herself, contradicted Monday's volunteer's advice; and then I found myself coming back a week later to undo a new set of contradictory advice that another random list of volunteers had given a student. This made long-term projects especially difficult, but even in math or foreign languages, which might seem easier to divide into bite-sized morsels, I often heard volunteers asking, for example, "Well, has your class learned the Pythagorean Theorem yet? ... Then what have you learned that could help you solve this?" or "You could do it this way, but I don't know if you've learned that [axiom, or formula, or verb conjugation] yet." And of course, some youth claimed not ever to have been taught anything, making the homework seem impossibly unfair, so that the volunteer would give up. Volunteers never knew when to believe the students, since they often did not even know the participants' names, did not know their schoolteachers, and had not been helping that participant when she or he learned that axiom or verb conjugation two months earlier.

A typical day shows this: A university student named Keith and I were volunteering at Community House, along with a loud volunteer, Josh (more about him later), and another volunteer who stayed quiet and needed help finding something to do, since there were more volunteers than youth that day. At various times throughout the afternoon, Keith, Josh, and I helped eleven-year-old Jeannette with her homework—an assignment on which she had been working for over a week, with new, contradictory advice from at least four different volunteers so far.

> Jeannette's homework was to write "Imagine you are a Loyalist, Patriot, or Undecided, in the War of Independence. How has the war changed your life?"
> I helped her today (Keith did, too), someone else had helped the day before, and yet a fourth person will help tomorrow. Yesterday's volunteer (probably trying to make the material "relevant" to Jeannette, who was black) suggested that she write about Crispus Attucks. Ok, but she didn't know what side of the war Crispus Attucks was on. I didn't want to risk making her do her whole assignment wrong and Jeannette did not know which was right. Besides, if she wrote it from the point of view of an actual, historical person, she'd have to make up inaccurate facts or else learn something about Crispus Attucks, and that was not part of the teacher's assignment. So I tried to convince her to follow the assignment directly: just make up a story about someone imaginary, who was either a "Loyalist, Patriot, or Undecided."
> She had been worrying all afternoon that her grandma was gonna just leave if she wasn't standing outside waiting for her. (Her grandmother just recently claimed custody of her, and is not eager to have an eleven-year-old again, according to Emily.) She was also distracted by Ana, and kept asking her questions about something else.
> Jeannette is a really poor reader, and the ancient encyclopedia had a lot of big words and awkward metaphors ("muskets revelled in the vallies," or something). Frankly, the tutoring was not going too well.

Keith, the university student majoring in Political Science and History, took my place when I got up to make a phone call. When I came back, I saw a problem that kept repeating: Keith had already contradicted the advice I had given Jeannette fifteen minutes earlier (and the rest of the afternoon, I could not get a song out of my head: "making love in my bedroom, I got up to wash my face . . . when I come back to bed, someone'd taken my place!"). Jeannette was receiving a wealth of help, but in a mess of bits and pieces that did not add up to a coherent whole. At first, I assumed that the conflicting advice was due to each particular volunteer's lack of skill, but it happened to most volunteers, and, as this example shows, it kept happening to me, too.

Keith was sitting on a desk, trying to convey some of his newly learned radical political ideas to Jeannette, while simultaneously talking to Josh.

Keith (speaking loudly to Josh, and whomever else wanted to listen): Her textbook (Jeannette's) was written in the most boring way possible. It's unbelievably boring—it's overloaded with irrelevant dates and places.

Josh: It's also wrong. It's a bunch of lies. You can look at disinformation.com to find all the lies.

Meanwhile, Keith kept asking Jeannette about the Boston Massacre: "Where were you?" At first, I was impressed (aside from noticing that he kept distracting Jeannette), by Keith's creative way of prodding her to think about history. This creative question completely confirmed my commonsense idea that volunteers reach young people in ways that dried up, dreary teachers would never imagine! "Perfect evidence for the importance of volunteers!" I thought. But it turned out that this wording, which I had not yet seen, came from Jeannette's schoolteacher, Mrs. Svensen, a strict, seasoned, gray-haired teacher: a paid professional. She had assigned a "point of view" story—a completely standard type of assignment. But anyway, in my notes at the time, I wrote, "The only part of the assignment that Keith really flopped on was that he didn't direct her to find someone who was a Loyalist or Patriot—someone whose opinions she would know!" Plus, Jeannette still had not actually written anything. Maybe she would tomorrow.

This pattern repeated over and over, often, in all the after-school programs: a volunteer is handed a student who received advice on a long-term project yesterday, and who will get some other advice tomorrow, and will get yet more, possibly conflicting advice the next day. The next week, when I still had high hopes, I wrote in my notes:

Now, *if* I were coming back tomorrow, perhaps we'd get somewhere. But this continuity isn't going to happen. Once a week for an hour or two just isn't enough. Even throughout the afternoon, kids get different helpers at different moments, like Jeannette last week. *Time* is of the essence: time spread out over weeks and days, while the student is writing that specific report, not for one hour here and for another hour there, with different volunteers working on the same report.

So, even if I come back every week, once a week for a year, Apache [the boy I had "helped" that day, who, like Jeannette, had had a long-term assignment and had, the day before, been given advice that reversed the advice he had received the day before that, and now had nothing written on his paper about Custer's Last Stand except: "Resolt: Custer dead."] might not be there every Wednesday for one thing. For another, that assignment will be done by next week, so even if we both come every Wednesday, we'll never get to complete an assignment to-gether. Plus, he'll be getting loads of advice from other people about how to proceed—someone else today, someone else later in the day today.

So, even though he *and* I both wanted to do this story and had really started to get somewhere interesting with it, for one day's work, we couldn't keep going. Sporadic volunteering is worse than no volunteer-ing at all! From this, I would gather that I was a bad teacher in one-on-one tutoring, and he would gather that he is a hopeless student.

So, is once a week for a couple of hours volunteering only totally tokenistic, a feel-good exercise for the volunteer, and useless for the kid? Or worse than useless, because the kids get to pull the wool over yet more stupid white volunteers—usually "sweet old ladies"—and reaf-firm the vast distance between them? And all the boatloads of "help" that amount to nothing must make them feel really dumb [...] My questions today are all about *time*.

Thirteen-year-old Carmen spoke about the problem of volunteers' lack of familiarity. She was the regal girl in a Youth Self-Government Board meeting at Chippewa Middle School whose Spanish-speaking immigrant mother held two different full-time jobs, till ten at night. As usual, her posture was perfect and her trademark glittery pink feather woven into her hair dangled elegantly on her shoulder. She said that after-school vol-unteer tutors were never, ever as helpful as her own mom, so she saved her questions for her mom, even if it meant staying up late to wait for her.

Roberta, the adult who is running the meeting, reads the agenda (no-tice: she is not trying to enact "family-like relations" here; she is doing something that does not require as much work against the grain, *and it works*): Question 2.a is about how to keep you guys on task about homework.

Carmen: The tutors, when they try to explain things, they start talking about something else, and it just doesn't help, they're confusing.

Karen, the co-leader of the after-school program (a new employee who will be moving to another state in two weeks!): It's nice to get it out of the way so you can really enjoy the rest of the afternoon.

[Carmen tries again to assert that the tutors are not helpful when she needs help. She cannot do the homework till she gets home. And again, the adults respond by saying that the kids should just try harder, "really knuckle down," they say.]

Was Carmen's explanation just an excuse? I did not think so. Next, some-one suggested asking the teachers to send the homework assignments to the tutors directly, so that the tutors would know first hand what the homework was, instead of having to rely on students' unreliable information which was often that "there was no homework" even when there was. However, the group decided that that would be too complicated since there were so many different tutors, and teachers, and students.

Carmen was lucky to have a mom who helped with homework; the others in the Youth Self-Governance Board did not have a mom like hers, or did not even have a "mom" at all:

> Dante asked Randy, when he said he was going to Kansas City to stay with his parents for the summer, "Oh, don't you live with your aunt and uncle?" "No, I live with my grandparents." And Veronica couldn't come, said Carmen, because she lives in a group home and Thursdays are the day she can visit her father.

So, for them, the after-school homework fulfilled more than one need; they needed not only "a safe place to go," but also, adults who could help them the way Carmen's mom helped her. Plug-in volunteers often said that they wanted to give young people the family-like relationships and family-like help that the kids' own families could not supply. Carmen's point was that the patchwork of advice did not work, and, indirectly, that the relationships were not as family-like as volunteers imagined.

CLUELESS VOLUNTEERS

One mission of Empowerment Projects is to drag volunteers "out of their boxes," to make them question their own lives, but this Jane Addams–like, fruitful perplexity was impossible to cultivate quickly. For example, when a group of church volunteers held a week-long summer program in a low-income housing project's park, they did activities that may have made the children's parents' lives more difficult.

> Kids were painting, and big blobs were getting on their clothes. I wondered aloud if their families had washing machines at home or if it would be a pain for them to go to the laundromat.
>
> [I had just read, in a textbook for preschool teachers, that dirty laundry was a big problem for parents who didn't have washing machines— the book said that teachers should keep this in mind when designing messy projects.]
>
> One volunteer said simply, "Don't worry, it's ok."
>
> Not wanting to sound stuffy, I said that it wouldn't bother *me* if it were *my* kids getting covered with paint, but maybe it would bother some *other* parents, like if they didn't have washing machines.
>
> Another volunteer said not to worry, because they had done messier art projects the day before.

Was it worth worrying about? After such brief contact, it would have been too awkward to ask the parents if they had washing machines, and hard even to imagine that such details might matter in the first place.

Downright Destructive Volunteers

More prickly than the problem of unhelpful volunteers was the problem of downright destructive ones. One afternoon, after finding that adult volunteers had merrily led a snowball fight in the middle of the street, at twilight, during a blizzard, Emily scolded her program participants, after the volunteer had left:

> If *anyone ever* leaves the building, you have to ask me first. If you go to McDonalds, if you go out with a volunteer, you have to come ask me first! And is it *ever* all right to have snowball fights out in the street?

Another afternoon, a volunteer bragged constantly about his dangerous and illegal exploits. Josh was thirteen years old, but since he was a good student, he could work alongside adult plug-in volunteers, helping Community House kids as if he were an adult; as he proudly declared, "I'm here to tutor, even though I'm smaller than most of the kids here." He was volunteering because his mother said he had to, as part of a bargain. While volunteering, he bragged about stealing music on the Internet; setting outdoor fires with his friends and spraying WD-40 on them to keep them going; almost burning down his kitchen while cooking; lavishly spending money on things that Community House kids could never afford; and doing other things that would have landed underprivileged Community House kids in reform school. Of course, most volunteers were not this harmful and distracting, but there were a few, and none got "fired."

Upon finding that a volunteer had made a big mess another afternoon, Emily yelled, "Someone has to pick up this mess on the floor! It doesn't matter whether you did it or not, you have to pick it up!" The organizational style was clear: as she did when discussing the snowball fight and many other similar transgressions, Emily tactfully did not say that it was the volunteer who had made the mess—not till he was gone, and even then, she did not mention him by name.

Intimacy with Permanently Open Doors

Where had Emily been when the volunteer was making a mess on the floor? Why had she not been supervising the plug-in volunteers and helping them have rewarding experiences? She had been fulfilling *another* of her program's civic missions, promoting *youth* volunteerism, holed up with three of "her girls" in her warm little office, to draw up an agenda for that night's Martin Luther King Day Planning Committee meeting. While doing this civic work, she was also fulfilling the mission of creating intimacy, with all four of them huddled inside, giggling, eating, and joking while writing the agenda for the meeting. When she emerged from her small office, heard the disorder, and saw the mess, she abruptly realized that she had neglected a third strand of the Empowerment Project's crisscrossed missions—the adult volunteers' civic empowerment.

That is, Emily was fulfilling many, but not all, of the Empowerment Project's missions at once: she was creating an *intimate, safe* atmosphere with her most *civically engaged youth* volunteers, so she was momentarily unavailable either to cultivate *adult volunteers' civic engagement* or to cultivate *intimate safety* for program participants who were not as civically engaged as her four girls were. In an Empowerment Project, safe, comfortable, long-term intimacy has to accompany open, breezy, temporary civic engagement; one of Emily's most challenging tasks was to balance all of them. Managing the adult plug-in volunteers was an especially difficult element in the mix.

PLUG-IN VOLUNTEERS WHO DESIRED A REWARDING EXPERIENCE VERSUS THE NEEDS OF YOUTH WHO ARE DIFFICULT TO HELP

As noted earlier, volunteers' quest for a "rewarding and satisfying experience" drove them away from ornery after-school homework club participants. At Nan's Casa Latina program in a huge basement cafeteria, participants sat in about eight groups of eight, at big tables. All volunteers quickly figured out that if they wanted a satisfying experience, they had to run to the table full of girls who actually wanted help with their homework, who actually *did* their homework, always had their textbooks, and never needed help that went beyond what volunteers could easily give. Most volunteers who came more than three times—that is, long-term, seasoned volunteers—learned to run to the good girls' table.

When policy analysts criticize governments for allowing for-profit schools or other agencies to focus on the needy people who are easiest to help, the critics call it "skimming the cream," "cherry picking," or "picking the lowest hanging fruit"—admitting only good students who will be cheap to educate, for example, or only patients who are basically healthy—and dumping the tougher students or patients onto government-funded schools and hospitals.[4]

Here, in contrast, the motive for cherry-picking was not money, but a quickly meaningful experience. The volunteers' quest makes sense. It was really discouraging to try to help teens who were hard to help or who disappeared. At Chippewa Middle School one day, for example, volunteers avoided or kept giving up on difficult students and moving on to easier ones. So it was like musical chairs. I stupidly persisted longer than anyone else with the difficult ones. One eighth grader, for example, had Spanish homework about seasons and weather, but he claimed not to know the words for spring, summer, fall, winter, hot, cold, rain, ice, or snow, and had not brought his textbook. I did not feed him answers, but got up to try to find someone else with the same textbook, so I could show him how to find the answers himself. While I was searching, another volunteer fed him the answers, so they could play outside and possibly "get to know each other," she told me. Next, I tried helping someone who said he was done when clearly he was not, and then I moved on to a table where homework club members were throwing crayons at each other. After a few weeks of similarly discouraging afternoons at Casa Latina one month, I wrote:

> I guess I didn't take notes on Casa Latina last week. Or one other week, either—both times, I didn't have much fun, for one thing . . . The one time, I was supervising kids in computer lab, and once again . . . I got stuck with the learning disabled kid. I don't mean just a kid who was fidgety, but one that teachers warned each other about, who really needed special services, or who was already getting them, or had just entered a new foster parent situation. "Got stuck" sounds harsh, and is. Who could take care of those kids? Volunteers, but it wouldn't be much fun for them . . .
>
> So, the popular adults end up playing with the popular kids. One kid was trying to do homework, and the volunteer kept interrupting her, in order to have fun . . . So, the adults tend to flock toward the outgoing kids who are getting along fine, or just getting in trouble in a fun way. The lonely kids stay that lonely. I can't see how this could change, because the last thing an outcast middle school kid wants is a grown-up's company in public.

At Chippewa Middle School, for example, under the glow of a bright, glossy mural showing a multiracial group rejoicing over a McDonalds Happy Meal, the chubby, greasy-haired boy who never took off his dirty windbreaker sat alone at a table meant for eight. I kept track for three weeks, two days per week, to see whether any volunteers ever sat with him. None did.

Imagine the alternatives to allowing volunteers to "pick the lowest hanging fruit," and to ignore the hard to reach ones: assign volunteers to students, no matter how discouraging and impossible it seemed to help students whom they feel unequipped to help. Most volunteers would never come back. Require training for volunteers? The organizations offered optional training once a year for four hours, but requiring it would be expensive, would take too much time, would risk imposing experts' cold, distant knowledge on grassroots volunteers, and might discourage volunteers who had only a few hours a month. It would violate Empowerment Talk's promises.

Partly because of the difficulty of finding rewarding teens to help, many volunteers came only two or three times and never returned. At one of the Casa Latina programs, one such volunteer spent most of the afternoon just sitting looking awkward. Since I had just given up, the week before, on trying to help kids who did not want help, and since the table with the good girls was already over-full of helpers, I plopped down next to this glum-looking college-age volunteer:

> He said to me, "I feel like all I do is policing." I agreed, and added that sometimes they make fun of us by telling us stuff like "Me llamo Pancho Villa." He agreed, and we agreed that we couldn't always tell what was true.

He came twice and then gave up.

One solution was to play along with the rowdy teens' jokes, or talk about clothes, music, and sports, or just praise teens for everything. The volunteers hoped that this would get them an emotional foot in the door, en route to more intimate bonding.

Paid organizers secretly, when talking amongst each other, remarked unhappily on this tendency to indulge young people rather than make them do their homework. The paid organizers were not pleased. Emily described to me a yearly training session for adult volunteers, about how to make volunteering fun and rewarding for both the volunteer and the recipient of aid. In it, an elderly volunteer asked how to make sure youth want to come back while also getting them to learn decimals, saying that just playing and being "fun" does not really help. Emily told me that it was "a really good question that they need to think about more." She added:

> It's the same with Homework Club—they really appreciate it when you really do make them do their homework. They do better in school; they don't leave things for the last minute, everyone's better. I told them, before Martin Luther King Day, that they'd better do their homework because I didn't want them to be leaving everything for the last minute, because I wasn't gonna do it all and 500 people [who were planning on coming to the event] were depending on them and would suffer if they didn't follow through on their promises. They got really angry at me. Marie and Samia haven't looked at me the same since.

Sometimes Marisol gets so angry at me, she won't speak to me—she leaves without saying goodbye.

What is striking about Emily's answer is that it shows just how much nagging she did. For her, a paid, long-term employee, the question was not just about how to make it fun, but about how to help, and for that purpose, she doubted that fun was always necessary. Volunteers did not consider nagging young people to "pick up this mess on the floor" to be rewarding, pleasant, or meaningful, so they did not have to do it. Furthermore, it was not clear whether volunteers even were authorized to nag and scold. Since they barely knew the participants, they lacked authority over them.

Emily was not always pleasant, sweet, or calm, and often flatly disagreed with her kids. For her, disagreeing with Benicia was a way of showing respect and dedication, and helping her. Once, Benicia complained to Emily that her teacher had unjustly made her write "I will not behave inappropriately in art class" 350 times. Emily interpreted her story through Benicia's previous stories and actions, and scolded her.

Benicia: It was the *other* kid's fault. The *other* kid scratched me. All I did was tell her not to scratch me, and the teacher said, "Get out of this class!"

A plug-in volunteer: But that's so unfair!

Emily(to Benicia, and kind of ignoring the volunteer): But see, that's what I always see, too—you say it's the other kid, but all I ever see is when you're the one who's acting up. That just shows that you should tell the teacher or whoever is in charge.

Benicia: Well, I don't want to disagree, but that's tattling [or some word for it that I had never heard before].

Emily (fiercely!): Well then *fine*, just *get* in trouble all the time!!

I had never heard any volunteer sound so direct and frustrated, or so engaged with a child for his or her unique characteristics, in such a personal relationship.

The most dedicated volunteers were in the Mentor Program. The brave founder of the Mentor Program made volunteers sign a form promising to stay with the "mentor/mentee relationship" for at least a year, for at least one hour a week.[5] Mentors were supposed to take mentees to the movies or bowling, to engage with "the whole person," and not just focus on developing skills. The mentor was even allowed to take the child out of school for a few hours, to go out to lunch or to the movies.

Emily liked the idea of mentors, but when speaking about any specific mentor rather than the principle of mentoring, she was critical. Here, she told a typical story:

> Benicia—have you met her? Whines and fights all the time and then wonders why she doesn't have friends? Well, her "mentor" always tries to "see the bright side." No matter what!! So, it was great to talk to Lizzie [a teacher at Benicia's school], about the other side, about how kids don't think Benicia likes them.

Emily went on to say that Benicia's mentor was "all about praise," even when Benicia needed to hear criticism. Lizzie, as a teacher, did not need to look only "on the bright side."

Teachers' and paid organizers' work is *supposed to be hard*; plug-in volunteers' work is *supposed to be rewarding* and not include nagging, scolding, or disagreeing. If a relationship is hard, even for months at a time, the schoolteacher or the paid leader cannot easily leave it, but the volunteer can. Most volunteers in Snowy Prairie aimed to be angels of mercy, which meant, to them, agreeing with the young person. "*The volunteer*," we were told at many volunteer training sessions, "*is there to be supportive*," and "The volunteer is there to support you *no matter what.*"

While I did not meet any of them, children who desperately lacked friendly, non-judgmental companionship surely must have benefitted from this program. However, from watching Emily, it became clear that separating supportive nurturance from disciplined nurturance risked making the mentor into the good guy who supplied all the fun, and the paid organizers and teachers into the bad guys who had to enforce homework, good manners, and discipline. The indulgent mentor made loyal paid organizers' and teachers' jobs harder. Fun and work split apart.

Children with "Special Needs": Volunteers, Employees, Families, and Professionals

Volunteers were supposed to become intimate with developmentally disabled or disturbed youth, and learn how to help them with homework, simply by being together, human to human, in a direct, personal relationship, and in the here and now. Volunteers were not supposed to need to know about the young person's home, school, or neighborhood, or to want second-hand impressions from teachers, families, or friends. Encountering the disabled youth with fresh eyes also meant that volunteers were not supposed to have little or no use for expert theories or training, either. Either long-term experience with that particular youth or training, or both, could have helped;[6] plug-in volunteers had neither.

Learning how to help a person who has "special needs" takes longer than learning how to help a less unusual young person. Volunteers dropped out or moved away before it could happen, or the program closed. Or volunteers avoided the participant with special needs, cherry-picking in order to avoid facing an unrewarding experience. Or the young person dropped out. After a few months with fourteen-year-old Desirée, for example, I finally managed to figure out how to help her, but then the school year ended and she left.

The first time we met in Chippewa Middle School, she and her brother and I painted with tempera paints and laughed. Her brother's caricatures were really funny, mine were pretty good, too, and we had a great time the whole afternoon. The next time, during homework hour, I helped her write a big research paper about England. Her project was supposed to have taken three weeks, and now was due the next day. So far, this was all that she had typed into the computer in the school library.

> England is a state that rich people that speak a diffrent langeauage living there. They are rich. They eat in a fast restarant. They speak a diffrent langeuage. They ware fancy clothes. They don't ware stuff like we be waring her.

She could not make the mouse go where she wanted it, so I showed her how to use the arrow keys. Actually, I was confused, because I was sure that she had been shown this before, since everyone else in her class had, but I thought, as a typical volunteer, that maybe I would find in myself a creative, magic inspiration for helping her that no one had tried before. I did not, apparently. Desirée started saying, "I used to have a computer, but . . . ." and then grew absorbed in her homework, from which I did not want to distract her.

The next time we saw each other, and the time after that, I figured out how to help her learn to multiply decimals, and by the end of those two weeks, she really grasped it. We were both really proud! We felt terrific! I imagined becoming one of those magical mentors who turns a kid's life around.

The next time, Desirée threatened a boy, almost throwing a pan of paint in his face. Then, the next time, she actually did throw a big handful of mud at a boy who had made fun of her new hair weave by yelling "Stevie Weavie" at her. Somehow, I still found her fascinating and funny, and after about four months like this, we were rather fond of each other.

After the school year ended, I never saw her again. The next fall, when the program started again, I was with a whole new set of volunteers and paid organizers: no familiar faces. Desirée was gone, too. The other volunteers had failed her by ignoring her. I may have tried harder, but I failed her, too, if attachment was the goal. If learning decimals was the goal, we were moderately successful, but future volunteers would not benefit from what I learned about how to teach Desirée. Each new volunteer would have to start from scratch.

In contrast, paid organizer Emily learned, over the course of months and years, the varied learning styles of her participants, conferred with their teachers, met their parents, and saw their homes. Patiently, she helped one girl overcome her odd phobias, and to chatter and scream less; and she tried to persuade other participants to be patient with her, too. Eventually, the girl felt confident enough to go on field trips—though on one trip, she spent an hour in the bathroom hiding from the dirt and worms outdoors, with her feet on the toilet seat to avoid touching the muddy floor.

When superhuman patience does not keep the terrified girl's feet on the floor, or time is short, one way to enhance or speed up the process is to learn from other people's experience indirectly: from professional training and books, and from records that professionals have kept on that particular young person. Many intertwined threads in our rug made professional knowledge about participants' unique disabilities unavailable to volunteers. As noted above, putting heavy medical/psychiatric labels on young people was thought to risk clouding volunteers' direct experience of them, eclipsing the warmth and intuition that was supposed to make the volunteers' presence so important in the first place. (Of course, this aversion to crude labels is not the special province of Empowerment Projects. We all want to see each person as unique, and the phrase "special needs" usually comes with a preemptive joke, "Of course, we *all* have 'special needs,' but . . ." When describing autism, school officials often say that autistic people can be very good at math, and have other unique and wonderful talents, but rarely mention why anyone would want to prevent autism. This delicate side-stepping is not unique to Empowerment Projects' plug-in volunteers.)

The difference between employees and volunteers was that employees could read the record and look for patterns *over time*; volunteers could not. As the director of the Boys and Girls Club (a program for disadvantaged youth) told the twelve-week youth workers' certificate program:

> We (in my program) treat all youth the same. . . . If you see "positive," you'll eventually only need to deal with positive issues. . . . None of our kids are identified as quote unquote "target outreach," but *we do keep a record on it for additional help* [my emphasis]. 'Cuz kids only get attention when they're in trouble, but all kids need it.

Paid organizers, social workers, schoolteachers, and other semi-professionals can look at the record. For obvious reasons, each child's personal, confidential profile—of their own and their whole family's mental and physical health, grades, employment, and residential history, legal and illegal drug use, sex partners, arrests, and abuse—are not open to random volunteers.

Imagine the other alternatives in Desirée's case: Holding the volunteers to a commitment of more than a year? No, volunteers had to participate voluntarily, and programs had to welcome them in great numbers, to show the program's grassroots support to funders. The closest anyone dared to pin a volunteer down with a time commitment was the brave coordinator of the Mentor Program, who, as noted earlier, required volunteer Mentors to sign a one-year contract, but the contract was not binding and many flaked out before their year ended. Forcing a year commitment would have scared many away. Monitoring Desirée's home to find out where she was and why she had not returned? No, sending monitors would have been coercive and intrusive, and expensive. Not allowing Desirée to attend? No, then she would not get any help and maybe would not have learned to multiply decimals at all.

Empowerment Projects do double duty, as social work agencies that help needy youth, and as civic associations that welcome volunteers. Simply because they stayed on site longer than volunteers, paid organizers like Emily were better at helping youth with special needs. A paid expert in special education—someone who could unobtrusively be there every day for members like Desirée, the boy in the dirty windbreaker, and probably several others whose troubles were less visible—might have been even better. But, even if Empowerment Project organizers had faith in experts' knowledge, paying for one would have been too expensive and complicated to justify quickly to hurried funders and voters.

White Volunteers Talking about Race with Non-White Participants

If a black or Latino participant claimed to have been a victim of racism, some white volunteers always believed it and some never believed it. White volunteers did not know how to sort through the evidence. They had never had to do so, themselves, and did not have the time to learn. For them, "racism" was an abstraction that they imagined either was never in play in everyday life or was always in play. Nearly all the volunteers in the homework clubs were white, nearly all Community House and Casa Latina participants were not (or at least, as noted earlier, usually did not classify themselves as white). Youth participants at Chippewa were about half and half.

On the one hand, some white volunteers never took the complaints seriously. They knew about racism as an abstract problem in society-at-large, but they did not see how it mattered in everyday life. So, they imagined that they could bond by peeling away the "black" part of the kid from the real inner person, without trying to learn much about the black kids' living conditions. Volunteers of this first type wanted to "treat kids as kids," they said, to "connect with them" as unique individuals, not as members of racial or class categories. On the other hand, many white volunteers also asserted that the whole society was racist and *always* agreed when young people complained of racism. Most volunteers swung abruptly between the two positions—always believing the kids and also never believing them—without noticing, and without trying to figure out how or if they could both be true.

Adult mentors in the meeting described earlier with the Ranscombe Scholars implicitly upheld the first position—that racism or poverty may be problems "out there," "in society" but are irrelevant in everyday life. They implied this when discussing the boy who could not do his homework: "He needs to learn self-discipline," "He needs to motivate *himself*," and "He needs to learn time management. We *all* do." They meant to sound sympathetic, to say that they could all relate to him, human-to-human, but they did not ask about his living conditions. By not even considering asking, they implied that his conditions were, or should be, irrelevant to his work habits.

When someone complained about racism directly, white volunteers in carefully tolerant Snowy Prairie tended to believe it without questioning the assertion. "Yeah, it's a racist society," as Keith often said, in response to a participants' complaint about a teacher or fellow student. Benicia, the African American nine-year-old who Emily said "whined all the time," was telling Keith that her teacher yelled at her for standing up in class, but did not yell at a white boy who was doing the same thing. Another white boy then accused the teacher of racism, and the teacher sent him out of the room. Keith exclaimed, "That's outrageous—sent out of the room, for saying that something is racist?"

She said yes and repeated the story.

He repeated, "For saying that something is racist? That's ridiculous!" Should Keith have agreed so quickly? What else had happened in that interaction, or right before it? What had the white boy, the teacher, and/or the white boy and/or Benicia been doing the rest of the morning, or week, or school year? Is being sent out of the room a really severe punishment in that school, or just a mild one? Was the problem due to a teacher's overt racism, or a more subtle racism, or a more general atmosphere at school? Or was Benicia in fact misbehaving, or had Benicia misunderstood the teacher? Why did Keith not tell Benicia that she should not have been standing up, no matter what the boy was doing?

Keith could not pursue such precise questioning, which would have required filtering Benicia's complaints through what he already knew about her and her schoolteacher and her classmates and her school, combing through evidence on a minute-by-minute, day-by-day, month-by-month basis, interpreting her stories through her previously told stories. Instead, Keith turned it into an abstraction and a commentary on Keith: agreeing with Benicia was a way of showing solidarity, displaying knowledge of racism, and, feeling superior to other whites. He was, in other words, doing Apolitical Structure Talk. It makes sense that the only adult I ever heard challenge a participant's complaint about a schoolteacher's racism, other than a paid organizer, was a black parent of a Community House participant, while she was waiting for her own kid to gather up her belongings.

From white plug-in volunteers in an Empowerment Project, youth participants could not learn how to do the endless puzzling and evidence-gathering that people of color routinely do to decide whether racism is in play or not.[7] My point is not to ask whether it was right to agree or disagree with the young people's complaints: the point is to ask how, or if, volunteers, youth, and paid employees sorted through *evidence* when trying to decide if something was an example of racism. Since they barely knew participants, white plug-in volunteers could not weigh the evidence in the specific situation, and since they themselves had not spent a lifetime weighing the evidence in their own everyday lives, they lacked practice. Whether sweet or stern, always agreeing or never agreeing, these evanescent volunteers did not go through the slow, painful process of gathering evidence.

After working at Community House for forty, or sixty, or even eighty hours a week for a few years, Emily, in contrast, got a strong taste of what life as a non-white teenager was like in Snowy Prairie, and she learned to pick apart the evidence. After years of taking her program members to public places, for example, she could joke with them about the suspicious gaze and surveillance that minority teenagers routinely receive in malls, in convenience stores, on sidewalks, in grocery stores—any time they are "shopping while not white."[8] Emily did not always agree with their complaints, since she, like them, was learning to sort through the scraps of evidence. Of course, not all paid organizers learn this—some might be stupid, insensitive, or racist—but, in contrast to plug-in volunteers, long-term, steady workers have the *possibility* of gaining first-hand knowledge.

A handful of paid organizers like Emily learned about participants' lives from the inside, over years of near-daily togetherness. Empowerment Talk promises a deep, intense kind of experience, not a comfortable one, but one that would jolt people out of their boxes, open them up, shake them up. If Jane Addams' idea of social ethics makes sense, then starting on the path toward becoming a good, helpful person requires completing this loop, or spiral, over and over, challenging one's own assumptions by growing intimately familiar with someone else's. Impossible to speed up, this soul-changing intimacy is very hard to mesh with Empowerment Projects' need to be flexible and always open to transitory volunteers.

So, Emily's and minority youth's judgments about racism were usually more nuanced and complex than white adult volunteers'. Emily and her program participants could switch sides in an argument, depending on which side was missing. This meant that the young people sometimes sounded surprisingly harsh, when, to take an example mentioned earlier, they argued that a boy whose drug-addicted mother kept getting kicked out of apartments and relatives' apartments was completely responsible for failing school. Hearing her group judge Dominic so harshly, Emily, who often told participants to take individual responsibility, now took the opposite side, explaining why he was *not* completely responsible. It was a move in a game—an *ongoing* game she and her participants played, switching sides when someone needed to supply the missing side of the argument. Participants did not want to let their own living conditions crush them, though some of theirs were similar to Dominic's, so someone in the game had to take the position that Dominic's failure was not inevitable. When organizers got a taste of the discrimination that their teens faced, they absorbed this ambivalent approach to the question of racism and poverty's personal effects. Without the plug-in volunteers' abstract certainty, organizers and participants alike learned to use concrete details, to expect both sides to have good points. They did not expect abstractly perfect answers.

While earnestly trying not to categorize people, white adults often could not distinguish one non-white kid from another. Erin, a white organizer, mentioned to Emily that Marisol was at a meeting; Emily informed her that it was Bonita. After having worked with them both in the Regional YEP for a year, Erin confessed to Emily that she could not tell them apart. Both had glossy black hair, but Marisol was four years older, about a foot taller, and a bit heavy, while Bonita was small, quick, and slight. The view was equally blurry from the other side of the racial divide: Community House members routinely mistook Sheila—willowy, blonde, big blue eyes—for Roberta—solid, brown hair, brown eyes.

When adults and youth were speaking to each other across vast social distances, there were stronger reasons for the adults to resort to abstraction than there would have been in a more socially homogeneous group. The greater the social distance between the volunteer's experience and the recipient's experience, the longer time the volunteer and recipient must spend together in order to get and give help.[9] Yet, in Empowerment Projects, it would be hard to demand a long time commitment.

When I first heard Emily's demands of evidence from Benicia, for her constant complaints of teachers', fellow pupils', and volunteers' racism,

I worried that maybe Emily was just racially insensitive. But then I caught myself echoing Emily, when I, too, heard Benicia's scattershot accusations often enough: One Martin Luther King Day, for example, the group had a contest, in which the emcee asked questions about King's life. Participants sat at big tables of about eight people each, and one person per table held up a big sign with the table's answer, A, B, C, or D, on it. As usual, participants sat with people with whom they felt comfortable, which meant that tables were fairly cleanly divided by race. For one question, the right answer was B. Benicia was in charge of holding up the cards for our table, which was mostly populated by black children from Community House. Benicia held up D, so another table won that round. Benicia complained to everyone at our table that the master of ceremonies did not pick her because she was black. I pointed out that most of the people at the winning table were black, too, including the person who held up the sign for the winning table. She was not convinced. Then, I pointed out that she, Benicia, had held up a D when the answer was B. She disagreed, but she was still holding the sign, so I said she should look at it. It said D. But, Benicia said, the emcee was probably racist, anyway.

PUZZLES OF GRATITUDE IN THE OPTIONAL SOCIETY

Organizers required participants to write "thank-you" notes to volunteers, even when the participants disapproved of a volunteer's offerings. The gratitude had to be explicit and rapid: explicit, since plug-in volunteers wanted very clear affirmation that their hard work was appreciated and did not know the youth participants well enough to understand anything subtle or understated; and rapid, since volunteers did not stay very long. Explicitness and speed destroyed gratitude's gracious cadence.[10] Expressions of gratitude sometimes seemed like forced declarations of dependence, as the Ranscombe Scholars event showed.

Fast, explicit expressions of gratitude always seemed to accompany a distance between the giver and the receiver. Instead of building intimacy, the fast, direct expressions of gratitude exposed an absence of intimacy. One day in one of the Casa Latina programs, participants were supposed to write thank-you cards for all the volunteers who had come that semester, but personalized gratitude was a little hard to muster toward volunteers whom the teens did not remember.

Unfortunately, the kids did not recognize the names of any of the volunteers except one, about whom one kid said, "Well I remember Alexi, but she doesn't come here any more" [Alexi was a flirtatious and pretty university student, who was really unfriendly to anyone she couldn't flirt with—in some other notes, I carried on in a crabby way about how rude she was to me, since I wasn't flirt-worthy to her, and how it was thus ruining my chances to "build community" with the volunteer community].

When Nan wasn't looking, I suggested that the kids make a thank-you card for her, Nan. Making the cards for the unremembered volunteers was difficult, ending up in a few sprinkles of glitter on a big "thank-you." In contrast, making the card for Nan was completely absorbing! They filled the card with pictures and writing, and everyone wanted to contribute. Some kids wrote or drew affectionate jokes, and others wrote expressions of simple affection: "Thank-you for being here every day for us," said one of the cards for Nan, the paid organizer.

The problem with writing the thank-you's to the anonymous volunteers was not just that kids don't like to write thank-you cards; when they knew the person to whom they were writing, and were grateful, they were lavish in their gratitude and affection.

Showing gratitude to beloved paid organizers was easy and fairly straightforward, but rarely this explicit.

What kinds of gratitude should they have displayed to volunteers who sat alone on a bench or wandered around the room awkwardly, not knowing what to do, or who came only three times? Or to adult volunteers who came as a form of personal psychotherapy, like a gloomy fellow from Argentina who had come to the United States for graduate school and was flunking out. He came to a Casa Latina after-school program a few times, hoping that volunteering would cheer him up, but dropped out after two or three visits. Participants had to craft a hand-made thank-you card with glitter and glue for him, too.

As a fairly typical volunteer myself, I wrestled with my own expectations of gratitude. I offered to bake once a week. The first time, I bought expensive, organic ingredients, and, with help from participants, made two pans of banana bread. When I stopped by the next day to fetch the pans, the bread had been all eaten up except for the pieces with walnuts. "Well, good! Walnuts are expensive!" I thought, but then regretted feeling good. I had snuck them in to give the bread more protein, so I should have felt defeated instead of feeling relieved. Furthermore, nobody thanked me. I then imagined how baffled I would be if my children thanked me for food, and then remembered that this is precisely the topic of a famous sociology experiment, in which college students were told, before a vacation, to treat their family home as if it were a hotel, offering thank-you's, or payments for services rendered.[11] Expectations of gratitude are part of what distinguish one institution's promises from another.

When kids did not need to thank the paid organizers explicitly, the silence signaled a longer-term relationship. As social researchers have long observed, giving and receiving gifts can stretch relationships out in a kind of temporal musical chairs, gracefully and subtly knitting people together through favors, gratitude, and aid. The gift-giver may very well never get a gift in return from the recipient, but probably will get one from someone else some day, round and round.[12] Gratitude has to have a gracious, slow rhythm; repaying a gift the hour after receiving one looks too much like payment, tit for tat—which is fine if it *is* a payment in a market, but clumsy if it is a gift.

Whether or not participants' gratitude was fake is not the point. Whether deeply felt or not, these fast and explicit expressions of gratitude are mandatory only when connections are precarious and optional. When you heard explicitness, you usually knew you were in the presence of a precarious connection.

Everyone's Institutional Intuition

Some paid organizers tentatively let themselves notice that plug-in volunteers were not always good for a program, mentioning the possibility under their breath, as a mild joke, or a quick aside, as if they felt sneaky and wicked not to feel gratitude, as if they could not let themselves believe what they saw. For example, in several noontime meetings, paid organizers said that adult volunteers needed training in how to treat youth with respect. When teen volunteers held a pizza dinner as a fundraiser, adult volunteers would not let them handle the money or order the pizza themselves. Caught between the obligation to promote civic empowerment among adult volunteers and to promote it among youth volunteers, these paid organizers were chagrinned at the *adult* volunteers' lack of sensitivity to the *youth* volunteers' spirit:

> Miriam, the leader of Grrl-illa Group: The volunteers didn't have any background in how to give youth the lead in things. That happened in Grrl-illa Group—the volunteers took over after the girls had planned it *all*! The girls were really mad—just because they're young didn't mean they can't handle money and decide how many pizzas to order. So there's a need to coordinate the training of volunteers.

> The leader of another program like Community House: The youth who are involved on big adult boards need training in how to deal with adults who don't listen to them. They don't want to be treated like little kids who don't know anything.

The leader of a program for troubled youth: If we train the adults, youth wouldn't have as much to complain about!

Similar discussion continued for months in the NOYO, with paid organizers wondering what to do when adult volunteers quashed youth voluntarism.

Many adult volunteers themselves intuited their own ineffectiveness. They stood around nervously at "volunteer opportunities" like Fun Nights; one muttered a typical sentiment for adult volunteers: "I'm not sure what I should be doing now." Paid organizers and youth participants also muttered the same thought about those volunteers, when out of their earshot. Here again, these programs' two civic faces—one asking adults to become volunteers, the other asking youth to become volunteers—clashed.

Two Contrasts: Paid Organizers' Intimacy, and Non-Plug-in Volunteers' Effectiveness

Two comparisons will show less potentially damaging ways of volunteering. While it may look as if this chapter is saying that all volunteer work is useless, it is not. Rather, the point is that the plug-in volunteers' combination of short time horizons and desire for intimacy were incompatible. Two *alternate* forms of volunteering reveal two different ways that volunteers can help: either by trimming their grand hopes, or by lengthening and intensifying their commitments. Let's take these one at a time.

Helpful Volunteers

Volunteers Who Did Not Try to Bond with Youth or Become Intimate

When volunteers performed tasks that did *not* involve trying to act like "beloved aunties," they could, indeed, be helpful. Community House's volunteer Board of Directors illustrates this point. Boards like this are required of nonprofits, and this Board consisted of about ten middle-aged or elderly women, including some retired social workers and teachers. They had a solid, reassuring, old-fashioned air; two even had half spectacles dangling on strings from their necks. These board members cut a less ambitious program for themselves than the plug-in volunteers did. They raised funds and provided oversight. Unlike plug-in style volunteers, board members did not aim to become intimate with individual youth. In fact, most had no ongoing contact with youth at all. Working quietly behind the scenes, they had a crucial effect on participants' lives nonetheless.

Part of Empowerment Projects' mission is to promote bonding not just between volunteers and the people they serve, but also between one volunteer and another,[13] to "build community." While such bonds did not materialize among the plug-in volunteers, they *did* form, to a degree, between the old-fashioned Board members. In contrast to the plug-in volunteers' anonymous, two-ships-passing in-the-night relations with one another, Board members *did* know each other's names, usually *did* get each other's jokes, and *did* know some basic facts about each other's lives—whether the other was married, employed, healthy, about to get a visit from her grown children, just back from the hospital, having a hard time at work, for some examples from the monthly conversation in the group. They worked as a group, in contrast to the plug-in volunteers, who worked on staggered schedules so that the programs could have lower child/adult ratios.

Like youth volunteers, the Board of Directors devoted a huge amount of time to fundraising, often in tandem with youth. Like youth-led fundraisers, most of the Board's efforts raised little money, but unlike the youth-led fundraisers, theirs were not laden with the need to empower anyone and did not need to be innovative. As described earlier in the story about the homey spaghetti or burrito dinners, these fundraising events' charm was to bring social workers, curious neighbors, and program participants in physical proximity with each other once every few months, over noodles or bins of used clothes, lamps, and appliances, board games in crushed boxes, faded plastic toys, and stuffed animals with matted pink fur.

These fundraisers also gave neighbors a chance to give money to Community House without making it look like charity—they could help the "needy youth" without fanfare, without drawing attention to the fact, and without demanding instant gratitude, or any gratitude at all. For example, at the Community House rummage sale every year, a few people gave us a five or ten-dollar bill to pay for cheaper items, and then told us, with a wink, to keep the change, which was sometimes worth more than the purchase itself—$4.90 in change for a ten-cent purchase was my first experience with this tactful gift-giving. The person at the cash register always thanked the customer, but since the donation was encapsulated in a market exchange, it made Community House look self-sufficient, not dependent. So, paradoxically, these exchanges of cold hard cash were more respectful than the plug-in volunteers' demands for personal gratitude for generosity that looked costless.

Some of the Board's fundraising was devoted to writing grants, the real source of money. Grant-writing can be a technical and boring affair, and everyone knew that it required mastery of certain buzzwords. Trudy (who, along with Emily and a very part-time bookkeeper were Community House's paid staff) did the grant-writing, and our job as Board members was to oversee her efforts. In practice, that meant just trusting Trudy.

At one typical meeting, none of us Board members could decipher the complicated charts and tables of the budget, though inspecting the budgets took over half of most meetings' time. Of course, we approved this budget anyway, as we approved every budget, since we trusted Trudy's judgment. These Board volunteers, working closely with the paid staff member, were quietly effective in their small territory; these volunteers, with less grandly personal ambitions than plug-in volunteers, did a great deal of good.

Dedicated, Long-term Volunteers

Volunteers who devote long, intense years to their work can also do a great deal of good. In the 1900s, upper-crust women volunteers often took their work just as seriously as professionals, sometimes working just as long hours, for just as many years.[14] Unlike the plug-in volunteers, these women's volunteer work did not feel optional and temporary to them. They did not wander off when volunteering grew difficult. Also unlike the plug-ins, old-fashioned volunteers got to know each other over their many years together as a group, not on the plug-in volunteers' staggered schedules. Over time, they often developed ongoing relationships, both with the people they served and with each other. Though the upper-crust volunteers may have used their volunteer work as a way of getting ahead in their social circles, their motives were probably no more mixed between selfish and selfless ones than Snowy Prairie's volunteers' were. Unlike the plug-in volunteers, who were very lightly screened, if at all,[15] old-fashioned volunteers were interrogated before beginning; because of tough screening processes, many of these volunteers dropped out before finishing the training.[16] Finally, they were heavily supervised, like the ones described in this study of a mental hospital, who were

> women who had had previous volunteer experience and were members of the New York Junior League. They had been carefully screened by the League and by the supervisory staff at the hospital and had been selected on the basis of their demonstrated capacity to learn, to take the direction of a supervisor, and to understand and work sensitively with persons in need of help.[17]

In contrast, contemporary plug-in volunteering included very little communication between volunteers and paid staff, or between one volunteer and another. The old-fashioned volunteers worked with the same family for years; Snowy Prairie volunteers usually worked with different youth each week.

Altogether, what a different world this old-fashioned volunteering was from contemporary plug-in volunteering! The upper-crust ladies' world of volunteering was no paradise. It had different problems from the world of the Empowerment Project—gender inequality, a condescending whiff of noblesse oblige, and ulterior status motives. The name "volunteer" makes us miss crucial differences between the everyday texture of volunteer work in the varied old conditions and the newly typical conditions of the Empowerment Project.

Conclusion: Hopelessly Clashing Time Horizons

The volunteers who had a two-hours-per-week-once-a-week-for-a-half-a-year to spare came to the homework programs to demonstrate that "we care," to show funders that a project enjoyed grassroots support, and to have a rewarding, intimate experience. How could it be that this hallowed symbol of good, caring citizenship simply did the opposite of what we Americans imagine?

Plug-in volunteers undermined a programs' intimate, family-like atmosphere, not because they were volunteers, but because of the plug-in *style* of volunteering. In an Empowerment Project, relationships between volunteers and needy youth are supposed to feel intimate and secure, yet also flexible, temporary, and optional. They are supposed to be deeply rewarding and challenging, yet also fast and easy to assemble and dissolve. When that proved impossible, organizers still had to welcome the plug-in volunteers so that their programs could appear to be open and grassroots. An organizer's success, paradoxically, brought tensions that sharpened to the extent that the success grew: the more they succeeded in attracting volunteers, the more volunteers were there, undermining a program's family-like atmosphere. Whether helping young people with homework or trying to bond, familiarity with the specific young person was irreplaceable. No organizational style could finesse that problem away. Intentions notwithstanding, plug-in volunteers who came as symbols of a caring community turned "care" into an abstraction.

CHAPTER 7

Paid Organizers Creating Temporally Finite, Intimate, Family-like Attachments

IN THE TWELVE-WEEK COURSE FOR ORGANIZERS, the teacher gave many rousing speeches about the dedication that youth work demands. Here, he came to a typical climax:

> Youth work is not just about coordinating resources for youth, or keeping youth occupied, but about our relationships with them. You as a youth worker are like an instrument for the youth. You're presenting yourself as a *whole person.*

Other times, he told them, "Give of yourself 100 percent." This short chapter will investigate the puzzles involved in creating this kind of attachment to youth, while also cultivating all the other goods of an Empowerment Project. Although organizers were told to cultivate a feeling of total devotion, to "give of themselves 100 percent," in the moment, no one expected their nearly family-like intimacy to last a lifetime, and this expectation subtly infused their relationships in the present. They were not family, and that could cause tensions with the participants' real families, which members expected to last forever.

It either would sound like a grammatical mistake or give a whiff of wrenching tragedy to hear, "She was once my daughter but I've lost track of her," while no one would wince to hear Emily say, in forty years, "She was once my favorite program participant but I've lost track of her." If you were a participant, you might, forty years from now, look back and realize with delighted surprise that you have been attached to your organizer since adolescence, but the informal prediction right now is that your mother would continue to be your mother, while Emily and any of her participants might easily and almost painlessly forget one another's names in a few years.

Yet, at the moment, as the many scenarios involving Emily have already shown, some paid organizers did give of themselves as close to 100 percent as anyone can. Some worked unpaid overtime on evenings, weekends, and vacations, when they were unemployed between jobs, and even after they had found other jobs. Some called youth work a mission that they did instead of having their "own" children.[1] This devotion could even become embarrassing, when, for example, Samia's mother teased Emily, saying she should "get a life" beyond Community House. Emily joked that she was very relieved when Samia's mom once saw her in public with a male friend. Even though he was not a boyfriend, Emily told me and her girls, at least it showed that she "had a life"—something that Emily herself doubted, telling me, another day, "This [working at Community House] takes all my attention. If I were married or in a serious relationship, I couldn't do this. I'll quit when that happens." However nebulous and hard to pin down "family" is, organizers and participants knew that they were not family to one another.

The puzzle: however intense their intimacy was at the moment, it was supposed to be temporally finite, because they were not "family."

Rules and the Risk of Getting Kicked Out

Before observing this explanation that focuses on unspoken ideas of "family" and "non-family," another seemingly obvious practical explanation needs to be dismissed. It may seem as if everyone knew that participants could easily be kicked out, and that this explained everyone's lack of long-term hopes for future intimacy. The rules regarding expulsion, and the fear of expulsion, were surprisingly unimportant and ineffective, however. There were too many compelling reasons to retain even disruptive members, as the following scenario shows.

At the beginning of each afternoon at Chippewa Middle School, Kristin stood in front of the sixty members, clipboard in hand, police whistle on a string around her neck, resembling my stringy, middle-school gym teacher, reading the rules about expulsion:

> "Be respectful. No fighting. No name-calling. If you violate the rules once, you get sent home for the day. Twice, you get sent home for the week. If you violate the rules three times, you lose the privilege of coming to the Recreation Program."
>
> "The main rule is: Be respectful. It's just like school. Like those kids over there (walking over and glaring at the Spanish-speaking kids) who are talking are being *sort of* disrespectful," but she said it with a glare and a tone indicating she thought they were being very disrespectful, but she couldn't *say* that because that would *have to* mean sending them home . . .
>
> She added, "I haven't had to do that to anyone yet. But I just wanted to let you know that it can happen."

However rule-oriented she was, and however much she relied on the risk of getting kicked out to enforce those rules, even Kristin could not easily expel anyone.

When she tried, it backfired. Some boys had broken into the soda machine, and were expelled for two weeks. These boys were the most popular with the girls, and temporarily kicking out the cute boys posed a huge problem: the girls who had crushes on them stopped coming, too. When these girls stopped coming, the group was filled only with unpopular boys and girls. It was like a stock market crash—a spiral that almost made the whole program collapse. Since size mattered for funding, the program's existence was in jeopardy. It took over six weeks to build the program back up to a decently fundable size. Expelling cute, popular boys was a bigger risk than kicking out non-cute or less popular ones, but organizers could not decree, "Kick out only ugly and unpopular members." So, no one ever got kicked out again as long as Kristin and Karen were in charge.

For different reasons, Emily almost never expelled anyone, either. She kicked only two kids out in her five years at Community House, both temporarily, both with anguish, both for very hand-tailored, personal circumstances, in which she was protecting one member against another. One was Jayson, a boy who was caught stealing. Emily's fury was not just about the fact that he had stolen, which had happened before, but that the victim, a thirteen-year-old named Crisco, was especially vulnerable.

> Crisco had really pulled himself together, he was really doing well, and now, suddenly his step-parents were ripping him out of his school and home, to move him to go live with his grandparents in northern Minnesota! And then, *the day before he leaves*—and he's already really upset—Jayson steals his Walkman [Crisco's one prized possession, as we both knew—he often needed to escape into a musical world]! And he knew perfectly well what he was doing.

Imagine this implausible rule: "If a child steals from someone who is having a hard time in life and who is currently pulling him/herself together, the punishment shall be stringent, whereas in a normal case of thievery, stealing shall be chastised only verbally."

Emily's anger came from her intimate knowledge of Crisco's very particular circumstances, her familiarity with the unique case.[2] It did not satisfy the Empowerment Project's mission of transparency.

A big program gets more funding, but here, we have seen that there are two other, possibly more important reasons for not expelling participants. In different ways, both group dynamics and strong feelings make it hard to kick members out. Kicking people out risked a market crash in Kristin's program. In addition, in a homey program like Emily's, kicking kids out would have felt too much like kicking out her own children. Rules, and the risk of being expelled, were very rare obstacles to intimacy in these programs.

No Shared Past or Future

The intimacy between Emily and her girls might, at any one moment, have felt more comfortable than the girls' relationships with their own parents, but here is our recurrent theme of temporal puzzles: no matter how loving Emily was, she and her program participants did not share a past and did not expect to share a future.

Casa Latina teens, for example, were Spanish-speaking immigrants. The organizer Laura, her two volunteer helpers, and I, on the other hand, were all white, native English-speaking, college educated, native-born U.S. citizens. One day, a professor came to invite teens to apply for scholarships, for Latinos to go to a summer camp to learn about engineering and physics.

After the professor left, one teenager, Alejandro, said:
I want to work at McDonalds!

Laura [the adult leader]: Don't say that! You're lying!

Alejandro: No, it's true!

Laura: No, you're lying. If you worked at McDonalds, your feet would hurt all the time . . . you would come home completely exhausted, they wouldn't treat you well at all!

Alejandro: Yes, I do!

Laura: This is not funny. You're joking about something that's not funny! These people are trying to give you an opportunity that normally doesn't go to Latinos, that usually goes to more privileged kids, who have more money than Latinos usually have. This is an opportunity to get work where you could make some money, where you'd be treated with respect. These engineering professors are giving you an opportunity to learn, to use your minds, so that you can go on to college and find decent work . . . where you'd be treated with respect.

Alejandro: Ok, fine, I don't want to work at McDonalds. I want to work at Pizza Hut!!

Laura: That is exactly what they want you to say! White society wants you [plural "you"] to work at McDonalds to serve them. White society wants you all to take the jobs that no one else wants. They'd be happy if you, you Latinos, took this kind of work. They don't want you to succeed. They don't want you [or "they don't like you! ¡No te quieren! She could possibly have meant "they don't love you," but her tone was less wry than that understatement would have required] [this dialogue is in Spanish, Spanglish, and bad Spanish, as were my field notes].

But you have a future, you can choose, it's a choice what you're going to do to make a living. It's not too late. There's still time to choose.

Alejandro: Who doesn't want me?

Laura: White people.

Alejandro: Which white people?

Laura: White society. They want you Latinos to serve them . . . more repetition, ending with Laura's encouraging Alejandro to seek a career that would be more lucrative than working at McDonalds.

Alejandro [later]: Make more money? Ok, fine [raising his voice, stretching a huge grin across his face]: I want to be a drug dealer!

Eileen, one of the volunteers, a university student who was volunteering partly to perfect her Spanish, mentioned, far into the conversation that took place after the teens had left, "His mother works all the time—at McDonalds. Oops! guess I shouldn't have said it's a terrible place to work!"

Laura's message traveled across lines of race and class, and, as the words made their voyages, their meanings transformed in surprising ways. When intimacy and diversity blend in the short-term conditions of Empowerment Projects, this is a likely result.

Laura and Alejandro had very different, separate pasts. Laura's protest about white society was not about herself or people like herself, but was in the third person. She was not Latino, nor did she count herself as one of the white people who hate Latinos. When Laura said, "White society doesn't want you," she thought of it as a protest; she was speaking out of principled indignation, stating something *general*: a political position. This was something that she could not do as easily if she were Alejandro's mother. If Alejandro's mother had issued the same statement, it would more likely have sounded like a complaint about her own conditions, but it would not have risked sounding like an insult to him, his family, poor people, Latinos, or people who had menial jobs. Talking about *his* conditions would have been the same as talking about her *own* conditions. Laura, in contrast, had to balance between offering advice and showing respect for Alejandro's real parent and her real conditions. The same words could never mean the same thing, coming from Laura's and the mother's mouths.

Laura and Alejandro also expected different, separate futures. She was only temporarily in his life. What they owed each other was different from what they would have owed each other if their fates were inevitably intertwined. If Laura were Alejandro's mother, then making *her* life tolerable would include making *his* life tolerable. If he ended up earning minimum wage at McDonalds, he might end up depending on her for rent.

Laura, of course, did not worry that Alejandro would depend on her in her old age, or vice versa. Organizers spoke about the young people's futures but did not imagine sharing them. Theoretically, a program organizer could choose to intertwine her fate with one or two of her program members for their whole lives, moving where they move, paying for their education and health care, helping them with rent, child care, and the rest when they are grown. But does anyone expect it? Conversely, parents sometimes completely lose touch with their offspring. Some families are "extended families," with biological relatives of many generations sharing a roof; some are "blended families"[3] with children of multiple divorces and remarriages, but nobody expects families, whether extended or blended, to be quickly and painlessly ended.

In twenty years, one might retrospectively say that Laura's or Emily's relationships with their youth (all of them? That would be impossible. Only a chosen few? That would make it not quite "family-like") was so caring all along, it was destined to last twenty years, thirty years, sixty years. But in year three, members' moral expectations did not stretch that far into the future, and those expectations, hopes, and intuitions are real, now, even if they are later proven wrong.[4] Despite Empowerment Talk's suggestion that people can transcend their roles and break out of their boxes, participants had implicit expectations and had to share them enough to protect their feelings. When a gawky minister started the process of adopting Benicia and her brother, he visited Community House regularly and focused his full attention on them, even showing them how to do headstands. The assumption had to be that he was planning something more long-term than a three-year or six-year stint as "father." After a few months, Benicia started treating him differently from the way she treated other adults, not just because he was willing to stand on his head.

During her years at Community House, Emily spent more time with her program members than most of their parents had during those same years, but the future expectations differed for her, for a volunteer, and for parents. Emily and her program participants had to keep their attention on the present and learn not to expect anything for the future. Her dedication had to wedge itself between the intrusions from plug-in volunteers and the teasing from participants' parents. And then, in various states of semi-embarrassment, within their clearly finite time horizons, hiding below the radar of their many publics, paid organizers sometimes succeeded in creating intimate, caring relationships—not when they were as open, infinitely unbounded, and voluntary as Empowerment Talk promises, but in spite of Empowerment Talk.

CHAPTER 8

Publicly Questioning Need: Food, Safety, and Comfort

PRIVATELY DECIPHERING WHAT TO COUNT as a "need" is often puzzling: Do I need that piece of cake? Am I even hungry at all? Do I need that boyfriend? However confusing it is for an individual engaged in solitary introspection to distinguish between needs and wants, participation in an Empowerment Project amplifies the difficulty. In these projects, comfort, intimacy, and safety are exposed to multiple audiences' gazes—funders, parents, organizers, plug-in volunteers, participants, and others. The desires have to make sense to many audiences. Painted into a corner, working fast, pleasing many onlookers at once, and proving their worthiness in time for the next budgeting decision, organizers had to make every activity justifiable according to these multiple audiences' multiple criteria. Organizers not only have to please all the audiences; if participants' desires seem unhealthful, organizers cannot blame any of the audiences.

Empowerment Projects' constant exposure to multiple audiences made it nearly *taboo* to distinguish between needs and choices, making it impossible to say that anyone "needed" anything, even food.[1] So, clever organizers learned how to get some of their program members' needs met without naming them as such. Organizers learned, for example, to write grants that described *food* as a means to better knowledge, empowerment, weight loss, brain gain, raising girls' self-esteem, lowering risk of disease, displaying love, attracting volunteers. Every activity had to be a means to an end—many ends—never simply an end in itself. When all attachments and needs had to be justified so constantly and publicly, any ground that may once have felt solid crumbled underfoot.

Writing this chapter was difficult for me, because I, too, could not locate any solid grounds for calling anything a need. Every time I wrote the word "need," I imagined an organizer gently correcting me: "No, do not say 'need,' but 'choice,'" hoping to empower me to take control and not take my presuppositions about "need" for granted. Of course, the organizer would be right, if, for example, I were a teen who "needed" drugs, fancy gadgets, or an abusive boyfriend.

Nutritious food seems like a good candidate for a "need" rather than a "choice," so this chapter starts there—though perhaps I should qualify this assumption by saying that I *personally feel* that nutritious food is a need. After hearing some of the effortful ways of justifying food, we will briefly see how the need for safety also melted under the multiple spotlights' heat. Next, the chapter argues that the constant demand for public justification could have a potential silver lining, if it forced participants to question themselves, to treat all needs as choices that should be well thought out, conscious, and reasonable. We see some hints of this approach, whispered in these programs: an approach that invited people to question what to count as a need—to subject "needs" to reasonable, conscious questioning—*without* necessarily making them all instantly vaporize as mere "choices" in this theater-in-the-round.

Tocqueville described a smooth transition from a purely domestic, private issue to a public concern; the man who learns of the highway being planned for his front yard has only to step out of his front door to make the transition. In Empowerment Projects, the move from private darkness to the public spotlight was not as easy.

PLEASING THE MANY AUDIENCES FOR FOOD

David, an educator at a nature education summertime program for disadvantaged kids, while the group is making its morning snack: The whipped cream is "organic" [but he does not say what organic means]
Then later:
David: Do you like whipped cream?
Kid: I never had it.
David: Have you had Coolwhip® [a frozen, whipped cream-like dessert topping]?
Kids, in enthusiastic unison: Yes!!!
David: It's like Coolwhip but tastes much better.
Linda, one of the elderly volunteers: *Much* better!

"In matters of taste, there is no dispute," of course. But as the Environmental Educator at Gardens of Hope, a public garden and meeting center, David had to try. It was his job. His job was to reintroduce children to the natural world—a world to which they may have never been introduced in the first place—and to teach them to love it. Every Thursday morning in July, the five- to nine-year-olds at Community House watched with amazement as David strenuously tried to convince them to appreciate worms, mud, bugs, and edible weeds like wood sorrel. David and the volunteer pointed out the smells of loam and flowers, and the sounds of birds, bugs, and breezes; they compared jagged-edged leaves and lobe-shaped leaves, the leaves' shiny top-sides and fuzzy under-sides.

David had to tiptoe around many invisible audiences, each upholding a different mission. While showing them the vegetable garden, David would have liked to convince children not to worry about getting their shoes muddy—*even if* their parents might get mad. He would have liked to convince children to like foods that their parents had never fed them, and to avoid foods that their parents often fed them—*without* appearing to criticize their families. He would have liked to inform them that their school lunches and fast-food meals were unhealthful—*without* appearing to denounce the schools and corporations that gave them the food, especially since some of those same companies donated food and soda to local Empowerment Projects. He would have liked to say that they needed to eat healthful food, but could not say what to count as healthful, could not explain why they had not had it in the past, and could not explain why he thought that they "needed" food that their families did not give them.

Not Offending Participants' Families

Each session at Gardens of Hope ended with an "educational snack"—an opportunity to connect nutrition with nature, their inner world with the outer. The children make the snacks themselves, in the center's kitchen, out of natural, sometimes organic ingredients. Today's educational snack would be crumbled-up fake Oreos—that is, made of natural ingredients, unlike real Oreos®, which have some fake ingredients. They mashed up the natural and therefore fake Oreos to make a pie crust, filled it with very sweet tofu pudding mix, and topped it with whipped cream.

> David (holding up a bag of natural imitation Oreos): These cookies are like Oreos but different, because they're made with *different* ingredients that make them taste better.
> [Another day, he held up a bag of candy that was like Gummy Worms but "natural," from Whole Foods, a "natural foods" supermarket chain], were "like Gummy Worms but made with *different* ingredients."
> Another day: "'Organic' means 'not sprayed with chemicals.'" [That day, he concludes his lesson by saying], "So I wanted to show you that organic food tastes *different* and *better*."

Organic food is "different and better" than what? That was what David could not say without blaming someone for having given them other food that was "different and worse." Avoiding that trap sometimes was impossible:

> Sienna [a seven-year-old girl, who always acted more "wired" than the other kids and who talked endlessly about money and sex to the other kids, and did lewd-looking dances—sticking things between her legs while in the van on the way back to Community House that day, for example. She clearly wanted to please David, though!]: David, this juice is good!

David: It has no processed sugar. It's 100% juice. That's why it tastes so good.

Sienna [again, trying hard to please David, looking straight at him—unlike her usual dismissive regard for teachers]: Yum. I drink soda.

Amy [whose parents soon pull her out of the program, saying she is "learning bad language"]: I drink water.

David: Water's really good for you. That's the best.

Sienna: When I get home, I always get a Popsicle, and candy.

David gives a polite, "Oh."

Something about David—was it the earnest smile? the 100 percent Indian cotton embroidered shirts on his skinny frame? the blond dreadlocks and rasta beads? the mere fact that he was a guy, unlike almost all the others adult leaders?—made the children always try hard to please him.

So, when David gave Amy a stronger vote of approval than he gave to Sienna, Sienna shot Amy a jealous glance, unsure why water was better than candy, but sure that David approved of Amy's snack and not her own; Amy's family, not her own. In our country's tense racial environment, there could easily have been the suspicion that race was an unmentioned part of David's unequal appreciation, Amy being Chinese and Sienna, black.

With love, Sienna's grandmother gave her Popsicles and candy. There was no easy way for David to say, "Your grandmother is feeding you food that is bad for you." That would have meant criticizing Sienna's grandmother, the corporations that made the food, or both. David wanted "comfortable" and "family-like" and "natural," but not what felt comfortable, family-like, and natural to Sienna or her grandmother.

Not Offending Corporate Donors

Organizers had to avoid criticizing another important audience: corporate donors. Donations of food from fast-food corporations and soda corporations were common, since they fulfilled the mission of sustainability, instead of relying on government funding or charity. David's grant for organic foods, fresh fruits and vegetables was rare. Grants for soda and chips gave fast-food companies publicity while giving the programs food, in what could easily look like a sustainable win-win situation: corporations get free publicity and Empowerment Projects get food. So, when Coke, Pepsi, and McDonalds donated soda and chips, Empowerment Projects accepted them.

Many organizers and youth participants alike called the chips, soda, and burgers "junk," acidly remarking on the corporations' self-interested motives, noting that corporate donors used the programs' civic events as charitable tax write-offs, to advertise to teens, and as general good-will publicity. At a Martin Luther King Day planning meeting, someone asks: What food should there be?

> Courtney, a youth worker: Coca-Cola donates a lot.
> Colette, another youth worker, ironically: Great, give 'em a bunch of caffeine.

> Sheila [the adult head of the Martin Luther King Day project that year, who later became more outspoken about all the caffeine and corn syrup that the programs fed people]: None of it is great but at least they'll be going out [to do a community service project] afterwards.

Many meetings included long discussions about which *kinds* of junk foods to get for events—Pepsi or Coke? McDonalds or Burger King? Do McDonalds' "salads" really have vegetables, or are they mostly just "globs of gross dressing," as two vegetarian youth volunteers insisted at one Martin Luther King Day planning committee meeting? The topic of the globby salads merited a detailed discussion, about whether they were filling, nutritious, too disgusting to serve, natural, just iceberg lettuce, high calorie, too small, equipped with a fork for the lettuce and a spoon for the dressing, or a spork, and more.

This was not the food that organizers promoted when wearing their social worker hats or their parent-like hats, but if McDonalds or Pepsi was giving it away for free, it was hard to say no, since the programs needed food. Or did they? Did Coke, chips, and globs of salad dressing fulfill the need for *food*? They looked like food, but with so many overweight youth, were they fulfilling the need or not? In their many discussions, it was clear that many organizers and youth volunteers doubted it. But whatever they personally felt, organizers and youth participants could not refuse corporate chains' free gifts without appearing ungrateful, overly critical and opinionated, and unsustainable.

Not Offending Experts and Invoking Expertise

Invoking expert knowledge was another way to justify food. As one NOYO member put it, requesting food in a grant application was hard, because "meeting basic needs" was never a good justification for a grant; grants were supposed to be innovative and exciting. To make eating more innovative, organizers had to cite research on rising obesity rates, rising diabetes rates, current brain development, behavior, ability to concentrate on homework, and other new scientific discoveries.

Getting a grant for a nutrition education program was a way to procure food. Getting the grant was, itself, a feather in the program's cap, showing that its organizer was innovatively, creatively ferreting out resources. Whether or not the education changed anyone's eating habits was less certain, though. Nutrition educators brought foods that they hoped to convince participants to like, but, as one educator explained to me, the five, one-hour sessions of nutrition education that she held at Community House one summer would probably not change anyone's eating habits. She recognized that changing their habits depended on steady, slow repetition.

Since she was not going to develop that kind of long-term relationship with the kids, she, like other organizers, focused on future potential: if kids heard a similar message in a number of different places, perhaps eventually, some of it would sink in. She had to mesh her mission of changing kids' habits with the mission of making kids feel comfortable and at-home, without depending on the long-term attachments and long calendar of a family, whose dinners might include a long-term, persistent cultivation of fondness for Brussels sprouts. Instead, she had to offer food that was immediately tempting to kids who had, she said, maybe never eaten fresh vegetables. One of the educational lunches she taught them to make was white flour tortillas wrapped up with cream cheese and cucumbers. Kids liked them (but were they nutritious, even though they lacked protein?). In the meantime, these short-term grants momentarily satisfied the need (if we can call it a need) to eat something.

To justify food in an Empowerment Project, it has to have other uses as well.

USES OF FOOD

Using Food to Symbolize Love

Organizers had spirited discussions about another justification of food: food can be utilized to evoke love and comfort, quickly. This use of food was only theoretical, though, since none of the programs I encountered received any grants for furnishing such abundant hominess.

"How can we make our community centers seem more like home?" asked the teacher in a twelve-week course for youth workers. The teacher had defined "family rituals" as habits that made us feel secure at home when we were children. "How can we make rituals like these for the kids we work with?" The discussion began with a discussion of hugs, which will be described later. Then it continued:

"Open door—leave the door of your office open."
"Meals [the speaker describes a program she once saw, which always started off with a hot meal, saying that nothing makes something more like home than the smell of good food cooking]."

"Honest and sincere encouragement."

"Keep it real—there will always be someone who doesn't like you. Don't try to please everyone and act nice when you don't feel it."

"Greeting. There's a rule at The Gap, and Blockbuster Video, wherever, that 'if we don't greet you, you get a free shirt or something.' Well, with us, they don't get a free anything. But the idea is the same—it's terrible to go into a youth center and not get a greeting, just walk in, nobody notices, 'oh, ok, that's ok.' Greeting is real important. But it *has* to be genuine."

"Consistency" ["Excellent" "Very good" chime in a participant and the teacher].

"Get their names right."

[. . . more suggestions . . .]

"Don't make promises you can't keep."

"Back to cooking, I think that's real important. There's a commercial with Sally Jesse Rafael and someone else, each one of them comes on and says, *'any time you eat together, you're a family.'* It's a cool commercial. That's my plug for television."

"It *is* a cool commercial."

The teacher: "We tend to bash it, but MTV researchers go into kids' homes and ask, 'Why do you like this shirt? Why did you put this poster up?' and etc. It's a marketing ploy but what's brilliant is that they get that information. We need to be doing more of that."

Others nodded and exclaimed emphatically, to echo the point.

It is hard to imagine a checklist of "things that make people in general feel at home," since, as we will see in the next chapter, what smells like home to one person may smell nauseating to another. Nevertheless, youth workers needed a definition of homey and family-like that could work in more or less the same way for everyone, fast. The Gap, Blockbuster, MTV, and the family dinner all seemed like models.

Later, a participant pointed out that there was no money, time, staff, or equipment to cook hot meals in her program. Again, almost all the others nodded and exclaimed emphatically, to echo her point. They had plentiful enthusiasm, but little food.

Using Food to Encourage Civic Engagement: "Whatever Gets 'Em Comin'"

Another use of food was to attract youth volunteers—not for nourishment, and not necessarily to make them feel at home and comfortable, and not to promote health or reduce diabetes risk or promote healthy body image or improve concentration or lower obesity rates, but "Whatever gets 'em comin'!"

That was how Erin, the bubbly paid organizer of the Regional YEP one year, put it. Participation in the evening civic engagement projects was optional, and a program's size mattered, so she always brought as much food as the Regional YEP's budget allowed, supplying every meeting with oozing, dripping chocolate chip cookies or other treats, and caseloads of soda, and chips. These desserts were supposed to attract volunteers, not just by being delicious. As a kind of benediction over the evening's offerings, Erin said that the food she brought to one meeting was "a reward" for all the good community service that youth volunteers were doing. Standing over a huge Tupperware container of about fifty big, warm, glistening brownies, four jumbo bags of tortilla chips, and thirty-six cans of soda for the group of sixteen people, she exclaimed, "You deserve it!!" One month it was brownies, the next it was chocolate chip cookies; she always pointed out that she *baked them herself*—a sign of her affection and respect for teens whose names she often could not remember.

Almost everyone came to these evening meetings ravenous: Most non-disadvantaged teens came straight from their afternoon rounds of sports, music, and other activities. Programs for disadvantaged youth had no filling food—expensive cookies, chips, and candy from brightly lit vending machines at Community House; free "fun-size" bags of cookies and chips in others; no food at all in others. Since they were teenagers, anyway, they were all always hungry.

The pop and cookies might be hard to square with the professional, educational goal of teaching participants to love broccoli and tofu, which they did not (yet) crave. It was also hard to square with another of the organizations' stated aims, which was of promoting "good body image" in girls, many of whom complained mildly, while devouring the irresistible cookies and brownies, that they were ruining their diets.

Another puzzle with using food to promote comfort and to allure participants was that everything is awkward for many teenagers, and eating in front of people is the worst. For example, Erin brought cookies to one Regional YEP meeting:

> As the plate of homemade chocolate chip cookies goes around the table, Bonita [age thirteen at the time] picks one up off the heap; then she puts it down; then she wraps a napkin around her fingers and tries picking it up again, but cannot grasp it; then she slides a napkin right up to the cookie and quickly flicks it onto the napkin. She mutters to herself, "I don't even know how to eat these."

The result of all this discussion about food, with all its symbolic uses, was . . . a great deal of discussion about food's potential, but hardly any food beyond the occasional deluge of chips, brownies, and soda.

QUESTIONING AND CODIFYING NATURE, COMFORT, FOOD

Food is somewhat exceptional, because it is hard to treat it as an abstraction without quickly getting hungry. Feelings of safety, or comfort, or a feeling of "community" are less tangible than food. Their absence is harder to recognize immediately than an absence of food is. But there was a proliferation of audiences surrounding these needs, as well, and justification of these "needs" resembled the justifications swirling around food.

Organizers complained about having to make an exciting case for something so basic as the need for safety. Funders were inspired by innovative participatory plans to help the needy and empower them, and that evoked an image of infinite future potential. As we saw earlier, fixing Community House's leaky roof, moldy carpet, or dangerous climbing structure was considered too remedial and obvious, not empowering and innovative enough to deserve funding. A good roof might be useful now, but it would not glow with the aura of infinite future potential. Organizers were pressed to focus on projects that glowed, and to neglect the duller ones.

Focusing on future potential also helped adult organizers avoid offending their multiple audiences. For example, a committee of the NOYO spent many meetings drafting a Letter to the Editor of the local paper aimed at showing that more funding for youth programs could prevent school shootings. Jeanne, a thoughtful, older organizer, mused aloud about whether the parents of the shooters knew about their own kids' problems, whether any parent can conceive of their own kid as a murderer, whether kids knew what resources were available, and whose job it was to tell them. Then, she caught herself, emphasizing that she did not want to blame anyone:

> We all have ideas about what parenting could be done, or done differently, or what schools could or couldn't have done. But I wanted to steer away from blaming or telling anyone "Here's what you should do that you're not doing," but to focus on what good we're already doing, and say "here's ways to get your kid involved."

> Kelly: Let's make sure it's not just another "we know what's best for people." There've been enough of those!
> Jeanne: Let's not blame anyone. We should talk about "investment in children,[2] rewards."
> [Kelly says we should give a list of what they are.]
> Jerrard [echoes Jeanne: not blame, accusing, keep it positive].

Our final answer was to build "the community," along with Jeanne's suggestions here, of "investing in children" and "rewards."

The hope was that if they drew on the current community's strengths, a better future community would emerge. As we have seen, Empowerment Projects' focus on future potential often made it hard to acknowledge any past or current problems and reflect on them, to figure out how to fix them, or to imagine any step-by-step methods of reaching the happy prophecy. For this history-less way of imagining a hopeful future, the past and present community—the one that had cultivated all those bad habits—had to seem irrelevant. In Empowerment Projects, no one could ask why bad eating habits and murderers were also products of the community.

Between all the audiences' crisscrossed spotlights, such questions often arose and immediately had to be put down. In a prairie nature education program, when the teacher said we should avoid pesticides, a girl chimed in with a story about her parents' spraying pesticides in their backyard. The teacher simply changed the subject, to avoid blaming anyone. Similarly, in one session at Gardens of Hope, David held up some apple grass that he had just picked from the lawn, as he sat in a circle with the children. With clear delight, he said that many foods were growing, right under our noses, freely and naturally. I was charmed, and started daydreaming of eating chives and apple grass as a child. They grew in a stinky, petroleum-filled stream whose mud oozed in rainbow-colored sludge in my housing development, and I would come home smelling like an onion-y gas station. As if he smelled my wistful, twisted, stinky memory, David added sternly:

> But don't *ever* eat them, unless you're absolutely sure you know how they were grown. Because they might have been sprayed with dangerous chemicals. Like these here probably were.

Even grass and roots are not as grassroots as Empowerment Talk suggests. While this is not Empowerment Projects' intended lesson, it is a useful one to ponder. However, organizers could not encourage such pondering, because it would require admitting that the community has problems, not just strengths, is the disease as well as the cure. Someone might feel blamed. If delighting in nature's bounty was a need, it was not one that David could speak about explicitly, or fulfill.

OPPORTUNITY AND THREAT: QUESTIONING AND JUSTIFYING NATURE; CONNECTING INTIMACY TO SOCIAL POLICY

Beyond the risk of offending all the many audiences, speaking so explicitly about "nature" and "needs" came with more potentially disturbing dangers—which were also potentially disturbing opportunities. Publicly justifying something by calling it "natural" or "a need" forces people to question it, to view it abstractly, from a distance—for better or worse.

For example, in the twelve-week certificate program's discussion, described earlier, on "how to make our centers feel like home," right before the topics of paid greeters at Blockbuster and the Gap, participants talked about hugs.

> One youth worker calls out a phrase that everyone except me knows [I asked several people later if she had made it up, and they all said no]:
> "Positive appropriate touch."
> The teacher (writing POSITIVE APPROPRIATE TOUCH on a big sheet of paper that is taped to the wall): "GOOD! Say more!"
> The youth worker, mildly chuckling: "Well, there's 'surfboard hug'—keep your body stiff like a board, don't get too close; there's 'hip to hip hugs,' that you can give to adolescent males in your program; there are face-on hugs that I give to females . . . [there were other hug categories, whose names I did not catch in my notes].

The list was not surprising; they had all heard it, or one just like it, before. This lesson on hugs is like the mandatory courses in many workplaces that teach employees how to avoid appearing to flirt or harass at work, or the elementary school classes that teach students to "take three deep breaths" or "count to ten" when angry, and to "use 'I' statements" in disputes. Like food, hugs could, in these conditions, under all these spotlights, start to feel less natural and more worth discussing, justifying, and scrutinizing. Of course, parents—those who might be tempted not to touch their children enough, or too much, or in the wrong way—*could* institute a similar regime, a similar codification of hugs, just to be on the safe side. But neither law nor custom requires families to codify their hugging practices.

On the one hand, this may be a travesty to the very nature of the hug. The very fact that organizers had to talk about their hugs so gracelessly made the hugs step partly out of the realm of utter familiarity, nature, charm, and intuition, and enter the realm of plans and laws.[3]

On the other hand, since we accept laws against brutal harassment in workplaces, we probably accept *some* codification of hugs and breaths. The codification of hugs could remind leaders to express affection, in case they forgot. It could protect teens against feeling lust for their caregivers, and vice versa. It could protect the caregivers from accusations of sexual abuse, in court, with lists of permissible and impermissible touches. Questioning natural feelings in this case presented an opportunity, not just a threat.

David, from Gardens of Hope, wanted kids to enjoy whipped cream, which he considered more natural, but is it? David hoped to find, in "nature," a solid bedrock of indisputable answers.[4] He hoped that participants had only to taste and see simple pleasures, and he trusted that they would directly sense which pleasures were natural. When writing drafts of this chapter, I went to the freezer aisle and bought a tub of the Coolwhip that David wanted kids to avoid, so I could tell you the ingredients. I was expecting a funny, incriminating list of polysyllabic plastics, plus a squirt of titanium dioxide for whiteness. Instead, I found:

> Water, corn syrup, hydrogenated vegetable oil (coconut and palm kernel oils), high fructose corn syrup, less than 2 percent of sodium caseinate (from milk), natural and artificial flavor, xanthan and guar gums, polysorbate 60, sorbitan monostearate, beta carotene (colors)

Is fat from hormone-fed cows who eat high on the food chain in a polluted planet more natural than Coolwhip's tasty melange of chemicals and vegetable fat? Since toxins in the environment concentrate in animal fat, even organic cream is not very natural anymore, so by standards that David himself *also* upheld, it may very well be more healthful and natural. Whipped cream was not rock-solid; upon questioning, it could melt.

These programs' exposure, transparency, and publicity sometimes forced open political questions that were both illuminating and disturbing. One sticky summer night, Emily was tired after one of her usual, long days. She said to the teenagers, who she took care of, and who, in turn, helped take care of the younger children, "I love the little kids, but—"

"You love me," says one of the teens.

"You love us, you do," says another.

Emily: If I'm tired, it's the kids who suffer. Because I yell more, which I don't like to do. Like today, I'm embarrassed at how much I yelled today. I talked to the county certifier who's really cool, and I told her we're short-staffed, and I was hoping they'd fund us more but then they probably would have to cut funding from somewhere else, from their own programs. But I'm telling people, there's 35 kids and just 2 staff. (Lots of indignant "oohs," from me and Sheila and kids). It's not enough. And if it's not enough, I end up yelling.

Community House's work of raising poor youth was publicly visible. Families and private agencies do not have to justify their caregiving to multiple, distant audiences, no matter how extravagant it is. Nobody has to justify the purchase of vans—or tanks. Parents or private organizations simply buy them, privately. Whether or not such purchases would be publicly justifiable is a question that families may *choose* to ask, but they are not *required* to ask or answer publicly. When close, daily relationships developed in an Empowerment Project's conditions, they almost had to reveal a connection between love and justice, intimate attachments and public policy. On the one hand, this could be a beautiful opportunity to cultivate a "sociological imagination," to connect their own personal lives to social structure, "to understand the larger historical scene in terms of its meaning for the inner life"[5] and vice versa. On the other hand, we can see how deeply risky it could be to complete that connection, because their attachment to Emily was up for debate. If they lost, they lost Emily.

CONCLUSION: ARE ALL NEEDS MERELY "CHOICES"?

The very act of telling, exposing, publicly justifying, was part of what made these intimate relationships what they were: possibly loving, always in need of public justification, and always disturbingly temporary and precarious, for as long as funding was temporary and precarious. If program participants grasp that their own intimate attachments and physical needs precariously depend on fickle funders and public opinion, perhaps the "sociological imagination" reaches its emotional limits.

Crisscrossed by so many different searchlights, the warm, dark nest of needs—for safety, comfort, and intimacy—comes up for relentless questioning. In these conditions, Empowerment Talk turned inside out: intimacy, comfort, and safety were supposed to provide solid, indisputable bases for the programs, but became topics of debate, not simple, indisputable needs.

On the one hand, no one can hide behind solid dogmas in such conditions, since even food and hugs have to be justified explicitly. Nothing can be taken for granted as permanent, natural, and obvious. On the other hand, there is one dogma: every need has to be justified in multiple ways for multiple audiences, and usually renamed "a choice," since most needs seemed to offend someone and always had to be ready to change if fickle funders changed their minds.

Drawing on Shared Experience in a Divided Society: Getting People Out of Their "Clumps"

MIRIAM [an organizer, at a lunchtime meeting of about thirty organizers and officials, discussing a plan to distribute a monthly calendar of events for youth]: The goal is to create a community so they can get to know each other. I know in our work [beckoning to her co-worker], we've spent a lot of time trying to get five communities together and ended up with five different *clumps*—kids from each community sticking together and not getting to know each other. It's taken time for us to realize that we have to structure it *very intentionally* to get them out of their clumps. Because people naturally tend to sit with who they know.

Another youth worker agrees about mixing them together.

A third youth worker [from a poor, rural community center]: Where do we want to go? Why is the goal to have youth get to know people from different communities?

A city official: The theory is that they are all segregated. By community, race, economic group, rural versus urban, whatever. And we were interested in breaking that down—whether it's youth from Stonington meeting kids from Snowy Prairie, so the kids from Snowy Prairie say, "Hey, they're not just rural hicks, after all!" So they wouldn't just see negative stereotypes. So they'll learn that there are other different kinds of kids who may look different or may live somewhat differently, but all are nice. The goal is to get them out of their "clumps," so they're not all isolated in their separate communities. And Janice Whittaker [an elected official] has said that her goal is to increase youth contact between communities [implicitly: so this is good to do, for funding purposes].

Roberta [city youth programming official]: And the surprising thing is that, when youth got together to talk about what they had in common, what they had that was different, what the ideal youth community would look like, what impressed me was that they didn't want to just stick with their own community. It was like "I'm sick of Stonington, I want to get out and find out what other kids are doing," and "Wow, I just met someone from [the nearest large city with a large black population—two hours away]! How exotic!" They're sick of their own place. . . .

Erin [leader of the Regional YEP]: Drug and alcohol prevention balance with how kids can improve their community—the two go together.

Empowerment Projects drew on shared tastes and a shared sense of fun, in the hopes that this would show participants that we are "all the same underneath," and they would eventually treat each other as equals. Trying to change feelings by drawing on feelings was hard to do quickly when members came from such different, unequal backgrounds, bringing such systematically different feelings to the group, and sometimes finding each other's desires disgusting. Participants were supposed to bond in the "here and now," without referring to any past, but they could rarely just get out of clumps and slice away their past feelings, when they were also being asked to draw on their feelings.

Organizers searched energetically for some activity or food that would bring all youth together, and said, partly in jest, that they had discovered precisely one Universal Good: Pizza. There were a few other shared tastes and topics of interest to all, but they were not the deeply personal inspiring feelings that Empowerment Project organizers were supposed to unearth. Learning to make impersonal small talk is an important skill, and sometimes, these projects taught it quite well. It just was not what they had planned to teach.

Trying to Coax Youth Out of Their "Clumps"

The Regional YEP made many plans aimed at pulling socially diverse participants out of their clumps to bond, including a slumber party, pizza parties, movies, dances. Erin explained the topic:

The County Youth Committee budget last year was $900: for Martin Luther King Day, for reserving spaces, renting rooms. So we didn't contribute much monetarily to Martin Luther King Day, but did do a lot of work!

This year I requested, don't laugh, $6,000!!—mainly for rewards for you guys, because you deserve it!! Like: a retreat, staying up late, talk about what makes you happy, what makes you sad, see how goofy you can be, how funny you can be. It's called 'bonding' and I'm into that!! You can't really just come to a meeting and feel connected. Because you don't know each other that well.

The next time Erin mentioned "bonding, getting to know you, getting to know what you like and what you don't like," a kid groaned sarcastically, so she added, "I'm also big into rewarding, combining work and fun, so I want the next event to be with *pizza*! [...] It'll be really fun, really low-key entertainment going on, really fun."

While the sleepover did not end up happening, some smaller events did—a Halloween party, a movie night, and another party that year.

No matter how hard organizers tried, youth volunteers stayed in clumps. Participants understood how hard organizers were trying to change their taste in friends, and they noticed that it kept not working, and they laughed. When, for example, I was helping three non-disadvantaged volunteers in the Regional YEP think up questions for a Martin Luther King Day Trivia Contest, they were facing a computer, looking at a website about Martin Luther King, while my job was to type what they had dictated to me earlier. While writing, I overheard them saying that the different groups *don't* get together, that the groups just stay completely separate, they never talk to each other. "So, it's not gonna work," one said. His observation seemed accurate to me.

Purely social events like the Halloween party seemed like auspicious beginnings, but got only as far as bringing diverse youth into the same building. When the non-disadvantaged Regional YEP members came to Community House for a party, one clump stayed in one room, while the other clump stayed in another. At one event, diverse youth sat in the same room on big couches, watching a movie, but they did not talk to each other; and there were no integrated couches. In all the social events I attended, I saw members of the two "clumps" exchanging more than a few words only three or four times in my four and a half years.

These conversations, reported in the chapter on politics, were teasing arguments about presidential and congressional politics. Focusing on impersonal public news that concerned them all was their superb solution to the puzzle of building bridges between people who were starting from very different places. Organizers did not encourage this solution, however; it did not yield the personal, deep intimacy that they hoped to cultivate.

Ice-Breakers

Since the Regional YEP met once or twice a month for the school year, the exercises were supposed to speed up the process a bit, by helping people take the first step. In groups with this combination of infrequent, optional meetings and vast diversity, efficient bonding was necessary. Organizers started most meetings with "ice-breakers," parlor games that organizers would find in books or on the Internet, aimed at tempting members to interact, based on the idea that even the longest journey starts with the first step. But participants rarely had a second chance to bond, or even see each other, again. In addition, taking a second step may have been upsetting, if participants were pressured to reveal and discover just how vastly different their lives were.

So, participants learned to act *as if* there would be a second step, but not to expect it at all. They learned, that is, to make small talk with strangers. A common ice-breaker helped. It was a musical chairs-type game, which the Regional YEP played before most meetings:

Everyone stands in a circle, with one kid in the middle.

The kid in the middle calls out, "I am on a train, and I'm taking everyone who does x/has x characteristic/likes x!" and this kid runs to take someone's spot in the circle, as the kids who do x/have x/like x give up their spots in the circle. Whichever kid has not grabbed a spot goes to the middle, and the process starts over.

The point was just to have fun running around and learning a bit about each other. Participants always called out unthreatening, bland qualities: "everyone who is wearing blue jeans, come out," or "everyone who likes music, has been to California, has green eyes, has white shoes, is wearing underwear, is wearing short sleeves, has brown hair, has a ponytail, is wearing a jacket, likes basketball, likes ice cream." The qualities all had to be impersonal or visible, and not associated with any social divisions or troubles. "Is wearing jeans or sneakers or the color blue" were okay; "is blonde" or "has straight hair," were okay, since they were not considered divisive or controversial in this largely blonde city. "Has kinky black hair" or "knows a millionaire" or "gets straight A's" or "has a relative in jail" or "has been to a welfare office" or "has ever gotten so drunk, they barfed," or "is gay" or "has parents who smoke dope" or "has been homeless" or "loves Jesus" were not okay. More precisely, no one ever tried ones like those. The closest anyone got to something personal or controversial was when one clumsy adult organizer, who dropped out after two meetings, said she would take "anyone who farts in the bathtub." No one jumped onto her "train," and every time I saw her after that, I imagined her bathtub farts. From this exercise, participants gained practice in mentioning inoffensive characteristics about themselves and others; not deeply "bonding," but staying nicely impersonal.

Other ice-breakers were just plain fun, whether or not they led to anything. One had participants crawling on top of one another till they fell over, collapsing in a heap of hilarious giggles. Still, participants knew that bonding exercises were supposed to lead to something, and were not ordinary *games*; everyone knew that more was at stake than mere fun, that it was silliness with a purpose.

After a few months of ice-breakers in the Regional YEP each year, teens grew tired of them, and many groaned loudly and conspicuously when organizers summoned them into another circle. The topics—"is wearing jeans," "likes ice cream," "has a belly button"—started to become repetitive.

Organizers Who Worked with Youth on Probation Trying to Bond with Those Who Worked with Girl Scouts

Like the youth volunteers, the adult organizers were socially diverse, and like youth volunteers, they had very diverse ideas of what felt comfortable, natural, and good. Their groups' diversity was a source of pride, and a potential source of insight, but was also an inexpressible source of tension and confusion.

Tastes and feelings of comfort often go hand-in-hand with different social backgrounds,[1] and teenagers, of course, use tastes—in food, music, clothes—as markers of identity. But something more visceral than status competition was in play: what felt like comfort food to one group tasted revolting to another, what felt like family to one group frightened the other, what smelled like home to one group smelled putrid to another. While disadvantaged youth managed to laugh the differences away, in jokes like the one about the baby blue cardigan with pearlized buttons described earlier, it was much harder for adults to do the same, since they were supposed to take the promises of Empowerment Talk seriously. An inspection of adult organizers' valiant efforts to do what they wanted youth volunteers to do shows why the youth volunteers could so rarely do it.

The twelve-week, four-hour-per-week certificate program for organizers included several women (mostly young, all white) who had bravely moved to the "big city" of Snowy Prairie from rural villages, and who now worked with young children in places like the Girl Scouts. There were leaders of centers like Community House for youth who were deemed "at-risk," on down to Reprise, a program for clients who were not just "at risk," but who had already been arrested or put on probation for violent crimes. The four Reprise staff members in the program were black men who had all grown up in extreme poverty. One was a former drill sergeant. Several other participants had become youth workers out of principle—feminist or Christian. Some expensive nonprofit and for-profit after-school programs were represented, too. Still other participants were looking for a change of pace, choosing youth work after profitable careers in business. It was quite a mix.

The teacher's explicit message, in every session, was that whatever a youth worker's background is, and whoever was in a youth program, the work is always, in a deep way, *the same*. All youth, he said, respond to the same treatment: cheery and warm.

The four black leaders of Reprise, the program for teens who had been arrested, kept arguing with the teacher, saying that their kids responded better to a more strict demeanor, but the teacher, who was white, kept repeating: "kids respond to warmth and friendliness." His message echoed Empowerment Talk's faith in comfort and gut feelings. In one such argument,

> the former drill sergeant and his three Reprise colleagues vehemently disagreed with others on the question of whether being nice and sweet to kids helps build a sense of closeness. He kept repeating over and over that acting too sweet with his kids was a mistake. Drawing on his military past, he said that when drill sergeants scream in the faces of cadets, it is a sign of love and respect, a willingness to take a risk of being disliked, in order to correct the other's defects.
>
> Some participants lightly mocked his argument; a few said that *they had never thought of it, that different kids' experiences mean you should show love to them differently.*

Most of the others, including the teacher, flatly disagreed, saying with equal vehemence that being nice and cheery is the only way to build closeness. To me, along with a few other sweet ladies like me, who exclaimed that they had "never thought of it that way," hearing the former drill sergeant was an eye-opening dispute about love in conditions of social inequality. It made me think that what feels comfortable, natural, affectionate, homey, and caring to one person may very well feel brutal to someone from another background. And vice-versa: keeping it friendly and sweet felt phony to the drill sergeant. It made me wonder if his tough love approach was a symptom of a problem, or maybe even not a problem at all.

Another session had a similar debate:

> Darren, from Reprise: Is it wrong to greet kids in a bad mood? Because if we greet them all chipper, they think, "Oh, he's in a good mood, I'm gonna have some fuuuuun today" [in other words, the kid comes in like a cat who's going to play with his mouse]!
>
> Teacher: So what would happen if they had a little fun?
>
> Darren: With our kids, you can't let your guard down, you can't be nice; these are kids who don't want to play by the rules.
>
> Teacher: There are different approaches that work with different kids. The key mantra is "keep it real. *Be yourself.*" If your approach is rough and tough, maybe there's a way to soften it up. If your approach is soft and fluffy, maybe there's some way to toughen up the edges.

Kelly, a young organizer from a program for YMCA non-disadvantaged youth: Isn't your program different from most of ours, though, because you have to get some work done and ours are mostly just for recreation?

Here, again, was one of those moments in which predictable mistakes were potentially more enlightening than the moments when the organization ran smoothly.

Promoting Instant Intimacy: We Both Like Birthdays!

Like teens' bonding exercises, adults' bonding techniques included ice-breakers, or breaking up into groups of three or four to talk or "role play." The organizers' diligent effort to *reveal* their feelings helps explain the teens' effort to *hide* theirs. In the twelve-week certificate class, quick bonding was easiest between participants from similar backgrounds—the soft pink women with the other soft pink women, the serious black men from Reprise with their fellow Reprise employees, etc. White participants became excited when they tried to bond across vast social distances. In one bonding exercise, we divided into small groups to talk about our "family cultures," and then reunited as a class to report on our discussions. One participant exclaimed with excitement that his small group had bonded so well, it was a "lovefest." As in the youth programs, the thrill was more over the very fact that communication had occurred, rather than about any surprising content of the communication, which in the case of the lovefest was about how much they liked Christmas when they were children.

Insisting on making oneself understood was out of place, if one wanted to communicate something unusual. People did not have enough time together to make fellow participants grasp any serious differences. For example, when we divided up to talk about our "family culture," I was in a group with three white youth workers and a black Reprise employee, Isaac. Linda and another participant had been decrying strict parenting styles, saying that being strict was *unfair* to children. Isaac kept gently disagreeing.

> You're talking fair, but you've got to remember, I'm over fifty years old, things were not fair in South Carolina in the 1950s and '60 s. That's the thing about a big family—we stuck together. We'd all heard about someone who died suddenly. No one ever said how but we all knew. So we knew not to delay getting home, just to walk straight home from school. All the kids in our neighborhood knew not to delay.

Later in the small group conversation, he tried to say that when his family stuck together, it was for different reasons than those that caused another participant's happy white farm family to stick together on the Northern plains:

> Isaac said his family of fourteen in South Carolina was just real different from now—he said, "You're talking about South Carolina in the turbulent '50s and '60s, you're talking about Martin Luther King coming to a town right near mine, my cousin knew Stokely Carmichael, I knew Malcolm X—you all know who he was??

Linda, a white youth worker, raised in Snowy Prairie, born in the 1960s, kept nodding along, interrupting, over-enthusiastically agreeing, but slightly missing the point. She chimed in, as if to complete his thought, saying: "Your family *was* community!"

Now Isaac chimed in, seeming simply to add to her last thought, but actually completing her sentence in a way that subtly argued against it:

> —"within the African American community,"
> which *she*, in turn, enthusiastically interrupted, saying,
> "—like a farm family—you stuck together!!!"

Isaac persisted, trying to say that his family stuck together partly out of fear of violence, but Linda kept chiming in, adding clauses onto his sentences. "Chiming in" can be a conversational method of signaling agreement, and that was clearly what Linda was trying to do here.[2] She could go through the motions of agreeing, in a conversation whose form signaled "agreement" to her. It *looked like* agreeable communication, which excited Linda in itself, so much so that she could not stop, even when Isaac started sounding annoyed at what he began to treat as interruptions.

Empowerment Projects threw diverse people together, potentially offering them a chance to learn about differences. Arguments like the one between the soft-touch YMCA women and the tough-love Reprise men showed that it was not easy to bridge these gulfs, but they potentially helped participants learn. Non-arguments, like the one between Linda and Isaac, or the teacher and Isaac, just confirmed to a person like Linda that we are all the same underneath.

A predictable organizational style, with predictable injuries, became clear: gently but persistently, people like Isaac tried to educate people like Linda, but rarely seemed to get through. All participants were supposed to dig down into their own souls to excavate feelings that could let them comprehend the other, on the Emersonian assumption that the most personal is the most universal. In the process, it looked like Isaac constantly dredged up intense, bitter feelings that were hard to explain quickly, and so, time after time, he was left swallowing the feelings that he had been encouraged to bring up. On the other hand, it is hard to imagine displaying such intense experiences so quickly for so many years to so many uncomprehending listeners; perhaps his frightening story was a well-rehearsed display that no longer felt intensely real.

Another day in the twelve-week certificate course showed me another way that these exercises in easy bonding lead to incomprehension. In the story reported earlier, about the well-off boy with the neglectful, Volvo-driving parents, it was hard for organizers to acknowledge that affluent youth could have any serious problems. Here, we were doing an exercise aimed at showing us, on a personal, experiential level, just how important it was for teens to have a close bond with a caring adult—just "someone who can *be there* for the child." The moral, the teacher insisted several times, was that "You can be *that person* for *that child*." We all had to describe the person who was like that for us when we were thirteen.

The twenty-five or so youth workers in the room all, miraculously, had one. One by one, they warmly described fond, loving memories of comforting, comfortable togetherness with an aunt, grandma, mom, dad, dance teacher, or guidance counselor, detailing peaceful times talking, cooking, going on walks, tinkering, or just being with them. When my turn came, I said, truthfully, that there really was no one.

The teacher said that it could not be true. There *had* to be someone. "Look, you're a professor now. There must have been someone."

I assured him that there was not. He insisted that there must have been. I almost started to explain, but, then, before any words left my mouth, I realized that any explanation would have been too personal, and thus, out of place. My feelings—which were really quite strong—led me to an insight:[3] This exercise had asked us to draw on deeply personal feelings in order to understand "youth" in general, but to make that work, those feelings had to be standard ones, ones that people in the room would easily and quickly recognize.

Eliciting gut feelings and then ignoring those that were hard to express quickly was a common pattern in the twelve-week certification program. Isaac and I fell off the edge, for different reasons, by having atypical stories that were not easy to tell quickly and publicly. Our personal stories were not impersonal enough.[4] In this strangely personal/impersonal world, adults like Isaac seemed continually frustrated about not being understood, but persisted, anyway. As these conversations wore on, Isaac enunciated every word more and more slowly; rage seemed to lurk just beneath the surface.

The merry, light joke at Community House about the "baby blue cardigan with pearlized buttons" was disadvantaged youth volunteers' skillful equivalent to Isaac's heavy explanations. Silence was probably another common tack. In these ways, disadvantaged youth participants learned a valuable lesson in these programs: not to be like Isaac, not to try too hard to make non-disadvantaged participants understand them.

Taste and Smell and Fondest Childhood Memories

Feeling pleasure and disgust from scents might seem completely physical, not social products, but they, too, divided people. Of course, tastes diverge in ways that do not always boil down to class or race differences or other inequalities. In Snowy Prairie, when they *did* correspond to these fraught distinctions, especially in organizations that aimed to overcome clumps, the mixture could be flammable.

When asked in the twelve-week class to talk about what made us feel "at home," DJ said that she felt most at home at Rainbow Garden, a homeless shelter, where she had spent many of her teenage years. The dance teacher there had been a real mentor for her—"that person" when she was thirteen. Now, DJ herself worked at Rainbow Garden. The thought of Rainbow Garden evoked, for me, a powerful odor of Lysol, Mr. Clean, or some other ammonia-based cleaning product, and reminded me of a conversation I had just had with a mother of a NOYO-affiliated preschooler. She had recently moved to a racially mixed neighborhood, happily hoping to teach her children to appreciate diversity. A half block from her new house was Ujaama, a community center with many programs for children. I asked if she ever went there with her three children.

> Sheepishly, she said that she really would like to, but "it feels so 'institutional,'" with those fluorescent lights and that horrible smell and those hallways.

> Just thinking of the intense smell of ammonia-based bathroom cleaning products made my nose sting; I said so, and she agreed, chuckling, "Yeah, it really stinks there!"

The white parent sincerely wanted to appreciate diversity, but the lights and smell of Ujaama made her uncomfortable, while DJ really felt at home there.

Similarly, on that day when we were drawing on knowledge of our own thirteen-year-old selves as a means toward understanding all thirteen-year-olds, DJ and I participated in an exercise about "making youth feel at home." It was hard for either of us to make the other feel "at home."

> We all had to role-play either being "a middle schooler" or being "an adult youth worker." My half of the room got the "kid" role. Everyone but me started bickering and yapping and throwing things and getting reeeeeaal silly. Sorry, but I was more the sort of teenager who was a quiet problem. My instant, automatic response to the suggestion "you are thirteen years old" was to put my head on the desk and almost start to cry. DJ came over to me, in the youth worker role, gently suggesting

all sorts of engagements for me: "How are you feeling? You're looking sort of sad. Do you like basketball? You could go play basketball. Or do want to play pool? There's some kids playing pool—you could join in. Or how about a snack? Would you like a snack? We have lots of yummy snacks in the kitchen, Cheez-Doodles, I think. How about Nintendo—would you like to play Nintendo, or other video games?"

The more she talked, the more miserable I felt. None were the morose, solitary, contemplative, subversive things I liked to do when I was thirteen. The goal was to get me active, moving, involved with other kids. She didn't suggest homework or reading a novel or playing music. She didn't ask 'what's wrong,' or ask if I wanted to talk about it. Or if she did, it wasn't long enough or eagerly and forcefully enough for the thirteen-year-old me to say.

Her list was interesting also because I started to feel sorry for her and finally just relented to having a snack, which is the only universal recreation—maybe why the Traffic in Snacks is soooo prevalent at every youth gathering . . .

I actually almost burst into tears, in my role as a thirteen-year-old, thinking, "She's suggesting video games and billiards! She'll *never* understand me!! Because all the things she's suggesting are the things I hate most about being a teenager. No arts and crafts—'that's for little kids.' No books—we're supposed to be 'having fun' and 'being enthusiastic,' not curling up with books." To my thirteen-year-old self, it all had that "public places" feel to it, the smell of Mr. Clean toilet cleaner and other cleaning products mixed with slightly rancid potato chips and personal hygiene products, and the bluish emptiness of fluorescent lights.

In retrospect, we were jumping a class and cultural divide, and since I would have been on top of the division, *I shouldn't have let my 13-year-old self be such a snob*. But aren't all cultural differences like that? Whether traveling from the top down, or from one ethnicity to another, there's that blank cultureless space that's filled with Mr. Clean and fluorescent light, where nobody lives. Or if anyone lives there, it's probably not you, and probably not like home. Or anyway, it's not me.

You're supposed to be able to cross boundaries of race, class, etc. with kids that you would never presume to cross easily with other adults. "You *all* like snacks, Nintendo, billiards." This is like the point black men make, that little black boys with big round heads and long eyelashes are called 'cute' and white ladies pat them fondly on the heads, till the kids get to be taller than the ladies, and then they magically become 'monsters' in the eyes of the same ladies. Kids are supposed to cross these boundaries with ease, as if they are unaware of the divisions and are not supposed to be curious about them.

We're all supposed to respect cultural differences and individual differences, but we're also supposed to assume that all kids like the same things, will like us and each other despite our and their social differences, and won't notice the differences.

Those were my gloomy reflections that day. If I did not like her tastes, I would look like a snob who felt superior to someone who had spent her teen years at Rainbow Garden. So, in my momentary incarnation as a thirteen-year-old, I finally gave in to her beseeching pleas, and tried to appear comforted and comfortable. To be acceptable in an open, inclusive civic organization, participants had to learn a quick, practical alchemy, to purify their messy feelings and make them just like everyone else's feelings.

MAKING SPEECH ITSELF INTO A POTENT SYMBOL, NO MATTER WHAT THE CONTENT: MYLAR VERSUS METALLIC GIFT WRAP

A typical organizational style smoothed over these tensions, seeming to make rapid bonding between diverse people possible: participants quickly had to find a topic that everyone would share—gift wrap, socks, pizza, blue jeans—any topic could suffice, as long as it had no divisive content. The very act of speaking itself in that kind of situation was a triumphant indication that "we are making contact; we are bonding," no matter what the content of the speech was, and no matter whether participants expected ever to meet again. The very act of having achieved a conversation was what mattered.

From this, participants learned how to produce and value conversation with strangers. For example, when the Regional YEP went to decorate the Pediatric Hospital before Christmas, there were four Regional YEP volunteers, about twenty students from a university-based Service Learning Club, and four sick children in pajamas. We all sat at a big table coloring wall-sized posters from *How the Grinch Stole Christmas*, to hang on the hospital walls. We were using small crayons, so we spent a lot of time just scrubbing swathes of color on the big posters. This did not require concentration, and was a bit boring, but it was hard to find anything to talk about.

One college-age volunteer kept up steady banter with a sick boy, maybe twelve years old, comparing nearby amusement parks first, and then comparing different kinds of gift wrap: Mylar vs. paper vs. metallic vs. tissue paper. She told the boy what state she was from, and answered his question, "When is Christmas?" The volunteer maintained a lightly kidding, friendly tone, unflappable even when the boy kept on asking when Christmas was, showing that he was not understanding the conversation entirely. Nevertheless, he clearly was enjoying it, and the talkative girl looked proud that she could keep the interaction afloat.

Everyone else at the table listened to their banter attentively, almost jealously. This volunteer was good at breaking the silence, but when she was quiet, no one could fill in, except to talk in undertones with the friends they had come with. They were talking in undertones because they knew that just talking to the friends with whom they had come was not the agenda. After a while, though, the volunteers gave up on conversing with the patients. Some college-bound teens started asking the university students about how to get into college, and about life in the dorms, while the younger or more shy volunteers, or those who had not thought about college, stayed silent.

Similarly, at several Safe Nights, the alcohol-free, tobacco-free evenings for teens, adult volunteers found no way to make conversation. Teens were absorbed with their own friendships, dancing, flirting and teasing, and playing basketball. Adults—except the enterprising, outgoing few who had managed to build a bridge by getting into a game of ping-pong or basketball—could always be found at these events wandering around embarrassed, looking like untethered boats, asking each other what they should be doing, and gazing with admiration at the adults who looked like they were having more success at connecting with youth participants.

In many volunteer activities, youth came and went; adults came and went; an adult could feel sudden momentary closeness to any random youth at any time, as they bonded over shared shoe sizes or shared tastes in candy, all without needing to know the child's name. In a week of free summer activities at a park in a low-income neighborhood, I seemed, on the face of it, to do what organizers would have happily called "forging a bond" with a girl (didn't catch her name) when we both laughed hard together about a talking necklace. Another volunteer managed to appear to bond with a child over a Happy Meals toy. To accomplish this instant bonding, it seemed that people were supposed to assume that they were all interchangeable, that anyone could do what anyone else could do, as long as someone did it. This intimacy had to be impersonal and universal, available equally to everyone quickly, no matter how far apart their starting points were.

To make such a quick, not-too-personal connection possible, organizers tried to initiate "positive" conversations. That sometimes meant making sure that disadvantaged youth did not talk about the particulars of their lives—the uncle in prison, the brother on drugs, the abused mom.

Paradoxically, in other words, trying to bond meant not letting participants talk about their own lives.

For example, at Chippewa Middle School, organizers tried to encourage bonding, by keeping the group "positive," as they often put it:

> It's the first non-freezing day of spring, and we're all happy to be out-
> side, even though we're sitting at one of those impossibly uncomfort-
> able picnic tables with built-in, plastic-coated wire-mesh stools that are
> all crooked and wobbly like bad teeth, surrounding a wire-mesh table.
> Carmen, Cerise, and some other kids [ages 11 to 15] are sitting at the
> table pretending to paint.

> But really, they are all talking about their friends and relatives who
> were in trouble: So-and-so got suspended from school for a month, and
> now he's back; another kid got arrested for lying about whether he was
> on probation, etc.

> They're animatedly talking about this when Kristin [an organizer who
> worked there for a few months] interrupts loudly, with a smile, *"Come
> on, guys, let's talk about something a little more positive now!!"*

> So they stop talking about their lives, and begin asking, "Where's
> the blue, do you have the blue?" and teasing each other for their pic-
> tures (a sunset with a long highway going back in perspective, another
> "I love so and so," etc.).

> Kristin keeps monitoring things. When a kid started mildly teasing an-
> other ("Oooh, that picture looks *ugly!*"), Kristin mildly, gently chas-
> tises: "That doesn't sound very *respectful.*"

Organizers begged participants to "be real" with them; they did not want
phony togetherness, but something deeper. Since people came from such
different places, though, there was implicit disagreement about what
could count as real. Kristin wanted intimacy, yet her job, as she understood it, was also to keep participants busy and happy, with activities and
conversations that were pleasant, not troubling, because she wished that
they had had happier childhoods—happier than the conversation about
jail and probation, absent parents, and mean uncles signaled to her. But
excluding their pasts, and their troubles, left little for them to say. Soon
after Kristin's suggestion, the girls all left the table. Most of them soon
quit the program, anyway, and Kristin moved away a month later.

Kristin often searched for tastes that she could share with participants:

> The "oldies" station was playing on the radio. Desirée wanted to change
> the station.
>   Kristin said she used to hate oldies but now that she's old (she is 27),
> she likes them [. . .]

Desirée [the girl who threw paint and learned to multiply decimals] said she didn't like the Beatles.

"Oh, sacrilege!" said Kristin, joking. "How could you *not like* the Beatles!" [...]

Kristin said she remembered where she was when John Lennon died.

I said I did too, and asked Desirée if she knew who he was.

She didn't [...]

Kristin tried to get Desirée to sing, when Desirée started humming along to the music.

Desirée politely declined.

After a while, Desirée asked again if she could change the station.

Kristin said, "Not while Aretha's on! She's great—the queen of soul!"

After Desiree left that afternoon, Kristin said that this whole conversation showed that Desirée really was a good kid, and Kristin said she felt good about having made the "connection." This was a bit puzzling to me, since Desirée had not said anything except what is quoted above.

As adults often said, *what* people said to each other did not matter as much as the fact that they were saying *something*, creating a tie—even if all Desirée said was "can we change the station?" For the purpose of building a bridge, the topic of gift wrap was just as good as any other building block. The kind of familiarity that Kristin was hoping to initiate would, however, have taken months to cultivate. Martin Luther King Day organizer Sheila, for example, told me that she was proud when Marisol said more than two words at once to her, after they had been meeting weekly for over six months.

These conversations were not like the comfortable, wandering chitchat and joking in Emily's program. When volunteers and sick children achieved a conversation, or Linda and Isaac bonded over a love of birthdays, organizers hoped that the very fact of speaking would help bring a bond into existence. The exchange of words in these organizations signaled that participants managed to pull off a conversation. Ironically, the result was a conversation that rarely made anyone comfortable; at the wire-mesh table at Chippewa, it could not be about the uncle's jail term or probation, which made the organizer uncomfortable, and could not be about happy, upbeat things, which made the girls uncomfortable.

CONCLUSION: PHATIC TALK

In Empowerment Projects, some participants and adult organizers learned that they were not quite the same underneath, and they simultaneously learned how to hide that knowledge. Participants had to learn how to use their knowledge of inequality while not talking about it. They learned to pretend to be living in the moment, where they could all momentarily be equal. They learned that we all like pizza. They learned to value the friendly chatter on its own terms without expecting it to lead to any intense future bonding; not to expect to make friends with the strangers, but just to trim their temporal horizons and feel comfortable with them. They learned to treat each interaction as if it had limitless future potential, and to accept that this potential would perpetually recede beyond the future's horizon. The lesson might sound unbearably empty, unbearably damaging to young people's sense of security, and unbearably undermining of Emily's heroic devotion. But it had a silver lining.

"Metallic wrapping paper or tissue paper?" "Aretha or the Beatles?" "Nice weather," "Skippy or Jif?" "Phatic" talk is the term for talk that is simply done in order to build an interpersonal bridge with words.[5] Such seemingly empty talk does important work, as any neighbor who says "Hello, looks like rain," or anyone whose teacher or boss did *not* say "hello" in the hallway can attest. The absent greeting can ruin one's day. When put to financial use, it can become the "warm chatter" that Mary Kay Cosmetics salespeople learn in training sessions.[6] But as elements of pure sociability, comments about the weather can continue for years and can be a fine basis of a friendly but distant relationship. Organizers and funders may have wanted something deeper, more "real" and "authentic," in their frequent words, but learning to make small talk is a crucial skill in any society. Learning how to do it with people who are very unlike oneself, and learning not to expect any deep connection ever to develop, is especially important in an unstable work world, with fast and temporary relationships between diverse, unequal people.

There was, then, a useful civics lesson here—the silver lining, lining the empty interior. A slightly cool, respectfully distant politeness that does not dredge up gut feelings or unify people in tight, hot, passionate bonds may be healthy for civic life.[7] When civic associations invoke metaphors of "family" and "tight-knit grassroots community," the result can be fanaticism and an inability to entertain discord, because such intense attachments—of family, local ethnic culture, or religion—are hard to put up for debate. One scholar's example is the former Yugoslavia where loyalties were too deep, old, and intense for diverse peoples to get along. On those terms, Snowy Prairie program participants were learning a good civics lesson in cool, respectful distance. These lessons were supposed to, but did not, harmonize quickly and effortlessly with the intimacy that Empowerment Projects aimed to provide.

PART THREE

Celebrating Our Diverse, Multicultural Community

An elected county official visited the county-funded Regional YEP. She exclaimed to me, while standing on the sidelines of a meeting: "What I really like about the Regional YEP is the diversity!"

I agree, nodding and smiling with genuine enthusiasm, but not wanting to talk loudly while the meeting is going on.

She continues, "It's diverse, not only by Snowy Prairie versus suburban communities, but also ethnically diverse! Just look around!"

If this were not available for her to say, what would there be to say? "I like it because it does a lot?" But it doesn't—they haven't done anything yet this year [since September, when the school year started, and it was now December]. Would she say, "I like it because there are a lot of kids?" But there aren't. What does this language do?

The Regional Youth Engagement Project's racial diversity was one of its crowning achievements—every visiting government administrator or NGO officer I met at a meeting remarked upon it favorably, and it was always very important in public events for visibly diverse youth to represent the youth programs, so that the audience could quickly see the group's diversity. The youth workers needed a working, practical definition of "diversity," to know what to appreciate, what to correct, and what to ignore.

"Culture" and "diversity" are used so often in the United States, they seem to mean everything and nothing. To understand what the mantra "celebrating our diverse, multicultural community" means, we have to hear what the phrase does, in action: precisely at what moments do people use these words? In reference to what people or activities?

Just to be clear at the outset: "celebrating cultural diversity" in Snowy Prairie did not require learning about any specific cultures. Learning about a culture would be too time-consuming. It might require learning history, customs, and manners, perhaps a set of prayers or a language for saying them. A culture is often too upsetting to be happily "celebrated." People sometimes want to embrace parts of their culture and shed the rest. *Furthermore, making distinctions between categories of people was taboo, but necessary in organizations that needed to promote diversity—people needed to know which differences to count as contributing to diversity. They had to know not to respond to a question about whether a group was "diverse" by saying, as my eleven-year-old said when I asked him about his funk band, "yes, because it had a saxophone player, a clarinet, and a flute."*

According to Rob Strauss, the well-read director of the county Youth Department, dreary bureaucrats of the past almost crushed America's colorful diversity, when they tried to make Italian immigrants eat Anglo-American food—beef and beans.[116] Haunted by America's near loss of garlic, today's Empowerment Projects demanded cultural diversity, but it had to be easy to see, taste, and hear, quickly, so it could be put on display to the multiple, distant, hurried audiences.

Since celebrating our diverse multicultural community could not mean highlighting and learning about deep, important differences, the question for this section will not be "what is multicultural diversity?" but "what did the act of naming something 'multicultural' or 'diverse' accomplish in these Empowerment Projects?"

"Getting Out of Your Box" versus "Preserving a Culture": Two Opposed Ways of "Appreciating Cultural Diversity"

THE CALL TO "celebrate cultural diversity" sounded different to different ears: For many adults and teens (especially white, native-English-speaking, non-poor, from a generally Christian upbringing), it was a call to be tolerant, curious, and brave, to mix with others, not "stay in your box." It was, above all, an invitation to discover that there *are* other cultures. Organizers at a lunchtime meeting of organizers were discussing diversity:

> Erin, the Regional YEP organizer for the year, was very excited about starting groups and classes about "ethnic diversity." They [the teens] *want* to learn.
>
> Rob Strauss, county director of youth programs: We saw that on our feedback forms. And it's kids from smaller communities, who are almost universally white.
>
> Erin: It's something we *have* to do, for the kids. They're asking for it!
>
> Nina: That's so cool.
>
> Erin: Yes, it really is.
>
> Later that meeting:
>
> Erin: I really believe that the only way we'll promote peace is to get kids out of their little communities. Kids in New Stockholm stay there with kids from there and don't really get to *interact with* kids from other communities, and don't learn about different cultures and different ways of living.

In contrast, for some organizers and participants in minority youth programs, the call for "diversity" meant *separating* from others momentarily, or teaching things that are hard to learn or that take time: teaching the Spanish-speaking teenagers good Spanish spelling and grammar, for example, or giving them a break from their long day's immersion in the English language, or giving black youth a chance to be together without having to feel as if they were under constant scrutiny as representatives of all blacks.

Two categories of people; two nearly opposite projects—the one aimed at *mixing* and dipping into lots of cultures but not spending a very long time in any one of them; the other aimed at *separating* and devoting a long time to learning details of a single culture. They sometimes worked at odds with each other.

In Snowy Prairie, the people who were the most committed to "diversity" were the members of the first category—the ones who were proud that they had voluntarily chosen to escape their all-white towns, to get "out of their boxes," when they moved to Snowy Prairie. The more they appreciated diversity, the more they wanted *everyone* to get out of their boxes. "Getting out of your box" to learn about others can be done publicly and is easy to communicate quickly.

Learning a language, or learning about a culture, in contrast, takes a long time. Since members had only a finite amount of time together, they could not learn much about each others' languages or customs. So the "protectors"—those who wanted to protect a specific culture that was hard to describe quickly—had to hide from the "mixers" who wanted to celebrate cultural diversity in a different, opposite way. The mixers' project fit Empowerment Projects' ideals and time lines; the protectors usually did not.

These two groups' agendas were not just different, but conflicted with one another. Thus: *The biggest promoters of "diversity" were usually the least interested in preserving distinct cultures.*

GETTING OUT OF YOUR BOX

At a midday meeting of mainly white, native English-speaking organizers, "diversity" meant "mixing with others":

> Rob, the government official in charge of youth programs, says that a new person, Cristina, is "starting a Hispanic Youth group." She had some association with a peace group in another state.
>
> Sheila, this year's adult organizer of Martin Luther King Day: Good, because that was the group (Latinos) that was not adequately represented at Peace Begins at Home Day.
>
> Rob: Well, there you have it. But they really want to focus on their *own community*. We'd have to encourage this new person, Cristina, to go broader, rather than ethnically specific. She wants to look out for her own, so we'll have to frame it as something that will benefit her kids. She'll want to know, "Will my kids will get something out of this?"
>
> Erin: They will! It's called *diversity!!*

Later, there is another disparaging reference to "Casa's focus on 'ethnically specific' projects'." So, what *these* (white, English-speaking) youth workers meant by diversity was inclusion and tolerance, leaving differences aside, uniting. As they often said, when encouraging young people to think up civic projects together, "You all face common problems as youth." They were annoyed with Cristina, not because they were against diversity, but exactly the opposite: they said that Cristina was *missing the point* about "diversity"! In this way, the word "diversity" absorbed different, sometimes almost opposite, meanings in different contexts.

Similarly, in a workshop for parents and teachers of preschoolers, on the topic of cultural sensitivity, taught by some of NOYO's most active members, a workshop leader brought up "language," saying that it is

> another whole concept that preschool kids might just *not have*. It's hard to tell a kid that someone isn't "talking funny" [as in a scenario that the teacher had given us, in which kids were saying that another toddler "talked funny" because he spoke to his parents in Chinese] when they don't have the concept of different languages.

> A parent of a young child said that it's easy to explain "language," because you can just point to cats and dogs and birds and say, when they want food, they say, "Meow, or woof, or tweet." When you want food, you say something else.

The preschooler who spoke Chinese to his parents did not need to be told that "other languages" exist; for him, it was obvious. He knew that English was one language among others, the same way that non-Christian Americans know about Christmas. Leaving aside the question of whether comparing non-English to barking and meowing is the best tack, the example tacitly shows whom the youth workers and parents had in mind when discussing "cultural diversity": The call to discover that different languages exist was aimed at children who routinely heard only one language.[1]

Getting Out of the Box as a Way of Becoming a Real Person

Many organizers had come to Snowy Prairie to escape small towns in the vast rural Midwest. Their relatives still lived in bleak, windswept, impoverished farm towns, wanting nothing more than to escape. Organizers from these backgrounds described those little towns as stifling, boring, and narrow. They had been brave enough to bust out and discover other cultures. For them, "getting out of their box" finally allowed them to breathe; it was synonymous with "becoming an individual." They were curious and rebellious, and treasured this spirit in themselves; this rebel spirit had been strong enough to propel their escape from the small town's comfortable "box." They "knew there was more to life," as they put it; they wanted something more cosmopolitan, edgy, and colorful. Organizers like these wanted to respect cultural traditions, but their own experience of escaping their little boxes told them that culture had to be a choice, and they wanted people to be able to participate in a variety of cultures.

These formerly rural adults' approach fit perfectly with Empowerment Talk. For example, in a discussion in the twelve-week youth workers' course, on how to appreciate cultural differences, my subgroup circled around and around to the idea that, as one member put it, "each person is unique, you can't tell just by looking. It's just what the teacher said: just because I'm white doesn't mean I'm a certain kind of person."

> "Yes," a suburban youth worker of northern European descent agreed, "like people in my small town, my town had 200 people in it. There are people there who've just never left and think that's all there is. And I'm the one who left, who went away. They can't imagine why I would have ever wanted to leave."
>
> Janet [another participant of European descent]: People who stay in their own little culture are like that little square on the carpet (a little metal outlet cover in the wall-to-wall carpet): they don't know anything else, they're afraid to leave their little square.

It may look as if they were members of a "dominant" culture,[2] but they did not feel that way; they felt that their route to survival was through rebellion against their culture. They were curious about blacks and Latinos, but did not expect blacks and Latinos to be as curious about their families' lives on icy, hardscrabble farms. Ironically, by rejecting their rural roots, and calling their small villages "little boxes," people like the women in my subgroup were part of a vast American rural exodus that is decimating rural America.[3] By *not* naming that rural way of life a form of "diversity" that deserved protection, and fleeing it, perhaps they were helping to end that way of life.

PRESERVING A DIFFERENCE

A very different approach to "celebrating diversity" appeared in some of Casa Latina's programs, which aimed to "promote Latino culture," as the central organization's brochure put it. In practice, in most of the ten Casa Latina-sponsored after-school programs, that did not mean much more than circulating Spanish translations of English-language children's books when it was reading time, and speaking in Spanglish. One month at Nan's Casa Latina program, for example, she circulated Spanish translations of *The Lion, the Witch and the Wardrobe*, *Winnie-the-Pooh*, and *If You Give a Mouse a Cookie* (the last two are also available in chewable vinyl for toddlers), since the eleven- to fifteen-year-olds' homework included fifteen minutes of daily reading, and Nan was trying to accommodate all levels of literacy.

While Nan did not try to teach participants about Latin American literature, organizers of some other Casa Latina after-school programs did. Laura, for example, said, in the twelve-week certificate course, that she tried to "empower the Latino community and preserve Latino culture." Lane, the other Casa Latina organizer in the certificate class, added that teaching good Spanish was important. Laura and Lane wanted these students to become fluent and literate in Spanish rather than half-Spanish, half-English "Spanglish."

To teach literacy, Laura staged a relay race that her middle schoolers found fun (I was amazed, but they really did): she would put a sentence in Spanish on the blackboard, and two kids would dash to the board, competing to correct the accent marks and the spelling ("sí" versus "si," "qué" versus "que," for example), throw the chalk to the next kid, who would dash to the board, and so on. Another day, she photocopied a poem by Pablo Neruda, and another day they read a short story from Spain; another day she photocopied a funny questionnaire about autos and air pollution in Mexico. To Laura, diversity did *not* just mean seeing how we are all the same and busting out of a box. It also meant working hard to preserve a difference, and learning a body of knowledge—about spelling, for example—that not everyone could or should share for all languages.

Puzzles of Preserving a Difference

At first glance, Laura's approach may seem more authentically appreciative of cultural diversity, but it presented some puzzles, too. First, it required freezing "your culture" more solidly than participants usually did in the course of a day. As noted in the Introduction, a teen like Veronica, at Community House, called herself Native American sometimes, Mexican at other times, American at others, and black at others; all were true, depending on the question and the context, on whether she was comparing herself to Euro-Americans, lighter-skinned Mexicans, people from other countries, or whites. Another girl at Community House was Puerto Rican sometimes, Latina at others, Black at others, and American at others, and again, all were true. What counted as "your culture" varied in the course of a day, depending on the comparison in that situation.

Second, there is, of course, no such thing as "Latin American culture," any more than there could be one culture for any other whole continent. Delving into the differences between the rural Guatemalan girl and the tall, sophisticated boy from Buenos Aires in Laura's group would have left one or two people in each category. If power comes partly from unity, dividing people into such small categories would not "empower" Latinos as a group.

Third, emphasizing the Spanish language and Latin American history did not help recent immigrants who did not speak Spanish but were having similar *experiences* to the Latin American immigrants'. A recent immigrant from Gambia, who spoke only Wolof, gave a touching speech at the annual Casa Latina dance, saying that Nan's Casa Latina program—the one that was partly in English—"saved his life" when he first arrived in the United States. That could not have happened at Laura's program, which was conducted entirely in Spanish. There, he would have felt just as foreign as he felt during the school day.

Puzzles of Breaking Out of Your Box

"Getting out of your box" emerged victorious as the most widely accepted approach. It was hard to disagree with, for reasons that will soon become clearer. Once, though, after some time spent listening to many enthusiastic participants in the twelve-week youth workers' course agree about the importance of getting out of your box, Isaac, the pock-marked, black program organizer who grew up in the rural South in the 1950s, suggested:

> At the same time, I know some black kids who won't talk to white adults. Period. They're afraid of white people. I know of kids like that. Because they had an uncle who was lynched by the KKK, a brother who was killed by the police, a grandfather who was murdered. I understand where they're coming from. They don't want to talk to any white person.

He thought that for them, distrustfully staying in their boxes was a matter of survival, learned after years of repetition, hard to unlearn, and *possibly still very useful*.

The whites with whom he was talking, who had fled their stifling rural villages, nodded sympathetically, but they were too busy arguing with their own ghosts to take Isaac's ghost very seriously. They quickly translated his statement into their own terms, switching back to the "people there who've never left" their stifling hometown, who "can't imagine why I would have ever wanted to leave," reinforcing their own urgent distinction between "staying in your box" versus "getting out of it so that we can really just treat each other as individuals."

CONCLUSION: BOTH APPROACHES MADE SENSE, BUT NOT TOGETHER

While both approaches to cultural diversity make good sense, they invite opposite action. The winning team's approach aimed to "break down walls." A big banner across Chippewa Middle School's entrance announced an art exhibit called "Cruzando fronteras/crossing borders." This made sense to white, middle-class people, who were curious about other people's lives. On the other hand, instead of "breaking down walls" and "getting out of their boxes," Laura's Casa Latina group required momentarily building walls up, creating an emotionally "safe space"[4] after a school day's immersion in Snowy Prairie's mostly white, Midwestern culture. Not everyone wants to exert the effort to learn another language and culture, and no matter how many languages one includes, *someone's* language will always be excluded.

The process of discovering "the other" can feel painful, coerced, and inescapable, or it can feel like a breath of fresh air, voluntarily satisfying curiosity, depending on the relationships between you and your "other." W. E. B. DuBois, writing in 1903, describes the harsh inner imagined white voice that tormented him as an African American, and the demand of "always having to see oneself through the eyes of the other." If, however, the inner "other" is not always so scornful, then learning to see oneself through the eyes of varied, plural "others" can be one of the prime sources of joy and wisdom in life, as Jane Addams, John Dewey, and their fellow reformers in 1920s Chicago made so clear.[5] These differences in degree and kind—forced or voluntary, constant or intermittent, in self-defense or out of curiosity, joyous or painful—made "celebrating our diverse, multicultural community" mean different things to the two different categories of people. In Empowerment Projects, anyone who wanted to preserve a culture had to *hide* from the proponents of diversity.

Why, in Empowerment Projects, did getting out of your box almost always sound more persuasive than creating a hidden, safe space? An obvious, but sloppy, explanation would be that the majority, or the "dominant culture"—the whites like the women from rural farms in this chapter—had the power to control the definition. That explanation is too simple. Rather, as the next chapter shows, navigating the crisscrossed missions of Empowerment Projects made it hard for participants to define "diversity" in any other way.

CHAPTER 11

Tell Us about Your Culture: What Participants Count as "Culture"

How did the approach that celebrated "breaking out of boxes" emerge as the usual practical meaning of "celebrating diversity"? To grasp this "how," we have to observe how naming something "diversity" worked in everyday conversations in Empowerment Projects. At each step in this naming process, puzzles arose, resulting in uncertainty about whether or not anyone could count *anything* as "diversity" or "culture." This chapter focuses on face-to-face conversational gambits—moves people made to categorize things as "cultural diversity."

I can call my *own* habit a sign of my "cultural diversity" to honor it or to bid you to refrain from judging it. Doing this required figuring out how to separate out "my culture" from "my own personal idiosyncrasy," and how to separate out the aspects of my culture that I deemed worth preserving from the unworthy elements. I may know, for example, that parts of my culture are sexist or non-inclusive, not empowering enough to sit comfortably in an Empowerment Project. I may not like parts of my culture. Doing all of this hair-splitting made almost everything that I could publicly count as "my culture" feel ambiguous and like a set of options, rather than a solid, safe home space.

I could call *your* puzzling habit "your culture" in order to refrain from judging it. White mainstream Snowy Prairians made this move often. The problem was that honoring all differences as "diversity" made it hard to see that some kinds of "diversity" were symptoms of inhumane conditions that were worth *changing*, not preserving, if, to continue the example just given, I saw that your black family feared white people in the rural south, and I called that fear "your culture" when you thought that mistrusting the KKK was a simple, rational calculation.

Hearing *me* name *your* habits "culture" or "diversity worth celebrating" could make you feel honored, but it could end up angering or embarrassing you, as well. You may not feel knowledgeable enough about this culture to stand up in public as a competent representative of it. It might take too long to explain important parts of it. Or I might be honoring an element of your culture that you detest and from which you have tried to "break free"—its folkloric lack of technology, its dogmatic religion, fear of outsiders, or sexism, for example.

To make your culture acceptable in these semi-civic Empowerment Projects, you had to purify it, to make it easy for viewers to grasp quickly. In the end, only visible differences could be displayed quickly, easily, and palatably enough, and the conclusion *had to be* that they did not matter. This lesson may sound like an empty cheer to appreciate "whatever" without understanding it. It may also sound internally contradictory, asking people to celebrate difference while pretending it does not exist. However, it was not simply as empty and contradictory as it may sound—though it did not do what organizers hoped.

"Excuse me for being different; it's my culture." Naming my own personal trait "my culture"

Calling my own personal habit part of my *own* "culture" could transform what may initially have felt like an odd idiosyncrasy into something honorable. In a presentation to youth workers and parents on "cultural sensitivity," Donna Yoshida-Dahlgren, a Japanese American social worker, invited the class to discuss ways of distinguishing between "cultural" and "personal." A youth worker said that her own mother was "warm," since she was American, while her father was "cold," since he was British:

> Donna paused for a long time [I thought she was going to say that the image of the stoic Brit was a stereotype. But something different happened]. She said that there are individual and family and cultural differences, and sometimes it's hard to distinguish between them.

> "Like I had a thing about gift-giving and thought I was just weird [a long story about how nervous gift exchanges made her]. But then I read this book about fourth generation Japanese Americans, and there was a whole chapter about gifts and (motioning turning the pages) I find myself in it! I found out that what I was doing around gifts was *cultural*—and I thought I was just being *weird*!"

The very act of naming the trait "cultural" revalued it. Naming it "cultural" not "personal" made its moral worthiness grow, in her eyes. This was Empowerment Projects' ideal use of "culture." Now we will see several converging currents that made this ideal hard to reach.

I Excuse You; It's Your "Culture": A Cultural Difference Worth Preserving or a Symptom of Horrifying Circumstances Worth Changing?

Calling someone *else's* habit "their culture" was often a way of refraining from criticizing it, even if it seemed irrational. This made it hard to distinguish between "cherished customs worth preserving" versus "rational, reasonable responses to horrible circumstances that should be changed." Both were honored with the name "culture." The result could confuse people.

For example, before she got her paid organizer job, Sheila worked as an unpaid volunteer at a park in a disadvantaged neighborhood. Trying to be respectful, she attributed the neighbors' puzzling behavior to "their culture":

> Sheila: The continuity is not there, it's never the same kids from one week to the next. The first week was mostly little kids, the next week it was a lot of older kids and some little kids, some of their brothers and sisters. One time it was almost all boys, but last time there were no boys . . .
>
> NE: How in the world do you do it? It must be so hard to think of what to do!
>
> Sheila: We have no expectations! Each time is not standing on its own; there's no continuity. So, this time, Joe Smeal from Vietnam Vets (an anti-war group) is coming to talk about war and what it's like . . . but he won't say anything that you needed to be there last time to understand. And then they'll maybe make some Vietnamese food, that some kids might like, and we'll paint the banners that kids made last time. But who knows if it'll be any of the same kids who made the banners!!"
>
> NE: Why do you think they're like that—coming just once like that?
>
> Sheila: *It's their culture*, the way their family life runs. Nothing is really stable in their lives; it's all run by what the parents are doing or what the older brother or sister who's taking care of the kid is doing. Life is chaos for these kids. I used to work in the day care there and sometimes an African American or Hmong family would just pull their kid out and move on without any warning, just say one day, "We're going to stay with relatives in another state," and that would be the end, with no time for the kid to have any kind of good-bye to the other kids or the teachers. We'd be like, "Oh, we've just cared for this child for the last year and now what do we do?"

Sheila was using the word "culture" as a gentle way of saying that even though it hurt her feelings when the families disappeared with hardly a good-bye, she was trying hard not to blame them. Calling it all "culture" was a way of avoiding judgment, but the word sounded so honorable, it made poverty hard to discuss or even to notice. Families moved often, needed to grab a free dinner, running all day; parents let older siblings bear too much responsibility for younger ones: Sheila quietly and patiently *observed* all of these difficulties of life in poverty. She *observed* more than the word "culture" allowed her to express. In an Empowerment Project, "celebrating diversity" and "ameliorating conditions" are both important missions. Naming it all "culture" made it hard for her to distinguish between what she would want to celebrate and what she would want to transform.

Don't Insult Me by Assuming I Need an Excuse: What You Just Called "My Culture," I Call "a Rational Response to My Dire Circumstances"

Naming differences in habits "culture" thus often insulted the people whose differences were being called "cultural," when they themselves considered their actions to be reasonable responses to horrific conditions—of, say, poverty or racism. For example, the twelve-week certificate course had two weeks on the theme of "appreciating cultural differences," during which those who had grown up in relatively comfortable, non-dangerous, stable conditions kept inadvertently offending those who had grown up in unstable or terrifying conditions. The two sets could not agree on what to count as "your culture"; people in the first category kept naming your fear (of lynchings, for example) as part of "your culture," while people in the second set wanted their fears to be seen as simply reasonable, not mysterious cultural quirks.

Let us go back to the discussion about "family culture" in the certificate program, as an example. The discussion started off agreeably, when the teacher asked participants to name some things that their families did together. People chimed in:

- "Seasonally appropriate holiday centerpieces" like three-dimensional fold-up paper accordion turkeys for Thanksgiving
- 3D fold-up accordion hearts and window dressings for Valentine's Day, too
- holly for Christmas
- baking our birthday cakes one way rather than another
- loving to go fishing
- even watching our favorite TV shows as a family together
- the way my dad would sit in the armchair, watching TV and drinking a beer

On this note, we divided up into subgroups. As described earlier, I was in a subgroup with Isaac, who had to defend his family's strict rules about walking straight home from school to avoid violence. The understated argument that we started in our subgroup continued when the whole class reconvened. The teacher posed more questions about what he called our "family cultures." One was, "Did your family live in constant fear and anxiety?" The teacher considered that an example of family culture, along with 3D turkeys.

Putting the question this way insulted Isaac. He asked the class (first mumbling, then aloud): "Is this about your 'family *culture*' or about your *community*, growing up in South Carolina in the 1940s and '50s?" The workshop instructor answered by reasserting what he had said at the beginning: fear is an element of a "family's culture." Isaac clearly considered the fear to be a rational response to dire circumstances, not a "culture" to cherish and celebrate.

Sometimes, new immigrants appreciated attention to something that organizers called "their cultures." Proudly, a very recent immigrant from Guatemala showed me a mural at her middle school's entryway. A nonprofit had partnered with the school, paying an artist to empower students to paint the mural. Proudly pointing to the section she had painted, she told me that it helped people learn about her "*culture*," since, she said, it showed her village's lack of running water, paved streets, and electricity. This practical definition of the word "culture" treated "the hardship" as if it were synonymous with "the culture." The word blurred a distinction that this girl, like Sheila and Isaac, may have needed to make: While she may not have wanted to forget the hardship, she may not have cherished it as something worth "celebrating," either.

PURIFICATION OF CULTURES

*Your Culture Might Be Too Sexist, Hierarchical, Not Open Enough,
Not Empowering Enough*

To be presentable in the civic arena, cultures had to be purified, because many elements of traditional cultures are incompatible with Empowerment Talk. Empowerment Talk puts "egalitarian and open" in the same breath with "cultural diversity," but not all cultures are participatory and open enough to fit. In fact, hardly any are. People had to perform careful surgery on their cultures before displaying them in Empowerment Projects. The only elements of anyone's culture considered worth celebrating ended up being those that matched the Empowerment Programs' culture.

For example, an evening forum on "youth and media" featured a speech by a local newscaster, Mai Jou, originally from Singapore. In the sea of mainly white faces and blonde heads, she stood for diversity. Discussion so far had revolved around two axes: lamenting that media are undermining traditional cultures, and asserting the importance of really deeply "listening and communicating": two key Empowerment Project missions.

> Most of Mai Jou's speech was about the same thing the others were about: "listening and communicating" was the refrain. But in her informal unprepared comments [after she stopped reading from prepared notes but was still at the microphone], she said, "My parents are wonderful people, and I—but I was born in Singapore, and the culture there is very much 'kids are not to be listened to; they're to be raised.' So I must have gotten it from somewhere else. I had wonderful teachers, a drama coach, wonderful people all along the way, and I'm thankful for that."

> But here's Mai Jou saying her culture wasn't about "listening and communicating" and yet it was ok. Or else she's ok because she left her culture!

Preserving traditional cultures did not mean upholding *those* aspects of traditions—those that did not value "listening and communicating." Mai Jou had to leave her family's culture behind. Publicly naming any specific trait as your "culture" could easily make it feel like a conscious choice. Mai's speech and Donna Yoshida-Dahlgren's soliloquy shared this nervous, temporary, ambivalent flavor; once you publicly named it your "culture," it became available for public scrutiny—*including your own scrutiny*—and started to look more like a personal choice that you should detach from yourself, rationally inspect, and could easily choose to discard.

The purification process had a silver lining, even if it seemed to strip cultures of everything that makes them different from one another. To see this silver lining, we can now go sit in rows of little molded plastic desk-chair combinations, in a classroom where a librarian is conducting a workshop in the optional yearly training event for volunteers. The topic is "Multicultural Literature," but after a short discussion, the audience still is unsure what to count as "multicultural." The librarian clarifies.

> Just make sure that once you find a book, it's ok. Just because it has images of multicultural kids doesn't mean it's a good book. Some of us might remember *Little Black Sambo*[1] from our own childhood: today, if we looked at it, we would see that *Little Black Sambo* is not giving kids a good image of themselves.

> An audience member asked her again how you could tell what counted as multicultural or "'authentic-ity,' or whatever you called it."

> The librarian began by saying that it is not easy, but quickly resorted to saying, "You have to go with your gut feelings. If you're reading along

and it makes you uncomfortable, go with your gut. You know the kids and what they like. Go with your gut."

The librarian could only repeat, "Go with your gut," because organizers who were trying to change your culture, community, or feelings had to do so in the name of your culture, community, and gut feelings. But certain gut feelings are not consonant with Empowerment Talk.

The librarian had to stop short of saying it, but what she was aiming for was not just for them to value all gut feelings, but possibly something better: to engage in civic-minded self-questioning, to doubt their feelings, to feel some "civic *dis*comfort."[2] Restringing "the string of the self,"[3] dropping some beads and reconnecting others, precisely distinguishing between "my culture" versus "my unique personality," might not always be a happy celebration, and certainly cannot be done quickly and publicly. At best, appreciating one's own "cultural diversity" required a very delicate procedure: the person who fondly remembered sitting on grandpa's lap reading *Little Black Sambo* had to uproot the warm memory of the storybook while leaving the lap intact.

Discomfort with Ignorance about the Culture That One Was Supposed to Possess But Did Not Know Very Well or At All

It was easier to feel sure about celebrating *someone else's* culture than to say what your *own* was. Organizers considered certain participants' cultures colorful and folkloric, but many participants did not, and most often, ridiculed organizers' folkloric idea of "their culture." For example, an organizer of one of the Casa Latina after-school programs, Nan, announced to her middle schoolers, "There's going to be an International Fiesta on April 2. Anyone who has things from their countries can bring them to the exposition: blankets, artisanal things, flags." One new immigrant joked about bringing his miniature Pemex (the national Mexican oil company) truck, saying it was his favorite toy when he was little. Another boy slyly said he could bring used wrappers from the Mexico City McDonalds where he used to love to eat. Cultural diversity was a vague cloud of a term, but everyone knew that Nan had not meant Pemex and McDonalds. At another event in a rural bar, an organizer told me that she hid guitars, sombreros, and words in Spanish for a hide-and-seek game. It was supposed to make Latinos feel welcome. This type of cultural cleansing sometimes made people nervous, but often just made them laugh at the irony.

Constantly being asked "Where are you from?" by adults who would not know the difference between one place and any other place, some participants gave answers like: "Yo soy de Chinga-tango-landia," which would mean "I'm from 'Fuck-you-tango-landia.'" Another participant introduced himself to volunteers as "Antonio Banderas" (this was when he was a soccer star, not yet a Hollywood star, so white Americans tended not know about him). This always got a big laugh from fellow participants, since the adult volunteers did not get the jokes.

Even when participants did want to display their cultures, many did not know much about them, so being asked to represent their culture and celebrate it made them nervous.[4] For example, organizers often tried to appreciate Latino teens' culture by asking them to speak Spanish, but some Latino teens did not know much Spanish:

> Erin [organizer, at an evening "multicultural dance celebration"]: What a beautiful dress! What did you say it's for—what's that thing you celebrate when you turn sixteen?
>
> Marisol: It's for my "quinceañara."
>
> Erin: I have to learn that word! Say it again!
>
> Marisol (pronouncing each syllable very clearly): Quinc-e-añar-a.
>
> Marisol's sister, Bonita: "You *idiot*! You don't know what you're talking about: it's quinceañera" ["-era," not "-ara"].
>
> And Bonita still doesn't bother to correct Erin: it's for when you turn fifteen, not sixteen [Erin had probably collapsed it, in her head, with the American "sweet sixteen" party].
>
> [Marisol did not talk for the rest of the evening.]

Instead of fulfilling Empowerment Talk's promises of comfort and familiarity, "celebrating diversity" could also deliver shame and discomfort.

A Solution: All the Same! "Let You Be 'You' and Me Be 'Me'"

The most common approach was to make all cultures sound the same. For example, in a city near Snowy Prairie, four parents, each representing a different "culture," with a translator when needed, gave a presentation about diversity in schools. A professionally dressed mom from Mexico City said, in beautiful, newscaster-perfect Spanish (that is, a relatively elite accent, I assumed):

> Our culture has been formed through generations, based on religious and spiritual values, where the most important is the family. My children are sensitive, friendly, active, and responsible. They're growing up with the same values I was raised with: respect to family and others. The most important things we want for our children in this community

are respect, equality, and feeling like they're on the same team, feeling effective together. We also want them to feel that they can also accomplish this within the Latino community.

All the parents in the audience nodded in appreciation, happy to learn that Mexicans value exactly the same things that other Americans value. This could be important to state publicly, since there were so many other, possibly insulting uses of the word "culture," as the story about the families who moved too often showed. The problem is that publicly and quickly describing such purified cultures made them all sound identical, all worthy on the same scale, for the same reasons.[5]

Viewing cultural diversity quickly, from a distance, summarizing them abstractly, risked repeating stereotypes, like the certificate workshop teacher saying that a hypothetical Latino man, in an educational vignette, had problems because of his "fatalistic Hispanic culture." Discussing a hypothetical Cambodian teenager, the teacher informed us that Cambodian families "value conformity." To use this bit of information, an effective youth worker would need to know how, if at all, they went about "valuing conformity" in everyday practice.

The puzzle was that noticing differences that are not just uniquely, idiosyncratically individual means categorizing people, and categorizing people can easily sound like stereotyping, so noticing any serious *cultural* differences was almost always taboo. In Donna's workshop on appreciating diversity, for example, a parent tentatively suggested that categorizing people was natural, saying that since her preschool-age daughter did it with birds and trees, why shouldn't she do it with people? I took the mom's question to mean that people think by using categories like cat vs. dog, pine vs. maple, hot vs. cold, up, down, tall, short, thin, fat, dark, light, etc. For Donna, the idea of categorizing people instantly set off alarms:

No, it's learned. It's environmental. They learn from their environment to think that different = bad, that blacks are inferior. They learn that.

[This was the first unequivocal thing she said the whole workshop—mostly she said, "That's a good question or ooh, that's hard, or what do you think."]

The mom: I mean, maybe kids are just looking for ways that things are different. Maybe that's how they learn, by putting things in categories.

Donna: Oh, I thought you were asking a different question, about how they learn that difference is bad.

Immediately, Donna returned to her original point, telling another story about teachers who discipline black kids for doing things that would not get white kids in trouble. She could not let herself focus on the mom's question.

Similarly, in the workshop on Multicultural Literature, held for adult volunteers, the librarian held up picture books showing "diverse" children. One book was peppered with Spanish words that English speakers would recognize—"burrito" and "piñata"—showing a girl with straight black hair having fun putting pitted black olives on the ends her fingers. The librarian said she liked this book because it did not "directly *say* that it was about diversity, but just showed *this girl* doing things that *all* children like." It showed, in other words, that no matter how different people may appear, they are the same underneath.

> Lots of posters at Community House like "It doesn't matter what is the color of your skin but the content of your character" (an indirect quote from Martin Luther King), and "Blue purple green, all the same underneath."

The point of all the posters was not that *individuals* are identical, but that no group-level, *category* differences matter, and it is only individual differences that matter.

In the two sessions on appreciating cultural diversity during the twelve-week certificate course for youth workers, we kept circling back to this theme of "being unique":

> The instructor: Even though I'm a white male American, my culture is completely different from any other white, male American. If I were a black male American, my culture would be completely different from any other black, male American.

Another white participant said, "We need to get beyond our own culture. Just because you see black doesn't mean you know anything, just because you see white doesn't mean you know anything about that person's culture."

A black participant complained that people see him and immediately assume that he likes rap music. Janet, a white participant, exclaimed, "I would *never* think that! I would love to just be 'me' and for you to just be 'you' and then everything will be all right."

In everyday conversation, then, celebrating diversity meant celebrating individuality and breaking out of your box, not celebrating cultural differences and preserving varied boxes. Several currents converged: in an Empowerment Project's time frame, there was not enough time for people to disentangle the differences they wanted to keep from differences that they rejected, either as symptoms of poverty or as stereotypes, or as overly confining or oppressive.[6] Rapidly and publicly describing and celebrating any complicated or disturbing differences was just too hard.

OTHER TRAITS THAT MIGHT PLAUSIBLY BE CALLED "CULTURAL DIFFERENCES" OR "DIVERSITY"

To round out our examination of everyday uses of the words "culture," "diversity," and "multiculturalism," we now can inventory some plausible definitions that did *not* fly in the Empowerment Projects.

Socio-Linguistic Differences: Not Noticed as "Cultural Diversity"

There is a form of diversity that might be called "cultural" but no one in the youth programs ever did: different judgments of what to consider polite, how fast to talk, how direct or deferential to be, how much or little to talk, how effusive or calm to sound, how much to tease and how much to praise, how much silence is acceptable. If, as some social scientists[7] have documented, these differences often fall along racial, ethnic, class, and linguistic lines, then here were *cultural* differences that caused conflict in the Empowerment Projects but went unrecognized. Celebrating them was nearly impossible.

In the twelve-week certificate class, a tall, sandy-blonde Midwestern organizer, Neil Norgaard,[8] described a troubling conversation he overheard between two teens in his program. He described some ways that he could have intervened, saying that whatever he said, he would bring it up *"without mentioning it directly."* He kept repeating that he would be indirect and then summarized with the punchline, "I *always* prefer to be indirect." Everyone laughed, because it was so obviously true, not just about Neil, but about many of the region's natives.[9]

Stylistic differences like these were topics of heated discussion, but were not named as "cultural difference." For example, in one meeting, organizers were talking about Sara Cantor, a member who was not there yet, saying that she "offended all the people" with whom she worked, because she was "loud" and "in your face," and "talked too much." They said—indirectly, of course, since they were like Neil—that her offensive behavior made it hard for her to get anything done.

> We were talking about how to pay for the food at the convention center, which usually had very expensive food, but had made an exception for them the year before:
>
> Sheila Lundgren [another soft-spoken, tall, blonde midwesterner]: They had done it for two years, but then Sara Cantor called and told

them to do it again, and they said no more donated space, so, I don't know, maybe it was the *tone*.

Rob Strauss: Tell them they gave it to you in the past, it's what they do.

Sheila: I mean, they got calls from three people, David Gustavssen, Sara Cantor, and me, and I don't know, somehow they changed their mind [when they talked to Sara].

Rob: Maybe it was the tone of one of the people who called (in other words, Sara's).

When Sara Cantor finally arrived, I saw that she did, indeed, wave her arms around and speak more quickly, emphatically, and directly than the others. Janet's words to describe "people from the East Coast" could have fit: "hyper and aggressive" and "in your face."[10] I had heard similar complaints about other women, who were also called "warm" and "energetic"—so it was not an unequivocally negative evaluation. Both times, I silently guessed they were Jewish, before having met them or gotten any cues other than the judgments from people like Neil, and in both cases, I was right. Perhaps my accurate guessing was just based on stereotypes, or perhaps the accuracy was pure coincidence. In any case, nobody asked the *question* of whether or not this linguist pattern was a form of cultural diversity (to celebrate). Instead, they took it as a personal defect.

Asking the question would have caused two problems: first, it would have risked evoking stereotypes, as already noted—"pushy Jews," for example. A second, more perplexing problem was that it would have shown that celebrating diversity is hard. The differences that caused anger here were not about values and ideas, but posture, vocal tone, and speed, microseconds between speakers, and gestures. Violations like these feel like visceral insults. Learning to change these intense, implicit feelings is like learning to play an instrument or to speak and understand a new language, skills one learns partly through theory and grammar, but mainly through practice. No one could have enough time to learn that for all of a program's participants, if they came from more than one culture.

The Secret Intuition . . . or Was It an Unjust Stereotype?

After many years of experience, many long-term organizers saw that different people had different styles of communication, but their jokes about this had an illicit tone, as if it were taboo to say that different interactional styles tended to fall along ethnic or racial lines. Members of the Community House Board of Directors—many of them former social workers who probably were the "Emily's" of their day—sometimes slyly, surreptitiously joked about such differences:

> They joked about one applicant for the position of program leader, when Emily was leaving the job; the director [who was white] said that this applicant was just "too white" for the teens, and we all knew what that meant, having seen overly nice, white volunteers try to get close to the teens. The term "too white" certainly is not about her race, since Emily is also white and all but two of the Directors were, too [and the directors were looking for someone who would be as good as we all thought Emily was]; rather, it was about her way of doing things. She was too culturally white.

When the director said that the applicant was "too white," she laughed, and the rest of us did, too. Many of us had seen those sweet white lady volunteers. We had also seen white youth volunteers often looked on in abject incomprehension, such as at one Youth Service Night, when quiet white youth volunteers from rural areas watched open-mouthed and aghast, while black volunteers teased and joked, yelling sexual innuendoes and friendly insults.[11] Was this crude stereotyping, or was it hard-won, practical knowledge about cultural diversity? The director was not saying that *every* white lady was sure to be a sweet pushover, but that it was *likely*, and so it was worth the effort to make sure that any particular white woman whom they hired was not in the middle of the curve. These elderly, long-term organizers and volunteers could not make their intuition public without sounding like they were stereotyping people, but they drew on it when choosing the new employee. These kinds of sociolinguistic difference remained almost impossible to speak about publicly.

Failed Bids at Classifying a Habit as "My Culture (Worth Appreciating)"

Since calling my habit "my culture" could positively reframe the habit as honorable, people sometimes tried to persuade others that their own habits were "cultural." The instructor of the twelve-week certificate course, for example, passionately described his own upbringing as working-class "white trash culture," citing its icons: "Hank Williams, trailer parks, fold-up lawn chairs on Astroturf, Pabst Blue Ribbon Beer, Kool-Aid," and more. He spat out this list angrily, resentfully, as an argument, because, he said, nobody ever counts it as "a culture." He told resentful stories of getting teased for his shabby clothes and aluminum fold-up chairs with yellow plastic webbing.

He wanted it to be named a "culture" so that people would respect him for having surmounted difficulties. The teacher's anger really made me think. Since he was white, his suffering was not visible on his skin: it was class—not color. It must be frustrating to be oppressed in a way that requires so much explanation, and that might be seen as your own fault or your parents' fault. It was hard to tell whether or not the teacher's gambit worked, because no one responded, and that, too, must have been frustrating.

Sometimes, it was clear that a speaker stretched the meaning of the word "diversity" too far and no one was convinced. In the certificate course, Janet made a bid for taking fat oppression as a kind of diversity. Her bid failed. It came after some black participants had been saying that they had not *chosen* to be black, so people should not assume that their skin color said anything about their identity. Janet slipped in a story about not having *chosen* to be big. She told of being a member in a support group, "the Outsized Club."

> "I'm six feet tall! I'm big! You might not think it's much, or enough, if you look at me, but I lost over 100 pounds! [. . .] I had to deal with being just big, and it wasn't a choice!"

> [later] Janet is regretting that she revealed her experience in the "Outsized" club, saying, "After I said that, I felt, gulp, what are they gonna think? But it's *not a choice*—I can't *help* it that I'm six feet tall! It's not like I ate *truckloads of food*! But still, even now, whenever I'm with a man who's shorter or smaller than me, all those feelings come out.[12]

Following each of the three times that she brought up the topics of height and weight that day, someone immediately changed the topic.

The teacher's and Janet's hope was that counting trailer-trash customs, or tallness and fatness, as "diversity" would help them gain recognition for a hardship.[13] In doing so, they confront a problem we saw earlier: Should we cherish it, or should we overcome it? She told us she had tried to lose the weight, was ostracized by fellow members of her "Outsized Club," and then gained it back anyway. She contrasted this with gang membership, the day's earlier topic; Janet reminded us that we had called gang membership "a choice," and therefore, something for which gang members should be held accountable (this is, parenthetically, not quite true when the alternative is getting beat up, or thrown out of one's home by a cousin who is in a gang). Her plight, she said in contrast, was "not a choice." Choice, not choice: Here, again, we see Empowerment Projects' tightly knotted grip of tensions surrounding the idea of "choice."

Blindly accepting categories and boundaries was considered rigid and unempowering. Your culture could be celebrated only if you did what Mai Jou did: choose pieces of your culture that empowered you, and leave the rest behind, or just leave it all behind. Such subtle feelings and troubling choices are too personal to describe quickly in public; as Janet eloquently put it, "I felt, gulp, what are they gonna think?" So, all that was left to celebrate was differences that were definitely not chosen: skin color, ancestry, height. And then the conclusion, in Empowerment Projects, had to be that those differences are not too hard to disentangle from other differences, only skin-deep and *unimportant*. The call to celebrate diversity becomes simply a call to overcome inequality, by ignoring it.

CONCLUSION: MAKING CULTURAL DIVERSITY QUICKLY AVAILABLE TO ALL

Empowerment Talk promotes two opposed ideals: on the one hand, to celebrate traditions, cultures, and local roots, and on the other hand, to innovate, experiment, cross borders, break out of boxes, make personalized, optional, temporary, and voluntary connections. Swallowing this mixture seems effortless enough, until we hear Mai speaking as a representative of diversity but having to reject her family in order to become empowered and egalitarian, or when we hear Isaac sounding insulted when someone calls his family's fear of being lynched an element of his family's "culture," or when we hear how hard it is to notice any differences that might be hard to change or leave behind, or that might make people really . . . different.

The terms "culture" and "diversity" had to be not just vague, but empty; if everyone is unique, no one but the person him- or herself could know what to count as his or her own culture. Like other aspects of Empowerment Projects, diversity had to be "open and undefined" and "up to you to decide 'whatever'." This defused potentially explosive differences: participants had to speak as if all differences were equally different and equally valuable.

Participants nonetheless had to act *as if* there were cultural differences that were deeper, but people in these organizations could not go delving into any ancient or darker complexities. Doing so would require dredging up too much ambivalence, it would be too personal and possibly painful. When Mai Jou said that she left her culture, it would have been hard for her to state publicly, clearly, and quickly whether she had wrenched herself away, or fled happily; whether she still retained traces of it, like Donna did with her nervousness about gift-giving; whether there were traces that she wanted to preserve but could not; or whether there were traces that she wanted to abandon but could not. Saying any of this would have required admitting that people's pasts can be hard to value and also hard to leave behind. Smoothing away one's difficult past, by pasting a big smile on it, could mean smoothing away one's self. Explaining why these pieces of selves are still worth understanding would require making ambivalence like Mai Jou's public—not happily "celebrating" it with a big smile, but respecting it. Isaac's family's strictness might not be cause for celebration, but the fact that it helped him stay alive could elicit respect—again, not a big happy celebration with an unequivocal smile. It is hard to imagine anyone wanting to turn themselves inside out in front of people and publicly expose this torn selfhood this way, and even if someone had wanted to do so, listening to a stranger's internal dialogue would probably exhaust any public's patience. It would certainly take more time than any Empowerment Project has. And so, for all the talk about appreciating differences, it was nearly impossible to appreciate or notice any differences that mattered to people.

There is, again, a silver lining: At best, the organizational use of the phrases culture and diversity were methods of avoiding passing judgment. To continue this attitude, participants could learn that appreciating diversity means that people of different backgrounds should expect *not to know much* about each other's cultures. They could even learn to consider misunderstandings expectable and acceptable, or even to welcome opportunities to learn about each other. They could learn to suspend judgment, to assume that they *would* judge all the diverse cultures to be "okay" *if* they spent the time learning about them, even though doing so was impossible in the busy Empowerment Projects. People did not learn about each other's cultures or appreciate them, but at best, judgments about other people's morals or habits kept moving ahead, into a perpetually receding horizon of future potential when you might theoretically learn more about the other person's culture.

Making one's *own* culture public had a similar silver lining: publicizing it tamed it. Nobody seemed quite sure what to count as "their own" but, at best, people scrutinized their feelings and categorized them as cultural or personal, never feeling completely certain that the classifications were correct. Sometimes, a person who could explicitly name something from their "own culture" could gain distance from it, make it an object—something external to oneself, that one could question, and decide to keep or to abandon. At their best, Empowerment Projects' celebration of cultural diversity meant exposing roots, if there were any, to the air; replacing roots and security and certainty with doubts and questions.

CHAPTER 12

Celebrating . . . Empowerment Projects!

"COME CELEBRATE OUR DIVERSE, MULTICULTURAL COMMUNITY!" Flyers advertising big public events in Snowy Prairie almost always included a line like that, and Empowerment Projects sponsored most of them. How could people publicly celebrate diversity if they could not describe the cultures they were celebrating, could not celebrate disturbing or puzzling differences, and frowned upon making distinctions between people anyway? What *did* these events celebrate?

In the dusty shade of a giant circus tent, about two dozen groups that sponsored Snowy Prairie's Juneteenth[1] celebration this year are distributing pamphlets, selling knick-knacks, and talking to the seventy or so passers-by under the big top. The sponsors include:

> Americans with Disabilities Coalition, National Association of the Mentally Ill, a pro-life group, a pro-choice group, Urban League, Black Labor Coalition, Rainbow Family Center, Hospice Care, AIDS Network, Snowy Prairie Area Anti-Drug Coalition, Tech-State University, another nearby State University, Snowy Prairie Technical College, the Boys and Girls Club, John Deere Corporation (makes tractors), Asthma Awareness Society, an alternative radio station, Casa Latina, YMCA, Legal Services, Tenants Resources Center, Snowy Prairie Area Peace Coalition (advocating an end to the war against Iraq, but also with a sign at the side of the table saying "Reparations Now!" referring to the movement demanding that blacks be repaid for the labor they performed while slaves or while underpaid workers).

> Also, you can buy handmade, locally produced soap made with African ingredients (like shea butter), other African American hair and skin products (the table is educational, because there is a sign reminding us that the first African American millionaire made her fortune selling such things), super-expensive African drums, batik fabric, and some second-hand housewares; these goods "say" "we are not corporate products, support your local community, support black businesses."

This odd assortment was typical: social service agencies, activist groups, health maintenance organizations, hospitals, the U.S. military, a local tractor factory, a local factory whose main product was spray-on cheese in a can, ethnicity-based businesses, educational institutions, and many,

many Empowerment Projects had literature tables at these events. The jumbles seemed initially jarring to me, but after attending a few of these events, I knew what to expect. It even made sense: these events inadvertently celebrated Empowerment Projects and the temporary, fast-moving, optional choices they offer. This chapter shows that the *form* of these celebrations perfectly echoed the Empowerment Projects' *form*.

Among all the tents at this day's Juneteenth celebration was a gospel tent, whose music had to be loud, since a lot of the other nearby tents also had music:

> The gospel singing is mesmerizing, even though there is a very loud drum sound coming from another exhibition tent that sells Africa paraphernalia, which fills up the silences in the gospel singing. There is the dramatic pause right before the climax, when the singer takes her final breath before the final long note. The atmosphere here is confirmed when Reverend Blanchard murmurs "Amen" and "hmm" in testimony. The Holy Spirit is in the tent.

The spirit was there. Before the singer's long final note faded into air, loud drumming from the tent next door filled the sacred silence. The gospel tent's walls were thin plastic sheets. Everyone could hear what was happening on all the stages at once; each performance threatened to drown out the others. In addition to these two stages was a third area, for a contemplative poetry reading, a fourth area for art projects involving glitter and glue for children, and a fifth for checking one's blood pressure and learning the signs of stroke, and more.

The event's form perfectly embodied Empowerment Projects, with their bewildering, over-stimulating inclusivity, with people milling around from all walks of life, with no center stage, no limit to the number or kinds of performances, foods, or activities. People freely milled in and out of whatever activity they selected for the moment. Focus was hard. Staying in one place was unnecessary.

About once a month, Snowy Prairie's youth civic engagement programs held a public event like this, to "celebrate our diverse, multicultural community," through holidays that are new, or new to most Americans—Cinco de Mayo, Chinese New Year, Día de los muertos, Juneteenth, Kwanzaa, Martin Luther King Day, and Cesar Chavez Day. These events always included literature tables that offered information on topics such as legal aid to families of prisoners and applications for reduced-cost home heating.

A prison rights project might not look like a very festive thing to celebrate, and is not the kind of "diversity" that anyone would *happily* celebrate. On the other hand, however lacking in glitter, color, imagination, and beauty they are, semi-bureaucratic complex organizations like

Empowerment Projects are where most of us spend most days. Here stalks the bureaucrat's ghost again, trying to hide and yet showing his face, despite organizers' best intentions. Here again, we find a silver lining to all the dizzying, attention disorder-inducing rush and noise: Americans fear, loath, and need complex organizations; these events inadvertently celebrated them.[2]

This chapter shows how it happened that organizations that set out to celebrate cultural diversity ended up celebrating Empowerment Projects. The first section shows that they celebrated "good things in general done by people of color," with the goal of boosting minorities' self-esteem and providing good role models, which was thought to lead to higher grades. This goal could not be said aloud without appearing disrespectful, but it was obvious, since nothing else glued the events together. The next section shows how hard it was to separate celebrating culture from celebrating religion, and the subsequent section shows how easy it was inadvertently to celebrate corporations. The result of all these subtractions, additions, and blends was a celebration of Empowerment Projects.

Your Culture Is a Prevention Program for At-Risk Youth

Celebrating . . . People of Color Who Have Done Things!

It may seem that in order to celebrate differences, it would be necessary to recognize their existence. However, it was taboo to recognize differences between different *categories* of people, as shown in the previous chapter; only individual uniqueness could be celebrated. Part of these events' goal was to fight inequality, to help the needy—not by celebrating their "difference" but by helping them overcome it. This mix of missions sometimes made it impossible for participants even to name the object they were celebrating! For example:

What Should We Call This Float?

Community House is going to enter a float in a parade for Juneteenth. It's going to be a pickup truck decorated with posters of "diverse" people. Sheila [the adult organizer of the Martin Luther King planning group that year] got photos for the posters off the Web of great—well, of great *what*? That was her question, and we couldn't say.

She asked, "What should we call this float? 'Great Americans who have served'?"

I said, "Well, that doesn't really fit Marion Anderson (an African American opera singer from a long time ago).

She said it sort of did, "She served people by singing so beautifully."

Marisol: "They're all role models." She said this twice, at different times. She was sure this was how they all fit together.

Emily, the Community House organizer, said, "It's 'I AM GREAT WEEK' at the summer program, so the 'role models' idea could fit with that."

Someone said "Famous African Americans"?

Sheila kept ruminating: "*Great* African-Americans? But it's not just that. Some of them aren't African Americans."

I said, "How about 'Great Americans'?"

"But," said Marisol, "Cesar Chavez isn't American, is he?"

I asked, "He's not??"

Sheila said, "Oh, no, he doesn't live here, does he? So we can't use 'Great Americans'." She keeps puzzling, "Americans who have done service?"

Bonita said, "Americans who have changed history." "People who have changed our lives."

Later, when we were away from the kids, Sheila said to me, "It's an African American *holiday*, but not all the people in the program are African American and not all the posters are, so, I don't know."

She had also brought the Dalai Lama and Mother Teresa [already included were Martin Luther King and Rosa Parks, of course]. Also Langston Hughes, but she did not know why he was famous [he was a poet and leader of the Harlem Renaissance in the 1920s]; and also there was Fanny Lou Hamer, a civil rights movement leader whose name had gotten cut off in the middle, so the poster just had her as "Fanny Lou" and no one noticed the problem; also W. E. B. DuBois, a social theorist and activist, but no one knew what he had done, either. There was no mention of why we did not know these people's names.

In the end, no one could think up a name for the Juneteenth float. Deciding which differences to highlight would require asking why we lumped together all these different "non-white people who did good things." We would have had to say that categories matter, and that some categories of people need more help than others. As we saw in the previous chapter, this approach to "diversity" made it hard to distinguish between differences that they wanted to preserve and celebrate, versus differences they wanted to abolish (like inequality). There were many similarly

confusing incidents, highlighting unexpected triumphs without mentioning the adversity over which they triumphed.

*Everyone knew, more or less, what sorts of people would fit on the
float, even though no one could provide any criteria.* One could not understand the float without knowing what held those people together.
People had to know how to use categories without talking about them.
This was a predictable organizational style in the youth programs. We
knew, and Sheila said to me later, that the goal was to give young people
"good role models" of people who were ethnically and racially like them
in some way. At another Juneteenth celebration, there were presentations,
saying, for example, that it was a black man who invented the fold-up
ironing board (making me wonder how proud it made young blacks to
know that fact). The problem was one we have seen earlier: this could
turn "your culture" into another prevention program, a means to an end.
It could be insulting.

When adults were discussing a series of multicultural dance performances—hip-hop, Mexican, generalized "Latino," African, drill teams,
and swing—everyone laughed when someone mentioned Norwegian folk
dance. Everyone laughed because organizers were not worried about
Norwegian Americans, and did not feel a need to raise Norwegian Americans' self-esteem by admiring their culture. It would be impossible, in this
context, to say why Mexican dances were more multicultural than Norwegian ones, but in everyday conversation, people drew the line between
categories that needed protection and those that did not.

Many of the region's farmers were of Nordic descent, and, as most
organizers knew, and repeated in a very surprised tone, each time they
repeated it, rural whites suffer ghastly rates of alcoholism, drug abuse,
spouse abuse, underemployment, and poverty. Their problem, however,
was not discrimination; their problem was just that they were poor, and
our society accepts large "differences" between rich and poor. We do not
call this difference "diversity," as the "trailer trash" teacher's lament made
clear. We just accept it as a difference not worth celebrating.

Celebrating . . . the Prevention of Statistically Predictable Risks!

These public events blended "diversity," poverty, and disease; the three
routinely went together often enough to be an obviously recognizable
trio. Celebrations of multicultural diversity usually took place in poor
neighborhoods, disseminating information about the illnesses that tended
to afflict people in the neighborhood. For example, one Juneteenth was a
scorching day.

> I am blinking in the bright sunlight, walking out from the cool shade of
> the "information tent," where the National Association for the Mentally

Ill and the other organizations have set up their literature tables. A strikingly beautiful teenage girl with golden skin and long, wavy black hair comes running over to me, with an air of urgency.

I wonder, "Do I know her? Why was she looking for me?" But no, she gives me a slip of bright red paper asking, "Do You Recognize the Signs of a Stroke??" She says that if I have any more questions, I can go over to the Health Tent. I say thanks and start reading the palm-sized sheet, befuddled. Now I'm wondering, "Do I look like I am about to have a stroke? Why did she run over to me? Let's see what the signs are: "Paralyzed side (and a picture of someone with a drooping mouth)?" (I wiggle both sides of my mouth) "No, not that," I reassure myself. "Confused (another picture, of someone with arrows swirling around their head)?" "Well, no more than usual."

Meanwhile, I see that she has run over to someone else who really does not look too healthy. Then I notice the giant stack in her hand. She is just giving these flyers out to all and sundry. In the Health Tent, you can get your blood pressure taken, your blood sugar tested, and more.

Distinguishing people on the basis of statistically predictable diseases may seem degrading and clumsy, but Empowerment Projects have to show that they help the needy by making them take responsibility for their problems. Since Americans do not have free health care, that means telling them how to take care of themselves. At every event like this, one could pick up pages upon pages of advice about diseases. The advice sheets usually ended with suggestions about when to see your doctor, but many people at these events had no doctor. That was part of why they needed to read all the advice, although not all knew how to read, either, and a person who actually was suffering a stroke would need a doctor, not a generic, do-it-yourself diagnosis.

At most public celebrations of diversity, legal aid activists also distributed information about how to avoid eviction. A sharp contrast between the legal and medical advice is instructive: here were two very different ways of resolving Empowerment Projects' typical tensions: in contrast to the do-it-yourself medical advice that came with only vague, inexpensive means of fulfilling it, the eviction information came with an offer of free, expert help from lawyers.

This jumble became predictable and normal; celebrating "multicultural diversity" meant celebrating the self-help that poor people were supposed to employ, to dodge illnesses in the face of precarious or absent medical care: through exercise, avoidance of tobacco, moderate alcohol consumption, fewer trans fats, and more servings of fresh fruits and vegetables per day. This is good advice, but when the overt agenda is a "celebration of your culture," the combination could make culture seem to be a prevention program.

Southeast Asian Recognition Event: A Valiant but Hopeless Effort at Explaining a Culture and a History

On a public scale, these events did what the personal conversations described in the last chapter did on a more intimate scale: they made it possible to avoid mentioning poverty and deprivation, while simultaneously recognizing their impact. Organizers hoped to show respect for people's hardships, without publicly trumpeting their deprivations. The "Southeast Asian Recognition Event," for example, gave awards to minority children who had been in "Regular School Attendance." Nobody mentioned why these (non-white) children were considered "at-risk," or who was doing the expecting. No one mentioned any connection between "Southeast Asian" and the unspoken prediction of school failure. And no one mentioned that the families at these events were mostly not Southeast Asian, but black and Latino—everything but white (except for three elderly church volunteers).

All this slithering between "celebrating cultural diversity" and implicitly acknowledging poverty had the effect of knotting minorities' "cultures" together with scientific, statistical, predictions of school failure:

> In a little bungalow-shaped church, out in a neighborhood on the "other" side of the interstate, near where the hidden slum was, amidst tiny, one-story houses, each with two windows and one door in the front, loud dogs, funny lawn ornaments, pickup trucks bigger than the houses, no sidewalks; behind the Lucky Limerick bar.

> Dan Lindmeier, a white school administrator, opens the event: I'm from the School District, and we want to congratulate you for setting a goal for yourselves, of being in Regular Attendance at school. We *know* that students who are in Regular School Attendance get better grades and score higher on standardized tests than students who are not in Regular School Attendance.

Making specific students' school records public is against the law, so this was not about predictions based on the "at-risk" status of these *specific* students—though no one mentioned how this conspicuously non-white crowd *had* been selected. Maybe the mere fact that their parents were black, Latino, or Hmong was enough to classify them as "at-risk."[3] I could not imagine how six-year-olds managed to skip school on frigid winter days, and wondered if the event was aimed at congratulating their mothers for making sure their children just got on the school bus.

After the school administrator's speech came a long lesson about Hmong culture, driving home to me just how hard it would be to describe a foreign culture in a snappy, short presentation. The lesson was impossible to follow. First, a Hmong immigrant gave us a fifteen-minute history, including an indecipherable story about "the war." Even though I already knew this tragic story of betrayal and exile,[4] I still could not follow his rendition of it, and started to wonder after a while if perhaps he was talking about some other war, in the more ancient past.

Another Hmong speaker told us about what she called "Hmong mating rituals," making joke after joke about the "sexism" in the ceremonies. Next, a spindly old man stood hunched over, alone in front of the rows of folding tables, demonstrating how to play a Hmong flute and shuffling along the floor. He said it was a dance that was done "at New Years," to comfort a family when someone died (did that mean that all the year's deaths were commemorated at the year's end, on New Year's Day?)

The master of ceremonies had the floor next:

> She said that New Year's used to be eight days and now it's three. There would be a march to the temple (what temple? Was there only one? Is the Hmong area that small?). She also said that New Year's is to celebrate the Hmong victory over the Chinese in the war and their long struggle. Neither Paul [my husband, who had come, too] nor I were sure what war she meant, nor could we figure out how New Year's was related to a war (could it be that Hmong people didn't have a New Year's celebration till the Viet Nam war?). We were really actually *trying* to listen, and we're pretty used to lectures.

Meanwhile, the black, Latino, and Asian moms were successfully managing to keep their tired six-year-olds quiet, sitting still for the whole two and a half hours (they would get home long past the bedtimes that Snowy Prairie schoolteachers recommended for a school night).

For the final act, eight girls performed a very slow "traditional Hmong dance," which was mesmerizing to the old white church ladies who were sitting behind me, but boring to the children in the audience, who became more and more fidgety.

> Finally, the dancing girls snapped into a rap/hip-hop music-and-dance routine. "If you wanna be with me . . . you better impress me." These little pre-teen girls, the same ones who had earlier worn these "traditional" outfits with pink beadwork and beaded fringed hats, now were wearing tight jeans and skin-tight shirts, stroking their hands up and down their sides and then moving their hands to the front, as if they were offering up a luscious tray of fruits Gauguin-style, but they didn't quite have the fruits yet . . . The eight- and nine-year-old black boys in

front of us started cracking up and dancing in their seats, as if they were mocking being at a rock concert, or watching MTV. The black moms in the audience started clapping along.

Finally, at 9 p.m., dinner began. It was "multicultural potluck," with many pots of Hmong food, including mercifully clear instructions about which sauce to put on what.

This event, more than any other I attended, made a valiant attempt to teach non-Hmong people about a foreign culture, but I could not follow most of the lesson. When using Hmong flutes to boost school attendance, organizers may have been taking a page from some current, controversial research which says that if immigrant youth stay loyally attached to their cultures, it can prevent them from dropping out; elders, churches, traditions, and families might keep them from a life of crime and poverty.[5] We just did not learn anything about Hmong culture, except that it was very foreign.

Youth Nazi Day: "Open and Undefined Up to You to Decide 'Whatever'?" Or "Changing the Culture of Death?"

In a mid-day NOYO meeting about producing a new Youth Activities Calendar, an organizer asked what to screen out. Rob Strauss, the regional director of youth programs, said that anyone should be able to put any event that they considered "a youth event" on the calendar. The organizers should not be in the position of "censoring," he said.

> But by the end of the meeting, he was convinced that there was a problem. Joking, he demanded: "Do we advertise Youth Nazi Day? Lick-an-Alien Day?" [making up names for events that he would not allow on the calendar]

> The group never arrived at a principle. But de facto, there were principles determining what counted as a "a youth event."

The question of "how to screen" arose a few times during that meeting. At first, participants rallied around a principle of being "open to any group that doesn't exclude anyone," thinking that that would rule out things like Youth Nazi Day. But then we realized that that would not work, either, because we thought that certain kinds of exclusion would be okay: for purely local, neighborhood-based groups, school-based groups, all-girl groups, skill-based groups like dance and music groups, and groups that had an age limit. Still, we kept coming back to the principle of being tolerant and open to everyone, and so we never finally agreed that exclusion was sometimes acceptable. In addition, organizers considered certain groups to be too racist or exclusive or unempowering to fit. They had to make judgments about what to include, but could not say what the judgment was. We just left the topic without deciding anything.

Though organizers were not supposed to judge, they did. An organizer from a black church told the NOYO about his church's program that would teach ballroom dance, etiquette, elegant dress, and makeup to young African American women. He said it would be like a cotillion ball, and they could dress up. Many wincing or quizzical faces led him to explain: it could teach them to respect and take care of their bodies, to be modest and to stand tall, and learn proper, lady-like manners—with only slight irony, he said that the body is a temple and people should not be showing everything to everyone. Faces relaxed and the workshop became part of the calendar.

Some organizers judged pop music's celebration of consumption, random sex, and violence. They called it "the culture of death," but they were not supposed to judge it. However, long-term organizers like Emily saw that just "open and undefined" did not suffice. She fairly directly told participants what they *should* want. So, as mentioned earlier, she offered a prize for participants who could "list forty rap songs with 'positive lyrics'"—songs that did not feature rape, drugs, or guns.

NOT CELEBRATING . . . RELIGION!

Empowerment Projects' public celebrations had to separate "cultural diversity" from "religious diversity." This was as hard as the precise surgical extraction that we saw in the previous chapter, when people delicately had to detach "culture" from both individual personality and social oppression.

In these semi-government organizations, it would be illegal to sponsor one religion or culture over another, but organizers did not think it would be right or fair, anyway, so the legal issue never arose. Several times, however, an African American musical group referred to Jesus in an Empowerment Project–sponsored celebration. Organizers quickly tried to fix the problem:

> Christian rap duo, Good Vibes: We're here to fulfill the dream of Martin Luther King and of Jesus Christ. In John: 17, he had a dream . . . " [Then came some other speakers, musicians and skits.] The program ended with the Christian rappers and break dancers. During the Christian rap songs, most of the white, non-disadvantaged members of the Regional YEP sat, while everyone else was summoned to step up to what began to seem like an altar—conversion, holy roller, baptism-style, to come up and be blessed. "You are blessed," one of the rappers said.

Some of the white, suburban YEP members were offended, and they said so on the evaluation forms that they filled out at the end of the day. Afterward, adults read the forms, and discussed them at a lunchtime meeting.

> They said that a lot of kids were turned off by the references to God and religion that Good Vibes had in its performance.
>
> Erin, grimacing ironically: Yeah, there's always gonna be *some* [that is, complainers who criticize everything].
>
> Rob: *Were they told* [that is, were the performers told not to sing about Jesus]?
>
> Sheila: It's in a lot of their performances. They could just take them out.

With all the amputations, not much of the body remained. It is hard to imagine separating culture from religion, but that was what organizers had to do when they celebrated African American culture.

It was also hard to slice away the Christian parts of Martin Luther King. Speakers at Martin Luther King Day echoed the idea reprinted on our pens and placemats, quoted here in chapter 1: that to serve others, we do not need to know about Plato and Aristotle but only a heart full of grace and a soul generated by love. This message sounds like one of Empowerment Projects' recurrent puzzles, between working to *change* people's conditions versus recognizing that we are all deeply the same underneath *regardless of* conditions. Christianity has its own ways of resolving this puzzle. If the quote had been given in a black church, most members would know that it was about recognizing that we are always more than our social conditions; that the sacred individual cannot be destroyed by worldly conditions, but is somehow always morally whole, morally worthy, despite it all.[6] Stripped of its sacred resonance, the message had to find resolution here without reference to any invisible, transcendent holiness inherent in all humans. Given in a black church, the message would have been about self-respect for the congregation as a whole: we should respect one another, and ourselves, despite our conditions.[7] The message shed meaningfulness as it traveled across races in this mixed-race crowd.

References to non-Christian religions probably slipped into events without too many people's noticing. For example, probably some aspects of the Hmong celebration were religious, depending on what one counts as "religion" versus "culture," but I did not know the references, and probably none of the rest of the non-Hmong audience did, either. In cases of complete ignorance, no one could be offended, because people did not recognize the religious references.

What surprised me in this overwhelmingly Christian part of the country, though, was how many organizers missed references to Christianity, as well. When a boy in the Gardens of Hope environmental education program referred to the Garden of Gethsemene, David, the organizer—the white guy in blonde dreadlocks—said, "What?"

James repeated, "The Garden of Gethsemene—you know."

David bent down, patiently and sweetly asking him if that was a garden in his hometown, in Alabama, where the boy lived during the school year. James informed David that it was "from the teachings of Jesus."

Sometimes, speakers seemed not to recognize what was specific to Christianity that other religions might not share. At one Martin Luther King Day event, a black lay pastor[8] offered a prayer—a personal, spontaneously invented prayer, which is already something that only certain religions do:[9]

URBAN LEAGUE BREAKFAST, 2001

A prayer:
   To all those who believe in God,
   whatever your way of praying to Jesus is [my emphasis],
   we will now pray:
   Oh, Lord,
   We ask you for guidance in little things,
   like saying "excuse me," and "thank you . . ."
   We stumble through life, trying to be good, but
   not always knowing how to be good citizens,
   not always knowing how to be good parents—
   how to be good.
   Whether we are parents, or teachers, or social workers,
   whether we serve in the mayor's office,
   the school board, or even the prison system,
   Oh, Lord,
   we ask you to teach us how to be who we are,
   how to be what we are,
   how to be together.

He was trying to confer respect upon all religions, but had not imagined that some religions actually have *no* way of worshipping Jesus. This prayer was unusual; usually, when a speech mentioned any one religion, it breezed through as many possible objects of worship as possible—Buddha, Mohammed, and "our Judeo-Christian heritage." Since that was hard to do, they were usually all excluded.

The usual way to resolve the tension between respecting diversity and avoiding religion was to dilute any religious messages until they all sounded the same.[10] At one NOYO meeting, a woman from an evangelical mega-church said she wanted more of a connection between the NOYO and her church youth group.

Church representative: There's a guy Rich Gibbs who puts on an event, where he gets kids from different youth groups to perform and church pastors: Our church has a group, and I know Mt. Zion does gospel, and kids really get into that (does a gospel-looking motion). And kids go, "Yay, we'll get to perform," and they really get a chance to see other kids from other communities (she describes a guy who organizes this event as "speaking as a church within the body of Christ. I think this event is really great."

Bing: bring 20–25 copies to the next meeting.

Church representative: Copies of what?

Bing: An info sheet.

Rob (uncharacteristically suspiciously): And what church is he with?

Church representative: He's just an independent, spiritual person who has a special [I expected to hear "calling" but didn't] *place* in his heart for kids.

Erin: What about kids who don't belong to church?? I'm always concerned that everyone is included.

Church representative: I think he'll have ways of transcending that—I'm sure he has ways of bringing them all together. This transcends youth group, church group, whatever. I think it's a lot about information, about just getting information.

Miriam, leader of a program like Community House: The goal is to create a community so they can get to know each other.

Deciding what to count as "diversity worth celebrating" is hard enough for a person to do alone, internally, as Donna's or Mai's internal dialogues with themselves suggested in the last chapter. When it is part of a public show, it is even harder, and could easily become offensive, when all cultures must be treated as if they are, deep down, underneath it all, identical. A city near Snowy Prairie got a grant for a visiting artist to teach classes in the local elementary school; in them, students designed personal "emblems" to represent their "cultures." People found the results to be so inspirational, a public gallery put them on display for months. Each emblem combined some of the following:

leprechauns and shamrocks (Irish), fleurs de lis (French), lots of spaghetti (Italian), other ethnic cuisines, European flags, baseballs, tennis shoes, lots of soccer balls ("I put in two soccer balls because my dad plays soccer and I do not see my dad" read the caption), dogs ("because I want a dog," the caption read), cats, crosses ("I chose to put a cross in the middle because I am Christian"), stars of David, light ("which represents my Quaker background," read the caption), skateboards, math symbols, bananas ("because I like them"), the sky ("so it would look cool" the caption read), fast cars, a Swastika ("because my mother is from Germany," said the caption!), coins, flames, dragons ("because in Vietnam, the dragon is like the strongest god"), the color blue ("because it's my mom's favorite color"), red, white, green, black, a leaf.

Putting a soccer ball and a cross in the same emblem, or even putting all these emblems' items in the same exhibit, might seem sacrilegious to a person who does not consider bananas, fast cars, swastikas, and sneakers to be equivalents. Glib multiculturalism blended together the stereotypic (the leprechauns and spaghetti), idiosyncratic (the bananas), commercial (the fast cars), national (flags), natural and/or spiritual (sky, mountain), hateful (swastika), and sacred (the crosses and stars).

Competent participants had to develop thick skins, not getting offended when their religion's most sacred symbols appeared on the same emblem with sneakers, spaghetti, or bananas, not getting perturbed when they heard their lord's name being taken in vain. Learning not to be ruffled when crosses and bananas are treated as equal symbols might be an excellent message, one that could help diverse people get along without necessarily having to learn anything about each others' religions or cultures. But it is not exactly what organizers had in mind when they proposed "celebrating diversity."

The public celebrations usually just blended everything together in one oceanic blur. At one event, one of the vendors, with a booth alongside the usual set of vendors and nonprofits, was selling jewelry that included random religious symbols, coins, and typewriter keys. This event featured folk dances from around the world. I arrived late, and Erin greeted me by rolling her eyes and saying, "It's bo-o-o-oring." I asked her which dance we were watching and she said it was the Israeli dance. In fact, it was the Italian dance. Did it matter that she mixed them all up? *No, of course not.* It would be considered nitpicking even to point that out, and that is my point: my even asking the question shows that my brain was on overdrive. The results were equal opportunity offenses to all traditions: de facto, the displays demanded an attitude of flexible acceptance.

A spectacular example of this jumbling was a performance by a dance troupe, "Peace is a Circle." This troupe performed widely, and its signature dance was spellbinding:

A circle dance, but an oddly populated one: hopping Irish dancers in plaid skirts and "bodies of ice," wiggling African dancers, "Aztec" dancers with giant feathered headdresses, elegant classical dancers from India, and more, *all dancing together*. The speaker said, "They are all one." And she is right: if you play enough drums simultaneously, the sounds all blur together into one continuous beat. But then, why bother to separate them?

The varied drumbeats blurred into one steady hum. Putting them all in the same dance is like putting a Tchaikovsky ballet, a Palm Sunday processional, a strip tease, a funeral dirge, a wedding march, Olympic gymnastics, and disco in the same show—not just in the same show, but the same dance.[11] I had fretted that strip teases and Masses might mean different things, but my worry could make sense only if the goal was to appreciate differences. That must not have been the goal here. The goal must have been to learn that we are all the same, no matter what we do or who we are.

CELEBRATING . . . CORPORATIONS! AND COMBATING "THE CULTURE OF DEATH"

All the public celebrations came with marketing. With Cinco de Mayo came Pepsi or Bud Light beer signs. The puzzle here was not the connection between commerce and culture in itself; in America, the two have often developed hand-in-hand.[12] Commercial sponsorship became a puzzle, however, when youth leaders objected to the sponsorship; if the youth were *leading*, were they allowed to lead the organizations to remove the corporate financial sponsors? No.

In a meeting of the Regional YEP, participants were talking about how to get free or cheap food and other donations:

Lots and lots of "Coca-Cola donates a lot," and debates about whether to get Coke or Pepsi; and

Erin [the adult leader of the Regional YEP]: "Home Depot is gonna donate $5,000 to Positive Youth Day! The only catch is that you all have to wear orange t-shirts.

Youth member: Bright orange??

Another youth member: Criminal orange [calling to mind the color of jumpsuits that prisoners wear]??

Erin: "It's *the* Home Depot, not just one store, but the Corporation [she meant that it is a big, important sponsor, not just a little, local one]! They're also gonna come to meetings, one person from the East side [of town] and one from the West."

There was no question about whether the group should be advertising for Home Depot, though Paul [a serious boy from a private Catholic school, whose comments often came with a quiet edge] kept up the [slightly critical] joke, "And will it have big letters on the front, "HOME DEPOT"?"

[The teens' light critiques were quickly preempted by an adult organizer.]

Karen (employee of United Way, one of the main sponsors): There's the problem of accepting food donations, because Home Depot wants to be the only one to donate food, they want full credit for the event.

Paul, the Catholic school boy asks: Why are they so greedy? Why don't they want anybody else to get credit?

Karen said: Because they donated $7,000 for the event!

Usually, no one criticized the groups' advertising on behalf of the corporation, not even as gently as Paul did here. Organizers most often treated the advertising as a way of getting money and free stuff. They hoped it would be just a means to an end. They did not ask if the advertising would, itself, be a message. In fact, the advertising was hard to ignore—it is one of the ways for people to locate a celebration of our diverse, multicultural community: it is where the loud music, Bud Light banners, and Pepsi signs are.

Later in this same meeting, after the discussion of Home Depot, another problem regarding corporate sponsorship arose. No youth volunteers spoke during this debate, but it was one of the frequent conversations about organizational logistics that gave participants a possibly boring but also possibly useful lesson about how Empowerment Projects gather money and supplies, and about how to navigate through organizational turf battles. The group had to solve a problem: an organizer from United Way told the Regional YEP that since Pepsi donates to United Way and United Way was co-sponsoring the event, Coke might not also want to donate. During the meeting, Erin and Karen discussed the issue for a long time, and finally figured out a very complex solution, while the youth volunteers sat in silence.

There was one form of corporate involvement that many NOYO organizers welcomed. They observed that company-sponsored volunteering—giving employees some time each week to volunteer as a representative of the company—sometimes solved the problem of typical plug-in volunteers' lack of steady, long-term commitment.

Some teens and organizers alike sounded queasy about helping corporations sell things that they considered harmful. At several meetings of the Regional YEP, youth were asked to generate ideas for charities' annual Christmas gift drives. "What would other kids want?" was the question:

> Paul [the thoughtful kid from a Catholic high school]: Like some poetry? Gary Paulson? or Shel Silverstein (writers whose work teachers assign)?
> A grown-up suggested video or computer games.
> Kids start naming some.
> About one of the games, VJ says, with a grin, "Violence is popular."
> Rob Strauss [this was four years after the "Youth Nazi Day" discussion—it appears that his opinion had not changed]—immediately chimes in with, "Throw it on our list. *It's not our job to say what they should want.*"

A bubbly discussion of participants' favorite violent movies ensued. Erin said she did not like one of the violent movies, but she was careful not to be preachy, saying her dislike was not because it was violent, but because it was "boring"—not "fun."

Some youth did not guess that they could be seen as cute, fresh-faced youth volunteers doing free advertising for corporations. In one Regional YEP meeting, Jenny exclaimed over and over again that two mega-malls had been "so generous" to us, we should shop in them and tell everyone to do the same.

This is not to say that organizers were completely at the mercy of corporations. There was a big exception to the acceptance of corporate funding. One organizer called a tobacco corporation's money "blood money." At length, his group had discussed applying for a tobacco-sponsored grant that they knew they could easily get, and they finally decided to refuse the easy money. Over time, others also had increasingly direct objections to giving "junk food" purveyors free advertising.

There also were some awards and sources of money that no one bothered to mine. NOYO organizers knew about this competition sponsored by the national Points of Light Foundation, but no local youth took up the offer for . . .

A Year's Supply of Toilet Paper

Subject: Georgia-Pacific to Honor Courageous, Selfless Children Across the Country

NEW YORK, JUNE 30 /PRNEWSWIRE/—Angel Soft(R) new and improved premium bath tissue will honor children under the age of 12 who have performed heroic or courageous acts in their communities through its first-ever "Angels in Action" awards program. The Angels in Action program will identify five children who have demonstrated remarkable courage, displays of emotional fortitude, or acts of selflessness. These actions might include saving a life, undertaking extraordinary volunteerism or facing a challenging situation with courage.

Each "Angel in Action" award recipient will receive a $5,000 U.S. Savings Bond (value at maturity) for future academic endeavors and a year's supply of new and improved Angel Soft(R) . . .

Angel Soft(R) bath tissue is the fastest-growing bath tissue brand in its category. New and improved Angel Soft(R) is 35% thicker, 35% more absorbent, and softer than ever! Initial tests revealed that consumers rank the improved product among the best in its class.

Georgia-Pacific, one of the world's leading manufacturers and distributors of paper and building products, makes the things that make you feel at home. Its consumer products include Sparkle(R) paper towels and napkins; Coronet(R) paper towels, napkins and bath tissue; Angel Soft(R) bath tissue; MD(R) bath tissue and Pacific Garden(R) antibacterial hand soap. In addition, Georgia-Pacific has created the Health Smart Institute, an educational initiative dedicated to improving personal and family hygiene practices, including the use of disposable paper products.

CELEBRATING VISIBLE DIVERSITY

Organizers needed to demonstrate that their programs served underprivileged, diverse youth, but the lack of privilege had to be *visible* so that sponsors could immediately see it without requiring too much elaborate documentation—of parental income or education level, for example. Non-white youth who looked white, or white youth who lived in rural poverty, or who were suffering in other ways—abuse, neglect, mental illness, for example—were hard to use in a public display, unless they declared to the audience, directly, that they were non-white, or were poor, abused, neglected, or mentally ill. The first—saying "I am not white"—was not uncommon; I never heard the second—making any particular teen stand as a representative of domestic violence, neglect, drug abuse, or the rest. This would require putting his or her personal problems on display. It would be too complicated, personal, weighed down with ambivalence, and not fun to celebrate. As a result, non-white faces were necessary symbols of the programs' utility in serving disadvantaged youth.

In order to have enough non-white faces appear in public events, organizers could not treat all youth participants equally, because more white boys were always willing to speak publicly than most of the non-white teens were. So, when planning one event, Rob Strauss cleverly asked, "Who would be willing to just go *stand* at the podium, if you *didn't* have to speak?" Several non-white youth raised their hands, and did indeed attend the public hearing (without speaking).

By the same token, Rob reproached organizers when they failed to make non-white faces materialize at public events. When Roberta asked members of the Regional YEP if any of them wanted to chair an upcoming public meeting, teens met her question with a long silence. Finally, one responded:

> Jim, a white boy who had come only a few times, tentatively, politely: I could try. I don't know. I could see if I can do it.

> At Jim's tentative statement, Rob Strauss seemed suspicious; the idea of these government-funded projects was to encourage participation from kids who were less privileged than this college-bound suburban kid. But Rob could not make this part of the program explicit. Instead, he turned, facing Polly head-on, to ask, out of the blue, how she generated the list to which to send this meeting announcement.

> Polly leaped to her own defense, protesting, "I *sent* the announcement to a list of over 30 places!"

Later, Rob told me that Polly should have tried harder to elicit participation from youth of color, confirming my suspicion that that was why he had pounced on Polly in the meeting.

The problem is, Rob did not know this particular white boy, and for all he knew, he was like the rich white boy portrayed in a public speech in an earlier chapter, who was neglected by his wealthy, alcoholic, Volvo-driving parents, and thus, the speaker said, more deprived than a poor kid with loving parents. Ferreting out and broadcasting the white boy's form of diversity/deprivation, if there was one, would be too embarrassingly personal.

Teens often mocked this attention to skin color behind the scenes. Of course, teenagers love to mock, even when they feel serious. Still, for it to be funny, the thing they mock has to be something they all recognize. Wild River Running Deer, an adult, spent hours a week for a month teaching Marisol, Bonita, and Marie a slow march to perform at one Martin Luther King Day celebration. The girls had to carry flags representing "their people" (black, red, yellow) and march around in circles. Each could carry only one flag, though some of them were multiracial. The girls found the rehearsals ridiculous, saying that they took time away from homework. One discussion of the event—outside of Wild River's presence, of course—began with a lot of muttering and giggling. Finally, when Marisol pulled herself together, Emily asked:

> Then you guys are gonna do the Youth Ambassadors Ceremony—with the flags?

Marisol: They're supposed to represent all the directions, or something. There's yellow, black, and red, I think. And white.

Emily (joking): That's right, don't forget me! It's supposed to represent all the cultures that are divided, coming back together.

Marisol (ducking her head down, smirking and muttering something to Samia about how 'it's supposed to represent Native Americans but you don't really want to know what it means,' wiggling her eyebrows and shrugging her shoulders with vigor, so now everyone's giggling without quite knowing why.)

Emily: Wild River wants to meet with you guys, because you guys don't know the history behind what you're doing.

Marisol, a little more audibly: I won't say what it's really about, it's supposed to be about bringing Native American nations together, supposed to be "recognizing" Native Americans, and that's good, but it goes way too far (rolls her eyes).

Emily: Well, you've been "very diplomatic" so let's stop there.

Roberta, the Snowy Prairie Recreation Commission head: The eyebrows say it all!

A few weeks later, Marisol told Emily that Wild River said "nasty stuff" about why there was no "white people's" flag, saying, "Its representation of white people was [even more eye-rolling] really bad!" In the first discussion above, we hear Emily and Roberta congratulating the girls, not on a beautiful performance or diligent practice, but on the fact that they had managed to be polite to Wild River. And, of course, after the celebration, Marie, Bonita, and Marisol were required to write very enthusiastic "thank-you" notes to Wild River, since she was called a "volunteer" (though she actually got paid through grants that she wrote for her productions), and volunteers always received thank-you notes.

Sometimes, the girls went beyond eyebrow-wiggling when they criticized local advocates of multiculturalism. In the privacy of Community House, amongst each other, with only me as an onlooker, after they had known me for four years, they exchanged detailed stories about the white organizer of a "multicultural theater group," laughing at how smug and proudly tolerant she was, calling her "a know-it-all," "a control freak," and a "racist." They had this conversation *while they were writing very sweet thank-you notes to her* for having led a workshop at an event that the girls had organized. The girls had invited her to lead the workshop, even though they thought, from previous experience, that she was "full of it." Nonetheless, the girls routinely lent themselves to public events, dutifully helping keep their program afloat financially by serving as representatives of diversity.

INADVERTENTLY CELEBRATING . . . EMPOWERMENT PROJECTS!

Rather than focusing attention on "cultural traditions," Empowerment Projects somewhat unintentionally focused attention on *themselves*. Before every event, organizers talked about the need for "visibility" and "good publicity":

> Jane [a city youth leadership administrator] also says "the original idea [for Good Youth Week] was to affect the city and county budgets that are drawn up in the fall, to shine a light on all the good things we *could* be doing if we had money."

> All of these events are all about coordinating the activities of church, city, county, school-based, volunteer, non-profit agencies, that all have different agendas.

The Regional YEP's project one year was a blood drive, held at a big mall. I had never heard Erin sound so serious. "What could be more important? Plus, the Regional YEP will be getting some *good recognition* for this."

Getting recognition was hard, partly because organizers themselves were not sure who the "they" was. Several NOYO meetings went like this one:

> Someone asked, "How many Youth Resource Centers have phones?"
> Rob Strauss didn't know.
> There was a question of what exactly counts as a Youth Resource Center: Rob says that that number is unclear.
> He says that the definition of a Youth Resource Center is vague "shades of gray," and gives examples. Glenwood House, he says, is not formally a Youth Resource Center, but is sponsored by the NOYO, and another center has started getting steady funding from a national non-profit and therefore stopped needing to come to NOYO meetings to find out about new grants.

This complicated list of "gray areas" continued quite a while longer.

With all of their inter-agency, inter-institutional blending, organizers diligently concentrated on sorting out which monies, individuals, projects, and organizations were coming from where—nonprofit, religious, government, donations, volunteer-led fundraisers, etc., with a wild mix of sizes, organizational structure, missions, clientele, locations, and calendars. Sizes ranged from regional school systems to tiny local art schools.

Members' organizations had various decision-making practices; vote, hierarchy, or informal decision-making. Some sent elected representatives to the monthly meetings; others sent the head, such as Rob Strauss; others had other levels of decision-making power; and others represented only themselves. Some could make decisions on the spot, while others had to report back to their organizations. Some organizations were purely local, while others were branches of national organizations. Coordinating schedules was hard between government calendars, religious calendars, commercial media calendars, school calendars, each with different rhythms and lead times and different durations, as well as young people's constant efforts to undermine and ignore all calendars.

For all these reasons, coordinating the different streams of organizations was extremely complicated and took a huge chunk of time at every meeting.

> Jerrard also wants Appreciating Teens Day [a big event, to be held in a convention hall that had stringent scheduling requirements regarding weekends] on Sunday, "because kids are already acclimated from church."
>
> Jeanne: Monday is good for the media.
>
> Sheila: Then would Appreciating Teens stay in the convention hall on the Saturday?
>
> Roberta: There could be a month-long Youth Engagement Week.
>
> Jeanne: It would be nice to tie in with the Youth Leadership dinner—to use the leadership conference as a start—on the other hand, trying to sustain interest over that long of a period can water it down.
>
> Jerrard: Halloween is on Wednesday, that's a problem.
>
> [Discussion of service opportunities related to Halloween, including UNICEF, gathering cans of food, and volunteering at the local Zoo for their Halloween Parade; discussion about whether kids can plan an early October event if they start working on it when the school year starts]
>
> Janey (a young new organizer): Trick or Treat so others can eat—is that like having an event that you have to bring two cans of food kind of thing?
>
> Jeanne (seemingly out of the blue): How can we organize a youth planning group so it's not so much adult directed?

Answering this last question would require teaching youth participants about how all of these different kinds of sponsors worked. A typical list of sponsors that organizers would discuss in NOYO meetings was full of acronyms (there is no point in reproducing one of the many alphabet-soup conversations here, because it would be incomprehensible), which were hard to decipher unless the listener already knew the organizations—where they were; whether they were government or NGO-based; big or small; schools-based or church-based; youth-led or not; whether they met monthly, weekly, or daily; were free-standing or branches of national organizations; for underprivileged youth or expensive; and all the other differences between the organizations.

These projects brought diverse populations together in one physical space, working on projects together. Sometimes, the incongruous blending was almost thrilling, in a city that was otherwise very segregated by race, class, and age:

> It was a snowy April evening, and the suburban high school buildings all looked closed. But deep inside the immense suburban high school complex, county bureaucrats, teenagers, undocumented immigrants, native English speakers, college student volunteers, social workers, babies, and paid nonprofit agency heads danced in the carpeted aisles of the brightly lit auditorium . . . kids *looked* like they were having fun, though it wasn't really sexy fun.

> They did not have to check in to register their names and worry that if they left, they would get locked out, like they did at Safe Nights [the events for teens in which the teens could not leave once they had entered, so that the adults could make sure they did not go outside to take drugs or contribute to an unplanned pregnancy]. At the Safe Night dances, kids who have babies themselves are the *only* ones with babies, and they look awkward, but here, a good many of the social workers and volunteers also brought babies and toddlers who darted between the dancers' legs. Unlike the last dance at Community House, this one had no gang violence in the parking lot. Unlike the dances at the Boys and Girls Club, this one had no police at the door. Rob Strauss got sweaty dancing.

Events like this could be important first steps toward the Empowerment Projects' goal of "building community."

CONCLUSION: FINDING PATTERNS IN THE "OPEN AND UNDEFINED" ORGANIZATION

EVERYONE WANTED THESE PUBLIC EVENTS to be authentically grassroots. Mentioning the ways that they were not purely grassroots could be offensive. At a Juneteenth celebration, an acquaintance, whom I knew in other contexts as a big advocate of grassroots organizing, exclaimed to me that it was:

> *impressive* that the local residents of this impoverished neighborhood managed to organize such a complex and elaborate event. She was really delighted. Her bubble burst when I pointed out the program, which listed all the corporate and government sponsors; she tried to argue and then looked annoyed at me for having pointed it out.

The acquaintance was annoyed because she liked the image of grassroots community initiative. Everyone did.

A celebration like Juneteenth was in some ways worse, and in some ways better than the local grassroots ideal she had in mind. Celebrations of "our diverse, multicultural community" had a complex job to do: to celebrate the organizations that brought participants together without drawing attention to the organizations themselves; to acknowledge that we live in a complex society full of formal organizations while focusing on something colorful, musical, and more appetizing than these semi-bureaucracies.

The typical event's esthetic form clearly echoed the Empowerment Project's form: no center stage, each stage optional, an overwhelming wash of sounds and smells, gospel singing on one stage interrupted midbreath by African drumming from another stage. In these celebrations, the form was the content—no sequence, no rhythm, all stages active at once, no unified mass audience, but events that are all about choices, options, overhearing, overlapping audiences. What made all the different projects and tractor parts and home heating programs for low-income families, and Jesus, spray-on cheese, the black man who invented the fold-up ironing board, free blood pressure tests, and Langston Hughes cohere was the simple fact that they kept appearing together, predictably, in one event after another after another, all at once. In the name of celebrating specific, unique roots, difference, and the beautiful, intricate details of this or that culture, these celebrations stirred together all the ingredients, to make them into a big Empowerment Project.

The three chapters on celebrating our diverse multicultural community have been like a theme and variations that finally resolve on the same chord: "getting out of your box" can be accomplished without investing huge amounts of time learning a language, or a set of customs for expressing emotions, or a body language, or intricate forms of politeness, or prayers. Everyone can feasibly do it vis-à-vis everyone else's culture, and it is easy to do instantly. In everyday interaction and in public events, celebrating our diverse, multicultural community meant separating oneself from one's culture enough, and purifying it enough, to expose it to the public spotlight. All of this seemingly thin celebration of empty diversity potentially taught some surprisingly useful lessons. It coaxed people into gaining critical, reflective distance from their own cultures, convinced them indefinitely to postpone passing judgments on other people's cultures or odd habits, and brought them all together to celebrate the thing they already shared: participation in Empowerment Projects.

Finding Patterns in the "Open and Undefined" Organization: Gray Flannel Man Is Mostly Dead

EMPOWERMENT TALK WAS ONCE a radical, potentially liberating constellation of ideas. Its once-radical exhortations have now become mandatory in many organizations. As a story that organizations tell about "what we do and why it is good," Empowerment Talk is unusual: it is a moral story that claims not to be one. Empowerment Project organizers insist that everything is "open and undefined, and up to you to decide whatever," that nobody is limited by roles or organizations or social differences, and that all missions can quickly and easily blend. We can easily dispense with this utopian ideal of limitless potential—an ideal that sometimes can, as this book has shown, become destructive.

Like any other kind of organization, Snowy Prairie's Empowerment Projects developed relatively predictable routines. Through their routines, the projects potentially arrived somewhere that may, potentially, in some ways, be better than where they had planned to go. The point of this final chapter is to see what those potentials may be, both in Snowy Prairie and in other parts of the world. To answer this, we start by asking how Snowy Prairie Empowerment Projects' everyday routines made it hard for organizers to notice those potentials. This questioning leads us to a list of concrete suggestions, to make Empowerment Projects work better. And finally, as a post-script, the chapter shows how these organizations' everyday routines are contributing to seismic historical transformations.

Here are some of the projects' detours from their original plans, and the potential insight that might, and sometimes did, come from the detours.

Rather than learning to catch a spontaneous personal inspiration that may waft in from somewhere outside of society, some participants inadvertently learn how governmental and nongovernmental bureaucracies work and how to use social statistics. Learning about expert-based bureaucratic decision-making is *likely* in Empowerment Projects because these organizations are results of such decision-making policies. These organizations also are the street-level creators of such policies. Just in order to get anything done, participants implicitly have to recognize the importance of complex organizations and begin learning to navigate their terrain—important lessons, since these are the kinds of organizations that run our world.

Rather than learning how alike we all are, some participants surreptitiously learn how different we are, and how hard and complicated it will be to overcome inequality. Learning how hard it is to leave inequality behind is *likely* in these organizations, because they are socially diverse; classic volunteer groups, in contrast, tend to be homogeneous, and thus do not have to face inequality so directly. Rather than bonding deeply with socially diverse people, participants learned to converse with, and to value light conversation with, diverse strangers—important lessons in how to summon a hopeful "as if" feeling, that could, in the right circumstances, allow participants to move ahead together, as if they were equals.

Rather than learning to create a feeling of togetherness by drawing on gut feelings, shared tastes, comfort, and nature, participants sometimes learn how radically different their tastes are, to question their own feelings of comfort, and to be unsure of what to count as natural.[1] Learning to feel puzzled about what to count as "natural" may very well be the only realistic attitude on a planet in which nature is changing. "Nature" and "tradition" both become projects and questions, rather than eternal ground beneath our feet. Learning to question one's own feelings of what is comfortable, natural, and traditional is *likely* in organizations that are supposed to challenge and improve people's desires and habits. Rather than resting comfortably, cultivating a bit of discomfort with ingrained habits can be an important lesson in a society, and a planet, that is quickly changing.

Rather than learning about each other's cultures, and feeling proud of displaying their own, participants inadvertently learn to treat cultural tradition as light and chosen. The more often they have to give clear and succinct public exhibitions of it, the more malleable, optional, and weightless it seems. In organizations that throw such diverse people together, and ask them to expose their cultures so publicly and transparently, it is *likely* that culture will start to feel like a puzzle, not a solid bedrock of shared values. Empowerment Projects' thin way of celebrating cultural diversity may be a useful lesson in a diverse society, in which no one can learn much about everyone else's religions, languages, customary ways of showing respect and gratitude, and everything else that constitutes a "culture." Perhaps trying to bond into one single, warm, tight community is not the only good goal after all; perhaps a more reachable goal is to learn how to keep an organization going *without* expecting to know very much about each other's religions and home habits. Cultivating this expectation might inoculate people against narrowness and dogmatism.[2]

Rather than learning to garden and to enjoy healthful food, participants learn abstract information about gardens and healthful food, without actually getting the food.

Rather than learning to trust the stream of plug-in adult volunteers who promise to become like beloved aunties but then vanish after a few months, youth participants often learn how to distinguish the real promises that organizers like Emily offer from the volunteers' usually false promises. This is a useful lesson in cultivating not too much, and not too little, but the right amount of trust[3] in a world whose organizations often promise the sun, the moon, and the stars.

Rather than learning to trust the plug-in volunteers, youth participants inadvertently might develop a bigger, more universalistic sense of trust. When youth participants learn that the whole society, with its tax policies and other abstract systems, help make the warm intimacy within their after-school programs possible, they learn a beautiful lesson about how contemporary societies build caregiving into their very structure—that whenever you go to a decent public school, drive on a safe highway, ride through a tunnel, eat uncontaminated food or drink clean water, you unknowingly have trusted and depended on thousands of strangers' careful work to keep you alive. Face-to-face trust would not be enough to keep you alive.[4] Participants learn that the program could end if funding is cut. Emily's group learns that she could feel more consistently loving, playful, and affectionate with them if the city government hired an assistant, so that she could work fewer hours. In these ways, they learn, perhaps somewhat brutally, that the personal and the political are inevitably intertwined. Learning to value complex organizations is *likely* in organizations that exist because of the funds and plans of distant others. Cultivating this sociological imagination may not have been the funders' main agenda, but it is a useful, profound lesson, nonetheless.

Rather than learning how to care about "the bigger picture," as some organizers hope they will, youth volunteers learn to ignore politics. Instead of learning how to connect their volunteer work with larger political debates, they learn technical skills of taking notes and running meetings. Learning civic skills minus politics is *likely* in organizations like these, which have to accept everyone regardless of viewpoint, and have to show results of action that all audiences will consider indisputably good. In most contemporary workplaces, in which turnover and insecurity are high and employees have to start getting along right away without waiting to get to know each other, employees need to know how to run meetings, take notes, and make small talk with strangers. Snowy Prairie's organizers recognized this, of course. This was not the stuff of their dreams, not the vision that inspired them to work so hard, but they were genuinely glad to help these underprivileged youth get a chance for better jobs than their parents had.

Through transformations like these, the more people had to talk about culture, grassroots, intimacy, and participation, and the faster they had to display them all, the lighter and more transparent, optional, and temporary they seemed. You might love your form of diversity enough to display it proudly, or fear that you do not know very much about it, or want to abandon it—including perhaps your religion, your language, your impoverished "trailer trash" upbringing, your sexist family, your fondness for *Little Black Sambo*. Perhaps you feel all three at once: love it, fear it, and want to abandon it, simultaneously. You probably volunteer for a similarly complex mix of motives.

Empowerment Projects ask you to display your feelings in the public arena, and the displays have to be fast and easy for distant audiences to digest. They cannot be ambivalent. When you make them so explicit and transform them into clear, quick action items, these tangled webs of feelings fall apart. Empowerment Projects demand that you be "yourself," but only a purified, simplified self that can easily fit in quickly with all the other selves. With all this exposure and speed, Empowerment Projects offer many chances to feel ambivalence and doubt—about one's culture, one's intimate relationships, one's inspiring volunteer spirit—but almost no chance to express, discuss, and possibly untangle the ambivalence and doubt.

Whether or not one would count these patterns as positive or negative, *however* one judges them, they show how Empowerment Talk materializes in these organizations' typical everyday conditions. It turns almost completely inside-out.

This might seem bleak and uninspiring, but there are many potential silver linings as well. *The bleakness and the silver lining both come from same source.* Participation gives youth an unexpected kind of knowledge: they might learn how to make things happen, not in a dream world, but in this dreary but fascinating, un-utopian world of complex institutions. These organizations' surprising opportunities and doubts both spring from their need to use Empowerment Talk in these organizational conditions, in ways that would be easy to convey rapidly and transparently to multiple, distant audiences. Participants have to prove that they are cultivating local roots, intimacy, inspiration and experimentation, and the performance have to take place in the glare of many spotlights shining through them in many crisscrossed directions for many distant spectators. All the thinness, doubt, constant explaining, and second-guessing make abstraction possible—necessary, even.

What these organizations potentially could do best is to teach members how to maintain a double vision: to feel spirits, roots, cultures, local communities, tastes, intimacies, and nature *and also* to turn them into abstract ideals, viewing them—even their *own* spirits, roots, and tastes—from a distance, in other words, to learn how to become fruitfully perplexed. Emily could love Bonita as a unique person with a unique smell, and *also* see how she fits into the larger society, even as "a statistic." With more time together, and less Empowerment Talk, participants could have done more of what they did best.

There were, however, good reasons that they did not have more time.

TEMPORAL CONTRADICTIONS

When Empowerment Talk materializes in these conditions of transparency, flexibility, blending, and openness, *time* itself becomes puzzling, with frequent tensions between

> treating participants as future potential leaders versus cultivating and nurturing participants who already are leaders
>
> drawing on "the community" in order to create "community," and drawing on gut feelings in order to change gut feelings
>
> creating programs based on statistical predictions of bad outcomes versus treating each youth as unique in the moment
>
> treating relationships between paid organizers and youth as family-like versus knowing that these relationships will be optional in ten years;
>
> treating plug-in volunteers as potential beloved aunties versus knowing they will not stay long, and will most likely not stay at all if the going gets rough
>
> treating volunteer work as soul-expanding versus scheduling one easy hour of it per month
>
> celebrating diversity by treating all as equal versus celebrating diversity by learning about and respecting different groups' different histories
>
> learning to enjoy any brief encounter for its future potential, while knowing that there would most likely not be time to fulfill the potential

Empowerment Project participants are exhorted to "be in the here and now," echoing a phrase that has resonated throughout society since the 1970s.[5] With this sentiment, human relations managers in businesses, schools, and government have urged people to drop their "baggage," let go of the past, be flexible and open, to treat the future as an open book rather than relying on the past as a model. Theorist Nikolas Rose traces this approach to mid-twentieth-century psychologists: key words in their approach were "aspiration," "becoming (as opposed to just "being")," "discovery, "self-actualization," "striving," among others.[6] These psychologists and management experts saw that people feel alienated when they cannot creatively and cooperatively make plans and implement them, both at work and in politics. They encouraged business managers and political leaders to design workplaces and political structures that would help people feel less bored, hopeless, and helpless, and to feel, instead, that their own thoughts and actions mattered. While not asking people to leave the past behind as avidly as Snowy Prairie's organizers did, the psychologists insisted that there are good reasons not to want to be trapped by the past, and insisted that even in hopeless circumstances, an individual can survive by being hopeful.

When these seemingly good management techniques became influential, new and different problems arose. Rose describes this less innocuous side to the story: these techniques enlisted the individual's whole psyche, whole imagination, whole sense of self in the cause of making the company productive and the government stable. A new kind of business, governance, and person emerged, intertwined, each partly constituting the other. Empowerment Projects, Rose would say, securely harness each person to the state apparatus. Rose asks us to investigate how this enlistment works, for better or worse, to create both governance and a citizen's loving attachments, culture and self, and that has been this book's goal.

Like many forms of participatory governance, youth programs tried to put these ideas in practice, and as is always the case when good ideas expand from the lab to everyday life, there were many slips twixt the cup and the lip. Here, letting go of everyone's past, being "in the here and now" together, and collectively imagining a hopeful future were hard to sustain for more than a few minutes, and success often caused more problems than failure. We can start with the past.

Letting Go of the Past, or Ignoring It Altogether?

Organizers had good reasons for encouraging participants to leave their pasts behind and try not to notice their inequalities. "Anybody can be great, because anyone can serve," as Martin Luther King put it, in the quote that appears on folders, pins, and t-shirts every MLK Day. This timeless message of universal love is always good to keep in mind, but its timelessness and universality make it hard to appreciate differences, to appreciate people for what they personally have been through. Discussing participants' vastly different and unequal backgrounds would be too bewildering, anger-provoking, politically controversial, and time-consuming for these organizations to handle.

Snowy Prairie's Empowerment Projects had good reasons for setting the past aside, but doing so caused a problem: it requires avoiding asking about the causes of the problems that volunteers hope to fix. The busy civic engagement programs gathered food for the hungry, but opening up discussion of "why is there hunger in the United States" could have provoked upsetting disagreements. The scene in the windowless conference room, in which the speaker encouraged each of us individually to use less electricity and then switched off the lights, showed that when people share wider political vision beyond "making a difference, one light bulb at a time" problems like hunger and pollution can seem insurmountable and eternal. Unless we could change the building codes, voluntarily turning out the lights just put us in total blackness.

Ignoring the past makes some of the organizations' other missions puzzling, as well: Though every visiting dignitary comments admiringly on the Regional YEP's diversity, it is forbidden to say what counts as "diversity" worth celebrating. Yet, beneath their colorful, five-minute exhibitions about diversity, difference, and culture, speakers sound insecure about what to count, if anything. Some "differences" are troubling and not worth celebrating, and many are hard to disentangle from the rest of one's self, but naming them all "culture" makes it hard to make these distinctions. Teens who are called upon to represent a "culture" often do not know much about it; for them, standing as its public representative makes them nervous rather than affirmed. When paid organizer Sheila calls poor people's habit of abruptly moving out of town their "culture," she was trying to sound respectful of their "differences," but the seemingly respectful word makes it hard for her to notice that their poverty is not a cultural difference worth celebrating.

Empowerment Projects multiply participants' chances to question their cultures, tastes, and feelings, but do not give them many chances to analyze their questions and doubts. Instead, when "celebrating our diverse, multicultural community" in Empowerment Projects, people have to conclude that no differences deeply matter.

Trying to cordon off the past to prevent it from touching the present does not stop people from making *guesses* about each other's pasts. Rather, people like the visiting officials and the plug-in volunteers rely on a more rapid, categorical measure: they guess based on eyesight. People are not supposed to invoke categories explicitly, but have to rely on them; this is most obvious when people stumble, when, for example, the girl with blonde hair who got the scholarship for minority youth has to tell the audience that even though she was blonde, she is Latina, and that that is why she won the scholarship.

Participants' divergent and unequal conditions keep bubbling back up in other ways as well, in the form of backstage jokes and muffled snickers, such as Community House teens' ongoing joke about the "baby blue cardigan with pearlized buttons." The repressed past reappears in the form of simple bafflement, when non-disadvantaged members cannot decipher disadvantaged volunteers' lives or families, and when the two sets of youth cannot fathom each other's habits, desires, jokes, goals, and tastes in food or clothes.

These organizations exist to transform unhealthful habits and feelings, but talking about the origins of these habits and feelings is taboo. The puzzle is that the organizers are supposed to draw on participants' feelings and desires in order to create better ones, but no one can say why participants ever had unhealthful ones to begin with. Analyzing the problems' origins would require criticizing youth participants' families, schools, the corporations that convinced them to enjoy food that organizers considered unhealthful, for example, or the vast inequality that made neighborhood segregation so prevalent.

TEMPORAL DISCORDS: THE FUTURE PERFECT

Empowerment Projects need to adjust and jiggle the future expectations of all the different audiences and diverse participants, and the schedules of the different kinds of organizations' calendars, and all the different aspirations—for intimacy, civic engagement, inspiration, appreciation of diversity, and openness to challenging preconceptions—that can unfold in different amounts of time.

A key element of their organizational style focuses on an abstract potential future: a safe place, where all the discordant clocks will harmonize, no audiences will feel blamed, and everything will be possible. "You are leaders" means "we hope you will eventually become leaders"; "we invite the community to attend this supper" means "we hope that by coming to this supper, you will eventually become a community." If people from different backgrounds can maintain a conversation about three-dimensional paper fold-out turkeys for a few minutes, the conversation becomes a powerful symbol of a potentially limitless relationship, and conversation partners grow excited. On the assumption that one never knows when the spark of intimacy will ignite, participants are supposed to be ready to bond quickly. Even though they know that this hard-won conversation will almost never lead to any future conversations, they learn to enjoy and treasure that kind of interaction.

Participants are perpetual future potentials: potential leaders, potential feeders of the hungry in the future, potential future risks, potentially intimate acquaintances. There is, however, rarely time to see if the potential or the prophesies will come true, because the organizations have to keep inviting new members, inventing new projects, not getting "old and stale" and "entrenched" for a long enough time to realize all those potentials. Not all relationships can survive such speed-up, though, so it makes sense in these organizational conditions to treat gut feelings and intimacy as perpetual future potentials. The potential future starts to feel as real as the present, or sometimes, even, more real than the present.

The double duty becomes a problem when *present* needs are hard to publicize as *future* potentials. Present needs—for food or a non-moldy carpet—and the needs of people who will never become self-sustaining—like the old, disabled people in one organizer's program—easily fall by the wayside, being too hard to justify. Volunteer work in Empowerment Projects has to improve the volunteer, not just help the recipients of the volunteer's aid, so the double duty makes sense. It blends Empowerment Projects' multiple missions. When organizers justify volunteering as means to a potential end—preventing the youth volunteers from becoming pregnant drug addicts or drop-outs—it is easier to fund than if organizers simply declare that volunteering is good because the recipients of aid need help. The double duty becomes a problem when present bonds between Emily and her program participants intimate bonds are disrupted by the projects' need to cultivate future potential bonds—between Community House participants and plug-in volunteers. Perpetually poised for photo ops, relationships tend to transform into ads for themselves. The double duty also means that whenever a young volunteer takes genuine pleasure in helping someone else, loud voices buzz in the background advertising the benefits that accrue to the youth volunteer him- or herself. Doubt is an Empowerment Project's constant companion.

The constant focus on potential makes it necessary for the after-school programs to welcome plug-in volunteers, and this is the only unequivocally harmful piece of the puzzle. They are supposed to represent the Empowerment Project's potential grassroots support, and potential cross-class and cross-race intimacy, but they almost never stay around long enough to realize this potential. Their presence does not *prevent* familiar, intimate, relationships from arising in these programs, in hidden places like Community House's third basement, protected from the programs' constant innovation and speed. It just makes them hard to maintain.

Temporal tangles like these are built into these organizations' very design. Empowerment Projects aim to put government in people's grasp, but bringing governance "closer" posed problems for coordinating everyday interaction. "We hold these truths to be self-evident . . . " begins our Declaration of Independence. Aimed at whole nations of distant citizens, an abstract, self-fulfilling prophesy like this works as a distant breath of hope, an alluring mirage on a faraway temporal horizon. As theorist Hannah Arendt points out, if we had to say it so explicitly, and get so many signatures affirming it, then maybe it was not yet quite as self-evident as we would like.[7] In person, up close, the same message easily provokes doubt. This kind of message can also work in religious settings, where people expect to hear counterfactual statements as metaphors. When shoeless slaves sang, "I got shoes, you got shoes, all of God's children got shoes! When I get to heaven, I'm gonna . . . walk all over God's heaven! I got a crown, you got a crown ... when I get to heaven ... I'm gonna shine all over God's heaven!" it reminded them that they could have, and in some sense, already did have, what all humans have, despite their current barefoot circumstances. They could see, however, that they did not have shoes at the moment. The song's realism is not empirical but "symbolic realism."[8]

Empowerment Projects aspire to translate this kind of hopeful metaphorical speech into everyday practice. The problem is that Empowerment Projects are now charged with the steady, nitty-gritty, reliably long-term work that states once did, of taking care of people who depend on the organizations, both now and over the long haul, not just in some far-away hologram of a future. When governance is supposed to be in the hands of the people, local and close to everyday life, then speaking *as if* all people already are equal and already have shoes does not help them get shoes today. It does not help them make plans for this afternoon together, or tomorrow, to plan just how they will overcome inequality. Instead, in the youth programs, it tends to eviscerate the present.

Guessing the Future through Different Sets of Equipment: Measurement or Intuitive Routine

When everyone is potentially anything to anyone and liberated from rigid roles—auntie, fellow volunteer, friend, social worker, plug-in tutor, person who "gives of oneself 100%" to youth—it is hard to get an informal feel for which relationships are supposed to last. The stories that one audience requires are undermined by the stories that another audience requires. A typical path through this thicket is to keep relationships "open and undefined" and to focus relentlessly on an abstract future. But hardly any action at all can be coordinated without an idea of how long it will last, so participants cannot, it turns out, leave it open and undefined and up to you to decide whatever.

As social scientists have long argued, people think and act by nearly instantly, intuitively recognizing patterns. "The baby cried; the mommy picked it up," for example, makes instant sense, and gives us strong hints of what to expect to happen next: we assume that the mommy picked the baby up to soothe it. We guess this because we have "filled in" the unspoken story, when we assume that the baby was *this* mommy's baby and not someone else's, and more. "The baby cried; the shortstop picked it up" leaves us unsettled, wondering if the shortstop plans on throwing the baby to second base.[9]

Categories like "family" or "baseball game" help people get a feel for *what they can realistically hope* to happen in the future: that the relationship should last as long as it takes to make a deal, between customer and cashier. Or to last exactly one year, between teacher and pupil in a classroom. Or forever, as a religion, tradition, or a parent-child relationship promises. How often, and for how long, can we expect or hope to be connected—how many minutes-days-years-decades-centuries?

If these distinctions were merely fictional, as organizers had to assume, then smashing them would require no more than making a conscious decision: program participants to *decide* to treat each other as "family," to *decide* to treat each other as civic equals, to *decide* to celebrate everyone's unique cultural tradition.

Despite Empowerment Projects' "open and undefined" "up to you to decide" refrains, participants have to guess how long they can expect fellow members to stay, and how often they might come. The projects' professed "boundary-less-ness" gives participants very weak tools for sharing aloud what they inevitably intuit—how long to expect plug-in volunteers to stick around, for example. The projects offer, on the other hand, very solid devices for orienting participants toward a distant, abstract future: predictions based on demographic categories like race; predictions of college acceptance for some youth, forebodings of drug abuse for others; constant forecasting and planning for the purpose of winning grants. These distant, expert-based, scientific techniques for anticipating the future are more powerful than members' informal ways of making predictions. Since organizers try to make planning seem irrelevant, and keep everything open and flexible, youth participants have to make guesses about the future on their own, by over-hearing, indirectly asking, second-guessing. The problem is that they have to do without benefit of warm-bodied, familiar intermediaries' guidance. When organizers invite young people to dream up ideas as if they "have a magic wand and anything is possible," they hope to empower youth, but youth participants second-guess what is possible, armed only with a magic wand, with no loyal, familiar adult acting as a realistic guide. The problem is not the long-range, complex planning; trying to make planning seem irrelevant is.

In other words, demonizing the bureaucrat and idealizing the volunteer lets the banished expert-manager-statistician-bureaucrat's ghost sneak back in, but this time he is invisible, silently demanding that young people act as if their own desires magically fit with various agencies' budget, logistics, and time lines, as if, in a sleight of hand, they have freely chosen his budget and time line. Through all of their guessing, without a warm adult guide, participants learn to adjust their expectations, to make them fit the requirements of distant planners.

Ironically, then, considering organizers' fear of the bureaucrat's ghost, Empowerment Projects can easily be *more* directive, impersonal, and abstract than plain old bureaucracies. In contrast to Empowerment Projects, bureaucracies usually have reliable experts who can take a long time to evaluate the bureaucrats' work. Empowerment Programs' judge is "the community"—an entity that organizers knew was vague, rushed, and full of non-experts who would not study the youth programs in depth. This entity's vagueness makes it even more powerful than any more sharply defined entity could ever be. It does not have to operate according to any rules or authority, but just on its own changing whims.[10]

Also in contrast to Empowerment Projects' participants, stodgy bureaucrats who worked side-by-side in their dusty offices for years usually developed habitual methods of getting things done. Participants in flexible, innovative, and transparent Empowerment Projects have much less time to settle in together, to grow set in their ways . . . or comfortable in their ways, or comfortable with each other. Their portable and impersonal routines have to be ready to use anywhere with anyone; they need relationships, tastes, desires, and traditions whose worthiness is easy to display fast.

Another difference between an Empowerment Project and a centralized, bureaucratic government agency is that Empowerment Projects cannot violate local folks' cultures and feelings, even when some local grassroots folks feel comfortable with Little Black Sambo and segregation. Empowerment Projects do not simply override the local racists, or local lynch mobs, directly, the way a central government can. Instead, Empowerment Projects have to make local communities want what the central government wanted them to want: local folks have to make it seem as if they have *freely chosen* equality and openness.

Running from the bureaucrat's ghost solves some problems but causes others, then. To combat the colorless ghost, the organizations develop devices for measuring and displaying cultural diversity. These standard measures and predictable displays—with their jumble of advice for preventing high blood pressure, ten-minute histories of Hmong culture, and multiple stages all playing loud music simultaneously, time-sheets for measuring volunteer work and the President's Hundred-Hour Challenge, rapid bonding exercises and fests——solidify the practical meaning of "cultural diversity," giving it a material incarnation.[11] Managing, controlling, planning, measuring, paying: the ghost's work continues, but in new, different forms, with new, different consequences. Fleeing the bureaucrat's ghost does not simply end impersonal surveillance and control of intimate lives. Inside these programs, social inequality feels just as strong as ever, but people have to learn to make it seem as if it has already melted away.

Cheerleaders and Critics Argue over Who Is the Rightful Heir to the Grassroots Throne

Probably the day the second American bureaucracy was built, our newly minted bureaucrat walked outdoors for lunch, blinked in the sunlight, and vowed to make his office more "participatory" and "in tune with the grassroots." By the same token, Americans have been bemoaning the "loss of grassroots community" since at least 1621.[12] One side cheers; the other mourns. Neither is quite right.[13] Volunteers do not necessarily live up to their image, and bureaucrats do not necessarily live down to theirs.

In Snowy Prairie, I heard more intense, thoughtful public-spirited dialogue among the paid organizers than I had ever heard in those classic volunteer groups. In earlier research, I heard classic volunteers' long discussions about how to build the throne for the Homecoming Queen and to transport cold soda to the high school dance—something hands-on, that would inspire a can-do feeling in members—but they could not talk about increasing funding for the school, even when its library's roof caved in! To maintain their can-do spirit, they tried to avoid even thinking about issues that they called "big" and "political," leaving them trapped within a narrow circle of concern.[14]

Americans' long-standing hatred of bureaucracy and love of grassroots volunteers, both miss the mark, yet contemporary cheerleaders for, and critics of, Empowerment Projects echo this black-and-white vision. Cheerleaders say Empowerment Projects nurture grassroots community; critics say that they crush the grass roots. Cheerleaders and critics share a presupposition: a deep faith in a community that they imagine to exist before the nonlocal, non-grassroots influences arrived—a noble, local community, better than bureaucracy and easy to disentangle from bureaucracy. The case of Snowy Prairie's youth programs shows just how untrue all of that can be.

Cheerleaders: In Snowy Prairie, the most vocal cheerleaders for Empowerment Projects advocated "asset-based community development" (ABCD). ABCD is, as described earlier, an influential program across the nation. Its advocates say that government money and experts "disempower" the grassroots community by ignoring these free, God-given assets; focusing on "needs" and "deficits," and spoon-feeding poor communities destroys their faith that they will ever develop the ability to sustain themselves. ABC developers hope to make local people realize how "rich" their community is in "resources."[15] In workshops, I learned that impoverished neighborhoods are *all* (if Snowy Prairie is any indication) "rich in loving grandmothers," for example. ABCD organizers remind us that family is priceless; love is priceless; grandmothers can offer home remedies and nurturance to the ill, bring mops to the crumbling public housing, volunteer in the local school, grow vegetables in a front yard plot, and teach children to garden and to read. "Everyone has God-given talents and gifts that can be used to benefit the community . . . Gifts are abilities that we are born with. We may develop them, but no one has to teach them to us."[16]

Critics of ABCD say that this kind of Empowerment Project aims to reform poor people's spirits without spending the money on reforming their living conditions—except possibly by cutting their funds even more.[17] These critics point out a few problems that caring grandmothers cannot solve—lack of health care, lack of textbooks and teachers in public schools, lack of public transportation, abundance of pollution, for example, that do not have simple, local causes, but are products of social policies that come from afar. These critics add that when corporations use donations to nonprofits as tax write-offs, then the government has less to spend on schools, parks, and the rest; nonprofits can control the money without democratic voters' supervision.[18]

A second sort of critic says that Empowerment Projects colonize poor people's informal relations of mutual aid—the warm, rich, hidden "community" that helps them survive poverty. Poor neighbors help raise each other's children, for example, sharing child care and food.[19] These exchanges often take place under the table, part of the hidden "informal economy," fixing cars and selling food on the street, sometimes illegally, without licenses, and always giving the downtrodden a feeling of pride in having cleverly triumphed in small ways over the powerful. Such "weapons of the weak"[20] survive precisely by being invisible to the powerful classes. Empowerment schemes might destroy those relationships by making them visible to authorities who can then control them, and give them a dollar value.[21] In Snowy Prairie, however, this is not an issue. Snowy Prairie's Empowerment Projects are not undermining a long-standing, loyal community that already exists. As Sheila noticed in her efforts to put on community suppers in a park, many impoverished families have no nearby kin or kin-like neighbors, and have to uproot themselves often, sometimes without even having time to say good-bye.

A third sort of critic argues that Empowerment Projects undermine radical political protest, because when activists get money from nonprofits and government, they have to cooperate with the mainstream, well-to-do people who hold the purse strings. Focusing on fundraising distracts activists from their grassroots base, without yielding any real political power.[22] These critics' examples come from radical black, Native American, feminist, and leftist social movements.[23] In Snowy Prairie's youth programs, in contrast, radical political protest is not a choice on the table. The only politically radical teens in the Regional YEP are on the far right, not the left—the passionately pro-capital punishment, anti-abortion girl, for example: not the kind of "radical" that these left-wing critics have in mind! True, there are a few leftist organizers who tame their radical political agendas to fit into their jobs. Bing is an elderly 1960s radical with a friendly, bald head and jack o'lantern smile. He is the one who gave little lessons on the different budgeting processes for nonprofits and government. He retired.

Both the cheerleaders and the critics' stories share a hero: the authentic grassroots community. The cheerleaders imagine it full of harmonious grandmothers; the critics imagine it full of explosive radicals. I did not meet either of those types in Snowy Prairie's youth programs. Cheerleaders' and critics' stories also share a villain: soulless bureaucrats who take power away from those good grassroots folks. The cheerleaders' and critics' usual sole question is, therefore, how Empowerment Projects draw on, or, conversely, crush, the grassroots community that they imagine to be already there, waiting to be resuscitated. The two sides are battling on the same turf. The battle is over who can claim to be *the rightful heir to the title "grassroots."* My point has been that playing this game is often an unproductive distraction. It often makes Empowerment Projects try to do what they do not do best.[24]

Empowerment: A Powerful Symbolic Constellation

This is how a powerful symbolic constellation like Empowerment Talk works: by making it hard to ask, in most public discussions, if "the diverse, grassroots, local, empowered community" is actually always better than experts, or bureaucrats, or paid organizers, or other possible candidates for goodness. Empowerment Talk works when, whether pro or con, everyone who is enmeshed in one of these Empowerment Projects has play the same game, arguing on Empowerment Talk's turf, using its language.

This book's stories have shown not just how Empowerment Talk works, but how it is transforming some of our society's most powerful keywords, as well. Words like "leader" and "community" change when people repeatedly use them in new ways, to do new things. When organizers repeatedly call young people "leaders," or say that they are inviting "the community" for supper, they assume that saying it often enough will coax it into existence, regardless of conditions. When organizers name an activity "bonding," or "a good choice," or "leadership," or "volunteering," they are trying to "do things with words,"[25] to bring relationships and desires into being, the way saying "I now pronounce you man and wife" marries you, or saying "you are under arrest" makes you so. Such pronouncements work in very specific conditions, with heavy equipment enforcing the words: when spoken by priests, high officials, and police, backed by churches, laws, and guns. But, in the youth programs, the words keep disobeying. The conditions in the youth programs weigh so heavily against the former meanings of the word "leader" or "choice," the words are simply changing meaning.

THE USES AND MISUSES OF HOPE: VARIED PATTERNS OF PACIFYING EMPOWERMENT PROJECTS' TYPICAL TENSIONS

Empowerment Projects come in many forms around the world. Wherever they appear, they face similar puzzles and potentials, but resolve them in different ways.

Many projects' implicit message is that "where there's a will, there's a way," regardless of conditions. When organizers ignore conditions, and just fix their eyes on a happier potential future, the result can be an exacerbation of existing problems. For example, an international NGO worker wryly tells a funny and/or tragic tale of his efforts at building civic associations in Albania, a very poor country that has never had much voluntary, empowered civic life. Our aid worker flies in to the capitol city for a few days, armed with a checklist that echoes Snowy Prairie's: a civic association worth funding is one that promotes local autonomy and community, equality and tolerance, empowerment, participation, sustainability—all the usual, unimpeachably good goals: "projectspeak," he calls them.

The foreign funds end up having a perverse effect: the Albanians who win money are those who can easily learn projectspeak, can draw up an expense account, and have access to the Internet, not to mention telephones: young, educated, relatively well-off go-getters. Our sheepish NGO worker realizes that he has undermined the community that was already there, widened the gap between rich and poor, urban and rural, young and old—inadvertently created a kind of civic life among elites, but not the kind he had hoped to create. In these material conditions, a nice moral mission turned into a harmful one. Old rural men, who had previously had local, kinship-based power, ask for money to help the handicapped, the ill, and the old, so they lose out to people who ask for money for people who will be more readily able to help themselves. For NGO representatives like this visitor to Albania, time for investigating concrete differences is short.[26]

Ignoring temporal conditions creates problems in many Empowerment Projects: Aiming for sustainability, participatory grassroots, and the rest, international aid organizations give a youth group in Botswana a water pump for their maize fields, but when hippos eat the maize crop that year, the locals sell the pump. Calling an organization "sustainable" is a kind of prediction; the aid workers base their predictions on the easy availability of equipment that is unremarkable in wealthier places—computers and telephones, not hungry hippos.

Many Empowerment Projects in the United States promote quick cross-class, cross-cultural bonding, another element of the "family resemblance" in these programs. Universities send eager, fresh college students into ghettos. Many of my own students have examined these university-based programs, echoing the tensions described in this book: The relationships start in October, after the students have settled into the semester's assignments, and end in early December.[27] In a project to help middle school girls, volunteers run to the "mentees" who want to be mentored, are easy to talk to, smile a lot, make eye contact, are not sullen, and do not smell bad. Mentors have no experience with the most serious problems that their mentees face, so if the mentee's uncle threatens to kick her out of her home if she does not join a gang, the university student changes the subject, since she has never heard of this dilemma, much less experienced it herself. Volunteer mentors rarely make these girls do their homework, preferring instead to forge an emotional bond. The "mentees'" school personnel blame the girls if they want to stop being mentored. In the cases that many student researchers report, volunteers often simply reinforce their own preconceptions: that poor, often black, kids are wired because their parents give them unhealthful food, do not make them do their homework, and do not protect them from gangs.[28]

A recurrent pattern is that Empowerment Projects ignore the material conditions that made the need for empowerment so urgent in the first place. This willful inattention is part of what turns Empowerment Talk inside-out. A terrifying ethnography of "alternative" women's prisons illustrates this. In this Empowerment Project, authorities talked about personal responsibility while making it almost impossible for the prisoners to take classes toward earning a high school degree or do anything else to become self-sufficient in the world after prison. Like the youth programs, the prisons relied partly on unstable NGO grants and so, staff turnover was high. Most of the teenage mothers in the prisons had had undependable or abusive parents, and encounters with an unstable staff of short-term prison therapists or teachers reopened their wounds. Preaching about choices and about letting go of the past absolved authorities from helping the prisoners.[29] Renaming conditions—such as time, money, availability of books, and transportation—"choices" is supposed to encourage even prisoners to recognize that they are not prisoners of past or current conditions. The prisons and Snowy Prairie's projects both show that focusing on potential by ignoring conditions is no answer.

Sometimes, however, critics make it sound as if conditions are the *only* problem. My point is that the messages—"Achieve! Work hard! Take responsibility"—by themselves are not the problem at all, when they are given in conditions that make it possible for listeners to achieve, work hard, and be responsible. Rather, the problem is the way the messages absorb meaning in practice, in the typical *conditions* of an Empowerment Project. In Empowerment Projects, the uplifting messages often do not come with any tools for enacting them.

From the above, it may be tempting to conclude that the university students and the earnest Danish aid workers should all stay home, and aid agencies should close up shop and keep their money, but those are not good solutions. *Not* planning would, however, be a way of abdicating— letting the video market, housing market, and job market make the plans— "letting the market decide," as policy makers who invest complete faith in the free market put it. Not planning would, itself, be a plan. Compared to this alternative, Empowerment Projects have the potential to do some- thing better, even if they rarely fulfill it.

Some Empowerment Projects depart from Snowy Prairie's, in four sig- nificant ways: they transform citizens into experts rather than trying to avoid the need for expertise altogether; they confront conflict rather than avoiding it; they require a long-term commitment; and/or they have very precisely spelled-out rules. In Snowy Prairie, these projects probably would have been judged too top-down, too rigid, and not open and limitless enough.

Tightly planned, time-intensive, narrowly defined projects can work by transforming ordinary citizens into experts, on the correct assump- tion that good citizens are made, not born.[30] But then, like any other way of balancing the tensions, this one is not perfect, either. These constrain participants' political imaginations, but in a different way from Snowy Prairie's; while Snowy Prairie's cut the connection between "civic" and "political" involvement altogether, these tightly planned projects pre- ordain a political agenda, beyond which participants' political imagina- tions cannot stretch.[31] They make it impossible for participants to go beyond following the experts' agenda, answering questions that experts already thought to pose. For example, volunteers in the 1990s in Chi- cago helped plan school curricula. They had to undergo a rigorous train- ing process with a huge commitment of time, energy, and thought, meet- ing for months to study national and state rules, and to pinpoint past successes and past failures.[32] They had very specific assignments and were not supposed to introduce issues, like hunger or air pollution, no matter how much the volunteers thought that those problems mattered for schoolchildren.

Another set of tightly planned projects that sever any connection to politics is the Grameen Bank's micro-credit operations, originally from Bangladesh and now replicated elsewhere.[33] These banks give small loans to poor people to start small businesses. I cannot draw out all the compari- sons with Snowy Prairie here, but two stand out: unlike Snowy Prairie's projects, these have clear, even rigid guidelines—no "open and undefined" here. *Like* Snowy Prairie's projects, these do not invite participants to ask themselves how global inequality arose or how to prevent it from arising in the future. Illustrating both contrasts, we read on the bank's website that recipients have to vow to uphold "16 Decisions," including: "We shall build and use pit-latrines," and "We shall drink water from tube-wells. If it is not available, we shall boil water or use alum"—matters that would not concern you, dear reader, who was probably wealthy enough to buy this book.

Ordinary citizens in some cities directly control the municipal budget. In some of these Empowerment Projects, people work together for a long time; they work with, rather than in annoyed opposition to, elaborate timetables, flowcharts, and well-defined ladders of increasing responsibility; and they work through conflict instead of avoiding it. Some of these "participatory budgets" are purely government projects with stable government funding, but many have hybrid, unstable funding. Their model is Porto Alegre, Brazil, a city of over a million. Porto Alegre's complex choreography precisely spells out how to develop the various forms of expertise necessary for effective participation. These Empowerment Projects resolve the nervousness surrounding expertise by demanding a time commitment that transforms ordinary participants into experts, even if in small ways. If they are on the street-paving committee, citizens learn about the different properties and costs of asphalt, cement, macadam, and tar.[34] Over time in Porto Alegre, citizens have learned to make deals, so that, for example, one neighborhood gets money to pave the whole length of its unpaved main street one year, and another neighborhood the next, instead of each neighborhood's getting only enough money to pave one block of one street per year (which would be useless, if you think about it).

Lest it seem such demanding projects can work for adults but not for youth, consider the Public Achievement program, run by long-time political activist Harry Boyte. In this program, youth in Minnesota work with coaches to generate a list of issues on which to work. So far, it sounds like the Snowy Prairie groups. Public Achievement's website very clearly states, however, that "*citizenship isn't easy*," describing it instead as "frustrating" and "difficult"—as well as life-changing and rewarding. The groups meet every week for a whole school year—another difference. Like Porto Alegre's process, Public Achievement clarifies conflict, rather than ignoring it. Participants are required to find power and conflict in the problem they have chosen to address: to ask "Who benefits from the problem?"—be it nasty school lunches or deforestation in Brazil.[35] Managing conflict is not the same as making it disappear. Participants call the experience frustrating and difficult. These projects aim to transform conflict into an invigorating source of mutual understanding. They are risky, less like picking up litter in parks and more like the soul-changing projects that Ezeky'el described in chapter 2: they can fail.[36]

These examples show how cultivating the grassroots from the top down can work when organizers stop trying to imitate grassroots voluntary associations. Unlike Snowy Prairie's projects, these all have strict rules and roles. They also demand a longer or more intensive time commitment. While they, too, shun *distant* experts, they address the need for expertise by making citizens *become* experts themselves. Finally, they invoke and analyze and accommodate conflict rather than submerging it. No one in those projects imagines relying very heavily on grandmothers' assets—unless, in Porto Alegre's road-building projects, they are argumentative grandmothers with expert knowledge of cement.

"Settlement houses" may be Empowerment Projects' most direct American ancestors; they contrast with Snowy Prairie's projects in ways that echo the differences we just heard. The continuity seems initially striking: Like Snowy Prairie's projects, settlement houses brought non-poor, native-born volunteers in contact with poor immigrants. Like Snowy Prairie's organizers, Hull House organizers hoped to value the immigrants' cultural traditions, to promote active political participation, to transform troubled families: to cultivate the whole person, in a many-sided way, as citizen, political activist, artist, parent, student, and worker.

There were some sharp differences. First, since their funding was steadier,[37] they could hold ongoing, serious classes in art, music, sewing, or sports. Jazz musician Benny Goodman learned to play clarinet in a settlement house.[38] In contrast, Snowy Prairie's programs did not develop talents that would take too long, be expensive, or require formal, top-down teaching. Instead, Snowy Prairie's programs just cultivated the skills necessary for staging fundraising events.

Another sharp difference concerns conflict: some settlement houses fought city hall; Hull House, for example, protested the neighborhoods' lack of garbage collection; Jane Addams, as described in the introduction, pushed for a minimum wage, and other legal protections of workers and poor families.[39]

The other sharp difference was introduced in the chapter on plug-in volunteers: like the projects just described, but unlike Snowy Prairie's projects, settlement houses made high demands on volunteers, often transforming them into experts, instead of ignoring the boundaries between professional and volunteer. A thorough 1950s report, based on the author's visits to over sixty settlement houses across the country, describes one in which volunteers worked with troubled families. First, volunteers attended four sessions of two hours each of training. The *mandatory* training sessions cautioned them "against attempting what a professional worker ought to be called in to do," and warned the volunteers, who were mainly middle-class housewives, to be very sensitive to "differences in class status." Next, the potential volunteer had a long interview about her motives, attitudes, her spouse's attitudes toward the volunteers' work, and how much time she had available. Dryly, the author notes, "As a result, a few volunteers who had taken the training courses were dropped, or rather, withdrew after facing up to what was expected of them."[40] Next, the volunteer had a case assigned to him or her—one family per volunteer, the same individuals each week, rather than a new child each week, as Snowy Prairie's volunteers usually had. Those volunteers then met weekly with a professional who supervised them and gave them advice.

While there were a few "trained professionals" in Snowy Prairie, I never heard any mention of any of them debriefing any volunteers. Even Emily was not a "trained professional" and when the Board had to replace her, we had almost no discussion of the applicants' training. Most had some hands-on experience, and a B.A. at most, usually in an unrelated field. Emily probably knew more than any professional with any number of advanced degrees, so what is the problem? Valuing Emily's natural talent sounds good until we notice the flipside of the coin: unlike saying that someone is a bad bureaucrat, or bad at some other specific role, saying that an adult cannot be a good mentor simply by "being herself" is to insinuate that she has a deep moral flaw. Emily's raw talent is considered a pure reflection of her inner character: egalitarian, brave, open. This makes it not just hard to imagine valuing training, but shameful even to need it. Nothing mediates between the person's whole self and the role: either a person has the "God-given gifts," or does not. If the organization had demanded training, that would have come perilously close to the bureaucrat's ghost, to imposing modernity's old, tired, bureaucratic divisions between one role and another. Settlement houses resolved the tensions surrounding expertise differently, in ways that more closely resembled the participatory democracy projects in Porto Alegre or Chicago.

Paradoxically, aid for Albania and Botswana can, in a fashion, bring local, empowered, grassroots community into being, in unexpected ways. The locals can become "empowered" . . . empowered to second-guess what their distant audiences from wealthier nations will consider "empowering (Bob 2001)." They get together to strategize about how to win grants from international aid agencies, forming a kind of civic association whose goal is to extract money from afar! Learning to navigate the galaxy of Empowerment Projects *is* members' direct personal experience. With a bit of reflection, they could learn how to navigate this bewildering, abstract, distant, global landscape.

PRACTICAL SUGGESTIONS

By hearing how Empowerment Talk materializes in typical real-life conditions, we can now specify if and how average citizens can be empowered, in ways that Empowerment Talk often rules out:

1. As organizers often say, these programs needed *more money, more stable money, and money for everyone to participate*, not just the poor. In addition to the reasons that many people give for more funding (more staff, lower staff turnover, a stable location), the programs' constant fundraising means that youth programs constantly have to come up with new, loud justifications—different justifications for different categories of youth. Hunger is, in the programs, not a good enough justification for food; organizers have to do gymnastics to justify food in terms of potential, hoped-for outcomes. *Constant fundraising risks turning all relationships into ads for the programs.*

2. *If participants learn the arts of abstraction, shifting, measuring, planning, and communicating at a distance to multiple hurried audiences, then organizers and funders should appreciate all the abstraction for what it is.* Constantly having the rug pulled out from under them, participants could develop a possibly healthy dose—or possibly fatal overdose—of doubt about and distance from their own feelings and cultures. If participation builds community, it will be abstract, based partly on information, expert knowledge, statistics, categories, reading, and doubt.

   If managing and planning is part of what makes these organizations possible, then make friends with the bureaucrat's ghost; it is not just a little gray ghost but "the elephant in the room." Even when it tries to hide, it whispers its big gray secrets.[41] Many Snowy Prairie organizers were real experts—they read widely in the literature on after-school and civic engagement projects and some had decades-long experience—but it was not cool to come off sounding like "an expert" in meetings. In other words, simply capitalize on what these organizations already do best.

3. *If transforming the community and its feelings is a reason for these organizations' existence, do not assume that there is a grassroots community voice or cultural tradition lying hidden and latent in every McDonalds parking lot*, waiting to be resuscitated. Sometimes, rarely, there is a community voice, clamoring to be heard, but it is usually too angry, resentful, deeply felt, tightly exclusive, or politicized for these programs—the high-strung, anti-abortion girl, or the participants who

find each other's tastes nauseating. In Snowy Prairie, the community voice comes into being when organizations bring it into being; the community does not exist before the managing, publicizing, and funding.

4. *If promoting diversity is a reason for the organizations' existence, then let the non-disadvantaged youth learn from the disadvantaged youth* about how everyday inequality works. The disadvantaged youth know about it but cannot talk about it in the community service projects; the non-poor youth often have no clue. Talking about inequalities within the group would probably be explosive and embarrassing. So we are thrown back on the need for experts who could help people learn from conflict and possible explosions—not to smooth conflict over, but simply to make inequality and difference intelligible to the non-disadvantaged youth. Organizers should be careful not to label all differences "cultural," and thus worth celebrating, when some are symptoms of poverty or oppression that no one considers worth celebrating.

5. *If promoting diversity is a reason for the organizations' existence, then acknowledge the distinctions that participants make between different categories of people.* There is a tension between quickly displaying "cultural diversity" to funders, versus appreciating and learning about harder-to-see differences. Diversity dissolves up close, when people are made to stand up in public as representatives for cultures that they have had to freeze and objectify and claim as theirs when they themselves often are not sure what to count as their culture.

6. *Since participants urgently ferret out information about differences between different organizations and different relationships, acknowledge the distinctions that participants already make.* Youth participants urgently needed to know if a new adult was a paid organizer or a volunteer. Within all the abstraction, publicity, measurement, and transparency, dense relationships *do* develop. Both kinds of relationships—public, transparent, and rapid, as well as intimate, slow, and dense—are important, and make sense only if people are permitted to make distinctions between them, so they can know how long to expect to together, or understand what just happened today in light of what happened yesterday.

And finally, an incendiary suggestion:

7. *If volunteering is supposed to lead to a deep transformation of both the volunteer and the recipient of aid, drop the plug-in volunteering.* It does neither. Plug-in volunteering is good for projects like picking up litter on a highway, because the litter does not care if a different, untrained volunteer comes next month, but the human recipient of

personal, face-to-face aid usually does. "Up close and personal" volunteering neither helps recipients nor teaches volunteers about the recipients' lives if it is sporadic or short-lived. It must either be time-consuming and long-term, or very firmly planned so that it is divided into foolproof morsels—reading a specific book aloud with a first grader, for example. Beyond needing the general, universal, symbolic love that the presence of a plug-in volunteer shows, recipients of aid need more. Someone like Benicia needs help from a person who knows and loves the densely detailed specifics of her own case: her teacher, her school, her family, her habitual moods. Theoretically, one dedicated plug-in volunteer can make a difference in one child's life, as organizers often say, but for every helpful one, I saw many harmful ones, and they, too, make a difference in children's lives. The consequences of treating plug-in volunteers as a symbol of goodness are grave.

Inevitably, treating volunteer work as a time-consuming, long-term, possibly difficult, and troubling commitment would mean saying that not everyone can be a leader, and that soul-changing civic engagement that goes beyond picking up litter cannot be easy and open for everyone. Volunteers who want to do something beyond making themselves feel good need time and training, or at least mandatory reflective discussion. Adults who have only Wednesday afternoon from 3 to 4:30 free should find something else to do to help society other than trying to forge a deep emotional bond with someone in that time slot.

All of these suggestions share a theme. They suggest letting participants make distinctions[42] aloud, rather than pretending that all kinds of people and all kinds of organizations and roles can quickly and easily blend. This includes temporal distinctions, so that participants can acknowledge the weight of past and present conditions. When participants cannot admit that relationships are limited, and that different types of relationships usually come with different future expectations, the only safe place is the blank canvas of the future, onto which participants can project abstract potentials that they doubt will ever materialize.

GRAY FLANNEL MAN

In the mid-twentieth century, people in wealthy nations worried that life was becoming too rigid, too predictable, not creative enough—you were trapped in your box. If rigid categories and boxes plagued organizations in the previous century, always claiming not to have any categories plagues Empowerment Projects. This plague's main symptoms are various forms of temporal disorientation.

The bureaucrat's ghost roamed throughout society back in the twentieth century. He had many incarnations: another was "The Man in the Gray Flannel Suit," in a 1955 novel and a 1956 Hollywood film, by the same name. Gray Flannel man with the job at Ford, in the office or on the assembly line, could count on having it for a long time, loyally supporting his family and having every weekend off, as long as he played by the rules: eating Wonder Bread and mayonnaise—nothing too ethnic—and keeping everything and everyone in the right box—public here, private there; men here, women there; whites here, blacks there. Not everyone was allowed into this arrangement, but those who were permitted entry could feel comfortably stable.[43] However, even for those who were allowed entry, there were problems: First, Gray Flannel Man's neat little box could feel monotonous and was full of conformists—or at least people who pretended to be just like whatever it was that Gray Flannel Man was pretending to be.

Everyone was pretending—which bring us to the deeper, more longstanding[44] critique of these falsely tidy boundaries. This critique says that the division between economy and politics is hypocritical, and as long as money rules, democracy is nothing but illusion. Hypocritically separating government, religion, and family has let a president be sweet with his own children while murdering far-away children; let the greedy boss be pious on Sundays and only Sundays; let the Nazi bureaucrat mindlessly claim, "I was just following orders."[45] The critics' advice: Smash these artificial borders between family, state, economy, and the rest, so the president, boss, bureaucrat, and everyone else all up and down the social hierarchy cannot hide in the boxes and are "at last compelled to face with sober senses his real conditions and his relations of his kind."[46]

While the critics accurately portray modernity's hypocrisy, their advice does not necessarily work out the way they imagined.[47] People do not have to worry about becoming "The Man in the Gray Flannel Suit" any more. Of course, there are still plenty of boring jobs, dreary marriages, and claustrophobia-inducing cultures, but do not worry about getting trapped in one for a lifetime. Try worrying, instead, about not even having a job, family, tradition, or a place that feels like a home. If you do manage to acquire one of these, you might worry about losing it tomorrow. No need to worry that everyone is becoming middle class and boring; trying worrying instead about the disappearance of the middle class, as the rich have gotten spectacularly richer and the poor dramatically poorer since the 1980s. You do not have to worry as much about losing your ethnic, religious, or racial identity in favor of Wonder Bread, but may, instead, be nervously trying to learn a language or culture that your parents already lost long ago, or displaying a culture that you left behind, or treating your culture as an object outside of yourself, in order to explain it explicitly and rapidly to impatient, uncomprehending audiences, in ways that make it feel unbearably light, optional, and empty.

Now, when the flexible, temporary job ends, the employee quickly has to end previous loyalties, re-package him- or herself, and apply for a new one.[48] Even marriage becomes temporary; when interviewed about their long-lived marriages, couples who came of age after the 1970s sounded amazed and baffled that the marriage *really has lasted* that long![49] Whether or not the marriage lasted, its permanence no longer just went without saying, as it did when older couples describe their marriages. Snowy Prairie's youth programs provided good preparation for the constant advertising and self-repackaging that the temporary job, civic group, and marriage require. This contemporary "break out of your box" world celebrates incongruous combinations. The more preposterous, the better. The soundtrack? World music, blending disco and Polynesian nose flute, Gregorian chant and hip-hop, or "omnivore."[50] The cuisine? Fusion. Both are space-traveling and time-traveling abstractions about roots. The scholarly discipline? Interdisciplinary, of course.

Theorists have analyzed this spirit in films, pop advice books, large-scale trends in employment and marriage,[51] calling it "liquid" and "optional," but in everyday interaction, however liquid and optional everything is supposed to be, organizations still have to become solid and predictable enough for people to make a plan together for next month, or at least for tomorrow afternoon. Back in "modern" times, people had sturdier guideposts for suggesting what to hope for or expect in a relationship, each marking a different emotional tone, a different set of equipment, on a different time frame. In Empowerment Projects, people have less firm grounds for acting, speaking, judging, predicting, or hoping from a position of "government employee," "civic leader," or "parent."

To become fluent in Empowerment Projects' organizational style, participants have to learn to appear not to care about categories that they have just used moments before. They have to learn to appear not to care about the past, and not to care about their future together. Participants learn how to appear to ignore distinctions that they know matter, to pretend that all people are instantly capable of all relationships. Noticing distinctions feels subversive.

Explaining their motives and internal lives so explicitly, quickly, and publicly pries open all sorts of questions, doubts, and ambivalence about them, while offering limited chances of expressing it. In this tentative, emotionally uncertain, optional world, where there are no apparent limits, the only taboo was against taboos; the only stated rule was to declare that there is no rule. Making rigid distinctions caused problems in "modern" organizations. Acting as if people could work together without making any distinctions causes predictable problems in Empowerment Projects.

A sense of what is appropriate to say and do where, with whom, and how, over what time horizon, is probably harder to learn now than it was in Gray Flannel Man's day. It is harder to learn now than in ancient Rome, when Cicero wrote about the importance of this practical knowledge, which he called "prudence," for knowing what you owed your slave versus what you owed your father. When "open and undefined" is the only rule, the need for prudence—for a feel for what to do, expect, and hope next—does not disappear, but knowing what one can realistically expect becomes more of a puzzle. The youth programs are especially good places for investigating contemporary people's groping quest for prudence, since these organizations provide such precarious grounds for finding it.

On Justification

On Justification argues that any organization has to represent itself to its publics, and to its participants—employees, parishioners, activists, customers, for example. Theorists[1] argue that these justifications are fictions because they never fully explain what people are doing together, but they are real because organizations have to make promises, and then, while never exactly meeting the promises, they at least put on a good show of meeting them. Each justification comes with its characteristic "devices" or "equipment," such as iambic pentameter and alters in the "inspired" mode, money in the "market" mode, or tax forms and flow charts in the "expert" mode.[2] The interesting puzzles are always in the ways that people try to keep the story going, because "out of place" things happen all the time.

In the hopes of making this book useful for comparative research on Empowerment Projects, I made my list of justifications closely correspond with Boltanski and Thévenot's. There are some differences, though. First, I never heard anyone using the "domestic" justification.

Second, I heard quite a bit of public speech about multiculturalism and experimentation; I trace this through Jane Addams and the fact that, unlike France, America is a nation of immigrants. Anyone who lands on our shore has to learn to present an acceptably public version of his or her "culture" to the people who landed here the year before; we have been "purifying" our culture for public palatability for a long time.

Third, I heard a great deal of very public discussion about intimacy, family-like relationships, food, needs, hugs, sleep, and comfort.[3] Thévenot says that such intimate attachments cannot be impersonally and publicly justified; my cases show when people often try, anyway. Moving them into the public arena usually forces people to strip their attachments of any ambivalence or doubt.[4] People have to sound more sure than they feel.

In the United States, while these intimate attachments' entrance into the public is never quite as easy as Tocqueville makes it seem, Americans recognize them as typical public justifications. In this kind of argument, people are supposed to "speak for themselves," to defend their own personal, even selfish choices, to show that they are not pretending to be better than they really are. This approach has a long history, going back to American colonists' aversion to the stuffy, high-toned speech of European intellectuals.[5] The good civic-minded person in this typical American[6] mode is someone who *gets their hands dirty*; that is, someone who hammers nails in buildings for homeless people, and cooks meals for hungry people, not only someone who speaks in universalistic ways about the common good.

Starting with the commonsense divisions that make sense in any one country may seem like a mistake, then, if what is taken for granted in France is not in Finland, Belgium, Italy, the United States, or Spain (to take some recent ethnographic studies).[7] However, starting *anywhere* is good, if only for this: noticing tensions that arise in Empowerment Projects in another country can sensitize us to ways that they do *not* arise in one's own. To make comparisons, their categories provide a good lingua franca.

Boltanski and Thévenot hint at what I have called "organizational style" when they ask about typical ways of smoothing out the tensions, but they do not do the empirical research necessary to develop the theory of styles further. Being American myself, I think that the proof of the pudding is in the eating. Tensions arise and are smoothed away in ways that theory does not predict. Empowerment Projects' constant issuing of hopeful self-fulfilling prophecies, for example, is not something that theory could have guessed.

Methods of Taking Field Notes and Making Them Tell a Story

I started with a different set of questions and objects of study, but once I decided that the "hybrid" Empowerment Project was my topic, I abandoned those notes. While it is not something that I suggest, the fact is that many ethnographers spend time in potential field sites without ending up using any notes from them.

For the same reason, I also set aside a chapter I had written on a for-profit summer program that I attended. However much the Empowerment Projects fell short of their own ideals, the for-profit program was much worse, I theorized, because organizers had no audiences for their work, and even lower pay. The for-profit program was a violent, frightening disaster, in an innocuous, clean building in a suburb. I discovered that an earlier book had already been written describing and explaining a similar program's failure.[1]

Taking notes: As many others have written, field notes document observable phenomena: "He crossed his legs," rather than "He looked uncomfortable"[2], for example.

In some meetings, when other people were taking notes, I did, too. Long quotes of dialogue are mostly from those settings, in which I could take notes the way news reporters take notes in shorthand (or did, before they started recording their sources). Some mnemonic devices help: remembering where people are, what they are wearing, how itchy or slippery their shirt's fabric seems, their posture, whether they look comfortable or not, remembering the order in which people spoke, and the scent and texture of their words, their emotional tone. Because of this tactile, practical approach to memory, speeches delivered from a podium are, I find, impossible to remember. That is, your body remembers when your brain does not. The long speeches I have quoted come from tapes—my own audio recordings, or videos that the organizations made.

From description to explanation, first step: noticing one's own feelings: Noticing what made one laugh or cry (or feel surprised, bewildered, outraged, joyous, or disgusted) lures the ethnographer from description to explanation:

> When descriptions are backlit by the strange glow of the absurd, they pulsate with demands for explanation. . . . When ethnographers

describe the operation of these enigmas, paradoxes, and little overt lies, they provoke curiosity about the big sociological "why?": what explains the sense of apparent coherence in the lives of the people studied? What makes it possible for them to take for granted that they live in a common social world? Why is social life not apparently coming apart at the seams constantly?[3]

Noticing one's own feelings sometimes can be perplexing. First, noticing one's own hypocrisy is unsettling, but a terrific technique for "making things strange," as the literary theorist Roman Jakobson described the work of the novelist. I grasped the organizers' multiple binds when I tried to do their job myself, as best as I could. Jane Addams suggests this as a mode of living; it also helps with refining social theory. Second, after a year in a field site, the ethnographer might become fond of some people, and try not to dislike others; I find myself surprised at how little this corresponds to any standard "variables" like class, race, age, or political affiliation, but is more about sense of humor, sensitivity, mood, intelligence—despite what I wrote in chapter 10.

From description to explanation, second step: putting puzzles together: I keep my field notes in many formats: First, I keep them in raw form. Based on these intuitions and a raft of constantly shifting social theories, I then "copied and pasted" them into vague categories that seem to be emerging, and I saved all the different formats, then hacked away and rearranged, trying out many different ways of dividing the field notes, and theorizing *around* them. In other words, the chapters began as *nothing but* notes that I stuck together for reasons that initially struck me as intuitively right, but then I moved notes around from one chapter to another as an interesting theoretical floor-plan became clearer. There is no need for a fancy software program for this; a word processing program suffices. In other words, I started writing long before I knew what I wanted to say, and while still doing fieldwork.

This is the specific beauty of ethnographic research: you develop your ideas and then go back to the field the next day to challenge them, refine them, make sure they are right, and/or discover variations on the themes.[4] "Ok, so does Erin really say 'fun' more than twenty times per meeting?" or "Do they really often spend more time talking about how to measure the volunteer work than doing it?" for two examples of ideas that came to me and that I then went back to check and even count or keep time, partly because they seemed so implausible. This is why it is important to start to write chapters before finishing the fieldwork.

I tried out various axes of comparison, testing them out and then realizing that they did not fit, or were boring. I tried comparing non-profit to for-profit to government-sponsored organizations, but quickly realized that almost all of my organizations were all three at once. I tried comparing programs that aimed primarily to make kids do homework with those that primarily made kids do community service, but the two bled into each other—kids in the first almost all had to be in the second. I also re-read my notes often, during each rewrite, of which there are an embarrassingly large number.

From description to explanation, third step: reading more, to find resonance: There is a constant back-and-forth between the story that the ethnographer is telling and the story that others are telling. One might start with a political ax to grind,[5] but while doing the research, the ax has to be lain aside momentarily. With ethnography, starting with an ax often is insufficient, because you are studying something that no one has noticed yet: I started this research just when these Empowerment Projects were becoming ubiquitous. A research literature was growing up around them, planning them, counting them, and criticizing them, and this book grew like a vine climbing on these new objects in the world: the projects and their critics.

From description to explanation, fourth step: so what are you gonna do about it?: For those social scientists who aim to critique current conditions, this last step is often important. Current social criticism often tacks on a hopeful vision as an abstract pie-in-the-sky afterthought, disconnected from the author's realistic description of current horrors. When Marx, for example, described the horrors of capitalism, his story was influential not just because it decried the horrors, but because, in his theory, the horrors and the hopeful vision arose from the same conditions.

Notes

INTRODUCTION: EMPOWER YOURSELF

1. An organization is called a "nonprofit" if it fulfills the following criteria: it uses some volunteers, does not operate primarily for profit, is not run mainly by the government, and does something for the public good. Harvard, Greenpeace, local, unfunded volunteer groups, most preschools, orchestras, soup kitchens, and hospitals fit this definition (Salamon and Anheier 1996: 11; for critiques, see Smith 1997; Eliasoph 2009).

2. Albertson's, a grocery store chain, has on its breakfast cereal boxes (between 2004 and 2009): "Imagine all the things you could do *instead of watching television! Unplug* the tube and grab your family! You could: volunteer your time at a soup kitchen . . . Work on a jigsaw puzzle . . . Catch fireflies . . . Plant some flowers . . . " These suggestions show a recurrent theme for this book: volunteering is good regardless of the timing of the recipients' needs (what if you unplugged your television at midnight?). For the toilet paper company, see chapter 12.

3. All names of people, places, and organizations have been changed, to preserve anonymity.

4. In a contemplative investigation, Sennett (2004) describes this and other twists of respect in conditions of inequality.

5. Williams 1974.

6. While not all Empowerment *Talk* happens in Empowerment *Projects*, these organizations may well be Empowerment Talk's "home turf" (as Alford and Friedland might put it; 1985).

7. See, e.g., Kunda 1992; Kameo 2009, on its use in high-tech firms; Adler, Kwon, and Heckscher 2008 in hospitals.

8. Hall 1992; Salamon and Anheier 1996; Salamon and Sokolowski 2005; Smith and Lipsky 1993. Excellent comparative overviews and critiques include Bode 2006; Boli and Thomas 1999; Clemens 2004; Dekker 2009; Dekker 2004; Edwards 2009; Edwards and Hulme 1996; Enjolras 2009.; Evers 2009; Sirianni and Friedland 2001; Hupe et al. 2000; Laville and Nyssens 2001; and Minkoff 2002.

9. This discussion summarizes similar ones put forth in Beem 1999; Esping-Anderson 1990, Schofer and Fourcade-Gourinchas 2001; Hall 1992; and Smith and Lipsky 1993.

10. I use the concept of "neo-liberalism," but not phrase. The phrase is just too confusing in American English, since what we mean by "liberal" and what theorists mean by it are nearly, but not 180 degrees, opposite. Using the term, Rose (1989), Cruikshank (1999), Gershon (2010), and Haney (2010), all describe precisely the same process that I portray here.

11. All types of organizations have built-in tensions. The classic example is bureaucracy. We like its impartiality, predictability, and explicit rules, so that we can try to enforce fair, universal treatment, but we dread the same: its impersonal impartiality, predictable monotony, and rule-bound "red-tape" (Weber 1946).

12. This is Kenneth Burke's recipe (1969) for investigating rhetoric, but I am expanding it to make it useful for mundane organizational life. The emphasis on "how's" comes from Katz (2001). "Organizational style" is from Eliasoph and Lichterman 2003; see similar ideas in Hallet and Ventresca 2006; Gouldner 1956. Lichterman and I called this "group style," but "organizational style" captures this actor's implicit methods of distributing what can be said in one part of the organization—to the needy youth at the luncheon, perhaps—versus what can be said in another part—on the grant form, or to the city youth department, for example. Within any complex organization there are many "groups" (Schein 1970), some corresponding to functional differences, some to personal affinities, each with its own style that has to fit into the puzzle of the larger organization.

13. The very useful concept is "typification" (Schutz 1967 [1932]; Cefaï 1997; Cicourel 1985). People implicitly "typify" the motives, people, or activities, grouping the disparate stars into constellations. People do not invent these typifications from scratch each time, but intuitively know when it is appropriate to retrieve them, in certain moments and not others.

14. The school day ends in the middle of the afternoon in the United States. Most places have no state-sponsored care after school.

15. But what were they, if "non-white"? Two Community House teens called themselves "Native American" when distinguishing themselves from other, whiter Mexicans; another girl whose parents were from the Caribbean called herself Latino when distinguishing herself from African Americans, but called herself black at other times; what they said depended on what they were doing with whom at the moment. This echoes Roth's (2009) observations of people's everyday, situational racial classifications.

16. Giddens 1991. Our rituals, even our "please's" and "thank-you's" and rituals of daily interaction, tend to fail, in the sense of feeling too "surface" and not deeply authentic (Alexander 2004). Here is a case of a permanently failing ritual, and its failure is what allows the organization to keep going. The rituals succeed by failing.

CHAPTER 1: HOW TO LEARN SOMETHING IN AN EMPOWERMENT PROJECT

1. The phrase "family resemblance" comes from Wittgenstein (1953). These missions are, with some modifications, drawn from *On Justification* (Boltanski and Thévenot 1991), and Thévenot's subsequent work (2001, 2006, 2007). For more, see Appendix 1.

2. As Goodwin, Jasper, and Polletta (2001) argue, sociologists routinely underestimate the power of passion as a source, not just a response, to social structure.

3. Neo-institutionalism theorizes this "decoupling" of projected images from members' everyday activities (DiMaggio and Powell 1991; Meyer and Powell 1991). They say that all organizations need "myths" (Empowerment Talk would

be one) to survive, that organizations need to project these noble images of themselves, and that no organization can live up to those lofty myths. The decoupling can never be complete, so we need to ask what happens instead; a wealth of recent institutionalist studies have begun to show how organizations "decouple" words and deeds "in patterned, systematic ways" (Eliasoph and Lo forthcoming; Morrill 1995; Heimer and Staffen 1998; Heimer and Gazley 2006; Swidler 2006; Swidler and Watkins 2007; Lounsbury, Ventresca, and Hirsch 2003; Rao 1998; Schneiberg and Lounsbury 2007). DiMaggio argues that knowing what one of these public stories means requires knowing where and by whom it is being invoked (2007; see also Brunnson 2002, for a more cynical rendition of the same).

4. This point echoes Boltanski and Thévenot's (2005) logic: the principles (of the market, bureaucracy, church, etc.) are not intrinsically helpful or harmful; what matters is how they play out in practice. How to judge whether an ideal is helpful or harmful in any given situation is part of a much longer debate of the potential discrepancy between the researcher's judgment and the research subjects' judgment. For a smart summary, see Burawoy (1991). I rely on my *observing organizers' and youth participants' mixed feelings*; if something feels somewhat wrong to them, *it shows*, and I can document how and when it hurts, empirically.

5. Power 1997; Strathern 2000.

6. Contrast this with Kramer (1994), Smith and Lipsky (1993), e.g., who ask if funders' mandates lead to professionalization and bureaucratization and a devaluation of grassroots volunteering. Again, my question is not about principles, but about how or if they materialize in everyday situations (Wacquant 2004).

7. This definition combines Booth and Jouve (2005).

8. The triad comes from Bacqué and Sintomer's neat summary of commonalities in such projects in Brazil, France, and the United States (2001).

9. In Cairo, see Elyachar 2005; in Santiago, Rius 2010 in rural Malawi, Swidler and Watkins 2007. For a superb overview, see Edwards and Hulme 1996. In general, projects in impoverished nations are less insistently concerned with cultivating a family-like atmosphere than European and other wealthy nations' projects, but they hope to transform gender relations and teach personal self-management—in Malawi, the lesson takes the form of "Life Skills" (Swidler and Watkins 2007: 1190).

10. Putnam 2000. See the conclusion for some severe critiques of this idea, especially Cohen and Arato 1996.

11. Swidler and Watkins 2007.

12. Haney 2010.

13. Marwell 2004: 274.

14. Thus, there might be Empowerment Projects in separate "wings" of an organization (Brunsson 1990; Clemens and Cook 1999; Cefaï and Joseph 2002; March and Simon 1958). A hospital (most hospitals are nonprofits in the United States), for example, might have an empowerment "wing" if it offers workshops in which groups of patients are taught to take responsibility for eating well and staying fit, or to manage their feelings about their disease.

15. Sampson 1996.

16. This nervous history of planning the grass roots partly from the top-down includes government programs in the 1920s, for example, that opened up public

schools at night, so average citizens could come discuss the issues of the day (Mattson 1998; Keith 2007).

17. Alexis de Tocqueville 1835: 151 (taken from the French version because the English translation of this sentence, in the text that most of us use [1968] is wrong).

18. Emerson's writing has had immeasurable influence on American writers, policy makers, institution builders, and philosophers (Stout 2003; Kateb 1992; Henkel and Stirrat 2001, e.g.).

19. "Self-Reliance," 1848: 107–110.

20. This way of thinking goes back further: Puritan theologians insisted that the only way to know God was directly, without a bureaucratic church's mediation, just as the only way to know the taste of honey is to taste, it, not by hearing someone talk about it, in Jonathan Edwards' famous image (1734).

21. Addams 2001 [1901]: 12. Dewey puts this image as civic engagement well: "The public," he says, "is not a thing, but an entity that is constantly in search of itself" (1926).

22. Erikson 1950; Wishy 1999; Tocqueville 1969 [1835]. As Mead (1967, quoted in Hulbert 2004: 207), put it, "So longstanding and so rapid have been these processes of change that expectation of and anxiety about change have been built into the very character of our people."

23. The phrase "make the road by walking it" comes from the Highlander School, for civil rights activists in the 1960s, thus showing that this influential approach to civic action is not just the property of one race or class.

24. This clearly does not apply only to Americans or children. Molinier (2005) and Traustadottir (2000), using mainly French and Icelandic examples, respectively, argue that this tact is necessary in any caregiving relationship—making, for example, the senior citizen feel as if the aid in inserting the catheter is freely given, and emphasizing the recipient's self-sufficiency, even if he or she needs help with basic tasks. On "prospectancy," see Gorney (1972: 497–502). See the conclusion for a dissection, following Rose (1989), of the uses and misuses of hope as a management technique in corporations and government.

25. The story I recount is very abbreviated. For more, see Alexander 2006; Bellah et al. 1985; Stout 2003; Eliasoph, Lichterman, and Cefaï in progress; Schudson 1998.

26. Jacobs 1993 [1961].

27. Wuthnow 1999; Hustinx 2001.

28. Boltanski and Chiapello 1991; Rose 1989; Steinmetz 2005.

29. Rose 1999: 173, paraphrasing Donzelot 1991.

PART ONE: CULTIVATING OPEN CIVIC EQUALITY

1. Warner 1992; Verba, Brady, and Schlozman 1956; Mcpherson and Rotolo 1996 ; Popielarz 1995, e.g. Historically, many were often downright bigoted (Kaufman 2002; Skocpol 2003).

2. Beck 1970 cited in Smith and Lipsky 1996.

3. Alexander 2006, 1998.

CHAPTER 2: PARTICIPATING UNDER UNEQUAL AUSPICES

1. Both groups were correct, as bounteous social research demonstrates: engagement in structured extracurricular activities, whether in a church, volunteer work, arts or academic clubs (Deschenes, McLaughlin, and O'Donoghue 2006; Eccles and Barber 1999;, Barber, Eccles and Stone 2001, e.g.), often lowers adolescents' chance of engaging in risky behavior and increases their chance of doing well in school. Whether or not there is a correlation is not my question, of course; rather, it is how the adolescents hear and understand their programs' uses of these correlations.

2. Handy et al., forthcoming; Friedland, and Morimoto n.d.

3. From a newsletter titled "The Afterschool Advocate."

4. Comparing costs of programs like this to the cost of a year in prison is common in these social service circles: "It costs more to send a kid to prison for a year than to Harvard," was the phrase I heard most often. Their point is, obviously, that an ounce of prevention is worth a pound of cure. But different people pay for prison (taxpayers) than Harvard (parents or trustees, not taxpayers). The comparison includes a neat switch of the verb's subject, that only makes sense when assuming that "we" will have to pay, one way or another.

5. Rosenblatt 2005.

6. We will "do better in math" and "increase our opportunities for everything," as a fifth grader put it on a video interview, explaining why the school district should not cut funding of her orchestra in Los Angeles (LAUSD 2008). Similarly, a city near Snowy Prairie had a program called "Arts are Prevention," to fund teen rock bands. See Rivkin-Fish (2003) on these mixed justifications.

7. More extreme and expensive examples come from bigger cities: Ordinary activities like fishing start to glow with the aura of potential cures for vast social inequality. They had statistics on music education in schools, but thinking of musicians from Charlie Parker to Judy Garland to Jim Morrison to Jimi Hendrix to Janice Joplin to Kurt Cobain to Ginger Baker to Serge Gainsbourg to Michael Jackson on down—suicides, overdose cases, or junkies all—it made me wonder: maybe it prevents suicide unless you get too famous? Or maybe it is another case of misaligned time frames: music prevents teen suicide but encourages adult suicide, so those adult suicides would not count against teen programs' success rates?

8. I was sitting next to Miracle and passed her a little note saying, "I never said a word a single word in school till my third year of college, and now I'm a professor!" This was easy for me to say since it was true, but it also indirectly sent a message upholding the usual organizational style. She looked really pleased and actually talked to me afterward, saying that she wants to be a tenth-grade math teacher. I felt the excessive pride that adult volunteers probably often feel in these situations. I saved her soul! Scouting out one's own hypocrisy is an important part of the ethnographic method.

9. The other main problem among non-disadvantaged youth was what organizers called workaholism. Scholars and activists (Lareau 2003; Wexler et al. 1992; Shor 1992, e.g.) have started to say that strenuous schedules are not as

harmless as they seem. Encouraging college-oriented to "do less" may seem to be an easier goal than fixing disadvantaged youths' problems, but puzzles abound: what about teens who enjoy their four AP courses?

10. As Morimoto and Friedland (n.d.) argue, someone like VJ knows that it looks good on his resume, but making this knowledge explicit undermines its power. If some kids volunteer for the wrong reasons, or list projects on their resumes but never actually do the work, then the investment's value goes down. Nationally, school officials have tried to codify voluntarism and other immeasurable goods, giving applicants extra points for having overcome adversity, played bassoon, excelled in sports (Stevens 2006). This "cultural capital" looks like it comes naturally to non-disadvantaged youth. Snowy Prairie youth workers were trying to level the playing field by making the unspoken rules explicit, but talking about it so explicitly kills its power—if everyone shares it, it is no longer "capital" (Bourdieu 1987).

11. This is very different from what Tronto (1994) describes as the "privileged irresponsibility" of a man who pays someone else to do his laundry, cooking, and cleaning, rendering invisible the care-work that went into making his life possible; he looks and feels independent. Caroline's case illustrates the other side of the coin: this feeling of independence does not have to breed irresponsibility, but may be necessary for developing enough of a sense of independence to take any responsibility at all.

12. Thévenot 1999.

13. Advanced Placement courses are university-level courses taught in high schools.

14. There can be two different "polities" (Boltanski and Thevenot 1991) in play simultaneously, when people enter a situation differently, through different doors, with different personal histories and futures (Lamont 2009).

Chapter 3: "The Spirit that Moves Inside You"

1 Americorps volunteers are paid, minimally, by the federal government.

Chapter 4: Temporal Leapfrog

1. Merton 1957.

2. Walker and McCarthy (in progress) find that organizations that hold little fundraisers tend to have more local ties; these dinners show the mechanism.

3. As oriented toward a future as everyone else in Empowerment Projects was, Sheila had organized the program partly to show future employers that she had experience with diverse youth. Once she found a paid job, she did not have time to continue volunteering, so she was trying to convince me to take over the volunteer position.

4. Describing anti-HIV work in Malawi, Swidler and Watkins (2007) show that while it is ineffective for encouraging condom use, it does create some Samia-like pride in some of the projects' young educators.

5. Culture critics (Hunter 2000, e.g.) say that this emphasis on pleasure and fun is an abdication of responsibility, inviting people only to obey their sensual whims, and making discussion of other moral motives rare, thus making morality hard to develop. The culture critics are partly right but miss the way that "fun" can become a prescription, not a description, because they would pay too much attention to the words without listening to what people were doing with words. Examining moral lessons that are given in texts, as culture critics do, makes it impossible to observe the temporal dimension of this moral dialogue: when Emily spoke about "fun," most participants knew that she did not mean simple self-indulgence. They knew this because they knew her.

6. Later that month, while dropping something off at my own kids' school, I saw a six-year-old girl miserably sitting waiting to see the principal, for punishment. A teacher breezed past to get her mail, taking time to scold, "What are you doing here? Did you make the wrong choices again?" Of course, the girl just hung her head. Asking "did you make the wrong choices?" simply meant "were you being bad?"

CHAPTER 5: DEMOCRACY MINUS DISAGREEMENT

1. Hamidi (2006).

2. Surprisingly unimportant after all of the above: taking sides would be illegal for these tax-exempt organizations. Nonprofit organizations can be tax-exempt in the United States, as long as they are non-partisan. Chaves, Stephens, and Galaskie-wicz' (2004) statistical sample is entirely consonant with what I found: despite this regulation, nonprofits are not necessarily more depoliticized than other voluntary associations; the tax regulations are surprisingly unimportant in nonprofits' everyday operations, except when the organizers exaggerate their importance.

3. McFarland and Thomas 2006, e.g., Hodgkinson, Gates, and Schervish 1995. Volunteering lead to a modest boost in the chances of political participation later in life, as many have demonstrated. The question is how. The mechanism may be the youth participant's interpretation of the community service (Jones and Hill 2003; McGuire and Gamble 2006), including, above all, thoughtful discussion of it (Youniss and Yates 1997; Baizerman, Rohoth, and Hildreth 2008).

4. The local food pantry program was unlike UNICEF: it was less educational (no mind-boggling lists of how much a few pennies could buy), and not connected to an international body. It did not aim to be democratic; the people who received the "can o' tuna" did not get to decide whether or not they wanted to spend the money on better preschools instead.

5. Poppendieck 1999.

6. Baizerman, Rohoth, and Hildreth 2008

7. Activists and scholars have long decried this depoliticized treatment: youth learn that Rosa Parks sat down on the bus "because her feet were tired," but do not learn about the political organization that taught her and her colleagues how to rebel, over the long haul. In local speeches, *civic* engagement was called good, natural, and simple; *political* engagement was, implicitly, bad, artificial, and complicated (Somers 1995).

8. Learning not to complain is, according to some research, more important in the American Midwest than in other places—in New York, for example, complaining is a method of bonding with strangers (Tannen 2005). But people complained in Snowy Prairie, just not in Empowerment Projects.

9. Laura knew both sides of the debate. In the 12-week workshop for youth workers, she argued with another Casa Latina organizer, Roland. He said that some teachers he respects are in favor of English immersion. Laura says kids can't learn math when they don't know the English words for numbers. Roland says the kids' parents all want them to learn English and that they quickly do learn it. He cites studies; she cites studies. It was really a beautiful debate between these two dedicated, long-term organizers, happening in this place that theorists would not predict: a certificate class for paid youth workers.

10. The teens left at 9 p.m., immediately after speaking, though many of the other people in the packed hall were still waiting to testify. Were they lacking courtesy, or was it that they were not treating this as a public event, where people are supposed to hear each other out to the end?

11. The phrase "civic skills" comes from Verba, Brady, and Schlozman (1995: 311): their list includes learning to take minutes, chair a meeting, speak in public, and write to a representative.

12. By echoing the form of political institutions, this organizational form appears to link the little local group to a long tradition of American democracy (Skocpol 2003). This symbolic link is only partly right; in these hidden, intimate, family-like conditions, this form did not feel one bit like Congress; it felt like dinner.

13. Over the same years that young people have become less politically active, they have grown more eager to address problems locally and personally, by volunteering, in a compassionate, one-on-one relationship in the United States (Delli Carpini and Keeter 2001; Lachelier 2007), in the Netherlands (Hustinx 2001), in Australia (Manning 2007) and elsewhere.

CHAPTER 6: HARMLESS AND DESTRUCTIVE PLUG-IN VOLUNTEERS

1. Such short-term relationships between adult "mentors" and youth are typical (Rhodes and Grossman 2002: 200). Long-term relationships with volunteer mentors can be very helpful, but short-term mentoring relationships are often harmful (Rhodes 2007: 4; DuBois 2007). DuBois, Holloway, Valentine, and Cooper (2002: 187–88) find that almost half of mentor relationships are either harmful or inconsequential.

2. Philipsen 1992.

3. Thévenot 2006; Breviglieri and Stavo-Debauge 2003.

4. For an excellent overview, see Smith and Lipsky 1993.

5. Only certain youth were eligible for mentors. Having an unstable or neglectful family was not necessary. Youth who had mentors all lived in a low-income neighborhood, were black, or had a Spanish or East Asian surname.

6. See again, Rhodes and Grossman 2002: 214. Relationships between volunteers and disturbed youth tend to end earlier than relationships with youth who

form bonds more easily; and for an adolescent who already has difficulty forming attachments, being abandoned by a mentor deepens the difficulty.

7. Essed 1990.

8. Anderson 1990; Lee 2000, e.g.

9. As interracial marriages and adoptions create racially diverse families, the families may have a chance to experience all the mind-opening perplexities that people in youth programs experienced (Galvin 2003). Like Emily, however, these parents can learn, incrementally, alongside their children, over a lifetime.

10. Viaud-Gayet 2008; Cottereau 1999.

11. Garfinkel 1966.

12. Mauss 2000 [1924]; Auyero 2001; Gershon 2010.

13. Putnam 2000.

14. Daniels (1988) and Ostrander (1984) give fascinating glimpses into these women's lives and long-term dedication.

15. Those who worked in the "mentor" program were screened lightly: since they drove kids places, they had to get background checks to make sure they were not criminals, and they were asked to make a year-long commitment, which they did not always fulfill.

16. Hillman 1960: 89. This historical difference will be discussed further in the conclusion.

17. E. Eliasoph 1959: 141.

CHAPTER 7: PAID ORGANIZERS CREATING TEMPORALLY FINITE, INTIMATE, FAMILY-LIKE ATTACHMENTS

1. "Giving of yourself 100%" is a puzzle, of course, for anyone, but becomes even more puzzling when money is involved (Hondagneu-Sotelo 1991; Hochschild 2003; Parreñas 2001; Macdonald and Merrill 2002).

2. It was not, in other words, what Stone (2000, describing paid care, calls "caring by the book."

3. "Blended family" is Stacey's (1998) term.

4. Boltanski and Thévenot 2005 [1991]; Barbelet 199; Hochschild 1983.

CHAPTER 8: PUBLICLY QUESTIONING NEED

1. Arendt (1958) says that bringing "need" into the public arena short-circuits reasonable dialogue. "Need" sounds too blind, raw, urgent, and irrational for a public discussion. Fraser (1989) shows that public "needs talk" is never quite so "raw"; societies have patterned ways that people can publicly press claims of "need." As this chapter shows, when a person has to make a public claim of "need," the process risks putting all needs up for debate.

2. Calling safety an "investment" seemed to be a neutral way to avoid offending all the potential audiences, but it also made it seem more like a rational calculation—a choice rather than a need.

3. Viaud-Gayet 2008.

4. Popenoe says that adults need to provide children with "a consensus of shared values" (1995: 73). Elshtain (1995) criticizes Arendt's similar idea of a hidden, dark place for the young to develop before entering the contested political arena; as Elshtain argues, no place is completely untouched.

5. Mills 1979.

CHAPTER 9: DRAWING ON SHARED EXPERIENCE IN A DIVIDED SOCIETY

1. This is amply documented by Bourdieu (1987), for example.

2. Gumperz 1988. Edelsky (1981) shows that what sounds like "chiming in" to one person in a discussion feels like "interruption" to another, depending on the "footing" (Goffman 1979).

3. The researcher's own feelings are useful if they can pry open a window onto theoretical insight (Blee 2002, e.g.), and especially if they are then confirmed by other means. In this case, I came down with a high fever a few hours later, so it was not even "I" who had this experience.

4. The denial of the story did not hold for another reason. Logically, if you do not become "that person for them," and no other organizers are available, some teens will have no one who is "that person."

5. Malinowski 1972 [1923]. More precisely, organizers like Kristin were trying to keep a phatic "frame" in play (Goffman 1974, Tracy, ed., 1991).

6. Eliasoph 1988; Biggart 1989.

7. Schudson 1997; Seligman 1991.

PART THREE: CELEBRATING OUR DIVERSE, MULTICULTURAL COMMUNITY

1. This worry has been almost as much of a constant in the United States as has been the fear of bureaucracy. For almost a century, schools have taught folk music of many lands (Olneck 1990). Like the potent symbol of "the volunteer" and the bureaucrat, the ideal of diversity transforms over American history.

CHAPTER 10: "GETTING OUT OF YOUR BOX" VERSUS "PRESERVING A CULTURE"

1. In the 1990s and early 2000s, a person could easily grow up in Snowy Prairie without hearing anyone routinely speaking another language outside of a language class.

2. Instead of presuming to know what the "dominant culture" was, as many sociologists easily would, I had to wait, to hear who needed to justify themselves in what ways, where, to whom; what needed justifying and what could be taken for granted.

3. Carr and Kefalas 2009, e.g.

4. Gamson 1996.

5. Du Bois 2003 (1903); Mead 1932, 1934; Addams 1901; Dewey 1926.

CHAPTER 11: TELL US ABOUT YOUR CULTURE

1. This example is doubly funny because *Little Black Sambo* is a book that has been deemed racist for so long, I doubt that anyone in the room younger than age fifty had read it.

2. Schudson 1997.

3. Mead, 1934: 135.

4. Many scholars and activists have criticized the "after-hours ethnicity" that includes only displays of beautiful clothing, appetizing foods, colorful and fragrant rituals, and folklore (see Rudrappa 2004, for a summary). See also the literary movement "McOndo," which satirizes the name of the village "Macondo" in the novel *100 Years of Solitude*.

5. Similarly, "There is a ready-made set of phrases people can turn to when explaining Samoanness . . . These terms are ones that people representing Samoanness readily produced in government training sessions . . . Explicating Samoan cultural values on this level is a far cry from understanding or conveying Samoan cultural knowledge" (Gershon 2010).

6. Bellah et al. 1991; Appiah 1996.

7. Classic essays are collected in Gumperz and Hymes 1973; Gumperz 1988; ; Giglioli 1972. See Jupp, Roberts, and Cook-Gumperz (1982) for a superb example of "crosstalk."

8. To make this point, I have to violate a key element of Empowerment Talk: I noticed qualities like hair and skin color, and the ethnic and age cues that go with names (Lieberson 2000). When I was in graduate school, I showed some field notes to my advisor *before* I changed the names of my research subjects, and my advisor gently chastised me for giving them names that she found ridiculous.

9. Literary images of the northern Midwest portray this reticence as a regional cultural style (Keillor 1985). For similar regional differences, see Tannen 2005.

10. In one small group discussion, I tried to say to Janet that everyone's culture is different, and that compared to people in the Midwest, people in the East seemed, to me personally, "warmer." But before I got to the word "warmer," Janet interrupted to say "in your face," and told a story about how rude New Yorkers are.

11. These situations echoed a study in which white and black jump-roping girls constantly misunderstood each other. The white girls praised each other no matter how poorly they jumped, while the black girls teased each other no matter how well they jumped. So, when they all jumped rope together, the black girls felt annoyed at the phony praise (which the white girls considered encouragement— part of what made jump rope enjoyable for them), while the white girls felt insulted at the put-downs (which the black girls considered to be fun teasing—part of what made jump rope enjoyable for *them*) (Goodwin and Goodwin 1990).

12. Earlier, Isaac had teased her about her giant feet, and she had responded with a wince and a nervous joke. Whether such comments are legal or not depends: in two California cities, it is, but it is just "inappropriate" in the rest of the state, as my university's anti-harassment training put it.

13. Some "differences" eluded the radar of "diversity," when, for example, youth volunteers and organizers alike traded mean jokes and stereotypes about old people ("They love pets," "They love cards").

1. Juneteenth commemorates the day that slaves in Texas found out that they were free, two years after the law had set them free.

2. Sullivan (2002) says that we need to learn to celebrate the current complex institutions that actually bring us together. These events may not have produced much collective effervescence, but at least they tried.

3. That was the basis of selection for the Mentor Program, no matter how much a child was surrounded by loving parents, aunts, and grandparents.

4. Hmong people fought on the side of the United States in the Vietnam War and were promised homes in the United States. They got them: on the coldest, most northern edges of the rural Midwest—colder than Moscow.

5. Portes and Zhou 1993. The theory is controversial, since it implies that culture, in addition to simple poverty and discrimination, is a problem. Critics call it a form of blaming the victim.

6. This tension between, on the one hand, wanting to appreciate each individual who "can be great because anyone can serve," regardless of "conditions," and, on the other hand, wanting to change the world, so that no one will be damaged by poor conditions, is what anthropologist Louis Dumont calls the "congenital Christian tension" (Dumont 1986).

7. Hodgkinson, Gates, and Schervish 1995.

8. A lay pastor is someone who the church authorizes to lead a congregation, without the full training that a real pastor has.

9. In a similar situation, Lichterman (2005), a Jewish researcher among Christians, describes being asked to lead a prayer and wondering if there was a Hebrew prayer about social workers, and if so, how to teach it to fellow supplicants.

10. Ammerman 1997.

11. As Taylor (1988) observes, something is lost if the listener does not know whether a song is sung at weddings or funerals (and whether funerals are considered sad or joyous releases in that society), or if it is an ironic take-off on an earlier tune, sacred or sexy or both.

12. A greeting card company invented Mother's Day. Christmas's focus on family gift-giving developed in the late 1800s, through active marketing (Gillis 1996). Starbucks' sugar skulls teach non-Mexicans in Nebraska about the Día de los muertos (Marchi 2006).

1. The Inuit diet . . . which includes marine mammals such as beluga whale . . . puts them at the top of a contaminated food chain. The toxins collect in the animals' fat and are passed on to the Inuit as they eat, or through breast milk . . . the

breast milk and tissues of some Greenlanders could be classified as hazardous waste (from Bluevoice.org, 7/12/05. See also Callon (1986) on nature as an ongoing project).

2. Seligman 1991: 145–98; Schudson 1997; Dekker 2009.

3. Cohen and Arato 1991.

4. This echoes Cohen and Arato (1991), Skocpol (2003), Beem (1999), Dekker (2009), and others, who criticize the overly face-to-face, personal vision of social capital that Putnam promotes. They say that we need the universalizing state to bring us together. Particularistic, local face-to-face interactions are not enough.

5. Boltanski and Chiapello (1991) underline this connection between the liberation movements of the 1960s and '70s, human potential movement, and new workplace relations.

6. Rose (1989: 110) lists some of these psychologists, including Erik Erikson, Kurt Lewin, J. L. Moreno, and Margaret Mead. Rose's story is already full of irony, but could be more so if he had observed that these four, along with many of their colleagues, drew on Marxist thought, and some were progressive, leftist activists. If the result of their ideas' influence was to bind workers more tightly to the capitalist firm, and citizens more tightly to the unjust state, this was very much an unintended consequence.

7. Arendt 1963.

8. Bellah 1970.

9. Sacks 1972: 332–34. The listener instantly and viscerally summons a pathway that is both personal and symbolically shared.

10. Freeman (1972) describes this "tyranny of structurelessness" and its origins in 1960s and '70s peace and women's liberation groups.

11. When modernity's ghosts haunt organizers, organizers' repeated responses become solid patterns. These patterned responses become more and more solidly predictable, in turn, eventually turning into brand-new ghosts that will haunt future organizations, round and round. The things are solid for the time being, the way a sedimentary rock feels solid, now that it is no longer mud, and before it dissolves into the river again (Krinsky 2007; Glaeser 2005; Thévenot 2006; Ricœur 1991: 430). These routines vary in their solidity; some feel rock-solid, have been the same for years, and would take years to rebuild.

12. Schudson 1998, 2006.

13. For a sensitive critique of this "Manichean" black and white approach to activism, see Boyte 2001.

14. See Eliasoph 1998, Evers 2009.

15. Kretzmann and McKnight 1993, e.g.

16. Kretzmann and McKnight 1993: 25.

17. Hyatt 2001, e.g. Does outsourcing government projects to volunteers and NGOs actually save the government money? This is a big debate, which depends on what monies are counted. If done well, coordinating volunteers and monitoring a myriad of nonprofits costs *more* than a smoothly running, centralized bureaucracy (Smith and Stone 1988; Smith and Lipsky 1993).

18. If corporate donors use the money for publicity, write it off as charitable tax deductions, and have indirect control over the donations, then it is an unelected "shadow state" (Wolch 1999). Without this escape hatch, the money

would have gone to taxes, and then, instead of being indirectly controlled by a corporation, it would have been controlled by an elected government.

19. Stack 1994, e.g.

20. Scott 1989.

21. Hyatt 2001; Sampson 1996; Elyachar 2005.

22. A. Smith 2007: 8; Gilmore 2007; Thunder Hawk, 2007, e.g.

23. The other clear illustration of these critics' point is the 1960s War on Poverty, in which the government tried to defuse inner-city riots by inviting poor people to "participate" in tame, peaceful forums. But when poor people demanded money for schools, housing, or health care, the invitation was canceled. Expensive or radical change was not the kind of "participation" that policy makers had hoped to find and fund (Van Til and Van Til 1970; Piven and Cloward 1978, e.g.); "empowerment" was not the programs' goal; control of the poor was.

24. Merton (1949) describes old-fashioned bureaucrats' need to hide behind roles, allowing for what March and Simon (1958: 164) call "the absorption of uncertainty."

25. Austin 1965, Cottereau 1999.

26. Sampson 1996; Sperling, Ferree, and Risman 2001; Swidler 2006, e.g.

27. These observations come especially from studies by my undergraduates at USC.

28. Hondagneu-Sotelo and Raskoff 1994. This sadly complements a study of NGO-sponsored racial sensitivity groups (Walsh 2007). Following a series of weekly dialogues between small groups of citizens of varied races, many black participants concluded that whites were not as racist as they had thought. No, they concluded: whites were even more racist than they had thought!

29. Haney 2010.

30. "New management" techniques presume this natural voice to be the best: "the deliberative practitioner" and the "responsive bureaucrat" (see, e.g., Stivers 2001; Fox and Miller 1995; Forester 1999), are supposed to specialize in "listening," as if the *vox populi* is the simple voice of truth.

31. Citizens' juries do not create ongoing places for engagement, but participating in one might incite conversation elsewhere, through "the questioning of everyday, apparently harmless practices, such as buying prawns or coffee" Luque 2005: 220). On the other hand, such organizations may have, over the past decade, become a "participatory-industrial complex," producing a quick and dirty simulacrum of participation (Lee 2007).

32. Fung 2004.

33. http://www.grameen-info.org/. The literature on micro-credit is vast. For good overviews of basic questions, see Schreiner 2005; Hashemi, Schuler, and Riley 1996.

34. Biaocchi 2002; Bacqué and Sintomer 2001. See Berger (2009) on similar projects in Belgium. Teenagers in youth programs do not control million-dollar budgets. But many "participatory budgets" also have "advisory power only"; those are more like Snowy Prairie's programs than like those of Porto Alegre.

35. Baizerman, Rohoth, and Hildreth 2008.

36. A striking example of this, and the risks involved, is in Carrell and Rosenberg 2002. They examine a series of "mutual qualification" projects, in which, for

example, disadvantaged low-income housing residents meet with building managers and planners, or immigrant youth meet with the bus drivers who often maltreat them. Over the course of a dozen long meetings, the groups become emotionally explosive. Through this "catharsis," the groups arrive at mutual understanding—when they do not simply collapse from the explosion.

37. Hillman 1960.

38. At Hull House, not surprisingly, his training was rigidly classical, not free, optional, or up to him to decide whatever (Glowacki and Hendry 2004: 84).

39. Addams 1960 [1910].

40. Ibid., 89.

41. Zerubavel 2006.

42. As Lamont (1992) shows, boundaries simultaneously divide up the world in ways that reinforce inequality, and also make thought possible. My suggestions here underscore that idea. The hope is that conscious recognition of the boundaries might lessen inequality.

43. This personifies the character that made what Harvey (1990) calls "The Fordist compromise" possible.

44. "Long-standing" here means at least 150 years old, since The Communist Manifesto criticized all these boundaries, and subsequent leftists and feminists have furthered the critique.

45. Arendt 1963.

46. As Marx put it in the *Communist Manifesto*. See http://www.marxists.org/

47. Steinmetz 2005; Boltanski and Chiapello 1991.

48. McGee 2005; Ehrenreich 2006.

49. Hackstaff 1999.

50. Bryson 1996.

51. Some colorful names include: "liquid modernity" (Baumann 1993)," "the bobo ethic" [short for bourgeois bohemian] (Brooks 2000), "the optional society" (Chalvon-Demersay 1996); Giddens describes a prison house in which we "have no choice but to choose" all the time (Giddens 1991).

APPENDIX 1

1. Alexander (1998, 2006); Walzer (1983); and Stone (1988) take somewhat similar approaches. Only Alexander shares *On Justification*'s essential, necessary emphasis on the pragmatic glitches that actors inevitably face when putting these justifications into practice.

2. All of the Empowerment Project's many missions, but especially the one for "transparency," had solidified into "equipment" (Thévenot 2003), or "props" (Burke 1969), or "material culture (e.g., Molotch 2000) or "things" (Latour and Weibel 2006). Sewell (1992) calls them "resources," but the word "resources" does not highlight the way that they *become* you—not a thing that you use, but that becomes part of the person's body, or defines the organization. See Stark and Girard (2007) for a creative use in an Empowerment Project.

3. Camus-Vigué (2000) argues that Americans, unlike French people, easily mix civic life with eating dinner, drinking beer, and socializing.

4. Thévenot 2007; Breviglieri, Pattaroni, and Stavo-Debauge 2003.

5. Cmiel 1991.

6. Luhtakallio (2010) says that the Finnish "civic" also includes getting one's hands dirty, building, hammering, and cooking.

7. Luhtakallio (2010), or Belgium (Berger 2009), Charles (forthcoming), or Italy and Spain (Talpin 2007).

APPENDIX 2

1. Suransky 1982.

2. Bogdan and Taylor1998.

3. Katz 2001: 454.

4. Burawoy 1991, 1998, 2000; Ragin 1992.

5. Burawoy 1991.

References

Abbott, Andrew. 2001. *Time Matters: On Theory and Method*. Chicago: University of Chicago Press.

Addams, Jane. 2002 [1901]. *Democracy and Social Ethics*. Urbana: University of Illinois Press.

———. 1960 [1910]. *Twenty Years at Hull-House*. New York: Signet.

Adler, Paul, Seok-Woo Kwon, and Charles Heckscher. 2008. "Professional Work: The Emergence of Collaborative Community." *Organizational Science* 18, no. 2: 359–76.

Alexander, Jeffrey. 2006. *The Civic Sphere*. New York: Oxford University Press.

———. 2004. "Cultural Pragmatics: Social Performance between Ritual and Strategy." *Sociological Theory* 22, no. 4: 527–73.

———. 2003. *The Meanings of Social Life: A Cultural Sociology*. New York: Oxford University Press.

———. 1998. "Introduction." In *Real Civil Society: Dilemmas of Institutionalization*, ed. Jeffrey Alexander. London: Sage.

———Alexander, Jeffrey, and Neil Smelser. 1999. "Introduction: The Ideological Discourse of Cultural Discontent." *Diversity and Its Discontents*, ed. Neil Smelser and Jefffrey Alexander. Princeton, NJ: Princeton University Press.

Alford, Robert, and Roger Friedland. 1985. *Powers of Theory: Capitalism, the State, and Democracy*. Cambridge: Cambridge University Press.

Ammerman, Nancy. 1997. *Congregation and Community*. New Brunswick, NJ: Rutgers University Press.

Anderson, Elijah. 1990. Streetwise: *Race, Class, and Change in an Urban Community*. Chicago: University of Chicago Press.

Armstrong, Elizabeth. 2002. *Forging Gay Identities*. Chicago: University of Chicago Press.

Appiah, K. Anthony. 1996. *Color Conscious: The Political Morality of Race*, with Amy Gutmann. Princeton, NJ: Princeton University Press.

Arendt, Hannah. 1977. "The Crisis in Education." In *Between Past and Future*, 173–96. New York: Penguin.

———. 1963a. *On Revolution*. New York: Penguin.

———. 2006 [1963b]. *Eichmann in Jerusalem: a Report on the Banality of Evil*. New York: Penguin.

———. 1958. *The Human Condition*. Chicago: University of Chicago Press.

Asset-based Community Development Institute. 2008. Institute for Policy Research, Northwestern University; http://www.sesp.northwestern.edu/abcd/.

Austin, J. L. 1965. *How to Do Things with Words*. Oxford: Oxford University Press.

Auyero, Javier. 2001. *Poor People's Politics*. Durham, NC: Duke University Press.

Bacque, Hélène, and Yves Sintomer. 2001. "Gestion de proximité et démocratie participative." *Les Annales de la recherche urbaine* 90: 148–55.

Baiocchi, Gianpaolo. 2002. *Militants and Citizens*. Stanford: Stanford University Press.

Baizerman, Michael, Ross Velure Roholt, and R. W. Hildreth. 2008. *Becoming Citizens: Deepening the Craft of Youth Civic Engagement*. New York: Routledge.

Bakhtin, Mikhail Mikhailovich. 1986. *Speech Genres and Other Late Essays*. Trans. Vern W. McGee, ed. Caryl Emerson and Michael Holquist. Austin: University of Texas Press.

Banting, Keith, ed. 2000. *The Nonprofit Sector in Canada: Roles and Relationships*. Kingston, Ontario: School of Policy Studies, Queen's University,.

Barbelet, J. M. 1998. *Emotion, Social Theory and Social Structure: A Macrosociological Approach*. New York: Cambridge University Press.

———. 1993. "Confidence: Time and Emotion in the Sociology of Action." *Journal for the Theory of Social Behaviour* 23, no. 3: 229–47.

Barber, B., Jacquelynne Eccles, and M. R. Stone. 2001. "Whatever Happened to the Jock, the Brain and the Princess? Young Adult Pathways Linked to Adolescent Activity Involvement and Social Identity." *Journal of Adolescent Research* 16(5): 429–55.

Battistoni, Richard, and William Hudson, eds. 1997. *Educating Citizenship: Concepts and Models for Service Learning in Political Science*. Washington, DC: American Association of Higher Education.

Bauman, Zygmunt. 1993. *Postmodern Ethics*. Cambridge, UK: Blackwell.

Beem, Christopher. 1999. *The Necessity of Politics: Reclaiming American Public Life*. Chicago: University of Chicago Press.

Bellah, Robert, Richard Madsen, William Sullivan, Ann Swidler, and Steven Tipton. 1991. *The Good Society*. New York: Knopf.

———. 1985. *Habits of the Heart*. Berkeley and Los Angeles: University of California Press.

———. 1970. "Between Religion and Social Science." In *Beyond Belief*, 237–59. New York: Harper.

Berger, M. 2009. Répondre en citoyen ordinaire. Enquête sur les engagements profanes dans un dispositif d'urbanisme participatif a` Bruxelles. Doctoral dissertation, Department of Sociology, Université Libre de Bruxelles.

Biggart, Nicole Woolsey. 1989. *Charismatic Capitalism: Direct Selling Organizations in America*. Chicago: University of Chicago Press.

Blee, Kathleen. 2002. *Inside Organized Racism*. Berkeley and Los Angeles: University of California Press.

Bob, Clifford. 2001. "Marketing Rebellion: Insurgent Groups, International Media, and NGO Support." *International Politics* 38: 311–34.

Bode, Inge. 2006. Disorganized Welfare Mixes: Voluntary Agencies and New Governance Regimes in Western Europe. *Journal of European Social Policy* 16, no. 4: 346–59.

Bogdan, Steven J., and Robert Taylor. 1998. *Introduction to Qualitative Research Methods*. New York: John Wiley and Sons.

Boli, J., and G. M. Thomas, eds. 1999. *Constructing World Culture: International Nongovernmental Organizations since 1875*. Stanford: Stanford University Press.

Boltanski, Luc, and Eve Chiapello, 1991, *Le nouvel esprit du capitalisme*. Paris: Gallimard.

Boltanski, Luc, and Laurent Thévenot. 2005 [1991]. *On Justification*. Princeton, NJ: Princeton University Press.

Booth, Philip, and Bernard Jouve. eds. 2005. *Metropolitan Democracies*. Burlington, VT: Ashgate.

Bourdieu, Pierre. 1987. *Distinction*. Cambridge, MA: Harvard University Press.

Boyte, Harry. 2001. "A Tale of Two Playgrounds: Young People and Politics." Annual meeting of American Political Science Association, San Francisco.

Breviglieri, M. 2007a. "Le "corps empêché" de l'usager (mutisme, fébrilité, épuisement). Aux limites d'une politique du consentement informé dans le travail social." In J.-P. Payet, F. Giuliani, and D. Laforgue. *Institutions : la voix des acteurs faibles*. Éditions Peter Lang.

——— 2007b. "L'insupportable. L'excès de proximité, l'atteinte à l'autonomie et le sentiment de violation du privé ." In Breviglieri, Trom, and Lafaye, *Sens de la justice, sens critique*. Paris: Economica.

Breviglieri, M., Luca Pattaroni, and Joan Stavo-Debauge. 2003. "Quelques effets de l'idée de *proximité* sur la conduite et le devenir du travail social." In *Swiss Journal of Sociology* 29, no. 1: 141–57.

Brooks, David. 2000. *Bobos in Paradise: The New Upper Class and How They Got There*. New York: Simon & Schuster.

Brown, Kevin, Susan Kenny, and Bryan Turner, with John Prince. 2000. *Rhetorics of Welfare: Uncertainty, Choice and Voluntary Associations*. New York: St. Martin's Press.

Brown, Roger, and Albert Gilman. 1972. "The Pronouns of Power and Solidarity." In *Language and Social Context: Selected Readings*, ed. P. Giglioli, 252–82. New York: Penguin.

Brunsson, Nils. 2002. *The Organization of Hypocrisy: Talk, Decisions, Actions in Organizations*. Norway: Abstrackt/Liber.

Bryson, Bethany. 1996. "Anything But Heavy Metal: Symbolic Exclusion and Musical Dislikes." *American Sociological Review* 16, no. 5: 884–99.

Burawoy, Michael. 1999. "The Extended Case Method." *Sociological Theory* 16, no. 1: 4–33.

———. 1991. *Ethnography Unbound: Power and Resistance in the Modern Metropolis*. With Alice Burton, Ann Arnett Ferguson, Kathryn J. Fox, Joshua Gamson, Nadine Gartrell, Leslie Hurst, Charles Kurzman, Leslie Salzinger, Josepha Schiffman, and Shiori Ui. Berkeley and Los Angeles: University of California Press.

Burchell, Graham, Colin Gordon, and Peter Miller. 1991. *The Foucault Effect: Studies in Governmentality*. Chicago: University of Chicago Press.

Burke, Kenneth. 1969. *A Grammar of Motives*. Berkeley: University of California Press.

Calhoun, Cheshire, ed. 2004. *Setting the Moral Compass*. Oxford: Oxford University Press.

Callon, Michel. 1986. "Some Elements of a Sociology of Translation: Domestication of the Scallops and the Fishermen of St. Brieuc Bay." In *Power, Action and Belief: A New Sociology of Knowledge?* ed. J. Law, 196–223. London: Routledge.

Camus-Vigué, Agnès. 2000. "Community and Civic Culture: the Rotary Club in France and the United States." In *Rethinking Comparative Cultural Sociology. Repertoires of Evaluation in France and the United States*, ed. Michèle Lamont and Laurent Thévenot. 213–28. Cambridge, UK: Cambridge University Press.

Carr, Patrick, and Maria Kefalas. 2009. *Hollowing Out the Middle: The Rural Brain Drain and What It Means for America*. Boston: Beacon Press.

Carrel, Marion. 2004. "Susciter un public local. Habitants et professionnels du transport en confrontation dans un quartier d'habitat social." In *Le public en action: Usages et limites de la notion d'espace public en sciences sociales*, 219–40. Paris: L'Harmattan.

———. 2004. "Faire participer les habitants? La politique de la ville à l'épreuve du public." Doctoral dissertation, Department of Sociology, University of Paris-V.

Carrel, Marion and Suzanne Rosenberg. 2002. *Face a l'insecurite sociale: desamorcer les conflits entre usagers et agents des services publics*. Paris: La Découverte.

Cefaï, Daniel. n.d. "Type, typicité, typification: Un essai de sociologie phénoménologique."

———. 2003. "Introduction." In *Les sens du public: publics politiques; publics médiatiques*. ed. Daniel Cefaï and Dominique Pasquier, 57. Picardie/Paris: Centre universitaire de recherches administratives et politiques de Picardie/PUF.

———. 2002. "Que'est-ce qu'une arène publique? Quelques pistes dans une perspective pragmatiste." In *L'héritage du pragmatisme: conflits d'urbanité et épreuves de civisme*, ed. Daniel Cefaï and Isaac Joseph, 51–82. Paris: Editions de l'aube/Centre culturel international de Cerisy-la-Salle.

de Certeau, Michel. 1988. *The Practice of Everyday Life*, trans. Steven Rendell. Berkeley and Los Angeles: University of California Press.

Chalvon-Demersay, Sabine. 1999. *A Thousand Screenplays: The French Imagination in a Time of Crisis*. Chicago: University of Chicago Press.

———. 1996. "Une société elective: scenarios pour un monde de relations choisies." *Terrain* 27 (September): 81–100.

Charles, Julien. forthcoming. "Des savoirs citoyens au raisonnement démocratique: La compétence politique à l'heure de la démocratie participative." In *Gouverner les mémoires. Le témoin, l'archive et le réseau*, ed. V. Tournay, F. Cantelli, and C. Routelous (dir.). Presses Universitaires de Rennes.

Chaves, Mark, Laura Stephens, and Joseph Galaskiewicz. 2004. "Does Government Funding Suppress Nonprofits' Political Activities?" *American Sociological Review* 69: 292–316.

Cicourel, Aaron. 1981. "Notes on the Integration of Micro- and Macro Levels of Analysis." In *Advances in Social Theory and Methodology*, ed. Karin Knorr-Cetina and Aaron Cicourel, 51–80. London: Routledge and Kegan Paul.

————. 1973. *Cognitive Sociology: Language and Meaning in Social Interaction.* New York: Penguin Books.

Clemens, Elisabeth. 1997. *The People's Lobby.* Chicago: University of Chicago Press.

Clemens, Elisabeth, and James M. Cook. 1999. "Politics and Institutionalism: Explaining Durability and Change." *Annual Review of Sociology* 25: 441–66.

Clemens, Elisabeth, and Debra Minkoff. 2004. "Beyond the Iron Law: Rethinking the Place of Organizations in Social Movement Research." In *The Blackwell Companion to Social Movements,* ed. David A. Snow, Sarah Soule, and Hanspeter Kriesi, 155–70. Malden, MA: Blackwell.

Cmiel, Kenneth. 1991. *Democratic Eloquence: The Fight over Popular Speech in Nineteenth-Century America.* Berkeley and Los Angeles: University of California Press.

Cohen, Jean, and Andrew Arato. 1991. *Civil Society and Political Theory.* Cambridge, MA: MIT Press.

Corporation for National and Community Service, in consultation with the MLK Center for Nonviolent Social Change, Inc., 2007: (http://www.nationalservice.org/whatshot/notices/801000mlkday.html).

Cottereau, Alain. 1999. "Dénis de justice, dénis de réalité: remarques sur la réalité sociale et sa denegation." In *L'éxperience du déni: Bernard Mottez et le monde des sourds en débats,* ed. Pascale Gruson and Renaud Dulong, 159–78. Paris: Éditions de la Maison des sciences de l'homme.

Cruikshank, Barbara. 1999. *The Will to Empower: Democratic Citizens and Other Subjects.* Ithaca, NY: Cornell University Press.

Daniels, Arlene Kaplan. 1988. *Invisible Careers: Women Civic Leaders from the Volunteer World.* Chicago: University of Chicago Press.

Delli Carpini, Michael, and Scott Keeter. 2001. "What Should Be Learned through Service Learning." *Political Science* 33, no. 3 (September): 635–38.

Dekker, Paul. 2009. "Civicness: From Civil Society to Civic Services?" *Voluntas* 20: 220–38.

————. 2004. "The Sphere of Voluntary Associations and the Ideals of Civil Society: A West-European Perspective." *Institute of Korean Studies* 35, no. 3, Seoul.

Dekker, Paul, and Loek Halman, eds. 2003. *The Values of Volunteering: Cross-Cultural Perspectives.* NewYork: Kluwer Academic/Plenum.

Deschenes, Sarah, Milbrey McLaughlin, and Jennifer O'Donoghue. 2006. "Nonprofit Community Organizers in Poor Urban Settings: Bridging Institutional Gaps for Youth." In *The Nonprofit Sector: A Research Handbook,* 2nd edition, ed. Walter W. Powell and Richard Steinberg, 506–522. New Haven, CT: Yale University Press.

Dewey, John. 1938 [1963]. *Education and Experience.* New York: Macmillan.

————. 1926. *The Public and Its Problems.* Denver, CO: Allan Swallow.

DiMaggio, Paul. 2007. "Culture in Organizations." Sociology of Culture Mini-Conference, New York.

————. 1997. "Culture and Cognition." *Annual Review of Sociology* 23: 263–87.

DiMaggio, Paul, and Walter Powell, eds. 1991. *The New Institutionalism in Organizational Analysis.* Chicago: University of Chicago Press.

Doidy, Eric. 2008. "Cultiver l'enracinement: réappropriations militants de l'attachment chez les eleveurs jurassiens." *Politix* 21, no. 83: 155–87.

DuBois, David L. 2007. *Research in Action* series, National Mentoring Partnership (www.mentoring.org), "Effectiveness of Mentoring Program Practices."

DuBois, David L., B. E. Holloway, J. C. Valentine, and H. Cooper. 2002. Effectiveness of Mentoring Programs for Youth: A Meta-analytic Review. *American Journal of Community Psychology* 30: 157–97.

Du Bois, W. E. B. 2003 [1903]. *The Oxford W. E. B. Du Bois Reader*, ed. Eric Sundquist. New York: Oxford University Press.

Dumont, Louis. 1986. "Genesis I: The Christian Beginnings." In *Essays on Individualism*, 23–59. Chicago: University of Chicago Press.

Eccles, Jacquelynne, and Bonnie Barber. 1999. "Student Council, Volunteering, Basketball, or Marching Band: What Kind of Extracurricular Participation Matters?" *Journal of Adolescent Research* 14, no. 1: 10–43.

Edelsky, Carole. 1981. Who's Got the Floor? *Language in Society* 10, no. 3: 383–421.

Edwards, Jonathan. 1734. "A Divine and Supernatural Light, Immediately Imparted to the Soul by the Spirit of God, Shown to Be Both Scriptural and Rational Doctrine." Northhampton, MA (found at Christian Classics Ethereal Library (www.ccel.org).

Edwards, Michael. 2009. *Civil Society*. Oxford: Polity Press.

Edwards, Michael, and D. Hulme. 1996. "Introduction: NGO Performance and Accountability." In *Beyond the Magic Bullet: NGO Performance and Accountability in the Post-Cold War World*. London: Kumarian Press.

Ehrenreich, Barbara. 2006. *Bait and Switch: The (Futile) Pursuit of the American Dream*. New York: Henry Holt.

Elias, Norbert. 1978. *What Is Sociology?* London: Hutchinson.

Eliasoph, Eugene. 1959. "Volunteers in Case Work." *Social Work*, 4: 139–45.

Eliasoph, Nina. 2009. "Top-Down Civic Projects Are Not Grassroots Associations: How the Differences Matter in Everyday Life." *Voluntas* 20: 291–308.

———. 1998. *Avoiding Politics: How Americans Produce Apathy in Everyday Life*. Cambridge, UK: Cambridge University Press.

———. 1988. *Making Cosmetic Change: Inside Mary Kay Cosmetics*. Radio documentary, Pacifica Radio Archives, Los Angeles.

Eliasoph, Nina, and Paul Lichterman. 2003. "Culture in Interaction." *American Journal of Sociology* 1008: 735–94.

Eliasoph, Nina, Paul Lichterman, and Daniel Cefaï. forthcoming. *Towards a New Sociology of Civic Action*.

Eliasoph, Nina, and Jade Lo. 2010. "Broadening Cultural Sociology's Scope: Meaning-Making in Mundane Organizational Life." *Oxford Handbook on Cultural Sociology*, ed. Jeffrey Alexander and Philip Smith. New York: Oxford University Press.

Elshtain, Jean. 1995. "Political Children." In *Feminist Interpretations of Hannah Arendt*, ed. Bonnie Honig, 263–84. University Park: Pennsylvania State University Press.

Elyachar, Julia. 2005. *Markets of Dispossession: NGO's, Economic Development and the State in Cairo*. Durham, NC and London: Duke University Press.

Emerson, Ralph Waldo. n.d. "Self-Reliance." In *The Works of Ralph Waldo Emerson in One Volume*. Roslyn, NY: Black's Readers Service.

Emirbayer, Mustafa, and Mimi Sheller. 1999. "Publics in History." *Theory and Society* 28: 145–97.

Enjolras, Bernard. 2009. "Between Market and Civic Governance Regimes. Civicness in the Governance of Social Services in Europe." *Voluntas* 20 (3): 274–90.

Erikson, Erik. 1994 [1964]. "The Nature of Clinical Evidence." In *Insight and Responsibility*, 49–80. New York: Norton.

———. 1950. *Childhood and Society*. New York: Norton.

Espelande, Wendy. 1998. *The Struggle for Water: Politics, Rationality and Identity in the American Southwest*. Chicago: University of Chicago Press.

Espelande, Wendy, and Mitchell Stevens. 1998. "Commensuration as a Social Process." *Annual Review of Sociology* 24: 313–44.

Esping-Anderson, Gosta. 1990. *The Three Worlds of Welfare Capitalism*. Princeton, NJ: Princeton University Press.

Essed, Philomena. 1990. *Everyday Racism: Reports from Two Cultures*, trans. Cynthia Jaffé. Claremont, CA: Hunter House.

Evers, Adalbert. 2009. "Civicness and Civility: Their Meanings for Social Services." *Voluntas* 20: 239–59.

Fazekacs, Erzsebet. 2003. "Scripting Nonprofit Sectoral Development in Hungary." Paper given at American Sociological Association annual meeting, Atlanta, GA.

Fishman, Robert. 2004. *Democracy's Voices: Social Ties and the Quality of Public Life in Spain*. Ithaca, NY: Cornell University Press.

Fishkin, James. 1991. *Democracy and Deliberation*. New Haven, CT: Yale University Press.

Fordham, Signithia. 1996. *Blacked Out: Dilemmas of Race, Identity and Success at Capitol High*. Chicago: University of Chicago Press.

Forester, John. 1999. *The Deliberative Practitioner: Encouraging Participatory Planning Processes*. Cambridge, MA: MIT Press.

Foucault, Michel. 1989. *The Order of Things*. New York: Routledge.

———. 1976. *Society Must Be Defended*, ed. Francois Ewald, Mauro Bertani and Alessandro Fontana. NY: Picador.

———. 1972 [1969]. *The Archeology of Knowledge*. New York: Routledge.

Fox, Charles J., and Hugh T. Miller. 1995. *Postmodern Public Administration*. Thousand Oaks, CA: Sage Publications.

Fraser, Nancy. 1989. *Unruly Practices: Power, Discourse, and Gender in Contemporary Social Theory*. Minneapolis: University of Minnesota Press.

Freeman, Jo. 1972–73. "The Tyranny of Structurelessness." *Berkeley Journal of Sociology* 17: 151–65.

Friedland, Lewis, and Shauna Morimoto. n.d. *"The Changing Lifeworld of Young People: Risk, Resume-Padding, and Civic Engagement."* Working Paper #40. Center for Research on Civic Learning and Engagement. http://www.civicyouth.org/?page_id=152.

Friedland, Roger, and Robert Alford. 1991. "Bringing Society Back In: Symbols, Practices, and Institutional Contradictions." In *The New Institutionalism in*

Organizational Analysis, ed. Walter Powell and Paul DiMaggio, 232–63. Chicago: University of Chicago Press.

Fundación del Estado para el Sistema Nacional de las Orquestas Juveniles e Infantiles de Venezuela. 2008. *La orquesta cómo instrumento de desarrollo comunitario*, http://fesnojiv.gob.ve/es/historia/el-milagro-musical-venezolano.html.

Fung, Archon. 2004. *Empowered Deliberative Democracy*. Princeton, NJ: Princeton University Press.

Galvin, Kathleen M. 2003. "International/Transracial Adoption: A Communication Research Agenda." *Journal of Family Communication* 4: 237–53.

Gamson, William. 1996. "Safe Spaces and Social Movements." In *Perspectives on Social Problems*, ed. Gale Millerand James A. Holstein. 8: 27–38.

Garfinkel, Harold. 1967. *Studies in Ethnomethodology*. Englewood Cliffs, NJ: Prentice-Hall.

Gayet-Viaud, Carole. Forthcoming. "La femme autonome et l'homme galant. Intransigeances du respect et acrobaties de l'égard dans la civilité urbaine." In *Penser l'autonomie*, ed. M. Jouan et S. Laugier. PUF (collection Questions d'éthique).

———. 2008. *L'égard et la règle. Déboires et bonheurs de la civilité urbaine,"* Doctoral thesis. Paris: École des Hautes Études en Sciences Sociales.

Gershon, Ilana. 2010. *Making Differences Cultural: Samoan Migrants in New Zealand and the United States*. New Brunswick, NJ: Rutgers University Press.

———. 2006. "When Culture Is Not a System: Why Samoan Cultural Brokers Can Not Do Their Job." *Ethnos* 71, no. 4: 533–58.

———. 2005. "Seeing Like a System: Luhmann for Anthropologist." *Anthropological Theory* 5, no. 2: 99–116.

Giddens, Anthony. 1991. *Modernity and Self-Identity*. Cambridge, UK: Polity Press.

Giglioli, Pier Paolo, ed. 1972. *Language and Social Context*. New York: Penguin.

Gillis, John. 1996. *A World of Their Own Making: Myth, Ritual and the Quest for Family Values*. New York: Basic/HarperCollins.

Gilmore, Ruth. 2007. "In the Shadow of the Shadow State." In *The Revolution Will Not Be Funded: Beyond the Non-Profit Industrial Complex*. ed. Incite! Women of Color Against Violence, 41–52. Boston: South End Press.

Glaeser, Andreas. 2000. *Divided in Unity: Identity, Germany and the Berlin Police*. Chicago: University of Chicago Press.

———. 2006. "An Ontology for the Ethnographic Analysis of Social Processes: Extending the Extended Case Method." In *The Manchester School: Practice and Ethnographic Praxis in Anthropology*, ed. T.M.S. Evens and Don Handleman, 64–93. New York: Berghahn Book.

Glowacki, Peggy, and Julia Hendry. 2004. *Hull House*. Chicago: Arcadia Publishing.

Goffman, Erving. 1979. "Footing." *Semiotica* 25: 1–29.

———. 1974. *Frame Analysis: An Essay on the Organization of Experience*. Cambridge, MA: Harvard University Press.

———. 1959. *The Presentation of Self in Everyday Life*. Garden City, NY: Doubleday.

Goodnight, G. Thomas. 1993. "The Reasons of Children and the Ethics of Institutions: On Tour in the Postmodern Library." Speech given at Wake Forest University, Great Teachers Program.

Goodwin, Jeff, James Jasper, and Francesca Polletta, eds. 2001. *Passionate Politics: Emotions and Social Movements.* Chicago: University of Chicago Press.

Goodwin, Marjorie. 2006. *The Hidden Life of Girls: Games of Stance, Status, and Exclusion.* New York: Blackwell.

Goodwin, Marjorie, and Charles Goodwin. 1990. *He-Said-She-Said: Talk as Social Organization among Black Children.* Bloomington: Indiana University Press.

Gorney, Roderic. 1972. *The Human Agenda: How to Be at Home in the Universe—Without Magic.* Los Angeles: The Guild of Tutors Press.

Gouldner, Alvin. 1954. *Patterns of Industrial Bureaucracy.* New York: Free Press.

Gumperz, John. 1988. *Discourse Strategies.* Berkeley and Los Angeles: University of California Press.

Gumperz, John, and Dell Hymes, eds. 1973. *Directions in Sociolinguistics.* New York: Blackwell.

Hackstaff, Karla. 1999. *Marriage in a Culture of Divorce.* Philadelphia: Temple University Press.

Hall, John A. 1995. "Introduction." In *Civil Society: Theory, History, Comparison,* ed. John A. Hall. Cambridge, UK: Polity Press.

Hall, Michael, and Keith G. Banting. 2000. "The Nonprofit Sector in Canada: An Introduction." In *The Nonprofit Sector in Canada: Roles and Relationships,* ed. Keith G. Banting, 1–28. Montreal and Kingston: McGill-Queen's University Press.

Hall, Peter Dobkin. 1992. *Inventing the Nonprofit Sector.* Baltimore: Johns Hopkins University Press.

Hallett, Tim, and Marc Ventresca. 2006. "How Institutions Form: Loose Coupling as Mechanism in Gouldner's Patterns of Industrial Bureaucracy," *American Behavioral Scientist,* 49, no. 7: 908–24.

Hamidi, Camille. 2006. "Eléments pour une approche interactionniste de la politisation. Engagement associatif et rapport au politique dans des associations locales issues de l'immigration." *Revue Française de Science Politique* 56, no. 1: 5–25.

———. 2002. "Les effets politiques de l'engagement associatif: le cas des associations issues de l'immigration." Doctoral dissertation, Institut d'Études Politiques, Paris.

Handy, F., and Ram Cnaan. 2000. "Religious Nonprofits: Social Service Provision by Congregations in Ontario." In *The Nonprofit Sector in Canada: Roles and Relationships,* ed. Keith Banting, 69–105. Montreal/Kingston: McGill-Queens University Press.

Handy, F., I. Hustinx, R. A. Cnaan, L. Hustinx, C. Kang, J. Meijs, A. B. Pessi, B. Ranade, N. Yamauchi, and S. Zrinscak. 2010. "A Cross-cultural Examination of Student Volunteering: Is It All About Résumé Building? *Nonprofit and Voluntary Sector Quarterly* (June), 39, no. 3: 498–523.

Haney, Lynne. 2010. *Offending Women: Power, Punishment, and the Regulation of Desire.* Berkeley and Los Angeles: University of California Press.

Hann, Chris. 1996. "Introduction: Political Society and Civil Anthropology." In *Civil Society: Challenging Western Models,* Chris Hann and Elizabeth Dunn, 1–26. New York: Routledge.

Harvey, David. 1990. *The Condition of Postmodernity*. New York: Blackwell.

Hashemi, Syed, Sidney Ruth Schuler, and Ann Riley. 1996. "Rural Credit Programs and Women's Empowerment in Bangladesh." *World Development* 24, no. 4: 635–53.

Heimer, Carol, and Lisa Staffen. 1998. *For the Sake of the Children: The Social Organization of Responsibility in the Hospital and the Home*. Chicago: University of Chicago Press.

Heimer, Carol, and J. Lynn Gazley. 2006. "Performing Regulation: Observations from Four HIV Clinics." Paper presented at the annual meetings of the Law and Society Association, July 6.

Henkel, Heiko, and Roderick Stirrat. 2001. "Participation as Spiritual Duty; Empowerment as Secular Subjection." In *Participation: The New Tyranny?* ed. Bill Cooke and Uma Kothari, 168–84. New York: Zed Press/St. Martins.

Hillman, Arthur. 1960. *Neighborhood Centers Today: Action Programs for a Rapidly Changing World*. New York: National Federation of Settlements and Neighborhood Centers.

Hochschild, Arlie. 2003. *The Commercialization of Intimate Life*. Berkeley: University of California Press.

———. 1983. *The Managed Heart: Commercialization of Human Feeling*. Berkeley: University of California Press.

Hodgkinson, Virginia, Margaret Gates, and Paul Schervish. 1995. *Care and Community in Modern Society*. New York: Jossey-Bass.

Hondagneu-Sotelo, Pierrette. 1991. *Domestica*. Berkeley: University of California Press.

Hondagneu-Sotelo, Pierrette, and Sally Raskoff. 1994. "Community Service-Learning: Promises and Problems." *Teaching Sociology* 22: 248–54.

Hulbert, Ann. 2004. *Raising America: Experts, Parents, and a Century of Advice*. New York: Vintage.

Hunter, James Davison. 2000. *Death of Character: Moral Education in an Age Without Good or Evil*. New York: Basic.

Hupe, Peter, Lucas Meijs, and Marianne Vorthoren. 2000. *Hybrid Governance: The Impact of the Nonprofit Sector in the Netherlands*. Work Document #65, Social and Cultural Planning Office, The Hague.

Hustinx, Lesley. 2001. "Individualisation and New Styles of Youth Volunteering: An Empirical Exploration." *Voluntary Action* 3, no. 2: 57–70.

Hustinx, L., and F. Lammertyn. 2003. "Collective and Reflexive Styles of Volunteering: A Sociological Modernization Perspective." *Voluntas* 14, no. 2: 167–87.

Hyatt, Susan Brin. 2001. "From Citizen to Volunteer: Neoliberal Governance and the Erasure of Poverty." In *New Poverty Studies: The Ethnography of Power, Politics and Impoverished People in the US*, ed. J. Goode and J. Maskovsky, 201–35. New York: New York University Press.

Jacobs, Jane. 1993 [1961]. *Death and Life of Great American Cities*. New York: Modern Library.

Jensen, Jane, and Susan D. Phillips. 2000. "Distinctive Trajectories: Homecare and the Voluntary Sector in Quebec and Ontario." In *The Nonprofit Sector in Canada: Roles and Relationships*, ed. Keith G. Banting, 29–68. Montreal and Kingston: McGill-Queen's University Press.

Joas, Hans. 1997. *The Creativity of Action*. Chicago: University of Chicago Press.

Jones, Susan, and Kathleen Hill. 2003. "Understanding Patterns of Commitment; Student Motivation for Community Service Involvement." *Journal of Higher Education*, 516–39.

Jupp, T. C., Celia Roberts, and Jenny Cook-Gumperz. 1982. "Language and Disadvantage: The Hidden Process." In *Language and Social Identity*, ed. J. Gumperz, 232–56.

Kameo, Nahoko. 2009. Empowerment in a Knowledge-Based Workplace: Its Intentions and Consequences." Masters Thesis, Department of Sociology, University of California–Los Angeles.

Kateb, George. 1992. *The Inner Ocean: Individualism and Democratic Culture*. Ithaca, NY: Cornell University Press.

Katz, Elihu, and Brenda Danet, eds. 1973. *Bureaucracy and the Public: A Reader in Official-Client Relations*. New York: Basic Books.

Katz, Jack. 2002. "From How to Why: On Luminous Description and Causal Inference in Ethnography." (Part I). *Ethnography* 3, no. 1: 63–90.

———. 2001. "From How to Why: On Luminous Description and Causal Inference in Ethnography." (Part II). *Ethnography* 2, no. 4: 443–73.

Kaufman, Jason. 2002. *For the Common Good? American Civic Life and the Golden Age of Fraternity*. New York: Oxford University Press.

Keillor, Garrison. 1985. *Lake Wobegon Days*. New York: Viking.

Keith, William. 2007. *Democracy as Discussion: Civic Education and the American Forum Movement*. Lanham, MD: Rowman and Littlefield.

Kharkhordin, Oleg. 2006. "Things as *res publicae*: Making Things Public." In, *Making Things Public: Atmospheres of Democracy*, ed. Bruno Latour and Peter Weibel, 280–89. Cambridge, MA: MIT Press.

Knijn, Trudie. 2000. "Marketization and the Struggling Logics of (Home) Care in the Netherlands." In *Care Work: Gender, Labor and the Welfare State*, ed. Madonna Harrington Neyer, 232–48. New York: Routledge.

Kramer, Ralph. 1994. "Voluntary Agencies and the Contract Culture: Dream or Nightmare? " *Social Service Review* (March): 33–60.

Kretzman, John, and John McKnight. 2005. "Discovering Community Power: A Guide to Mobilizing Local Assets and Your Organization's Capacity." by Assets-Based Community Development Institute, Northwestern University/ Kellogg Foundation (www.northwestern.edu/ipr/abcd.html) Evanston, IL.

———. 1993. "Building Communities from the Inside Out: A Path Toward Finding and Mobilizing a Community's Assets." Evanston, IL: Institute for Policy Research, 19–25.

Krinsky, John. 2007. *Free Labor: Workfare and the Contested Language of Neoliberalism*. Chicago: University of Chicago Press.

Kunda, Gideon. 1992. *Engineering Culture: Control and Commitment in a High-Tech Corporation*. Philadelphia: Temple University Press.

Lachelier, Paul. 2007. "Democracy, Individualism and the Civil-Civic-Citizen: Young American Professionals Talk about Community, Politics and Citizenship." Doctoral dissertation, University of Wisconsin, Madison.

———. 1998. "The Best Party on Campus: Political Detachment in a Political Association." Master's Thesis, University of Wisconsin, Madison.

Lamont, Michele. 2009. "Critères d'évaluation et structures culturelles." *Compétences critiques et sens de la justice*, ed. Marc Breviglieri, Claudette Lafaye, and Danny Trom, 437–46. Paris: Economica.

———. 1999. *The Cultural Territories of Race: Black and White Boundaries*, Chicago: University of Chicago Press, and New York: Russell Sage Foundation.

———. 1992. *Money, Morals, and Manners*. Chicago: University of Chicago Press.

Lamont, Michele, and Laurent Thévenot, eds. 2000. *Rethinking Comparative Cultural Sociology. Repertoires of Evaluation in France and the United States*. Cambridge, UK: Cambridge University Press.

Lareau, Annette. 2003. *Unequal Childhoods*. Berkeley and Los Angeles: University of California Press.

Latour, Bruno, and Peter Weibel, eds. 2006. *Making Things Public: Atmospheres of Democracy*. Cambridge, MA: MIT Press.

Laville, Jean-Louis and Marthe Nyssens. 2001. *Les services sociaux entre associations, etat et Marché: l'Aide aux personnes âgées*, La Découverte, Paris.

Lee, Carolyn. 2007. "Is There a Place for Private Conversation in Public Dialogue? Comparing Stakeholder Assessments of Informal Communication in Collaborative Regional Planning." *American Journal of Sociology* 113, no. 1 (July): 41–96.

Lee, Jennifer. 2000. "The Salience of Race in Everyday Life: Black Customers' Shopping Experiences in Black and White Neighborhoods." *Work and Occupations* 27, no. 3: 353–76.

Leiberson, Stanley. 2000. *A Matter of Taste: How Names, Fashions, and Culture Change*. New Haven, CT: Yale University Press.

Lévi-Strauss, Claude. 1963. *Structural Anthropology*, trans. Clair Jacobson and Brooke Grundfest Schoepf. New York: Basic Books.

Lichterman, Paul. 2005. *Elusive Togetherness: Church Groups Trying to Bridge America's Divisions*. Princeton, NJ: Princeton University Press.

———. 2002. "Seeing Structure Happen." In *Methods of Social Movement Research*, ed. Bert Klandermans and Suzanne Staggenborg, 118–45. Minneapolis: University of Minnesota Press.

———. 1996. *The Search for Political Community: American Activists Reinventing Community*. Cambridge, UK: Cambridge University Press.

Lorentzen, Hakon, and Lesley Hustinx. 2007. "Civic Involvement and Modernization." *Journal of Civil Society* 3, no. 2: 101–18.

Los Angeles Unified School District. 2008. Accent on Performance (DVD of 2008 Honor Orchestra).

Lounsbury, Michael, Marc Ventresca, and Paul M. Hirsch. 2003. "Social Movements, Field Frames, and Industry Emergence: A Cultural-Political Perspective on US Recycling." *Socio-Economic Review* 1: 71–104.

Luhtakallio, Eeva. 2010. *Local Politicizations: A Comparison of Finns and French Practicing Democracy*. Doctoral thesis, Department of Sociology, University of Helsinki.

Luque, Emilio. 2005. "Researching Environmental Citizenship and its Publics." *Environmental Politics* 14, no. 2, 211–25.

Macdonald, Cameron, and David Merrill. 2002. "It Shouldn't Have to Be a Trade: Recognition and Redistribution in Carework Advocacy." *Hypatia* 17, no. 2: 67–83.

Madsen, Richard. 2002. "Comparative Cosmopolis: Discovering a Path to Moral Integration in the Modern Ecumene." In *Meaning and Modernity: Religion, Polity, and Self*, ed. Richard Madsen, William Sullivan, Ann Swidler, and Steven Tipton, 105–23. Berkeley: University of California Press.

Malinowski, Bronislaw. 1972 [1923]. "Phatic Communion." In *Communication in Face-to-Face Interaction*, ed. J. Laver and S. Hutcheson, 146–52. Harmondsworth: Penguin.

Manning, Nathan. 2007. *Young People and Politics: Apathetic and Disengaged: A Qualitative Inquiry.* Doctoral dissertation, University of Flinders, Flinders, Australia.

March, James, and Herbert Simon. 1958. *Organizations.* New York: John Wiley and Sons.

Marchi, Regina. 2006. "US Day of the Dead: Communicating Politically Through Culture." Annual meeting of National Communication Association, Boston, MA.

Marwell, Nicole P. 2004. "Privatizing the Welfare State: Nonprofit Community-Based Organizations as Political Actors." *American Sociological Review* 69: 265–91.

Mattson, Kevin. 1998. *Creating a Democratic Public: The Struggle for Urban Participatory Democracy During the Progressive Era.* University Park: Pennsylvania State University Press.

Mauss, Marcel. 2000 [1924]. *The Gift: The Form and Reason for Exchange in Archaic Societies.* New York: Norton.

McFarland Daniel, and Reuben Thomas. 2006. "Bowling Young: How Youth Voluntary Associations Influence Adult Political Participation." *American Sociological Review* 71, no. 3: 401–25.

McGee, Micki. 2005. *Self Help, Inc.* New York: Oxford University Press.

McGuire, Jenifer, and Wendy C. Gamble. 2006. "Community Service for Youth: The Value of Psychological Engagement over Number of Hours Spent." *Journal of Adolescence* 29: 289–98.

Mcpherson, J. Miller, and Thomas Rotolo. 1996. "Testing a Dynamic Model of Social Composition: Diversity and Change in Voluntary Groups." *American Sociological Review* 61, no. 2: 179–202.

Mcpherson, J. Miller, and Lynn Smith-Lovin. 1987. "Homophily in Voluntary Organizations: Status Distance and the Composition of Face-to-Face Groups." *American Sociological Review* 52, no. 3: 370–79.

Mead, George Herbert. 1934. *Mind, Self, and Society.* Chicago: University of Chicago Press.

———. 1932. *The Philosophy of the Present.* Chicago: University of Chicago Press.

Mead, Margaret. 1967. "The Story of the White House Conference on Children and Youth." U.S. Department of Health, Education and Welfare, Social and Rehabilitative Children's Bure 18, quoted in Ann Hulbert, *Raising America: Experts, Parents, and a Century of Advice.* New York: Vintage, 207.

Melucci, Alberto. 1996. *The Playing Self*. Cambridge, UK: Cambridge University Press.

Merico, Maurizio. 2008. "Construire un rapport à l'espace public. Légitimation, participation et conflit dans un centre d'accueil et dl'insertion en Italie du Sud." In *Adolescences méditerranéennes: L'espace public à petits pas*, ed. Marc Breviglieiri et Vincenzo Cicchelli, 277–96. Paris: L'Harmattan.

Merton, Robert. 1957. "The Self-Fulfilling Prophecy," in *Social Theory and Social Structure*. New York: Free Press of Glencoe.

Meyer, John. 1994. "Rationalized Environments." In *Institutional Environments and Organizations: Structural Complexity and Individualism*, ed. W. Richard Scott and John W. Meyer and Associates, 28–54. Thousand Oaks, CA: Sage.

Meyer, John, John Boli, and George Thomas. 1994. "Ontology and Rationalization in the Western Cultural Account." In *Institutional Environments and Organizations: Structural Complexity and Individualism*, ed. W. Richard Scott and John W. Meyer and Associates, 9–27. Thousand Oaks, CA: Sage.

Meyer, John, John Boli, George Thomas, and Francisco Ramirez. 1997. "World Society and the Nation State." *American Journal of Sociology* 103, no. 1: 144–81.

Meyer, John, and Brian Rowan. 1991. "Institutionalized Organizations: Formal Structure as Myth and Ceremony." In *The New Institutionalism in Organizational Analysis*, ed. Walter Powell and Paul DiMaggio, 41–62. Chicago: University of Chicago Press.

Meyer, John, Joanne Nagel, and Conrad W. Snyder. 1993. "The Expansion of Mass Education in Botswana: Local and World Society Perspectives." *Comparative Education Review* 4: 454–75.

Mills, C. Wright. 1979 (1940). "Situated Action and Vocabularies of Motive." In *Power, Politics and People*, ed. Irving Horowitz, 439–52. New York: Oxford University Press.

Minkoff, Debra C. 2002. "The Emergence of Hybrid Organizational Forms: Combining Identity-based Service Provision and Political Activism." *Nonprofit and Voluntary Sector Quarterly* 31, no. 3 (September): 377–401.

Minkoff, Debra C., and Walter W. Powell. 2006. "Nonprofit Mission: Constancy, Responsiveness, or Deflection?" In *The Non-Profit Sector: A Research Handbook*, 2nd edition, ed. Walter W. Powell and Richard Steinberg, 591–611. New Haven, CT: Yale University Press.

Mische, Ann. 2008. *Partisan Politics*. Princeton, NJ: Princeton University Press.

———. 2003. "Crosstalk in Social Movements: Reconceiving the Culture-Network Link." In *Social Movements and Networks: Relational Approaches to Collective Action*, ed. Mario Diani and Doug McAdam, 258–80. Oxford and New York: Oxford University Press.

———. 1998. "Between Conversation and Situation: Public Switching Dynamics Across Network Domains." *Social Research* 65: 695–724.

Mische, Ann, and Phillipa Pattison. 2000. "Composing a Civic Arena: Publics, Projects, and Social Settings." *Poetics* 27: 163–94.

Molinier, Pascale. 2005. "Le care a` l'épreuve du travail: vulnérabilités croisées et savoirs-faires discrets." In *Le Souci des Autres: Éthique et Politique du Care*, Vol. 16, ed. Patricia Paperman and Sandra Laugier, 299–316. Paris: Éditions de l'École des Hautes Études en Sciences Sociales.

Molotch, Harvey. 2000. *Building Rules: How Local Controls Shape Community Environments and Economics*. Boulder, CO: Westview Press.

Morrill, Calvin. 1995. *The Executive Way: Conflict Management in Corporations*. Cambridge, MA: Harvard University Press.

Moynihan, Daniel Patrick. 1970. *Maximum Feasible Misunderstanding: Community Action in the War on Poverty*. New York: Free Press.

Musso, J., with C. Weare, N. Oztas and B. Loges. 2006. "Neighborhood Governance Reform and Networks of Community Power in Los Angeles." *American Review of Public Administration* 36: 1.

Nussbaum, Martha. 2001. *The Fragility of Goodness: Luck and Ethics in Greek Tragedy and Philosophy*, 2nd edition. New York: Cambridge University Press.

Olneck, Michael. 1990. "The Recurring Dream: Symbolism and Ideology in Intercultural and Multicultural Education." *American Journal of Education* 98 (February): 147–74.

Ostrander, Susan. 1984. *Women of the Upper Class*. Philadelphia: Temple University Press.

Parreñas, Rhacel Salazar. 2001. *The Migrant Filipina Domestic Workers in Rome and Los Angeles*. Stanford: Stanford University Press,

Philipsen, Gerry. 1992. *Speaking Culturally: Explorations in Social Communication*. Albany: SUNY Press.

Phillips, Susan, and Graham, Katherine. 2000. "Hand-in-Hand: When Accountability Meets Collaboration in the Voluntary Sector." In *The Not-for-Profit Sector in Canada: Roles and Relationships*, ed. Keith Banting, 149–90. Montreal and Kingston: McGill-Queen's University Press.

Piven, Frances Fox, and Richard Cloward. 1978. *Poor People's Movements*. New York: Vintage.

Polletta, Francesca. 2002. *Freedom Is an Endless Meeting: Democracy in American Social Movements*. Chicago: University of Chicago Press.

Popenoe, David. 1995. "The Roots of Declining Social Virtue: Family, Community, and the Need for a 'Natural Communities' Policy." In *Seedbeds of Virtue: Sources of Competence, Character and Citizenship in American Society*, ed. Mary Ann Glendon and David Blankenhorn, New York: Madison Books.

Popielarz, P. A., and J. M. McPherson. 1995. "On the Edge or in between—Niche Position, Niche Overlap, and the Duration of Voluntary Association Memberships." *American Journal of Sociology* 101, no. 3: 698–720.

Poppendieck, Janet. 1999. *Sweet Charity: Emergency Food and the End of Entitlement* New York: Penguin.

Portes, Alejandro, and Min Zhou. 1993. "The New Second Generation: Segmented Assimilation and Its Variants." *Annals of the American Academy of Political and Social Science*, vol. 530: 74–96.

Power, M. 1997. *The Audit Society: Rituals of Verification*. Oxford: Clarendon.

Putnam, Robert. 2000. *Bowling Alone*. New York: Simon & Schuster.

Ragin, Charles C. 1992. *What Is a Case? Exploring the Foundations of Social Inquiry*. New York: Cambridge University Press.

Rao, Hayagreeva. 1998. "The Construction of Nonprofit Consumer Watchdog Organizations." *American Journal of Sociology* 103, no. 4: 912–61.

Rhodes, Jean. 2007. "Fostering Close and Effective Relationships in Youth Mentoring Programs." *Research in Action* series, National Mentoring Partnership (www.mentoring.org).

Rhodes, Jean, and Jean Grossman. 2002. "The Test of Time: Predictors and Effects of Duration in Youth Mentoring Relationships." *American Journal of Community Psychology* 30: 199–206.

Ricœur, Paul. 1991. "Life: A Story in Search of a Narrator." In *Reflection and Imagination: A Paul Ricœur Reader*, ed. Mario Valdés, 482–90. Toronto: University of Toronto Press.

Rius, Pia, 2010. "Le sens du juste, les conceptions de l'activité et du travail du mouvement des sans-emplois en l'Argentine des années 90." Doctoral thesis. Paris: École des Hautes Études en Sciences Sociales.

Rivkin-Fish, Ziggy. 2003. "Planning Civil Society: Putting Value on the Arts Through Cultural Planning." Paper given at American Sociological Association Annual Meeting, Atlanta. ust.

Rose, Nikolas. 1999. *Powers of Freedom: Reframing Political Thought*. Cambridge: Cambridge University Press,

———. 1989. *Governing the Soul: The Shaping of the Private Self*. New York: Routledge.

Rose, Nikolas, Pat O'Malley, and Mariana Valverde. 2006. "Governmentality." *Annual Review of Law and Social Science* 2: 83–104.

Rosenblatt, Susannah. 2005. "Mariachi Has Them Playing a Different Tune." *Los Angeles Times*, February 6, p. A26.

Roth, Wendy D. 2009. "'Latino Before the World:' The Transnational Extension of Panethnicity." *Ethnic and Racial Studies* 32, no. 6: 927–47.

Rudrappa, Sharmila. 2004. *Ethnic Routes to Becoming American: Indian Immigrants and the Cultures of Citizenship*. Piscataway, NJ: Rutgers University Press.

Sacks, Harvey. 1972. "On the Analyzability of Stories by Children." In *Directions in Sociolinguistics: The Ethnography of Communication*, ed. John Gumperz and Dell Hymes, 325–24. New York: Blackwell.

Salamon, Lester. 1995. *Partners in Public Service: Government-Nonprofit Relations in the Modern Welfare State*. Baltimore, MD: Johns Hopkins University Press.

Salamon, Lester, and Helmut Anheier. 1996. *The Emerging Nonprofit Sector: An Overview*. New York: St. Martin's Press.

Salamon, Lester, and Wojciech Sokolowski. 2005. "Institutional Roots of Volunteering: Toward a Macro-Structural Theory of Individual Voluntary Action." In *The Values of Volunteering*, ed. Paul Dekker and Loek Halman, 71–90. New York: Kluwer.

Salamon, Lester, and Wojciech Sokolowski. 2005. *Monthly Labor Review* 128, no. 9: 19–26.

Salamon, Lester, Wojciech Sokolowski, and R. List. 2003. *Global Civil Society: An Overview*. Baltimore: Johns Hopkins Center for Civil Society Studies.

Sampson, Robert, Doug McAdam, Heather MacIndoe, and Simon Weffer-Elizondo. 2005. "Civil Society Reconsidered: The Durable Nature and Community Structure of Collective Civic Action." *American Journal of Sociology* 111, no. 3: 673–714.

Sampson, Steven. 1996. "The Social Life of Projects: Importing Civil Society to Albania." In *Civil Society: Challenging Western Models*, ed. Chris Hann and Elizabeth Dunn, 127–42. New York: Routledge.

Schein, Edgar. 1970. *Organizational Psychology*. Englewood Cliffs, NJ: Prentice-Hall.

Schneiberg, Marc, and Lounsbury, Michael. 2007. "Social Movements and Institutional Analysis." *Handbook of Institutional Theory*.

Schofer, Evan, and Fourcade-Gourinchas, Marion. 2001. "The Structural Contexts of Civic Engagement: Voluntary Association Membership in Comparative Perspective." *American Sociological Review* 66: 806–28.

Schor, Juliet, 1992. *The Overworked American: The Unexpected Decline in Leisure*. New York: Basic Books.

Schreiner, Marc. 2005. "A Cost-Effectiveness Analysis of the Grameen Bank of Bangladesh." *Development Policy Review* 21, no. 3: 357–82.

Schudson, Michael. 2006. "The Trouble with Experts—and Why Democracies Need Them." *Theory and Society* 35: 491–506.

———. 1998. *The Good Citizen: A History of American Civic Life*. New York, Martin Kessler Books.

———. 1997. "Why Conversation Is Not the Soul of Democracy." *Critical Studies in Mass Communication* 14: 297–309.

Schutz, Alfred. 1967 [1932]. *The Phenomenology of the Social World*. Evanston, IL: Northwestern University Studies in Phenomenology and Existential Philosophy.

Schweiker, William. 1995. *Responsibility and Christian Ethics*. New York: Cambridge University Press.

Scott, James C. 1989. *Domination and the Arts of Resistance*. New Haven, CT: Yale University Press.

Scott, W. Richard, John Meyer, and John Boli. 1994. *Institutional Environments and Organizations: Structural Complexity and Individualism*. Thousand Oaks, CA: Sage Publications.

Seligman, Adam. 1991. *The Idea of Civil Society*. New York: Free Press.

Sennett, Richard. 2004. *Respect in a World of Inequality*. New York: W. W. Norton.

Sewell, William Jr. 1992. "A Theory of Structure: Duality, Agency, and Transformation." *American Journal of Sociology* 98: 1–29.

Sirianni, Carmen, and Lewis Friedland. 2001. *Civic Innovation in America: Community Empowerment, Public Policy, and the Movement for Civic Renewal*, Berkeley: University of California Press.

Skocpol, Theda. 2003. *Diminished Democracy: From Membership to Management in American Civic Life*. Norman: University of Oklahoma Press.

Smith, Andrea. 2007. "Introduction: The Revolution Will Not Be Funded." In *The Revolution Will Not Be Funded: Beyond the Non-Profit Industrial Complex*, ed. Incite! Women of Color Against Violence, 1–20. Boston: South End Press.

Smith, David Horton. 1997. "The Rest of the Nonprofit Sector: Grassroots Associations as the Dark Matter Ignored in Prevailing 'Flat Earth' Maps of the Sector." *Nonprofit and Voluntary Sector Quarterly* 26, no. 2: 114–31.

Smith, Steven Rathgeb, and Michael Lipsky. 1993. *Nonprofits for Hire: The Welfare State in the Age of Contracting*. Cambridge, MA: Harvard University Press.

Smith, Steven Rathgeb, and Deborah A. Stone. 1988. "The Unexpected Consequences of Privatization." In *Remaking the Welfare State: Retrenchment and Social Policy in America and Europe*, ed. Michael K. Brown, 232–52. Philadelphia: Temple University Press.

Sobieraj, Sara, and Deborah White. 2004. "Taxing Political Life: Reevaluating the Relationship between Voluntary Association Membership, Political Engagement, and the State." *Sociological Quarterly* 45, no. 4: 739–64.

Somers, Margaret. 1995. "Narrating and Naturalizing Civil Society and Citizenship Theory: The Place of Political Culture and the Public Sphere." *Sociological Theory* 13, no. 2: 229–74.

Sperling, Valerie, Myra Marx Ferree, and Barbara J. Risman. 2001. "Constructing Global Feminism: Transnational Advocacy Networks and Russian Women's Activism." *Signs* 26, no. 4: 1155–86.

Stacey, Judith. 1998. *Brave New Families*. Berkeley and Los Angeles: University of California Press.

Stack, Carol. 1997 [1975]. *All Our Kin: Strategies for Survival in a Black Community*. New York: Basic Books.

Stark, David, and Monique Girard. 2007. "Socio-technologies of Assembly: Sense-making and Demonstration in Rebuilding Lower Manhattan." In *Governance and Information: The Rewiring of Governing and Deliberation in the 21st Century*, ed. David Lazer and Viktor Mayer-Schoenberger, 145–76. New York: Oxford University Press.

Steinberg, Marc. 1999. "The Talk and Back Talk of Collective Action: A Dialogic Analysis of Repertoires of Discourse among Nineteenth-Century English Cotton Spinners." *American Journal of Sociology* 105, no. 3: 736–80.

Steinmetz, George. 2005. "The Epistemological Unconscious of U.S. Sociology and the Transition to Post-Fordism: The Case of Historical Sociology." In *Remaking Modernity: Politics, History and Sociology*, ed. Julia Adams, Elisabeth Clemens, and Ann Orloff. Durham, NC: Duke University Press.

———. 1999. *State/Culture: State-Formation After the Cultural Turn*. Ithaca, NY: Cornell University Press.

Stevens, Mitchell. 2006. *Creating a Class: College Admission and the Education of Elites*. Cambridge, MA: Harvard University Press.

Stivers, Camilla ed. 2001. *Democracy, Bureaucracy, and the Study of Administration*. Boulder, CO: Westview Press.

Stone, Deborah, 2000. "Caring by the Book." In *Care Work: Gender, Labor and the Welfare State*, ed. Madonna Harrington Meyer, 89–111. New York: Routledge.

———. 1988. *Policy Paradox and Political Reason*. Glenview, IL: Scott, Foresman.

Stout, Jeffrey. 2003. *Democracy and Tradition*. Princeton, NJ: Princeton University Press.

Strathern, Marilyn. 2000. *Audit Culture*. New York: Routledge.

Sullivan, William. 2002. "Politics as 'The Public Use of Reason.'" In *Meaning and Modernity: Religion, Polity, Self*, ed. Richard Madsen, William Sullivan, Ann Swidler, and Steven Tipton, 236–54. Berkeley and Los Angeles: University of California Press.

Suransky, Valerie Polakow. 1982. *The Erosion of Childhood*. Chicago: University of Chicago Press.

Swidler, Ann. 2006. "Syncretism an Subversion in AIDS Governance: How Locals Cope with Global Demands." *International Affairs* 82, no. 2 (March): 269–84.

———. 2003. "The Politics of Aids in Sub-Saharan Africa." Paper given at American Sociological Association Annual Meeting, August.

Swidler, Ann, and Susan Cott Watkins. 2007. "Ties of Dependence: AIDS and Transactional Sex in Rural Malawi." *Studies in Family Planning* 38, no. 3 (September): 147–62.

Talpin, Julien. 2007. "Schools of Democracy: How Ordinary Citizens Become Competent in Participatory Budgeting Institutions." Doctoral dissertation, European University Institute, Florence.

———. 2006. "Jouer les bons citoyens: les effets contrastés de l'engagement au sein de dispositifs participatifs." *Politix* 79, no. 75: 13–31.

Tannen, Deborah. 2005. *Conversational Style: Analyzing Talk among Friends*. New York: Oxford University Press.

Tavory, Iddo. 2009. "The Structure of Flirtation: On the Construction of Interactional Ambiguity." *Studies in Symbolic Interaction* 33: 59–74.

Taylor, Charles. 1988. *Sources of the Self*. Cambridge, MA: Harvard University Press.

Thévenot, Laurent. 2007. "The Plurality of Cognitive Formats and Engagements Moving Between the Familiar and the Public." *European Journal of Social Theory* 10, no. 3: 409–23.

———. 2006. L'action au pluriel: Sociologie des régimes d'engagement. Paris: La Découverte.

———. 2001. "Pragmatic Regimes Governing the Engagement with the World." In *The Practice Turn in Contemporary Theory*, ed. Karin Knorr-Cetina, T. Schatzki, Eike Savigny, 56–73. London: Routledge.

———. 1999. "Faire entendre une voix; regimes d'engagement dans les mouvements sociaux." *Mouvements* 3 (mars–avril): 73–82.

Thompson, E. P. 1967. "Time, Work-Discipline, and Industrial Capitalism." *Past and Present* 38: 56–97.

Thompson, J. D. 1967. *Organizations in Action; Social Science Bases of Administrative Theory*. New York: McGraw-Hill.

Thunder Hawk, Madonna. 2007. "Native Organizing Before the Non-Profit Industrial Complex." In *The Revolution Will Not be Funded: Beyond the Non-Profit Industrial Complex*, ed. Incite! Women of Color Against Violence, 101–6. Boston: South End Press.

To, Clara Wai-Chun. 2005. "Intergenerational Contract, Women's Labor and So-
cial Change in Contemporary Rural South China." Ph.D. Dissertation, Univer-
sity of Wisconsin-Madison.
Tocqueville, Alexis de. 1969 [1835]. *Democracy in America*, ed. J. P. Mayer. New
York: Anchor Books.
———. 1961 [1835]. *De la démocratie en Amérique*. Paris: Editions Gallimard.
Tracy, Karen, ed. 1991. *Understanding Face-to-Face Interaction: Issues Linking
Goals and Discourse*. Hillsdale, NJ: Lawrence Erlbaum.
Traustadottir, Rannvieg. 2000. "Disability Reform and Women's Caring Work."
In *Gender, Labor and the Welfare State*, ed. Madonna Harrington Meyer,
249–69. London: Routledge.
Tronto, Joan. 1994. *Moral Boundaries: A Political Argument for an Ethic of Care*.
New York: Routledge.
Ullman, Claire. 1998. *The Welfare State's Other Crisis: Explaining the New Part-
nership between Nonprofit Organizations in France*. Bloomington: Indiana
University Press.
Van Ausdale, Debra, and Joe Faegin. 2001. *The First R: How Children Learn
Race and Racism*. Lanham, MD: Rowman & Littlefield.
Van Til, Jon. 2001. *Growing Civil Society: From Nonprofit Sector to Third Space*.
Bloomington: Indiana University Press.
Van Til, Jon, and Sally Bould Van Til. 1970. "Citizen Participation in Social Pol-
icy: The End of the Cycle?" *Social Problems* 17 (Winter): 313–23.
Verba, Sidney, Kay Schlozman, and Henry Brady. 1995. *Voice and Equality: Civic
Voluntarism in American Politics*. Cambridge, MA: Harvard University Press.
Vitale, T. Forthcoming. "Contradiction and Reflexivity in Social Innovation: A
Case Study from the De-Institutionalization Movement." *European Urban and
Regional Studies*.
Vygotsky, Lev. 1986. *Thought and Language*, trans. and ed. Alex Kozulin. Cam-
bridge, MA: MIT Press.
———. 1978. *Mind in Society: The Development of Higher Psychological Pro-
cesses*. Cambridge, MA: Harvard University Press.
Wacquant, Loïc. 2004. *Body and Soul*. New York: Oxford University Press.
Wagner-Pacifici, Robin. 2001. *Theorizing the Standoff: Contingency in Action*.
New York: Cambridge University Press.
Walker, Edward, and John D. McCarthy. in progress. "Legitimacy, Strategy, and
Resources in the Survival of Community-Based Organizations."
Walsh, Katherine Kramer. 2007.*Talking about Race: Community Dialogues and
the Politics of Difference*. Chicago: University of Chicago Press.
Walzer, Michael, 1983. *Spheres of Justice: A Defense of Pluralism and Equality*.
New York: Basic Books.
Warner, Michael. 1992. *The Letters of the Republic: Publication and the Public
Sphere in Eighteenth-Century America*. Cambridge, MA: Harvard University
Press.
Waters, Mary C. 1990. *Ethnic Options: Choosing Identities in America*. Berkeley
and Los Angeles: University of California Press.
Weber, Max. 1946. "On Bureaucracy." In *From Max Weber: Essays in Sociology*,
Hans Gerth and C. Wright Mills, 196–244. New York: Oxford University Press.

Wexler, Philip, with the assistance of Warren Crichlow, June Kern, and Rebecca Martusewicz. 1992. *Becoming Somebody: Toward a Social Psychology of School*. Washington, DC: Falmer Press.

Williams, Raymond. 1974. *Keywords: A Vocabulary of Culture and Society*. New York: Oxford University Press.

Wittgenstein, Ludwig. 1953. *Philosophical Investigations*. New York: MacMillan.

Wolch, Jennifer. 1999. *The Shadow State: Government and Voluntary Sector in Transition*. New York: The Foundation Center.

Wuthnow, Robert. 1998. *Loose Connections: Joining Together in America's Fragmented Communities*. Cambridge, MA: Harvard University Press.

———. 1991a. "The Voluntary Sector: Legacy of the Past, Hope for the Future?" In *Between States and Markets: The Voluntary Sector in Comparative Perspective*, ed. Robert Wuthnow, 3–29. Princeton, NJ: Princeton University Press.

———. 1991b. "Tocqueville's Question Reconsidered: Voluntarism and Public Discourse in Advanced Industrial Societies." In *Between States and Markets: The Voluntary Sector in Comparative Perspective*, ed. Robert Wuthnow, 288–308. Princeton, NJ: Princeton University Press.

Yang, Guobin. 2005. "Environmental NGOs and Institutional Dynamics in China." *China Quarterly* 181 (March): 46–66.

Youniss, J., and M. Yates. 1997. *Community Service and Social Responsibility in Youth*. Chicago: University of Chicago Press.

Zerubavel, Eviatar. 2006. *The Elephant in the Room*. New York: Oxford University Press.

Index

ABCD. *See* asset-based community development

Addams, Jane, 7–9, 189, 250, 259, 262

adults: professionals (*see* paid organizers); volunteers (*see* Community House, Board of Directors; plug-in volunteers)

affluent youth. *See* non-disadvantaged youth volunteers

Albania, 246

Albertson's, 265n.2

Alexander, Jeffrey, 260, 279n.1

Arato, Andrew, 277n.4

Arendt, Hannah, 239, 273n.1

asset-based community development (ABCD), 243–44

audiences: corporate donors, 155–56; experts and granting agencies, 156–57; families, 154–55; multiple, focus on future potential to avoid offending, 160–61; multiple, justification of nutritious food as a need and, 153–57; multiple, the problem of justification and, 152–53

Bacqué, Hélène, 267n.8

Baumann, Zygmunt, 279n.51

Beem, Christopher, 277n.4

Boltanski, Luc, 259–60, 267n.4, 277n.5

Botswana, 246

Bourdieu, Pierre, 274n.1

Boyte, Harry, 249

Brady, Henry, 272n.11

Brooks, David, 279n.51

bureaucracy: Empowerment Projects and, comparison of, 241–42; grassroots volunteers vs., 243, 245; rigidity of, embracing the opposite of, 9–10

Burke, Kenneth, 266n.12, 279n.2

Camus-Vigué, Agnès, 279n.3

Carrell, Marion, 278–79n.36

Casa Latina programs, xii, 186–87

celebrations: corporate marketing associated with, 220–23; of Empowerment

Projects, 226–28; form of, Empowerment Projects and, 206–8, 229; grassroots, desire for, 228–29; lessons from, 229–30; Martin Luther King Day (*see* Martin Luther King Day); religion, avoiding, 215–20; of selected differences, 208–10; of Southeast Asian (Hmong) culture, school failure and, 212–14; of statistically predictable risks, 210–12; visible diversity at, 223–26

Chalvon-Demersay, Sabine, 279n.51

Chiapello, Eve, 277n.5

choice: conditions for, need to consider, 81–83; needs vs., 152–53, 164; self-fulfilling prophecy, as subject of, 79–81

Cicero, 257

civic education: classroom discussion at school, 107–8; institutional intuition, developing, 108–13; interpreting and applying rules, experience at school in, 103–4; through intimate attachment to a paid organizer, 104–7

civic empowerment, 20–23. *See also* leadership

Cohen, Jean, 277n.4

community: creating bonds across separate communities of volunteers, 165–66 (*see also* volunteers); as a need, justification of, 160–61; self-fulfilling prophecy, as subject of, 68–72

Community House: Board of Directors, 142–44; community-building dinners at, 70–71

Cooper, H., 272n.1

corporate sponsorship, 155–56, 220–23

cultural diversity: appreciating one's own, 196; categorizing things as, 190–91; celebrations of, 206–8 (*see also* celebrations); individuality as the source of difference when celebrating, 199–200; measuring and displaying, 242; sociolinguistic differences, 200–2

culture: agendas of mixers vs. protectors regarding, 183–84; celebrating one's own, discomfort at, 196–97; emptiness of in Empowerment Projects, 204–5; framing habits as, 202–4; Hmong, 213–14; as a moving target, 187–88; naming one's own traits as, 191; naming others' traits as, 191–93; naming something as, 190–91; preserving differences in, 186–87; purification of, 194–96; purified, ignoring differences to produce, 197–200; rational response to dire circumstances vs., 193–94; rebellion against one's own, 185–86; religion, separating from, 215–20; unacceptable definitions of, 200–4; variations in tastes and childhood memories, assumptions of similarity and, 174–76. *See also* cultural diversity; multicultural diversity
culture critics, 271n.5

Dekker, Paul, 277n.4
Dewey, John, 189, 268n.21
DiMaggio, Paul, 267n.3
disadvantaged youth volunteers: fundraising by, 31–33; non-disadvantaged youth volunteers, distinguished from, 1–2, 17–18; non-disadvantaged youth volunteers, joking about, 43–45; politics, discussion of, 35; as the problem, 18–20; reasons for participating, 18–23, 30–31; statistics and self-perception for, 33–34
diversity, 181–82; breaking out of your box, 184–86, 189; celebrating, potential discomfort from, 197 (*see also* celebrations); emptiness of in Empowerment Projects, 204–5; naming something as, 190–91, 237; preserving differences in the name of, 186–87; puzzles of, 186–89; religion not included in, 215–20; two approaches to promoting, 183–84; unacceptable definitions of, 200–4; visible representatives at public ceremonies, 223–26. *See also* cultural diversity
DuBois, David L., 272n.1
DuBois, W. E. B., 47, 189
Dumont, Louis, 276n.6

economic development, Empowerment Projects and, 4–5
Edelsky, Carole, 274n.2

Edwards, Jonathan, 268n.20
Elshtain, Jean, 274n.4
Emerson, Ralph Waldo, 6–9, 58
Empowerment Projects: American history, rooted in, 6–9; blending that occurs in, viii–ix, 1–2; bureaucracies and, comparison of, 241–42; celebrations of (*see* celebrations); characteristics of, viii, 4–6; cheerleaders for and critics of, 243–45; conditions/context, disregard for past and present, 5–6, 246–48; detours/unintended consequences of, xv–xvi, 2–4, 231–35; doubt, increasing feelings of, xiv–xv; emptiness of culture and diversity in, 204–5; the "future potential" and temporal issues in (*see* temporal issues); inequality, impact of and on, 46–47; inequality, organizational style regarding, 40–46; intimate comfort and safety promised by (*see* intimate comfort and safety); multicultural diversity of (*see* multicultural diversity); pacifying the typical tensions of, patterns/examples of, 246–51; practical suggestions for, 252–54; rejecting the distinctions of the Gray Flannel Man's box, problems resulting from, 254–57; rise of, ix; self-fulfilling prophecy and (*see* self-fulfilling prophecy); soul-changing intimacy promised by Empowerment Talk, clash of speed and flexibility with, 137–38; tangled hopes and unintended consequences, 2–4 (*see also* morally magnetic missions)
Empowerment Talk: civic empowerment a theme of, 20–23; hopes, inversion of, xiv–xv; inside-out impact of, 231–35; mantra of, viii; opposed ideals of, 204; politics and, 98–100 (*see also* politics); practical suggestions in tension with, 252–54; transformation of keywords by, 245–46; volunteering, positive impacts of, 20–23, 48–49 (*see also* volunteering)

food: junk, nutritional status of, 155–56; need for nutritious, justification of, 152–53; nutrition education programs, grants for and impact of, 156–57; pesticides and natural status of, 161; pleasing the many audiences for, 153–57; as symbol for love and family, 157–58; uses of, 157–59

Princeton Studies in Cultural Sociology

Paul J. DiMaggio, Michèle Lamont, Robert J. Wuthnow, Viviana A. Zelizer, series editors

Origins of Democratic Culture: Printing, Petitions, and the Public Sphere in Early-Modern England by David Zaret

Bearing Witness: Readers, Writers, and the Novel in Nigeria by Wendy Griswold

Gifted Tongues: High School Debate and Adolescent Culture by Gary Alan Fine

Offside: Soccer and American Exceptionalism by Andrei S. Markovits and Steven L. Hellerman

Reinventing Justice: The American Drug Court Movement by James L. Nolan, Jr.

Kingdom of Children: Culture and Controversy in the Homeschooling Movement by Mitchell L. Stevens

Blessed Events: Religion and Home Birth in America by Pamela E. Klassen

Negotiating Identities: States and Immigrants in France and Germany by Riva Kastoryano, translated by Barbara Harshav

Contentious Curricula: Afrocentrism and Creationism in American Public Schools by Amy J. Binder

Community: Pursuing the Dream, Living the Reality by Suzanne Keller

The Minds of Marginalized Black Men: Making Sense of Mobility, Opportunity, and Future Life Chances by Alford A. Young, Jr.

Framing Europe: Attitudes to European Integration in Germany, Spain, and the United Kingdom by Juan Dez Medrano

Interaction Ritual Chains by Randall Collins

Talking Prices: Symbolic Meanings of Prices on the Market for Contemporary Art by Olav Velthuis

Elusive Togetherness: Church Groups Trying to Bridge America's Divisions by Paul Lichterman

Religion and Family in a Changing Society by Penny Edgell

Hollywood Highbrow: From Entertainment to Art by Shyon Baumann

Partisan Publics: Communication and Contention across Brazilian Youth Activist Networks by Ann Mische

Disrupting Science: Social Movements, American Scientists, and the Politics of the Military, 1945–1975 by Kelly Moore

Weaving Self-Evidence: A Sociology of Logic by Claude Rosental, translated by Catherine Porter

Economists and Societies: Discipline and Profession in the United States, Great Britain, and France, 1890s to 1990s by Marion Fourcade

Reds, Whites, and Blues: Social Movements, Folk Music, and Race in the United States by William G. Roy

Privilege: The Making of an Adolescent Elite at St. Paul's School by Shamus Rahman Chan

Making Volunteers: Civic Life after Welfare's End by Nina Eliasoph